The Four Gospels and the One Gospel of Jesus Christ

The following books by Martin Hengel are also available from SCM Press

Between Jesus and Paul (1983)

The Cross of the Son of God (1976)

Earliest Christianity (1974)

The Johannine Question (1990)

Paul Between Damascus and Antioch
(with Anna Maria Schwemer) (1997)

The Pre-Christian Paul (1991)

Studies in the Gospel of Mark (1985)

The Four Gospels and the One Gospel of Jesus Christ

An Investigation of the Collection and Origin of the Canonical Gospels

Martin Hengel

SCM PRESS

Translated by John Bowden from the German.

Translation © John Bowden 2000

0 334 02759 4

This edition first published 2000 by
SCM Press
9–17 St Albans Place London N1 0NX

SCM Press is a division of
SCM-Canterbury Press Ltd

Printed in Great Britain by
Biddles Ltd, Guildford and King's Lynn

To John Bowden

publisher, translator and friend

Contents

Contents

Contents

Contents

Preface

This book goes back to a lecture which I gave in November 1998 at the invitation of the Institute of Biblical Research in connection with the SBL conference in Miami. In preparation for it I had composed a substantially longer text which John Bowden translated into English and which I gave in four lectures at the Trinity Divinity School in Deerfield, Illinois. I have successively expanded this basic study into an investigation of the historical genesis of the collection of four Gospels, the significance of the term 'Gospel' and the central role of the Gospel of Mark. A concluding chapter comprises a critical discussion of the relationship between Luke, Matthew and the Logia tradition. In the book I have attempted, starting from Irenaeus and Clement of Alexandria and applying all the references from the early church and the New Testament textual tradition, to give a plausible historical account of the development of this collection and to evaluate its historical and theological significance. Here I have brought together in one place reflections which have occupied me for decades.

I am grateful to Frau Dr Hanna Stettler and Vikar Matthias Hennig for producing the difficult manuscript in its slow growth and to Frau Privatdozentin Dr Anna Maria Schwemer and Matthias Hennig for reading the proofs.

Most of all I am grateful to the translator, the Revd Dr John Bowden, who for almost thirty years now in a masterly way has translated numerous books of mine into English, beginning with *Judaism and Hellenism*. In reading through the English manuscript Luther's remark in his 'Letter on Translating'

xi

(1525) came to mind: 'I have experienced what an art and a labour translation is.'

This book is dedicated to John Bowden with gratitude.

Tübingen, April 2000   Martin Hengel

I

Introduction:
An Aporia and Two Questions

The *Novum Testamentum Graece* of Nestle-Aland (twenty-seventh edition) with the twenty-seven writings of the New Testament canon comprises 680 pages including the critical apparatus. These writings were composed in a period of about seventy or eighty years, roughly between AD 50 and 120/130. The earliest are the seven authentic letters of Paul, which were written approximately between AD 50 and 60, and the latest can be called 'pseudepigrapha', the Pastoral Letters attributed to Paul and II Peter. The four Gospels and Acts, which stand at the beginning of the New Testament and which in contrast to the letters at least in their outward form set out to narrate above all 'history' or 'stories', of course including shorter and longer speeches and dialogues, were written in the middle of this period, roughly between AD 70 and 100.

Thus the New Testament has a similar division to the Greek Old Testament, the Septuagint, with its distinction between 'historical' and 'didactic books'.[1] However, there is one difference. In the Old Testament the historical books set out to extend from the creation to the time of the Maccabees in the second century BC, i.e. according to contemporary ancient Jewish chronology over almost five millennia,[2] whereas the stories of the narrative writings in the first part of the New Testament – with great gaps – merely cover a period of less than sixty years, from the birth of Jesus to the arrival of Paul in Rome (c. 6 BC–AD 60).[3] Moreover – and this is the new feature

– they tell the same story of the activity of Jesus four times, in part in very different ways.

As is shown by the beginning of his work, ἀρχὴ τοῦ εὐαγγελίου Ἰησοῦ Χριστοῦ, 'beginning of the Gospel of Jesus Christ', Mark, the earliest evangelist and narrator known to us, here already calls his written account of the activity and passion of Jesus εὐαγγέλιον, message of salvation. In so doing he uses a word that had already been a key term for Paul, the first Christian author, before him, which the earliest evangelist can use for both the preaching of Jesus and for that of the church.[4] Paul used it from the beginning as the embodiment of his missionary message, i.e. the oral preaching with which he founded communities. In his genuine letters we find it 48 times (and 15 times in the Deutero-Pauline letters), and in the original Mark 7 times,[5] whereas it does not appear at all (apart from the title) in Luke and John; and although Matthew is almost forty per cent longer than Mark, it appears there only four times. So for Mark, too, the word must have had a quite special significance, though at least externally it differs somewhat from Pauline terminology (see below, 90f., 145ff.). That applies above all to the opening sentence and the title of the work. According to the Letter to the Galatians, Paul received his 'Gospel', which was of a rather different kind, not narrated but proclaimed as teaching, through a 'revelation of Jesus Christ', i.e. a quite special revelation independent of human tradition, at his call before Damascus, and according to him there is no other 'message of salvation' than this one.[6] At the beginning of Romans (1.16) he defines it thematically as 'the power of God for salvation to everyone who has faith'.

It is part of the riddle, one could even say the offence, of the New Testament corpus that in it this one message of salvation through Jesus Christ, narrated in stories with a historical sequence, which Mark 1.1 already called εὐαγγέλιον, has found written expression in four writings of more or less biographical, narrative character which often differ considerably from one another, indeed sometimes contradict one another (not to mention the 'Gospel' that Paul proclaimed, which he received directly from Christ and which seems to be rather different in form). Each of these four writings bears as a title the designation τὸ εὐαγγέλιον, supplemented by the name of the author in a way which was quite unusual in antiquity (see 48ff.): κατὰ Μαθθαῖον, κατὰ Μᾶρκον, κατὰ Λουκᾶν, κατὰ Ἰωάννην, i.e. Gospel according to Matthew, Mark, Luke, John. Thus basically we have four written versions of the 'message of salvation' as an account of Jesus from very different authors, which in part differ widely. Only much later – after the time of Irenaeus (c. AD 180) – do the church fathers speak without embarrassment of four 'Gospels' in the plural, although the New Testament and the Apostolic Fathers up to the middle of the second century were quite rightly strict in using the singular and never the plural. For while there were indeed many kinds of 'good news' in the Greco-Roman world, which therefore preferred the plural εὐαγγέλια,[7] there can be only one message of salvation, whether in oral or in written form, at least in early Christianity. This message was identical with the one Gospel of Jesus Christ son of God (Mark 1.1), as both objective and subjective genitive, because its contents and its author were Jesus Christ alone.

Basically it describes the central message of primitive Christianity. Therefore in his sermon to the high-priestly aristocracy, according to Luke Peter confesses that 'salvation' is given from God only in him and 'in no other'. Paul has received the Gospel not from man but 'through a revelation of Jesus Christ', and in founding the community of Corinth he 'decided to know nothing among you except Jesus Christ, and him crucified'.[8] By contrast, in profane Greek usage, not least also in the quite rare testimonies to the emperor cult, the plural is by far the more dominant, and nowhere does the word mean 'message of salvation' in this exclusive sense, but 'good news', in the sense of the message of a victory or the accession of an emperor. The exciting story about the report of the victory over Absalom to David in the LXX is typical of this older political-military usage as 'news of victory': already in I Sam. 18 the plural εὐαγγέλια is used once or twice, the very rare feminine singular εὐαγγελία two or three times, and the corresponding verb εὐαγγελίζεσθαι four times.[9] In comparison with the Greek and Jewish parallels, the Pauline and Markan use of εὐαγγέλιον takes on a much deeper, even unique significance.

Justin, after AD 150, is the first to use the plural for our four Gospels – but still with a bad conscience. He does so just once in his *Apology*.[10] Elsewhere he avoids this form, which he evidently still felt to be inappropriate, and in 15 instances he prefers to use the formula '*reminiscences of the apostles*',[11] ἀπομνημονεύματα τῶν ἀποστόλων instead; the emperor, whom he was addressing, and other pagan readers, would understand it better than the specific Christian term εὐαγγέλιον, which otherwise he uses only twice, in the singular. Once he makes the Jew Trypho confess: 'That your teachings, which stand in the so-called Gospel, are so powerful and so wonderful that no one can observe them. I have read them with interest' (*Dial.* 10,2). The Jewish conversation-partner knows that Christians call the writing which contains their message 'Gospel'. At another point Justin quotes Matt. 1.27/Luke 10.22 relatively freely with the formula 'it is written in the Gospel' (*Dial.* 100,1). But this terminology, which is specifically Christian (see above, 3) remains a rare exception with him. He took over the term 'reminiscences of the apostles'[12] from the famous four books of ἀπομνημονεύματα Σωκράτους, the reminiscences of Socrates by Xenophon which he, a former Platonist philosopher, quotes in his *Second Apology*.[13] This restrained use of a 'theologically impossible' plural is maintained until Irenaeus. Irenaeus is the first writer who can also sometimes speak with a relative lack of concern about the Gospels in the plural; indeed, he has to do this, because he is the first author known to us who deliberately develops a 'theory of the four Gospels'. However, he himself still prefers the singular. Before him we find the plural only in the passage of Justin already mentioned and in a fragment of Apollinaris of Hierapolis, a contemporary of Marcus Aurelius.[14] Even Augustine can still begin his praise of the Fourth Evangelist in his *Commentary on John* with the sentence: 'In the four Gospels, or better in the four books of the one Gospel.'[15] Therefore he cannot tolerate any contradiction in them (see below, 23).

Two problems arise over this aporia, namely that while there can be fundamentally only one 'Gospel' as the message of salvation through Jesus Christ – whether oral or written – , in the New Testament canon in reality we have four 'Gospels' as separate biographical narrative writings which, at least according to a modern critical understanding, are both rival and mutually supplementary, and which narrate the life and teaching of Jesus in sometimes quite divergent ways.

1. What is the relationship between what is systematically and doctrinally the one Gospel that Paul preached and the narrative, biographical, written report about Jesus' life, teaching and death, and how, after Mark, could the two, the earlier preaching of Paul and the later 'kerygmatic biography of Jesus', be given the same designation? Behind this lies a deeper opposition which is still a matter of dispute today. Harnack, for example, spoke of a double form of the Gospel. By this he meant the difference between 'the Gospel (of the kingdom) of God', which the Galilaean Jew Jesus of Nazareth announces according to Mark 1.14,[16] and which we find in the story of the Synoptic Gospels, and the apparently quite different Gospel of Paul and the later church about the divine Christ, Son of God and Kyrios. For him 'the higher righteousness and the commandment of love' was the 'embodiment of the message of Jesus', for one can 'depict the whole Gospel . . . as an ethical message'.[17] He summed up this difference in the polemical statement, 'The Gospel as Jesus proclaimed it has to do with the Father only and not with the Son', a statement directed against the high christology of the church first developed in our earliest Christian written testimonies, the Pauline letters.[18] In his view, this simple ethical Gospel of Jesus was recorded in the plain narrative of the three Synoptic Gospels, especially in Luke. In Paul, however, the Gospel is 'the message of reconciliation through the crucified and risen Christ'.[19] Thus according to Harnack there was a threat that 'the formation of a correct theory of and about Christ threatens to assure the position of

direct importance and to pervert the majesty and simplicity of the Gospel'.[20] In between stands the Gospel of John, as 'the greatest riddle that the earliest history of Christianity offers', in which Christ 'preaches as his testimony to himself . . . what his disciples felt about him', i.e. he appears as a 'Pauline Christ walking on the earth, speaking and acting . . .'[21] Harnack's differentiation corresponded to that gulf which had been created in the earlier liberal study of Jesus and which – despite Karl Barth and Rudolf Bultmann – still preoccupies us today. But was Harnack really right with his supposition of two totally different forms of the Gospel? A more modern and much more naive form of this famous 'liberal' distinction is the alleged contradiction between Jesus as the 'peasant Jewish Cynic' or the Galilean Socrates and the Christ of the kerygma.[22] There is nothing new under the sun. In Chapter 5 we shall finally return to this basic question: whether, how and why there were really two contradictory forms of the 'Gospel', as Harnack and his modern and still more radical successors thought, and how the term εὐαγγέλιον could relate to them. But before that we shall be concerned with the second question:

2. How is it that we have the narrative of Jesus' activity in a fourfold and often contradictory form in the canon of the New Testament, and how old are these four Gospels? A single, correspondingly longer, Gospel about Jesus would have already spared the early church, and even more modern New Testament scholarship, which is still young[23] – the chair for the discipline in Tübingen was founded precisely a century ago by Adolf Schlatter – to the present day much racking of its brains.

Thus we have only one biography of Muhammad (who died in 632), by Ibn Hisham (who died in 834, 212 years after the Hijra), which has incorporated parts of the lost earlier biography by Ibn Ishaq (died 767).[24] Although the chronological distance from the historical subject in the Muhammad biography is much greater, the historical scepticism of critical European scholarship is substantially less here. Basically, two questions overlap. First, what was the 'Gospel', the 'message of salvation', originally? Was it the narrative of the closest disciples about Jesus, his teaching, his activity and his passion, or doctrine about him as 'christology' and 'soteriology', the doctrine of salvation? Or is the opposition formulated here a false one? Could the Gospel perhaps – necessarily – contain both? And secondly, why and for how long have we also had this Gospel in such different narrative forms? How did these different forms develop, and why were they not summed up in *one* normative narrative?

II

The Authors of the Four Gospels and the Temptation towards Harmonization or Radical Reduction

1.*Historical narrative in the New Testament*

Let us turn first to the second – simpler – question. Here it is striking how much weight the four parallel narratives about Jesus have in the New Testament canon itself: they make up almost half of the New Testament text – 319 out of 680 'Nestle' pages. The earliest church evidently preferred vivid narrative to abstract letters with their 'pure doctrine' or paraenetical admonition, for if one adds the δεύτερος λόγος ('second writing') composed by the evangelist Luke, the Acts of the Apostles,[25] also a narrative, which to some extent goes with the Gospels as an appendix and occupies a unique historical intermediate position between the Gospels and the Letters, the proportion of the writings which narrate 'history/stories' increases to almost two-thirds of the New Testament.[26] Basically, the visionary accounts of the Revelation of John, with their 'utopian' depiction of the history of the present, the heavenly world of God and the divine future, need also to be counted among the 'narrative' writings. Revelation is also connected with the Gospels through the 'Synoptic apocalypses'. Even Paul narrates parts of the earliest 'church history' in Gal. 1 and 2; I Cor. 15.1–11 or Rom. 15.14–32 and his own biography in Phil. 3.4–7.[27] On the other hand, the 'narrative writings' abundantly contain 'teaching and admonition' in the form of discourses. No fundamental opposition may be constructed at this point.

Primitive Christianity has no knowledge of the abrupt distinction between 'dogmatics' and 'church history' which is so popular, or even between 'faith' and 'facts of history' in that form. New Testament studies in particular has done badly by this distinction. The truth lies between a 'historicism' which is hostile to theology and a 'dogmatism' which is hostile to history; John 1.14 opposes such false alternatives. The 'incarnation of the Son of God' and the history of Jesus in space and time, which is then narrated and at the same time proclaimed as Gospel, cannot be torn apart.

At any rate, the parts which narrate 'history' in the form of more or less consecutive 'stories' or summaries – mainly about Jesus (with the 'words of the Lord' and 'speeches' interspersed) – are predominant in the New Testament. However, since the days of Reimarus and Lessing, and even more since the old Tübingen School of F. C. Baur and his disciple D. F. Strauss, the historical evaluation and classification of them have led to never-ending controversies. The Life of Jesus written by the twenty-seven-year-old Repentent in the 'Tübinger Stift' (1835), with its radical historical criticism of the Gospel of John in particular and 'myth' in the Gospels generally, served as a springboard and changed research into the Gospels over the next 160 years. The same can be said about the debate concerning the historical value of Luke-Acts, even though the more radical suppositions of the old Tübingen school were revised again later in the nineteenth century, not least by the greatest German theological historian Adolf von Harnack, who was also a great New Testament scholar, like the more – or even too – conservative Theodor Zahn, who was at the opposite pole from him.[28]

However, the aporia of separate Gospels that tell stories about Jesus which are often different, indeed contradictory, which has been exposed here, is not new in this form: it was already an intensive preoccupation of *the* early church; indeed it is fundamentally inseparable from the origin of the Gospels themselves.

2. *The defence of the number four in Irenaeus*

Around AD 180, Irenaeus was the first church teacher we know to use as a basis something like a 'canon', i.e. a collection of recognized 'apostolic' writings, the four Gospels in particular. He certainly did not invent this collection himself; it had already existed for quite a long time in the mainstream church, largely recognized and used in worship. However, he is the first church author known to us to make an effective defence of it as an exclusive collection.[29] In this connection it is worth noting that even in Irenaeus the use of the singular 'Gospel' far exceeds that of the plural. In the third book, which is crucial for this topic, the plural appears only five times out of the seventy-five occurrences of the word, and is concentrated in the remarks about the 'fourfold Gospel' in 3,11,7–9.[30] For Irenaeus the collection forms a unity and therefore he can still call it the 'Gospel'. Here contradictions in the chronology of Jesus between John and the Synoptics do not trouble him. He accuses the Valentinians of not having studied 'in the Gospels (*in evangeliis*) how often the Lord went up to Jerusalem at the time of the Passover'. Here he keeps to the plural visits in John and rejects the duration of Jesus' activity in the Synoptics as a year, along with the age of Jesus as thirty when he appeared as a teacher. He says that the thirty years were only his age at the baptism (Luke 3.23); Jesus first taught at the 'age of perfection' between thirty and forty (John 8.56f.). This is all done with reference to the earlier tradition in Asia Minor.[31] Unimpressed by such contradictions, he regards all four Gospels together as the *principia evangelii*, as containing the basic teachings of the one 'saving message of God, creator of the world, attested by the prophets, who through Moses gave the ordinance of the law and who is (none other than) the Father of our Lord Jesus Christ'.[32]

All the evangelists – Matthew, Luke, Mark and John – bear witness against the heretics to the identity of God in the Old and New Covenant and his son Jesus Christ: 'But none of the heretics teaches that God has been made flesh.'[33] Indeed, the 'reliability' (*firmitas*) of the Gospels is so great that by their predilection for individual Gospels the heretics must confirm this and at the same time be convinced: the Jewish-Christian Ebionites by Matthew, Marcion by Luke, whom he 'circumcised', the Docetists (like Cerinthus) who claim that Christ as incapable of suffering, by Mark, and the Valentinians by John.[34] Nevertheless, in what follows Irenaeus must energetically go on to defend the fact that there are only four apostolic Gospels. He does this with a variety of arguments and images from creation and revelation, for example the four cardinal points of the world and their four universal winds, the four covenants of God with mankind,[35] and especially the four 'cherubim' who are bearing the throne of the Lord (lion, bull, eagle and man),[36] taken from Ps. 79.2 (LXX), Ezek. 1.5–12 and the Apocalypse of John 4.7,[37] a text which Irenaeus quotes. This indicates not only that the existence of the four-Gospel collection was older, but at the same time that it was still being attacked or even was not recognized without reservations in Christian circles. Irenaeus himself makes a virtue of necessity and argues, in apologetic terms, that the εὐαγγέλιον τετράμορφον,[38] 'the Gospel in four forms', given by the creator of the world and Logos incarnate, expresses the perfection of apostolic tradition about Christ. Thus there may be neither more nor less than these four, since the Gospel in its divinely-willed fourfold form is in turn 'held together by one spirit'.[39]

Cullmann's criticism of Irenaeus and his grounding of the number four in an ontology of creation and in salvation history misses the point. A modern theological-historical understanding, namely that the evangelists could not exhaust the wealth of the revelation of the incarnate Christ and 'therefore . . . had to bring together all the depictions of the life of Jesus that were available from the apostolic period', would have played straight into the hands of their Gnostic opponents, who claimed that in their writings they were handing on such a diversity, including the secret revelations of the Risen Christ. The argument from the order of creation and the Old Testament tradition which were both denied by the main opponents could seem quite convincing to the readers of the time.[40] It was decisive for Irenaeus, as it was a little later for the Muratorian Fragment, that the four Gospels are governed by the one Spirit of God.[41] This is directed both against the production of a single written Gospel, whether that of Marcion, who regarded all other Gospels than the one which Paul received from Christ as forgeries,[42] or the Harmony of Tatian,[43] who *de facto* combined the four into one, and also against the challenging of the authenticity of the Fourth Gospel, i.e. against Gaius, the conservative presbyter, and his friends in Rome, and even more against the variety of 'apocryphal' Gospels which were appearing in the second century.[44] Origen, in his *Commentary on John*, asserts against the criticism of Marcion 'that just as the Gospel which several people preach is one, so (too) that which has been written by many is in its spirit-gifted significance one, and therefore in truth the Gospel, which consists of four texts, is one'.[45] Eusebius in his *Church History* speaks briefly and succinctly in enumerating the 'writings of the new covenant' of the 'sacred fourness' of the Gospels[46] without listing them again individually according to their authors.[47] By the third century they had long become an unassailable entity.

3. *Serapion of Antioch and the Gospel of Peter*

How necessary it was for Irenaeus to defend the fact that there were four Gospels which were now becoming 'canonical' is shown by the controversy of a contemporary, Bishop Serapion of Antioch, with the community in Rhossos on the Mediterranean coast of Syria.[48] When he had visited the community, a group had presented to him the Gospel of Peter with the urgent request that it might be read in worship. Trusting in their 'orthodoxy' and without examining the writing further, he allowed them to do so. Later he heard in Antioch that this Gospel was treasured by Docetists and that those members of the community in Rhossos had similar tendencies. Now he got hold of the work from heretics and read it: in doing so he noted 'that while most of it agrees with the right teaching of the

Redeemer, some deviates from it'; he lists the deviations at the end of his letter. Unfortunately the bishop has omitted this conclusion with the critical points. Because of the heretical tendencies in the community Eusebius announced that he would be visiting it soon. At the same time he emphasized his 'allegiance to Peter, the other apostles and Christ', but also his resolve to reject writings under a false name,[49] 'because we have not received such writings' (from the tradition).

This episode shows that 'apocryphal' Gospels – decked out in keeping with the fashion – recognized beyond those which towards the end of the second century were regarded as traditional, were still very attractive to some members of the community. This applied in a special way to the Gospel of Peter, which knows and presupposes all four Gospels, because here Peter spoke in the first person, and because in it miracle was depicted to the point of a dramatic description of the resurrection of Jesus, and at the same time hostility to the Jews was quite substantially intensified. Thus here it is exclusively the Jews who crucify Jesus. The Akhmim Fragment begins with the scene in which Pilate, as opposed to the Jews, washes his hands (Matt. 27.24) and rises to withdraw; King Herod (cf. Luke 23.7ff.) gives orders to take Jesus away to be crucified. Serapion could hardly take offence at all this, but he was offended by features which could be interpreted as docetic. On the other hand the bishop of the Syrian metropolis of Antioch shows an amazing ignorance about this makeshift work, a sign that it was not disseminated widely and – contrary to some modern assertions – must have been composed at a relatively late date. Here Serapion's judgment is based solely on the content of the work. His generosity in initially allowing it to be read in worship is amazing. Certainly the Gospel of Peter was not the only one to be read aloud in Rhossos; rather, around this time we must presuppose a knowledge of all four Gospels. However, by comparison with the traditional Gospel writings it had attractive, more 'contemporary', indeed downright sensational features.[50]

This whole process, as it was played out in Syria, shows

how the situation in the church required Irenaeus' energetic advocacy of the fourfold Gospel. His work spread in the church from Gaul with amazing rapidity. This is an indication of the various lively connections between communities in the second century. An Irenaeus fragment from Egypt perhaps comes from as early as the end of the second century;[51] Clement of Alexandria also knew the work of the Bishop of Lyons well and the same goes for Tertullian. Here the knowledge of a widely recognized collection of the four Gospels which is used in worship is certainly substantially older than Irenaeus. His work found such a response because it so emphatically defended what was known and tested, but in part still attacked or not fully recognized. In keeping with his tendency Irenaeus used virtually no 'apocryphal' Gospel tradition.[52]

That people in Syria were more generous towards the use of 'apocryphal' Gospel tradition even in the third century is shown towards the beginning or middle of this century by the original Greek version of the Didascalia, composed by a bishop, which has been preserved in Syriac (and partly in Latin). Thirty per cent of these instructions, which were allegedly given at the Apostolic Council in Jerusalem, consists of biblical quotations. Matthew is quoted the most extensively; then follow Luke and Acts, Mark, and most rarely John. The Pastoral Epistles and I Peter enjoy especial popularity among the letters. Nevertheless, in this 'orthodox-apocryphal' pseudepigraphon traditions from the Gospel of Peter and midrash-like elaborations are not dispensed with completely.[53] But such brief escapades no longer damage the absolute validity of the four Gospels; on the contrary, they are an expression of certainty. According to tradition the apostles had already laid down 'that except (for) the Old Testament and the Prophets and the Gospel, the acts of their triumphs, nothing should be read on the bema of the church'. But here the Gospel was given the highest status. The apostles also laid down 'that at the conclusion of all the Scriptures, the Gospels shall be read as being the seal of all Scriptures; and let the people listen to it standing upon their feet, because it is the good tidings of the redemption of all men'.

This custom too does not indicate an innovation, but may already have been church practice for some time. It could also have been a liturgical custom in Antioch and Rhossos around AD 200.[54]

4. *Clement of Alexandria, the fourfold Gospel and the apocryphal tradition*

A relatively generous attitude towards apocryphal Gospel tradition is also evident in Clement; this clearly distinguishes him from Irenaeus. On the other hand he takes the authority of the four Gospels quite for granted and emphasizes the uniqueness of the apostolic tradition. Thus one could say that he speaks with some ambiguity about the authority of the Gospels.[55] However, this ambiguity seems to me to be less than is sometimes assumed. Here Hans von Campenhausen first emphasizes the difference.[56] Certainly according to him Clement is also 'a fighter for the true church against heretical error' and a 'scriptural theologian' who 'lives and moves in the words of the Bible. Nevertheless, apart from this most general characteristic in relation to the canon and to canonical thought, hardly a greater difference is conceivable than that between Irenaeus and Clement.

The difference arises from the difference in personality, which includes Clement's unique philosophical and literary education, and from the special intellectual situation in Alexandria and its quite different theological tradition. Nor is Clement a bishop, but a free Christian teacher, practised in open discussion with educated pagans and all kinds of Gnostic 'heretics'. On the one hand his Middle Platonic education brings him close to them, but he attempts to defeat them, if possible with their own weapons. His aim is not one-sidedly a tie to the institution and authority of the church, but education to become the true – Christian – 'Gnostic'. As such, according to Mehat, he became the 'founder of academic theology in the church'.[57] However, for him, too, 'holy scripture' (γραφή), consisting of 'prophecy', i.e. the Old Testament and the New

Testament, Gospels and apostolic writings, is the 'supreme authority'.[58] He has in common with many Christian writings of the early period a way of quoting scriptures as a rule 'from memory' and here can also allow himself great carelessness;[59] however, this need not tell against a fixed authority of scripture. The quotations 'flow' from the abundance of his learning.[60] This becomes evident in particular in his treatment of the four Gospels. Among other things he also has a 'historical' interest in them. Thus in Book 6 of his *Hypotyposes* he hands down a tradition of 'the elders' about the ordering and at the same time the sequence of the origin of the Gospels. According to this, those with a genealogy will have come into being first; by that he means Matthew and Luke, without mentioning them by name. Then follows Mark, who put down in writing the preaching of Peter in Rome, and 'lastly John, when he recognized that the human side of Jesus (σωματικά) is described in the Gospels, inspired by the Spirit composed a spiritual Gospel'.[61]

That is how people thought in Alexandria – as did Irenaeus, though he came to a different conclusion – about 'historical' questions relating to the four Gospels. Evidently Clement took it for granted that the collection of four Gospels was based on recognized church tradition and was unchallenged, since he does not have to defend it anywhere. Presumably it had also been used in worship in Alexandria for a long time. That is confirmed by the earliest papyrus finds in the interior of Egypt, which go back to around the middle of the second century.[62] Accordingly he can sometimes quote all four Gospels with their fixed titles; this happens once each with Matthew and Luke and twice with John.[63] Clement refers twice in connection with the story of the rich man and the dialogue with the disciples which follows in Mark 10.17–31[64] to the agreement in meaning,[65] despite slight differences, with the other 'acknowledged' Gospels.[66] That means that he was also aware of the problem of the possible contradictions between the different versions of the one Gospel and had compared the texts like a skilled philologist.

Nevertheless, Clement speaks explicitly of the *four* Gospels only once. This is in an argument with Julius Cassian who, coming from the school of Valentinus, like Tatian (see below, 24f.), called for radical sexual continence and in so doing referred to a conversation between the Lord and Salome about the abolition of the differences between the sexes. Clement rejects this, giving as a reason, among others: 'We do not have this saying in the four Gospels that have been handed down to us, but [it stands] in that according to the Egyptians.'[67] In contrast to Irenaeus, however, he does not reject such a Gospel in principle; rather, he has quoted this saying of Jesus to Salome twice before, and on the first mention he emphasizes that it must be expounded to the Encratites in the correct way so that they are confounded and refuted by it.[68] In other words, although it does not come from a recognized Gospel it must be taken seriously because of the discussion with the opponents.

Elsewhere, too, he seems to quote from the Gospels without giving the title. He can quote the Gospel of the Hebrews in the same way. First comes a reference to Plato's *Theaetetus*, that wonder at things is the beginning of philosophy; this is confirmed by an apocryphal apostolic tradition, the 'Traditions of Matthias', and finally by the Gospel of the Hebrews: 'Anyone who is amazed will become king; and whoever has become king will find rest.'[69] He gives the same quotation once more later, expanded and with no indication of source, inserted between a passage from the *Timaeus* and a saying of Thales.[70] With no mention of an author, an unknown Gospel appears: 'For it was not out of envy that the Lord in some Gospel commanded: "My mystery is for me and the sons of my heart."'[71] According to a quotation of Matt. 5.10,9, which is not wholly precise, he presents a second more extensive version of the same text with the remark 'or as some of those say who alter the Gospels', by which he probably means the followers of Marcion.[72] By citing this text, probably from the 'Gospel of Marcion', Clement wants to show off his learning, like Justin to Trypho. At the same time he indirectly emphasizes the binding character of the text, which he first cites. Last of all he adduces two further 'Matthias traditions'.[73] Perhaps they are connected with Basilides and his school, who according to Hippolytus 'maintain that Matthias handed down to them secret sayings', which he received in personal instruction from the Redeemer.[74] Clement himself also rejects an appeal to leading Gnostics, 'who boast that they are presenting the opinion (τὴν δόξαν) of Matthias'. He does this with a sharpness and clarity reminiscent of Irenaeus: 'for just as there was only a single teaching of all the apostles, so too there is only one tradition'.[75] But this does not prevent him from citing such Matthias traditions when it seems appropriate. Moreover one could refer to a number of real or supposed agrapha, the origin of which is unknown.[76]

On the other hand, Clement himself can say that 'after the resurrection the Lord handed on "*gnosis*" to James the Just and John and Peter; these handed it on to the other apostles, and the other apostles to the Seventy'. However, here *all* the 'apostolic' emissaries of Christ share in the 'secret teaching' of the Risen One, and thus it benefits the whole church. Contrary to Gnostic claims, there is no special revelation to individual disciples; this is reserved only for a few elect.[77]

In his 'Gospel' terminology, as a rule Clement makes a clear distinction between the saving message that is preached, i.e. the teaching of the Logos or Kyrios,[78] and the Gospel writings. Usually, in a very similar way to Irenaeus, Clement speaks of the Gospel in the singular, frequently with the formula ἐν τῷ εὐαγγελίῳ; this is quite often associated with a discourse or action of the Lord. For him, too, the plural still remains an exception. He is also fond of associating the term with the Old Testament in order to express the unity of the revelation in scripture, for example with formulae like 'the Gospel and prophecy'. That means that 'the Gospel' has come to stand alongside the prophetic writings as holy scripture,[79] for 'the one God is proclaimed by the law, the prophets and the Gospel'.[80] Here it is striking that the Gospel is mentioned first.

Clement's relative generosity towards 'apocryphal' texts and traditions,[81] which is connected with the unique spiritual milieu in Alexandria and his constant controversies with many kinds of discussion partners to whom he wants to present the true apostolic 'gnosis' of the Gospel, should not obscure the fact that even for him the apostolic origin and special church authority of the four Gospels was already unassailable. On this point, for all the differences there is no fundamental opposition between him and Irenaeus. Now that means that the four Gospels as a recognized authoritative 'apostolic' collection of writings certainly do not derive from an initiative of the bishop in distant Gaul. It must be essentially older. That applies in the second half of the second century to both Alexandria and Lyons, Antioch and Carthage. It is grounded in liturgical use, which had long been the tradition in all these places. On the other hand, Clement's relative openness in dealing with texts of uncertain origin also illuminates Serapion of Antioch's initial generosity towards the wishes of the members of the community in Rhossos. However, the sovereign teacher Clement seems to be better informed about such writings, in some circumstances suspect of heresy, than the initially unsuspecting Bishop of Antioch. We might almost say that precisely because the unique authority of the four Gospels was indispensable for him, he could sometimes bring himself also to use 'apocryphal' texts which helped him in his argument, indeed turning the very texts of the 'heretics' against them, as is evident from the example of the Gospel of the Egyptians. Thus Clement is not arguing from a position of uncertainty but rather from one of strength. Nor should we forget that interest in apocryphal Gospels, oral agrapha and midrash-like elaborations of the Gospel material continued, on the one hand out of learned or even heresiological 'curiosity', and on the other in the form of popular elaborations and hagiographical legends based on the reports in the Gospels, which seemed too simple. The source continued to bubble powerfully, basically right down to modern times.[82]

5. *Justin as the first witness to the collection of four Gospels*

Justin, the contemporary and bitter opponent of Marcion, and – as I have remarked – the first to use the plural 'Gospels' in his *Apology* (after 150) once (reluctantly), is a witness to this essentially earlier respect for the collection of the four Gospels in the church in Rome and probably also in Asia Minor, where he was converted around 130. About a decade later than the *Apology*, in the *Dialogue with Trypho* (c.AD 160), he says that the reminiscences 'were composed by apostles (of Jesus) and their successors',[83] and by the use of the plural he indicates that he recognized at least four Gospels as 'reminiscences of the apostles':[84] in all probability he is therefore already thinking of the 'apostolic' Gospels of Matthew and John and, in the case of the 'successors' to the apostles, of Mark and Luke. In other words, he knows not only the names of the authors of the Gospels – probably four – but for him they already embody the apostolic, i.e. authoritative, tradition, regardless of whether the authors were real 'apostles' or only their 'successors'. Only for that reason can he also already speak in the *Apology* and then again in the *Dialogue* of 'Reminiscences of the Apostles' instead of Gospels, although only two really 'apostolic' authors were known to him. He certainly knew the Gospels of Matthew and Luke, and very probably those of Mark and John.[85] Whether he uses apocryphal Gospels is disputed. However, their use in the extant work of Justin cannot be demonstrated convincingly. The divergent passages could also be free quotations, oral tradition or midrash-like elaboration. His practical use of these 'reminiscences of the apostles', especially of Matthew and Luke, in quotations is already 'harmonizing'. Probably he already possessed notes of some sort of private 'Gospel harmony' without John for his personal use in catechesis, to which he resorted freely and which may have inspired his pupil Tatian to write his new precise and more elaborate literary Gospel Harmony (see below, 24ff.). On the other hand, the 'reminiscences of the apostles' in Justin had already long been read aloud in worship. We shall be returning several times to this point, which is decisive for our topic (see below, 37).

6. *Criticism of the Gospels and the contradictions between them*

That there was still a dispute even a generation after Justin as to whether there were really four Gospels is shown by the conservative Roman presbyter Gaius, who has already been mentioned. Towards the end of the second century he was still denying and contesting the authenticity of the Gospel of John (and of the Apocalypse). He argued that both were forgeries by the arch-heretic Cerinthus, who according to Polycarp and Irenaeus had been a bitter adversary of John in Ephesus. In other words, for Gaius the Fourth Gospel was an impudent forgery by this Jewish-Christian and gnosticizing opponent. The reason given for this assertion is not so much that later in the second century the Fourth Gospel became popular among the Montanists and the Valentinian Gnostics; rather, it is 'historical-critical'. The Gospel deviates all too much from the Synoptics, above all in its chronology: 'The Johannine account contradicts . . . the recognized witnesses.' Irenaeus already knows a criticism of the Fourth Gospel directed against the Paraclete in radical anti-Montanist circles and rejects it sharply.[86]

The heretics' criticism of the 'scriptures' to which Irenaeus refers immediately after his catalogue on the origin of the four Gospels is of quite a different kind. It emerges from the context that the keyword 'scriptures' primarily refers to these: 'If one refutes them [i.e. the heretics who do not agree with the Gospels] from the scriptures, then they make accusations against precisely these scriptures, that they are neither reliable nor do they possess authority, that their language could be understood in different ways and that the truth cannot be discovered from them by those to whom the [secret oral] traditions are not known.' Here they referred among other things to I Cor.2.6, where Paul speaks of the 'wisdom for the perfect'. In reality, by this wisdom each is said to understand his own system.[87] Here Irenaeus mentions first Valentinus and then Marcion, Basilides and Cerinthus; however, in reality the charge above all applies to the school of Valentinus. He is wrong to mention Marcion, because Marcion rejected all oral secret tradition and appealed only to his written Gospel and a doctored Paul. Presumably he knows from his own experience that in discussions Gnostics cannot be convinced by arguments from scripture, not least from the Gospels, which they allegedly recognize,[88] because they have 'deeper' knowledge. The Bishop of Lyons contrasts their criticism of scriptures which according to them are inadequate because they are unclear with the 'apostolic tradition', which stems from the apostles and – as the continuation of his discussion of the disputed question shows – attests the clarity, reliability and perfection of the Gospels. The later old Protestant dogma spoke here of the *claritas* or *perspicuitas* and the *sufficientia sacrae scripturae*.

We get a fundamental criticism of the Gospels from the Middle Platonist Celsus, the first pagan literary opponent of Christianity, whom we know more closely from Origen's refutation *Contra Celsum*. He carefully read all four Gospels and the letters of Paul around the time of Irenaeus and found rich ammunition in them for his sharp attacks. He probably wrote against what in his eyes were the insolent assertions of the Christian Apologists like Justin, because he supposed the new religion to be a danger to the Roman state and humanity in general.[89] One argument in his accusation against the Christians is that 'some of the faithful, as though coming from a drinking bout, fight one another and alter the Gospel after it had first been written down three or four times, indeed many times, and falsify it, so that they can reject arguments against it (better).'[90]

Here he is arguing that the Christians deliberately altered their original 'message of salvation' to avoid accusations. In so doing he is basically adopting Marcion's radical standpoint, that the apostles of the group of twelve had corrupted the original Gospel 'in order to please people'. The very fact that there are several 'Gospels' already indicates a falsification of the original message.[91] The 'three' or 'four times' is probably a reference to the 'canonical' Gospels, the number of which was not yet clearly recognized everywhere, as is also shown by

Irenaeus' defence; the 'manifold' forgeries refers to the relatively numerous 'apocryphal' Gospels or Gospel-like writings which were composed in the second century, above all by Gnostics. In his answer Origen here refers particularly to Marcion and the Valentinians. This charge is continued by later enemies of the new faith, from the Neoplatonists Porphyry, Hierocles and Julian the Apostate up to Faustus, Augustine's Manichaean opponent; it compelled Augustine to write his defence, *De consensu evangelistarum*, between AD 397 and 400.[92] In it he tries daringly to defend the inerrancy of all four Gospels:[93] only differences in style and form of presentation are possible; real contradictions must be excluded.

In the time of the Reformation, the Nuremberg theologian Andreas Osiander (1498–1552), who was a contemporary of Luther, expressed himself even more strongly in his great harmony of the Gospels on the basis of an extremely strict theory of verbal inspiration. Even Augustine was not consistent enough for him. According to him, because of the differences between the Synoptic accounts Jesus had performed two stillings of the storm in two different years of his activity, and had healed two different possessed men at Gerasa and Gadara and twice the slave of a centurion; similarly four blind men before and after his visit to Jericho; he had been anointed three times and had driven the traders out of the temple three times.[94] In other words, he follows the principle: 'If two or more evangelists differ from each other even in small details in the account of a work, the only conclusion can be that they are not speaking of the same but of different matters.' 'In contrast to the Augustinian tradition . . .' he could not 'concede any distinction between essential and inessential in holy scripture'.[95]

This may seem to us to be a quite extreme case, but a similar sort of unbiblical, and ultimately rationalistic, apologetics remains the rule in Protestant orthodoxy until the beginning of historical criticism in the eighteenth century, and indeed in some evangelical fundamentalist circles to the present day. Such a 'fundamentalist rationalistic' exegesis which makes the New Testament a law book does as little service to the real historical and theological understanding of the Gospels (the two cannot be separated) as the radical ahistorical scepticism which seeks to investigate the text only by a literary approach in terms of its aesthetic value or by a dogmatic approach in terms of its unalterably fixed 'truth content' and prohibits any authentic historical investigation, or at least is not interested in it.

With its most prominent representatives from Origen to Eusebius,[96] the early church investigated this question particularly intensively, and through John Chrysostom and Ambrose to Augustine in his famous writing which has already been mentioned. On the whole it dealt with the problems of the differences and contradictions in the Gospels in a more reasonable way[97] than Old Protestant dogmatics, which was imprisoned in its rigid doctrine of inspiration and absolute inerrancy.

Nevertheless the explanation of so many manifest contradictions,[98] like the different genealogies of Jesus in Matthew and Luke, and the chronologies of the Synoptics and John, which diverge so greatly that they date the day of Jesus' death either on 14 (John) or 15 (Synoptics) Nisan, and other similar problems, compelled several church fathers to attempt learned explanations, offering more or less apologetic but always unconvincing harmonizations.[99]

7. Harmonization, uncontrolled diversity of texts or radical reduction

7.1. Tatian

So it is all the more a near-miracle that the early church resisted the temptation to replace the four Gospels, which in parts are so different, with a unitary Gospel Harmony. This would have met practical catechetical needs better and done away with all these problems. As in the case of Muhammad we would have only one 'valid' biography of Jesus. Historical criticism since Reimarus, Lessing, Semler and D. F. Strauss would then have found things much more difficult. Around AD 170 Tatian, a pupil of Justin, who came from Syria and later returned there, created, possibly in the steps of his master, a perfect Harmony of this kind, now of all four Gospels in Greek and Syriac. This was the so-called διὰ τεσσάρων (εὐαγγέλιον),[100] i. e. 'the (one) Gospel from the Four'. Tatian worked all the Gospel material like a mosaic into the framework of John with scrupulous accuracy, beginning with the prologue and ending with chapter 21. In his method he differed fundamentally from his teacher, who still used the Fourth Gospel with relative restraint and did not put it on the same level as the Synoptics; he also dealt with the text in a way which was amazingly free. Perhaps Tatian's interest in the Fourth Gospel was based on the influence of the school of Valentinus, which also forced him into an Encratism which was hostile to creation.[101] At all events the Fourth Gospel, which was also treasured among the Valentinians,[102] seemed already to be the most important for him. Initially this Harmony became established in the Syriac-speaking East as a work read aloud in worship, and this led to the four 'separate' Gospels not being translated into Syriac until probably towards the end of the third or the beginning of the fourth century. The Diatessaron still had a commentary written on it by the important Syrian theologian Ephraem (306–373). However, from the fifth century on, even there this popular Harmony was more and more displaced by the four Gospels of the mainstream church.[103] This later repudiation of the Diatessaron, which in part led to direct acts of destruction by orthodox bishops, may have been governed, among other things, by certain insertions and omissions by the author which were hostile to marriage or ascetic and Encratite, and other smaller changes. Thus for example he passed over the genealogies of Jesus, presumably because the Lukan and Matthaean versions could not be harmonized by the best means (see n.99 above). Nor did he attempt to harmonize the appearances of the risen Christ; he put the reports of the evangelists one after the other.[104] We have many quotations of the original Syriac text in the commentary on the Diatessaron by Ephraem (306–377);[105] we also possess a small fragment of the Greek text from Dura Europos, which shows how carefully Tatian worked.[106] By contrast, versions revised in the mainstream church were later translated into numerous languages: from Arabic, Persian and Armenian through Latin,[107] Old Italian to Old High German, Middle Dutch and Middle English. This is a sign that a completely unitary work continued to be valued for popular reading and learning. It is quite probable that Tatian's work was already stimulated by a 'harmonizing' use of the first three Gospels by his teacher Justin, above all of Matthew and Luke, for practical teaching. Individual apocryphal insertions in Justin, like the appearance of light at the baptism of Jesus,[108] and a few non-Synoptic sayings of Jesus[109] indicate that he exercised a degree of freedom, which presupposes that in the midst of the second century there was as yet no inviolable text which was strictly fixed on a philological basis. This developed only from the second half of the second century on, in Alexandria, the old citadel of ancient Christian philology and its first centre.[110] Neither Justin nor his pupil Tatian already presuppose a fixed '*canon* of the four Gospels'. However, we can say that in them there is a *collection* of Gospels which is already widely recognized; this represented the decisive preliminary stage to the later formation of the church canon. Irenaeus, with whom our investigation began, is then a further important stage on this way.

7.2 *The textual tradition*

Here we come up against a further problem of the early period: its Gospel texts were still to some degree 'fluid'. They could be changed – perhaps influenced by a 'richer' parallel tradition[111] – as is evident from the numerous harmonizing supplements and also from isolated additions of an interpretative and supplementary kind.[112] This is true of relations both between the Synoptics and also, less strikingly, between them and John. The weakest member, Mark, is most strongly affected by these supplements; the most influential Gospel, Matthew, has the greatest effect. The most striking of them are the different endings to Mark,[113] since the original ending in Mark 16.8 about the flight of the women from the tomb and their silence with the explanation 'for they were afraid' seemed intolerable as the last sentence of the Gospel. Matthew 28.8 already changes it to 'with fear and great joy, and ran to tell his disciples' – a clear correction of his source. The conclusion, Mark 16.9–21, in particular, is very probably a cento made up of material from the three other Gospels, Matthew, Luke and John, and apocryphal traditions, composed in the first third of the second century.[114] In general, in the first half of the second century, before Justin, sayings of Jesus were still not quoted too frequently, and in addition there was some lack of concern in quoting them exactly, i.e. a relative freedom in wording. They were not yet untouchable 'sacred text' in the strict sense (see below, 61f.). In this early period, however, this free way of quoting also applied in part to quotations from the Old Testament, even in Paul,[115] although the text of the main works of the Hebrew Old Testament, the Pentateuch, the Psalms and the prophetic books had already been laid down in Greek since the third or second century BC in the Septuagint translations which were gradually proceeding, including later revisions. From the beginning the LXX was regarded as 'holy scripture' in the Greek-speaking communities of earliest Christianity.[116] In other words, as a rule the first Christians often quoted from memory and were fond of adapting the text to the catechetical situation. For this purpose people not only used the original texts but also prepared extracts from the Old Testament scriptures and the new Christian scriptures, in some circumstances mixed with oral or 'apocryphal' material, so-called *testimonia* or ἐκλογαί.[117] The Christian teachers had this freedom because they themselves were inspired by the eschatological gift of the Spirit of God, who was the true expositor of the biblical text. There was also a further problem. A considerable number of members of the community could neither read nor write, so reading the scriptures and a lecture expounding them – sometimes in the form of a dialogue – in Sunday worship and in the freer catechetical instruction were more important than private reading for theological education or personal edification. This latter activity was limited to a relatively small circle of educated people, acknowledged teachers and leaders of the community.[118]

The reading of scripture, the sermon related to it and teaching, on the other hand, served to provide concrete instruction; in other words, the actual life of the community was orientated on a fixed, stereotyped form of Christian existence and ethics. Here above all the practical application for fundamental questions of life stood in the foreground. The 'scientific' precision in the tradition of the text which we take for granted was still completely unknown. Exactitude in the use of scripture grew in parallel to the intellectual challenge by the opponents and a raising of the level of education in the communities. The Roman Shepherd of Hermas, the Didache, a Christian apocalypse like the Ascension of Isaiah or, still before 150, the *Epistula Apostolorum* are typical examples of this early period – theologically simple and to some degree theologically indifferent.[119] The 'Christian philosopher' Justin is the first to begin to attempt cautiously such theological and philological precision, using different forms of the LXX text in his dialogue with the Jewish scribe Trypho, since each side accused the other of 'falsifying the text'.[120]

However, that does not mean that the textual tradition in the manuscripts was arbitrary. On the contrary, here we have to differentiate between relatively free quotations still influenced by oral tradition or catechetical praxis and the transmission of the text itself by early Christian scribes. We will have to assume that there were already Christian *scriptoria* around the turn of the century in the major communities like Rome, Ephesus or Antioch. These show certain typically Christian scribal customs like the use of the codex, the *nomina sacra*, and also the titles of the Gospels and the beginnings of letters. The Christian scribes worked relatively independently of the rest of the literary world of antiquity and at the same time in a conservative way.[121] It is highly improbable that Christians in the early period had their 'sectarian literature' copied in pagan scriptoria. Here they must rapidly have built up their own 'codex production' also for the LXX text (see below, 118ff.). The text of the Gospels is the best transmitted in the whole of antiquity: about six Gospel papyri go back to the period around

200 or to the second century AD,[122] and a further nineteen to the third century; of course most of them are only small fragments, but some contain larger parts of the text.[123] Together with the great uncials since the fourth century, the numerous later manuscripts, and the early translations, the attestation of the original text is so strong that practically all the secondary alterations to the text and interpolations can be picked up in the unbelievably multiple textual tradition.[124] It is therefore extremely rare for conjectures or the removal of hypothetical glosses to be necessary.

The text of the earliest Gospel 'according to Mark', which can be dated quite precisely to around the year AD 69/70, and which was first used between around AD 75–80 by Luke and then around 90–100 by the author of the Gospel of Matthew, was not demonstrably very different from the form of the text which we possess in the twenty-seventh revised edition of Nestle/Aland 1993. The hypothesis of an 'original Mark' (Ur-Mark or Proto-Mark), or of a later Deutero-Mark, occasioned by the so called 'minor agreements' between Luke and Matthew against Mark, which has been put forward time and again, has thus proved quite unnecessary.[125] The textual tradition, which despite countless variants is relatively reliable, gives no occasion for such conjectures. Codex Bezae (D), a Greek-Latin bilingual text of the fifth century, and the witnesses of 'Western' text with their numerous omissions and expansions, above all in the Gospel of Luke, the much-discussed 'Western non-interpolatives', are an exception here. In Acts this form of the text offers a distinctive, quite new and independent revision, which may go back to the middle of the second century. The riddle of this form of the text is still unsolved, but it is the exception which proves the rule.[126] The philological recension of the text which is to be presumed to have been made in Alexandria around the end of the second or the beginning of the third century did not create a completely new text, but merely corrected the text, sometimes abbreviated it slightly and improved the style. On the basis of the earliest papyri, the Old Latin translation and the large number of variants, we can get behind it. It would be completely misleading on the basis of this fact to want to claim that we may no longer speak of an 'original text' in the New Testament generally; rather we must speak initially of an almost 'chaotic' diversity to which order was first brought in an 'orthodox' way, i.e. a violent way, by the process of canonization in the mainstream church.[127] Such a judgment would be far too one-sided.

Here no sufficiently clear distinction is made between *textual criticism*, which is founded on the uniquely broad manuscript tradition of the text in antiquity, and modern *literary criticism*, which investigates behind the text that has been handed down and thus seeks to clarify the origin of the works of New Testament literature which came into being before the manuscript tradition which has come down to us, but as a rule works in a much more hypothetical way than textual criticism, which is based solely on textual evidence and above all on manuscripts. K. and B. Aland have given a convincing description of the task and methods of textual criticism, i.e. of the most thoroughgoing restoration possible of the original text.[128] The borderline between literary criticism and textual criticism runs right through the decisive point at which the Gospels 'begin their literary existence through copies', i.e. from the time when they were deliberately disseminated. 'It [textual criticism] has no access to what there was before this.'[129] That is the field of literary criticism, with what today are often abundant hypotheses which can no longer be verified; this has become all too much a favourite child of New Testament scholarship.[130] As for the relative chronological proximity to the original text, not only do we have a series of papyrus fragments which still belong to the second century or the time around 200, but we must also remember that a large number of the forerunners of the numerous Gospel texts from the third century can go back to the second century and not all need have come from Egypt. The no less early Gospel papyri of John and Matthew are hardly more than between one and three generations removed from the original writings.

The relative consistency of the Gospel text despite all the

appearances of its running wild up to the end of the second century may be connected with constant reading in worship, which on the whole required fixed forms of text. Liturgical usage is more 'conservative'; the same goes for the scribal customs in the early Christian scriptoria. The difference at precisely this point from the often romance-like apocryphal literature, say the apostolic acts, but also the Gospel of Thomas, in which the Greek fragments and the Coptic translation are often substantially different, is striking. Once again: no ancient text is as well attested as the Gospels.

7.3 Marcion

As well as the manifest contradictions in the Gospels, which must have surprised any attentive reader and which presented opponents with arguments, this relative freedom in dealing with the earlier Gospel writings that was still widespread in the second century may – *inter alia* – have caused Tatian to compose his Gospel Harmony with such scrupulous accuracy. Here a new 'theological and philological' tendency may be pointed out by comparison with his teacher Justin, who could still be relatively generous in his quotations of the Gospels (as distinct from his use of the Septuagint). Tatian wanted to sum up as precisely as possible the 'apostolic testimony' of the Gospels about Jesus, which for him was split into four versions, in a really unitary work, and thus at the same time create a superior counterpart, much richer in content, to a quite different unitary Gospel. This was the Gospel of the arch-heretic Marcion, who around AD 144 had been expelled from the church in Rome because he attributed the Old Testament to an inferior, only 'just' god, and claimed that all the Jewish-Christian apostles except Paul had falsified Jesus' original message of the 'unknown God' and 'gracious Father' 'in a Judaizing way'.

Marcion adopted the opposite approach to both Justin, with the 'Reminiscences of the Apostles', and, in his footsteps, Tatian, with the Harmony of all four Gospels. His approach was not that of synthesis but of rigorous reduction: he wanted to purge the Gospel of Luke of all Old Testament Jewish leaven, claiming this refined version as the only true one, which according to Gal. 1.12 Paul had received personally through 'a revelation of Jesus Christ' (cf. above, 3). Together with a heavily purged collection of ten letters of Paul, the 'Apostolikon', his 'Gospel' represents the earliest form of a 'New Testament canon' known to us.[131] However, perhaps this combination already had a kind of forerunner in the Gospel of John and the three Letters of John; I assume that these were published together at the beginning of the second century,[132] and in quite a different form, even before the collection and publication of the letters of Paul, in the two-volume narrative work Luke-Acts. With a pinch of salt one could also call this 'Gospel' and 'Apostolikon'.[133] Even here we owe more to Luke than modern 'critical' scholarship dares to credit him. He is the first author – at quite an early stage (see below, 99ff., 186ff.) – to connect by means of two writings the life and ministry of Jesus with the apostle(s), thus preparing for a first step in the direction of the later New Testament canon. Marcion also rejected Acts because of its tendency to harmonize the early Christian preaching, especially that of Paul, and because of its use of the Old Testament, but accepted the 'purified' Gospel of Luke, *inter alia* without the birth stories,[134] because he knew that Luke had been a follower of Paul and attributed his purged text simply to the apostle himself. In itself, a purged Gospel of Mark or John would have served his purpose better than Luke. But here the attribution to a disciple of Peter or a Judaizing apostle ruled out their use. That – as far as we can see – he does not mention Luke is understandable, since he regarded Luke too as a forger; Marcion in fact wants to restore the original Gospel of Jesus Christ preached by *Paul*. Without the connection between Luke and Paul it would be quite incomprehensible why he chose this particular Gospel. He was probably of the same view as Irenaeus and others later, that Luke wrote down the Gospel preached by Paul. It simply had to be 'purged'.

Thus Marcion too already wanted radically to do away with the offensive diversity of the Judaizing Gospels, which in his view had come about through forgery and falsification, and by means of theologically-motivated aggressive 'literary criticism' tried to regain the original form of the Gospel revealed by Christ to the one true apostle, Paul, before it had been corrupted by Judaizing forgery. It is understandable that he gained some sympathy in latently anti-Jewish modern liberal German Protestantism, a sympathy which was still lasted to the middle of the twentieth century. People did not want to be dualistic Marcionites any more, but they could understand Marcion all too well in the light of his repudiation of the Old Testament, parts of which were allegedly so questionable in religious and ethical terms.[135] That the church – fortunately – did not take the way of either Marcion or Tatian (both could have seemed seductive and in a way still do so today) is shown us for the first time by Irenaeus, not only with theological arguments, but also with historical arguments which must be taken seriously.

III

The Four Gospels, Their Authors, and the One Gospel

1. *The testimony of Irenaeus and the Roman community*

Around AD 180, Irenaeus, the first deliberately 'biblical theologian' in the full sense that we know,[136] no longer refers primarily to the Septuagint, but presents the earliest form of the 'New Testament' in the making known to us in connection with the salvation-historical scheme which he developed against Gnosticism. Here he opposes what in his view is real 'apostolic tradition' to the radical reduction in Marcion's Gospel, making the not wholly unjustified accusation against Marcion that he has 'circumcised' the Gospel of Luke and 'handed on to his disciples not the (whole) Gospel, but only a *particula evangelii*'.[137] Over against Marcion's claim that only the 'apostolic' testimony of Paul is valid, he sets what he considers to be the whole genuine 'apostolic tradition' of the divinely-willed unity of the four Gospels, the Acts of the Apostles and the letters of the three most significant apostles: thirteen by Paul,[138] one by Peter, and two (or three) by John.[139] Accordingly, in his argument against Marcion and the Gnostics he can speak both in the plural about 'the Gospels of the apostles' and in the singular about the 'Gospel which is given by the apostles'.[140] At the beginning of the third book of his anti-Gnostic work, the Bishop of Lyons has preserved for us the most important external evidence for the historical order of the four Gospels. These reports were much discussed and argued over in the past, and even today they are usually underestimated

34

or indeed completely ignored in judging the origin and dating of the Gospels.

According to him, the apostles first preached the Gospel, 'but later by God's will also handed it down to us in scriptures'. However, as preachers of the message of salvation 'they all equally possessed the Gospel of God, each for himself'.[141] Then follow individual items of evidence about the four Gospels and their authors:

> Matthew composed his Gospel among the Hebrews in their language, when Peter and Paul were preaching the Gospel in Rome and founding the church (there). After their death, Mark, the disciple and interpreter of Peter, handed down to us the preaching of Peter in written form. Luke, the companion of Paul, set down the Gospel preached by him in a book. Finally John, the disciple of the Lord, who also reclined on his breast, himself composed the Gospel when he was living in Ephesus in (the province of) Asia.[142]

This account of the origin of the 'fourfold Gospel' has all too easily been dismissed to the realm of later apologetic legends, and sometimes Irenaeus has even been branded a liar.[143] However, Claus Thornton[144] has shown that this is an earlier tradition, which must be taken seriously; as the geographical references and references to persons show, it is written throughout from a Roman perspective. This will be clear from the mention of 'Peter and Paul preaching the Gospel in Rome', when Matthew wrote the first Gospel book 'among the Hebrews in their language'. According to him the first written Gospel was already composed in Jewish Palestine by the apostle Matthew when it was still being preached orally by the two leading apostles Peter and Paul in the pagan capital of the Empire. How Irenaeus, who also knows and treasures the Acts of the Apostles, imagines this time of the 'preaching of the Gospel' by 'Peter and Paul' remains unclear. That Paul taught there successfully for some time follows from Acts 28.30f.; Peter's stay from I Peter 5.13. The later tradition in Eusebius has Peter coming to Rome at an early stage, shortly after the accession of Claudius, but the historical value of this piece of information remains uncertain.[145] Ignatius, too, 'not like Peter and Paul do I command you' (Rom. 4.3), and above all I Clement 5 indicate that both were active in Rome, a community which took on unique significance after the destruction of Jerusalem. For the Roman community both apostles belong inseparably together from earliest times. Galatians 2.11ff. was no longer an obstacle for it. Very soon it felt especially honoured by the residence and the martyrdom of the two 'princes of the apostles'.[146] It is striking that despite the special significance of Rome, which he acknowledges, Irenaeus nevertheless moves the earliest Aramaic Gospel writing to Jewish Palestine and attributes it to an apostle, i.e. a member of the most intimate circle of disciples: there, in Jewish Palestine, is the homeland of the Gospel of Jesus Christ. This text of Irenaeus' is relatively independent of Papias' two earlier pieces of information about Matthew and Mark,[147] around two generations before Irenaeus, which we have yet to investigate. The Bishop of Lyons knew Papias' work,[148] but simply does not quote it here. He knows substantially more about the origin of the Gospels than is reported by Papias, who in turn has partially quite different things to say. His reference to Matthew has rather a different character from the utterly enigmatic Papias text (see below, 68ff.).

The form of this information is also interesting. As Thornton has demonstrated, it corresponds to the short notes about authors in the catalogues of ancient libraries, of the kind that we know, say, from the Museion in Alexandria. Presumably this information comes from the Roman church archive. As I Clement, around AD 100, shows, the Roman community had a respectable library, even containing 'apocryphal' books like Esther, Judith, Wisdom and Sirach, which are still alien to the New Testament.[149] There in Rome where, after the destruction of Jerusalem in AD 70, all the threads of the communities in the empire came together, in the first decades of the second century they must already have had the four Gospels, even if they did not recognize them all equally. Probably the latest Gospel, that of John, was not so highly esteemed in Rome in earlier times as Matthew, Mark and Luke. This is still evident in Justin, who also presupposes quite a large community library.[150] Though the tradition which is already to be presupposed in Marcion (i.e. again in Rome) that Luke wrote down the 'Gospel' that Paul preached may be questionable, it was known there that Luke had been a travelling companion of Paul for many years.[151] The relevant information about each writing, its author and its origin were kept in the Roman church archive; this was important for reading them aloud in worship, since people had to know what they were reading there and also had to convey this to the community. Anonymous public readings were hardly tolerable because each reading needed an 'authoritative' or even 'inspired' text, and author.[152] If all the Old Testament writings had their titles which were given before they were read in worship and sometimes also mentioned in quotations, this was also necessary for the new writings of the Christian community.

This is again confirmed again by Justin around 150 in Rome: according to him the 'reminiscences of the apostles or the writings of the prophets' [153] were read aloud in worship on Sunday, a custom which may go back to the last decades of the first century, for the Gospels of Mark and Matthew were written above all to be read out in worship (see above, 20). It is interesting that Justin here already mentions the Gospels before the prophetic writings, i.e. the Old Testament, which was understood throughout as a prophetic work focussed on Christ. One might almost assume that already in his time in Rome the reading of the Gospels occupied a role like that played by the Torah of Moses in Jewish worship, and that this reading had already had such a role for a considerable time. Probably Mark 13.14 – which was written in Rome – already presupposes a public reading of the Gospel in the community: the person reading it out was to raise his voice at this point.[154] As I have already pointed out (see above, 4), the designation 'reminiscences of the apostles', skilfully chosen in this particular context, presupposes that the Apologist understood the reading of the

Gospels to be a normative testimony of the messengers of Christ to their Lord in the worship of the community.

That Irenaeus in his famous report about the Gospels is referring back to the Roman community archive is also suggested by the fact that a little later he refers once again to the 'community in Rome founded and organized by the apostles Peter and Paul whose fame is everywhere', and lists its bishops from Linus, the immediate successor to Peter, to the twelfth member, his contemporary Eleutherus.[155] He had visited Eleutherus in Rome in AD 177, the year of persecution, when he was still presbyter of the community in Lyons,[156] and had possibly had stayed for some time in Rome about two decades earlier, at the time when Polycarp, the bishop of his home town Smyrna, had visited the capital. His way from Asia Minor to Gaul certainly took him through Rome. He was therefore familiar with Asian and Roman customs and traditions and explicitly emphasized the special authority of the community in the imperial capital.[157] At least the first seven or eight 'bishops' of Rome mentioned in the list need not have been 'monarchical' bishops in the later strict sense, but presbyters who could legitimately represent the Roman community (or communities) to the outside world,[158] thus e.g. Clement, who wrote the famous letter to the Corinthians about AD 100. The names of these 'leading presbyters' must similarly have been recorded in the Roman archive. That means that this list, too, need not simply be an invention, but will come from the Roman archive. It is certainly older than the author Irenaeus, and the same also goes for his list of four Gospels.

2. The historical order of the Gospels and the Gospel collection

The order of the four Gospels in Irenaeus's list is also an important indication of the age of the collection, which for him was already an 'apostolic', authoritative one, and which is still a matter of dispute today. It shows that the names of the evangelists cannot be separated from the Gospels.[159] If we leave aside the problematical Hebrew 'Matthew',[160] historically it corresponds precisely to the chronological order of their origin: Mark, Luke, John. This shows some kind of historical remembrance about the making of the Gospels. Mark is the earliest, followed by Luke, who uses it; John, who presupposes both but deliberately gives a quite different account, is last. As the beginning of the Muratorian Canon, which is mutilated, has been lost, its account only begins with the last sentence about Mark; it mentions Luke the physician as the author of the Third Gospel and has John follow him.[161] Further evidence is the version of the old Gospel prologue to Luke, which has also been preserved in Greek; this explicitly emphasizes that Matthew and Mark came into being before Luke, and John after these Gospels.[162] The divergent later information of Clement of Alexandria, which he claims to have received from the 'Elders', i.e. especially his teacher Pantaenus, that those Gospels which contained a pedigree of Jesus, i. e. Matthew and Luke, are the oldest, already shows the tendency to devalue Mark in the time after Luke and Matthew, who are later and have worked his Gospel into theirs. Thus Mark soon became unimportant, but nevertheless remained in the Gospel collection because his work was backed by Petrine authority (see below, 78ff.).[163] On the other hand it is significant that throughout the whole of the early church there is never a real commentary on Mark. From now on Mark leads to some degree a shadow existence between Matthew and Luke, but because of a conservative attitude was kept, and not lost. As I have remarked, the Gospels were composed between around AD 70 and 100. The Greek Matthew (we have no other) is, as we will see, quite late and is to be put between Luke and John around AD 90–100 (see below, 169ff.). Neither an extremely early nor an extraordinarily late date for John (Klaus Berger around 50/60, F. C. Baur and W. Schmithals around 170)[164] is historically justified. In other words Irenaeus, or probably the Roman archive, is amazingly well informed about the circumstances and chronological order of the composition of the Gospels.

He knows, for example, that Mark wrote his Gospel after the

deaths of Peter and Paul, i. e. as martyrs, presumably in Rome in the Neronian persecution of AD 64.[165] He does not say directly that Mark wrote his Gospel in Rome,[166] as Clement of Alexandria reports soon afterwards, since this fact was generally known there and is presupposed in the statement 'Mark . . . handed down to *us*', i.e. the Roman community. On the other hand, again correctly, he emphasizes the origin of the Fourth Gospel at a foreign place, Ephesus in the province of Asia. This precise geographical detail would have been unnecessary had Irenaeus, who himself comes from the province of Asia, received the information about John there. By contrast, in Rome people's geographical knowledge was not so good. This information cannot come from Papias either. The emphasis on the fact that John is the Beloved Disciple (John 13.25) and composed the Gospel himself is probably an indication that this was still a disputed question. John is not called apostle but only the 'disciple of Lord' according to the old stereotyped tradition of Asia Minor which goes back to John the elder, whom Papias already calls 'disciple of the Lord' [167](see below, 67f.). The conclusion of the Gospel (chapter 21) indicates, rather, that it was edited by disciples after his death.[168] By contrast, the place of origin of the Gospel of Luke was presumably already uncertain at that time.[169] Nevertheless, towards the end of Acts, in 28.14, 'and so we came to Rome. And the brothers when they had heard of us came out from there to meet us', it proves that Luke had links with the Roman community and was not unknown there. Perhaps 'Theophilus', the 'friend of God', was a prominent Roman whose real name had to be kept secret.[170] That would explain why Luke ends his second book with the arrival of Paul in Rome. From now on the recipient knows the story himself. The later information in the so called Monarchian Gospel prologues[171] that Luke wrote his Gospel in Greece (Achaia) seems to fill the geographical gap between Mark in Italy and John in Asia Minor.

Contrary to Irenaeus, for apologetic reasons Clement of Alexandria relates that the Gospel of Mark was composed in Peter's lifetime, at the urgent request of his hearers. There are two versions of the reaction of the prince of the apostles: according to the first he just remained neutral and made no objections; according to the second he was delighted and 'confirmed the writing for reading in the churches'.[172] The first 'neutral' or restrained verdict on Mark may be connected with the fact that immediately afterwards Clement praises John, who, he says, recognizing that the three earlier Gospels had treated only τὰ σωματικά i.e. the more external events of the life of Jesus, composed his 'spiritual Gospel' on the admonition of his disciples and seized by the Spirit.[173] By contrast, the other verdict gave full 'apostolic legitimation' to the Second Gospel, which it urgently needed in the face of the overwhelming rivalry of the major Gospels. The twofold, contradictory tradition in Clement and the difference between it and Irenaeus, who is a little earlier and whose work he knew, show that even the status of the earliest Gospel was still not completely undisputed around AD 200 (or rather, was being disputed again). That becomes even clearer in the note in Papias, which is two or three generations earlier (see below, 65ff.).

This order of the Gospels in Irenaeus' famous report, orientated on the chronological order of their composition, is also confirmed by their order in most of the earliest codices. So in the great uncials of the fourth/fifth centuries, Vaticanus, Sinaiticus, Alexandrinus, Ephraemi Syri rescriptus and nearly all later majuscules and minuscules, but also in a papyrus, the very early P 75 from as early as the beginning of the third or the end of the second century, the order Luke/John is shown, and it is demonstrated that the four Gospels could also be divided between two codices. The first, which is lost, very probably contained Matthew and Mark.[174] This order also corresponds to that of the Muratorian Canon and the earliest Gospel prologue (see above, 39).

This matching order of the four Gospels in Irenaeus, Origen, Eusebius, Athanasius and the later church fathers,[175] at least one very early Egyptian papyrus, nearly all later parchment codices since the fourth century, and later canon catalogues,[176] is all the more striking, since in the earlier part of the second century an individual codex for each Gospel was certainly still the most frequent practice.[177] It indicates an earlier tradition about Irenaeus' order, substantially similar, to which the order of the Gospels in the church archives of leading communities corresponded (see below, 123ff.). Other orders remain more or less exceptions. The most important exception is the so called 'Western order': Matthew, John, Luke, Mark (and Acts), probably in P 45[178] shortly after 200, in some old Latin manuscripts (e a b ff² f g), in the Apostolic Constitutions and in the outsider Codex D (fifth/sixth century), in W (fourth/fifth century) and X (Monacensis ninth/tenth century).[179] This is easily explained by the priority of the apostolic authors to the disciples of apostles;[180] in the case of the latter, the order is determined by the greater length and thus also significance of Luke by comparison with Mark. Here the historical 'miracle' was that after the composition of the great Gospels Luke and Matthew, which largely reproduced it, Mark was not lost, like all others of the 'many' mentioned in Luke 1. The earliest Gospel had really become the least important after the three later ones.[181]

In this early period of the second and third century the frequency of the use of the Gospels and therefore the dissemination of manuscripts of them was still strikingly different. It was very closely connected with the high value attached to content and authority and the use in worship which resulted from them. The most widespread Gospel writings were those which were allegedly apostolic and in reality later (see below, 76f.); those of disciples of the apostles were less important, although they were earlier. According to the papyrus tradition known to us so far, of the around twenty-five Gospel papyri before Constantine eleven are of John, nine of Matthew, four of Luke and only one of Mark.[182] That is according to the twenty-seventh revised edition of Nestle/Aland, 1993. However, in the volumes of the Oxyrhynchus papyri for 1997 and 1998 there are a further nine presumably pre-Constantinian Gospel fragments, so that the total increases to thirty-four, more precisely twelve of Matthew,[183] five of Luke and fifteen of John. John was evidently particularly popular in Egypt in the second and third centuries – as opposed to Mark and Luke. Only in the case of Mark does this number remain limited to one, i.e. to P45 as the one great composite codex from the beginning or the middle of the third century. This discrepancy in the frequency of the four Gospels is striking.

Therefore despite this extreme subordination of the Second Gospel it is surprising that Papias already reports its origin and that fundamentally already in Justin (see above, 19ff.) and then in Irenaeus, Clement of Alexandria and Tertullian it could appear quite naturally as a fixed part of the 'four-Gospel collection'. Its importance within this collection must rest on a very old and authoritative tradition – towards the end of the second century – which could not be shaken, despite its rare appearance. This also means that it was rarely found in the smaller community libraries. We have papyrus examples only from the province of Egypt and not from the Nile Delta, above all from Fayyum, the place where the Oxyrhynchus papyri were discovered; here evidently smaller communities could dispense with the Second and sometimes also the Third Gospel. The community libraries in Alexandria, where appeal was in fact made to Mark, the founder of the community, must have had a copy of his Gospel.[184] By contrast, the predilection for John in Egypt is probably connected with an early spiritualizing, indeed 'Platonizing', thought in Alexandria which had already been typical of Alexandrian Judaism since the second century BC, with Aristobulus and later the book of Wisdom and Philo. With good reason Clement, the first 'orthodox' Alexandrian theologian that we know more closely, described John, as opposed to the 'Synoptic Gospels concerned with bodily things', as 'the spiritual Gospel'.[185] These numerous Gospel fragments and texts on papyri are a clear indication of the scale of the significance of the Gospels, especially Matthew, John and Luke, for the early churches and their theology in the Egyptian Chora, of which we know almost nothing before the end of the second century.[186] However, in other areas of the church the numerical ratio of the Gospels could have been rather different. Thus in

Rome Matthew may have predominated, but the number of the earliest Gospel quotations in the fathers like Irenaeus, Tertullian and Clement to some degree confirms the ratio given by the papyri of the second and third centuries (see n.55 above).

The rival order Matthew, John, Luke, Mark, especially in some manuscripts of the 'Western' text, is in any case an exception, although it must seem theologically more 'rational'. Intrinsically one would expect that as the Gospel which was later to become the most insignificant, Mark would always stand at the end. But remarkably, that was not in fact the case. Evidently this order could no longer gain a footing, because the earlier 'historical' order was already largely firmly established. The order of the old Syriac Gospel discovered by Cureton – Matthew, Mark, John and Luke – is also irrelevant: possibly Luke appeared as an 'outsider' by comparison with the apostolic Gospels of Matthew, Peter-Mark and John. The old Syriac Sinai palimpsest, however, has the usual order.[187] At all events, the order Matthew, Mark, Luke, John, which appears for the first time in Irenaeus, which is meant to reflect the chronological origin of the Gospels, and which, apart from Matthew, in fact does, rests on very old tradition. In my view this goes back to the beginnings of the second century; otherwise it would never have been able relatively quickly to become the dominant order almost everywhere, despite the striking retreat of Mark.

It is also striking that while Irenaeus and even Justin refer to the apostolic character of all four Gospels, nevertheless not all four Gospels are attributed to apostles, i.e. to members of the group of the Twelve, who according to the view of the teachers of the second century were the authentic bearers of the 'apostolic tradition' that constituted the church. As Justin already emphasizes (see above, 20), they were also attributed to two disciples of apostles, Mark and Luke, whose works were manifestly the oldest.[188] Given the emphasis that was attached to 'eyewitness' in the second century, because the tradition was running wild, one might have expected only apostolic titles with a late, unhistorical 'invention' of the author's names. From the beginning of the second century this then really became the rule in 'apocryphal' Gospels (see below, 59ff.). What would have prevented the copyists or the communities in a secondary attribution in the second century from transferring the Gospel of Mark to Peter and the Gospel of Luke to Paul? In the second century they would certainly no longer have come up with the relatively remote names of Mark and Luke. This possibility of a direct apostolic origin related for Mark is indicated in Justin[189] and completed with Marcion. With Marcion Paul really suppresses the alleged forger Luke and the real author of a Gospel becomes – even more clearly than in 'orthodoxy', which was developing gradually – Christ himself. Far too little attention has been paid to this basic question in 'critical' scholarship and nowhere has a satisfactory solution been offered.

As the quite unequal numerical attestation of the four Gospels in the Egyptian papyri from the second to the fourth centuries shows that before Constantine the Gospels were predominantly disseminated as individual codices,[190] the dominant order in the codices containing several Gospels and in the canonical lists corresponding to the lists of authors in Irenaeus – Matthew, Mark, Luke, John – cannot, as is still constantly assumed, be attributed simply to the central introduction of a codex of the four Gospels, which contained all four texts in one volume, say in the early second century. This thesis, which we already found in Zahn and Harnack, is now again being advocated with an extensive justification by T. K. Heckel,[191] who wants to associate the collection of all four Gospels with John 21 and the Johannine school, and in this connection refers among other things to Eusebius' report of the origin of the collection of four Gospels, which is said to rest on earlier tradition, possibly even that of Papias. In Eusebius, first of all there is a report of the composition of the Gospel of Matthew in Hebrew for the Jewish Christians in Palestine, before the apostle left the Holy Land. He then goes on:

After Mark and Luke had produced the Gospels (named) after them, the tradition goes that at the end John too, who over the whole period had used the oral message, saw himself occasioned to write for the following reason. After the three Gospels composed earlier had already reached all, and also him, he accepted them positively, as the tradition goes, and confirmed their truth. The writings lack only the report of what Christ accomplished first at the beginning of his preach-ing. And this word is really true.[192]

This tradition, composed very much in the style of Eusebius, certainly does not belong in the second century, but to Alexandria or Caesarea in the third. It has the three earlier Gospels legitimated by the beloved disciple and is meant to resolve the chronological conflict between the Fourth Gospel and the first three Gospels. This piece of text hardly has any-thing to do with Papias (and the elder John). Papias' fragments produce quite a different picture; above all he does not yet identify John the son of Zebedee with the 'elder John', who provided his tradition. It is interesting that here the general dissemination of the three earlier Gospels, i.e. a collection of three, is presupposed. Moreover Heckel has paid too little attention to the testimony of the early papyri: in the pre-Constantinian texts of the Gospels the codex of the four Gospels by no means predominates; on the contrary, if it did, Mark would be represented far more frequently in the Gospel texts and John and Matthew more rarely. That means that this form of codex was still the rare exception in the second century, even if we must assume quite special circumstances for the Egyptian chora.

The question of the order of the Gospels must be separated from the question of the origin of the first composite codex. Moreover there were also intermediate stages, like P 75 with Luke and John in one codex (see above, nn.123 and 174). Knowledge of their attribution to an author and the chrono-logical order of their composition must be substantially older than the collection of the four in one codex. It is best explained with Thornton as deriving from historical knowledge which was recorded in the lists of books in larger and more influential communities. Now in the last three decades of the first century, according to the end of Acts, I Peter and I Clement, the Pastoral Epistles and the letters of Ignatius, Rome had become by far the most important community. It was constantly visited by Christian teachers and travellers (see below, 138f.) and was in uninterrupted contact with the leading communities throughout the empire. The order of the Gospels in its 'bookcase' may have become normative for the larger communities in the Roman empire in the course of the first half of the second century (see Chapter IV).

Given the theological significance, the later 'Western' order – Matthew, John, Mark, Luke (or Luke, Mark) – which perhaps played a role in the province of Africa and in part in Egypt would have been more obvious as the real 'apostolic' order.[193] That this 'Western' order too, following the apostolic status, does not exclude knowledge of the historical order, is shown by the Latin prologues to the Gospels, where despite the order Matthew, John, Luke, Mark (or Mark, Luke), in the prologue to the Gospel of Luke the 'historical' order of composition (Matthew, Mark, Luke, John) is explicitly attested.[194] Now the question of the origin of this order is indissolubly bound up with the Gospel superscriptions, the significance and age of which Heckel underestimates. Here we must not forget that the historical books of the LXX up to IV Kingdoms and the prophetic books from Isaiah to Daniel had a fixed order, orientated on the history of the people of God, although in the synagogues they were not kept in composite codices but in individual scrolls. The scrolls must have lain side by side in the 'Torah shrine' in a fixed order, so that the correct book was immediately to hand (see below, 116ff.). Therefore in the case of the Gospels, too, from the beginning a relatively fixed 'historical' order was likely. The Christians took over from the synagogue not only the LXX but also the need for simple book titles and a fairly fixed order in the bookcase. It *must* have been possible to be able to find the books for reading in worship quickly and with no danger of confusion (see below, 118). Every scholar knows this problem from his or her own library.

3. *The superscriptions of the Gospels*

3.1. *Their new form and its meaning*

The unusual list in Irenaeus in turn presupposes the superscriptions of the Gospels, which have similarly been completely neglected in recent scholarship. Sometimes there are still crude false judgments here. That may be connected with the fact that even in the more recent editions of Nestle-Aland the textual evidence for the *inscriptiones* and *subscriptiones* is in part quite incomplete.[195] These titles are widely attested in a variety of ways: by some of the earliest papyri, by reports in the second- and third-century church fathers, and by the earliest translations. They too were already completely uniform in the second century.[196]

Their original form, which is also demonstrated by earlier papyri as *inscriptio* or *subscriptio*, is always the same: εὐαγγέλιον κατὰ Μαθθαῖον or Μᾶρκον, Λουκᾶν and 'Ιωάννην, etc., i.e. 'the Gospel *in the version of* Matthew, Mark, Luke or John'. This goes against the form customary in ancient book titles, in which the name of the author is put first in the genitive and followed by the title of the work; we find this title even in the New Testament, for example in the Catholic Epistles.[197] The usage was probably disseminated generally, at the latest through the famous library of Ptolemy II, the Museion, in Alexandria. As a rule these titles have the same form regardless of whether they were added at a secondary stage or are original. Anonymous works were relatively rare and *must have* been given a title in the libraries. They were often given the name of a pseudepigraphical author. In other words, in the Hellenistic and Roman period almost all books which were duplicated by copying, disseminated in the book trade and collected in libraries, also had a title which had similarly been structured by the model of the inclusion of the book in the Museion of Alexandria and other great libraries. Works without titles easily got double or multiple titles when names were given to them in different libraries. This is also evident from individual pseudepigrapha of the Old and New Testaments, for example.

48

Both the authors and later editors could change or supplement titles.[198]

The unusual titles of the Gospels already indicate that the evangelists are not meant to appear as 'biographical' authors like others, but to bear witness in their works to the *one* saving message of Jesus Christ. As is already shown by the beginning of the oldest Gospel, Mark 1.1, 'beginning of the Gospel of Jesus Christ', the title of this Gospel could not be 'Gospel of Mark' because the content of his book was the 'Gospel of Jesus Christ', the saving message of Christ – as subjective genitive (or *genetivus auctoris)*, 'coming from Jesus Christ' and objective genitive, 'about Jesus Christ' – but only 'the Gospel (of Jesus Christ) *according* to Mark'. The real 'author' of the one Gospel was Jesus Christ himself.[199] In addition, a double genitive like 'Gospel of Mark of Jesus Christ' would have been stylistically almost intolerable.[200] Moreover such a title with the genitive of the author would have put too much emphasis on the author by comparison with the real author and content of the Gospel, Jesus Christ. The closest parallel to this linguistic usage is to be found in the church fathers, when they speak of the Old Testament prophetic writings κατὰ τοὺς Ἑβδομήκοντα, according to (the translation of) the seventy (or, more precisely, seventy-two) legendary translators in Alexandria, as opposed to the later Jewish 'recensions' according to (κατὰ) Theodotion, Aquila or Symmachus.[201] The seventy-two were indeed not authors, as Moses, the prophets, David or Solomon were regarded as authors; but already the Jew Philo and later the church fathers regarded the translators as prophetic interpreters of the Old Testament word of God himself, given by the inspiration of the Holy Spirit.[202] It may, however, be that this terminology relating to the 'seventy' and the later editors is already formed in imitation of the title of the Gospels, since it is to be found only in the Christian tradition. If we might call the Gospel writings a new literary 'genre', i.e. of 'religious' or 'kerygmatic' biography, the titles in particular, which took a novel form, would be an indication of that.

3.2. *They were not secondary additions but part of the Gospels as originally circulated*

It follows from this that these superscriptions were not added to the Gospels secondarily, at a later time, long after their composition, as e.g. Zahn and Harnack still believed, say when the four Gospels were first brought together in a great codex – a view which is still widespread today but on closer inspection is untenable.[203] Although they belonged together by their content, in the second century – as I have already said – they primarily still circulated in codex form as individual writings. This form, which during the first and second centuries AD was quite rare in pagan usage, was a typical Christian achievement. It is certainly substantially older than the first collection of more than one Gospel in a codex and in my view goes well back into the first century.[204] It set the sacred books of the new community apart from the scriptural scrolls of its Jewish mother. Therefore the Old Testament scrolls in Christian use were relatively quickly copied on to codices. We can distinguish the few Jewish and the numerous Christian manuscripts of the LXX on papyrus with no difficulty, because the former are always on scrolls and the latter nearly always on codices. Thus the Gospels were probably written on codices from the beginning.[205]

The first collections of two, three and possibly, somewhat later, four 'Jesus biographies' together into one Gospel codex still remains obscure and is a matter of dispute. It probably began in larger communities in which several Gospels were read in worship.[206] For practical considerations these were made into a larger codex to read aloud from. Here the order could still be variable, but it was plausible for Matthew to stand in first place as the most important and allegedly oldest Gospel, and John, probably at some distance in time, to stand at the end as the latest of the four. The order Mark, Luke, John would then have corresponded to the chronological order of composition. The other order, wrongly described as 'Western', with the two apostolic Gospels Matthew and John at the beginning, seemed to be more sensible theologically and corresponded to the frequency of usage, but in the long run it could no longer really assert itself in the face of the 'historical' order. Here too people were amazingly conservative. Presumably such a collection came into being for the first time in Rome in the first decades of the second century and then spread from there; however, perhaps there was also a certain parallelism to Asia Minor, the home of the Fourth Gospel and the Johannine corpus, where there was a special interest in disseminating the Johannine writings. Indeed throughout the second century Christian teachers and authors travelled frequently between the imperial capital and the province of Asia. Theologically, as a result of the impulses stemming from the Johannine corpus, the province of Asia played a leading role until towards the end of the second century. By contrast, the community in the imperial capital enjoyed the highest respect and correspondingly the greater influence. However, such a development was not possible as an act of force, but needed some time. Be this as it may, it was preceded by the gradual collection of the codices of the individual Gospels; here, as is shown by the papyrus discoveries in Egypt, even in the third century the individual codex still predominated. For a long time the composite codex remained the rare exception, probably for technical reasons. Only gradually and probably first as an exception were two or three and finally four Gospels with their already existing title εὐαγγέλιον κατὰ . . . as *inscriptio* or *superscriptio* combined in a larger codex. In Chapter IV I shall attempt to give a hypothetical reconstruction of this development starting from Rome (see below, 116ff.).

That in the early period the individual codex of a Gospel tended to predominate and, at least in Egypt, mainly the 'apostolic' Gospels Matthew and John were disseminated is shown by their absolute predominance in the papyri of the Gospels before Constantine (see above, 42f.). On the other hand, no complete canonical Gospel appears in a mixed codex together with letters or edifying writings of various kinds.[207] At best later shorter texts from the Gospels, taken out of context, appear in such a connection, for example for liturgical use.

Passages as well known as, say, the Our Father, could also be used later for magical purposes.[208] This separate tradition of the Gospels, particularly in the earlier period, shows that they played a prominent role relatively soon, i.e. already in the second century, as Justin confirms. It is also striking that, although initially they were disseminated only as individual writings and it took some time for the collection of two, three or four in a codex to become established, the 'historical' knowledge of the order of their origin which is evident from the reports about the evangelists in Irenaeus, the Muratorian Canon, the prologues to the Gospels and the order in many codices of the Gospels was preserved as fixed independent tradition.

As is shown by the titles of the New Testament books, Justin and Papias, at a very early stage – not to say from the beginning – there was an interest in the authorship and therefore at the same time in the 'apostolic authority' of the writings read aloud in worship. By reading such texts there was a desire to make present the proclamation of the first witnesses who founded communities. Therefore already from the last decades of the first century more and more writings were composed under the direction of an apostle, whether this was Paul,[209] Peter[210] or – in the case of the first evangelist – Matthew. In the second century this tendency continued with greater force in the overabundant 'apocryphal' literature. In the case of one writing handed down anonymously, the Letter to the Hebrews, people likewise scratched their heads over the absent author. Tertullian attributed the letter to Barnabas,[211] in the Greek-speaking East it was put in the proximity of Paul; by contrast the Muratorian Canon, presumably from Rome, simply omits it (see above, n.41).[212] This ascription to Paul was probably already made by the editor of the Pauline corpus around AD 100. However, it says much for the conservative character of the textual tradition that here people did not simply invent an appropriate author and add a correspondingly brief introduction to the letter, but preserved the enigmatic title πρὸς Ἑβραίους and the lack of a prescript.[213] We meet with the combination of the title of the work and the authority of the author throughout the second century, both with the authentic writings and with the constantly increasing 'apostolic' pseudepigrapha.[214]

3.3. The Gospels did not first circulate anonymously and their collection is not the result of an official decision in the church

It can therefore also by no means be assumed that at some time in this dark period, before Irenaeus or even more before Justin, there had been a kind of general 'council' of a number of churches in a province at which the four hitherto anonymous writings gained recognition, were given their titles, and were then brought together as a 'four-Gospel canon'. Such an idea would be completely anachronistic. The first local synods known to us are only in connection with the origin of Montanism towards the end of the second century, in the province of Asia, and did not concern themselves with questions of the canon.[215] Far less could the 'four-Gospel collection' be the work of a single Christian authority or school,[216] because no person, school or even community in the early second century possessed the authority and power to establish its own Gospel collection throughout the church by one decisive action. The acceptance of single books and even more of a collection of books for use in worship and catechetical instruction simply could not be enforced; as a rule it needed a longer development and depended upon the authority of the writer(s), its (or their) acknowledged theological and paraenetical content, and the example of influential and leading churches.[217]

At all events, the rapid increase in the production of 'Christian' literature in the second century, which is already lamented by Papias, made a critical survey of the texts involved in readings in worship in the individual communities increasingly more urgent.[218] Here not only were the Gospels or particular letters of apostles read in worship, but also other didactic writings composed with a certain authority like I Clement in Smyrna in the case of Polycarp and in Corinth still in the time of Bishop Dionysius in the middle of the second century,[219] and later also Acts of martyrs, which were sent out as letters.[220] Other writings, like the Shepherd of Hermas which was popular in the second century too, or some 'apocrypha' of the LXX like Tobit, Wisdom or Sirach, were useful for catechetical and moral instruction, for example in baptismal teaching. In the second and third centuries their use in worship and instruction still in no way meant 'canonicity' in the later dogmatic sense. Before the fourth century there was as yet to be no talk of a clearly fixed 'canon' [221] of the New Testament in the strict sense. However, the collection of the four Gospels is the most important step towards the formation of the canon. The redaction of the letters of Paul was a further important development.

At the same time, the strange uniformity and early attestation of the titles of the Gospels excludes the possibility that for a long time they had been circulating anonymously in the communities or even that, as in the case of some apocryphal texts from Nag Hammadi, they had received their titles as a secondary addition or that these titles had even been changed. For if they had first circulated anonymously and had been given their titles only at a secondary stage and independently of one another in the different communities, because a title was needed for announcing the reading in worship, this must necessarily have resulted in a diversity of titles, as can be illustrated by many examples from antiquity. On this assumption the question why these particular titles, Matthew, Mark, Luke and John, i.e. of very different authors, were added also remains quite unexplained. There is no trace of such anonymity.[222] Not only the complete uniformity of the titles from Alexandria to Lyons and from Antioch to Carthage[223] before the end of the second century and their 'historical sequence' (Matthew), Mark, Luke, John, but also manifold references in the later second century itself, whether to the Gospels as authoritative scripture or to its authors, show their great age, indeed in my view their original character. At least in the second half of the second century after Justin the references to author, title and Gospel text accumulate to such a degree that I need not go into the matter further.[224]

There is, however, a dispute over the fate of the Gospels and their titles in the most obscure part of church history, the first half of the second century, the decades before Justin's *Apology* shortly after AD 150 and the editing of the fourth and last Gospel, that according to John, around the turn of the century in the time of Trajan (AD 96–117). In this connection we should not forget that simply of the second-century Christian writings known to us by title, around 85% have been lost. The real loss must be substantially higher.[225] Our knowledge is therefore very fragmentary and the extant witnesses are more or less chance ones. Therefore the argument from silence, which is popular in the history of early Christian literature, and indeed in some circumstances is necessary, easily leads to false judgments. Nevertheless the fact remains that it is utterly improbable that in this dark period, at a particular place or through a person or through the decision of a group or institution unknown to us, the four superscriptions of the Gospels, which had hitherto been circulating anonymously, suddenly came into being and, without leaving behind traces of earlier divergent titles, became established throughout the church. Let those who deny the great age and therefore basically the originality of the Gospel superscriptions in order to preserve their 'good' critical conscience, give a better explanation of the completely unanimous and relatively early attestation of these titles, their origin and the names of authors associated with them. Such an explanation has yet to be given, and it never will be. New Testament scholars persistently overlook basic facts and questions on the basis of old habits.[226]

Thus – as I have already said (see above, 32) – contrary to a widespread view, Marcion with his single Gospel and the one Apostolikon was not the first to prompt the bringing together of the εὐαγγέλιον τετράμορφον[227] in one collection[228] in the mainstream church. The four-Gospel collection did not result from the attempt to defend the 'apostolic' Jesus tradition against his radical attack. It was the other way round. As the examples of Justin, especially Tatian and perhaps Theophilus of Antioch[229] show, Marcion's provocation and his radical reduction encouraged the production of Gospel harmonies on the basis of (three or) four works; however, after Marcion such harmonies could no longer establish themselves because the (three or) four Gospels had already largely found recognition before him, and because from the beginning names from the apostolic age were connected with these Gospels. The 'apostolic' authority of the four (or three) Gospels and their collection is not a consequence of the Marcionite reduction to one Gospel but its presupposition. This rejection of all attempts to produce a Gospel harmony came about although such an authoritative, generally recognized, work would have been very helpful in the controversy with Marcion, Gnostic opponents, pagan critics like Celsus and Jewish conversation partners. But in the second half of the second century the 'apostolic' authority of the four Gospels which partially differed in such an offensive way was already so strong, despite all the personal generosity to be found, say, in Clement of Alexandria and individual conflicts in the church, as with Gaius in Rome or in Rhossos in Syria (see above, 12f., 21), that it was not longer possible to take this course.

In Irenaeus the question of a harmony of the Gospels is no longer a topic of discussion; he is concerned solely with establishing, in principle, the number four which has already largely been recognized long before him. There may be no more and no fewer 'apostolic' Gospels than these four. For him there is no longer an alternative. Marcion as an independent thinker chose the Gospel of *Luke* from the Gospel writings known to him, since he knew that Luke had accompanied Paul on his travels, and he believed that by 'purging' it he could get at the true Pauline Gospel of Christ. He had to reject the Gospel according to Mark, the disciple of Peter, and that attributed to John, regardless of their content, because for him these names were associated with the Judaizing apostles in Jerusalem; this was even more the case with Matthew and his stronger Jewish-Christian and in some way seemingly anti-Pauline theology. He already had no other possible choice.

4. 'Gospel commentaries' and 'apocryphal' Gospels

4.1. 'Commentaries'

The first 'Gospel commentaries' known to us were also written in the second century, some time before Irenaeus. They show the early authority of the Gospel texts commented on. Their authors were educated Christian thinkers interested in a Platonizing philosophy of religion and engaged in theological 'experimentation', whom later the Bishop of Lyons condemned as 'Gnostics'. He is the first to use the term *gnostikos* for his enemies. Commentaries presuppose a reading public with a higher education. Heracleon, a disciple of Valentinus, wrote a commentary on John, probably in Rome, which was later quoted with 48 fragments by Origen in his own commentary on John's Gospel,[230] and Ptolemy, who came from the same school, produced a commentary on the Prologue of the Gospel which was sharply criticized by Irenaeus. But Ptolemy also quoted in his Letter to Flora the beginning of the Fourth Gospel against the repudiation of the creator God in Marcion and for the first time called the author of the Gospel 'disciple of the Lord' and apostle.[231] More enigmatic is the earlier 'commentary' by Basilides of Alexandria, 'Twenty-Four Books on the Gospel', which like the work of Papias still belongs in the time of Hadrian (AD 117–138).[232] According to Clement of Alexandria, who quotes from it, it probably bore the title ἐξηγητικά.[233] It seems to have expounded not only Gospel texts, but even more strongly those relating to the Pauline 'Gospel'. Evidently for him the Gospels and the Pauline Gospel were not in opposition, but a theological unity. The singular 'Gospel' is typical of this early period. Basilides 'did not yet recognize a canonically safeguarded and limited plurality of Gospels, but simply commented on the Gospel'; however, he seems already to have known several Gospels.[234] According to Origen there was even an εὐαγγέλιον κατὰ Βασιλίδην. Jerome, quoting Origen, censures him for having ventured to produce this under his own name (*suo nomine*).[235] There are some indications that Basilides especially used the Gospel of Luke, but also other

Synoptic texts and even perhaps John in this commentary. He already follows the Synoptic chronology of the period of Jesus' activity, namely one year;[236] Hippolytus at the beginning of the third century also attests that in the view of the disciples of Basilides 'everything with the Saviour happened precisely as it is written in the Gospels (!)'.[237] In other words, he or his disciples were already using Gospel (and Pauline) texts which were generally known; they are not accused of using apocryphal Gospel writings, but they did also refer to unknown oral traditions which allegedly go back to the apostle Matthias[238] or to Glaucias, an 'interpreter of Peter'.[239] That means that like his earlier contemporary Papias, whose work he presumably knows, he still wants to make a connection with earlier bearers of oral authoritative tradition, apostolic and post-apostolic, and is probably also attempting to collect such traditions; this is done by Papias in an even more intensive way. Possibly the Gospel text underlying his great 'commentary' is, like that used by Justin, a harmonizing mixed text which may have later circulated among his pupils as εὐαγγέλιον κατὰ Βασιλίδην. Quite a different possibility would be that Origen and Jerome used this title only in a polemical sense, to castigate the arrogance of the heretic. That would mean that this title never really existed. Certainly it does not come from Basilides himself. 'Gospels' have indeed also been attributed to other heretics, though with the exception of Marcion such reports are difficult to verify. That Gnosticizing Christians required the reading of Gospel texts is shown by the so-called Letter to Rheginus from Nag Hammadi, which could come from a contemporary of Ptolemy: 'For if you remember reading in the Gospel that "Elijah appeared and Moses with him", do not think that the resurrection (ἀνάστασις) is illusion (φαντασία). It is no illusion, but it is the truth.' The author is referring here to the reading of the story of the transfiguration according to the Markan version.[240] It is interesting that in this intellectual milieu a private reading of the Gospel is pre-supposed.[241]

4.2. 'Apocryphal' Gospels and 'apostolic authority'

That the unusual form of the title εὐαγγέλιον κατὰ . . . already served as a model in the first half of the second century, also follows from the titles of individual apocryphal Gospels from this period, the majority of them Gnostic or gnosticizing: they imitate an already existing, recognized form of title, thus already in the midst of the second century in the case of the 'Gospel according to Peter', 'according to Thomas', 'according to Philip', 'according to Matthias', and many more. Irenaeus even speaks of a *Iudae evangelium* which he attributes to the Cainites and which is otherwise unknown.[242] Presumably here he is deliberately deviating from the usual form of the title. In addition the *Decretum Gelasianum* from the beginning of the sixth century AD also lists Gospels under the name of Andrew, Bartholomew, James the Less[243] and Barnabas; we also know Gospels which were attributed to the Twelve[244] or the twelve apostles, and there was also a Gospel of Mary.[245] Epiphanius even mentions a Gospel of Eve.[246]

This conclusion cannot in any way be reversed. The title 'Gospel according to . . .' was certainly not first formed as a defence against Gnostic Gospel writings or, as Helmut Koester conjectures, taken over by his opponents in imitation of the title εὐαγγέλιον in Marcion. It is absurd to assume that the community in Rome or elsewhere transferred the new title, immediately after the appearance of Marcion's Gospel, to its anonymous writings which were read in worship. In fact Justin presupposes that it has long been acknowledged, and is generally known and used in worship. The opposite course is far more likely. The 'apocryphal' Gospels of the second century, whether Gnostic or not, imitated it together with the attribution to 'apostolic' authors because they too sought recognition in the church by their appeal to 'apostolic authority'.[247]

So as a rule, primarily the names of apostolic or apostle-like figures of early Christian times were put at the head of these manifold later 'Gospel writings', the production of which extends from the first decades of the second century up to the

Middle Ages.[248] All this indicates that the new, exclusively Christian designation εὐαγγέλιον, hard for a pagan reader to understand, used for a genre of writing connected with the teaching and activity and passion of Jesus, quickly attained great popularity in the church and that thus as a rule the name of an apostolic author was associated with it. Sometimes, as in the gnosticizing 'Gospel of Thomas' and in the fully Gnostic 'Gospel of the Egyptians', the title seems to have been added at a secondary stage. In the predominantly Gnostic Library of Nag Hammadi the title 'Gospel' is no longer prevalent, because the circles which preserved such esoteric books there were not interested so much in the teaching ministry of the earthly Jesus and stories about it, which were read publicly in worship, as in the hidden dialogues and speeches of the Risen One or in 'secret' protological or heavenly revelations and speculations.[249] Above all – and this already applies in part to the Gospel of Thomas – the eschatological character of his preaching and references to his messianic authority were eliminated in favour of a Platonizing dualism with an ascetic colouring. Some writings with the title 'Gospel', like the Gospel of Truth or the Gospel of the Egyptians, no longer have much to do with the person of Jesus, but are Gnostic theological treatises, the first with a typical Valentinian character, the second with a relatively confused Sethian character.[250] Here the Gospel titles have completely lost their original reference. That is already true, at least in part, of the Gospel of Philip and the fragment of the Gospel according to Mary. They all presuppose the four Gospels and their tradition. All in all the Nag Hammadi texts – the Gospel of Thomas excepted – contribute relatively little to the understanding of the Gospel tradition. Furthermore, particularly in the case of the Gospels 'according to Thomas', 'according to Philip' and 'according to Mary', it is striking how the form of the title already imitates in a stereotyped way the Gospels which later became canonical.[251]

5. *'Euangelion' or 'the Kyrios'?*

Nevertheless, in the first half of the second century references to the 'Gospel' as a writing are relatively rare, and we do not find all that many literal quotations of the Gospels. This is connected with the fact that, first, the sources from this most obscure period in church history are particularly sparse and, secondly, that the word εὐαγγέλιον was largely understood, as already by Paul, in the sense of the living 'message of salvation', preached orally and with a christological stamp. The word still has this meaning in I Clem. 47.2, where Clement refers the Corinthians to the letter of Paul to them which was also in the archive in Rome and at the same time probably alludes to the letter to the Philippians, which Paul wrote from Rome.[252] Around AD 100 he still does not quote sayings of Jesus as 'Gospel' but invites his readers to recall 'the words of the Lord Jesus'.[253] For I Clement, only the Old Testament in the form of the LXX is 'scripture'; in it the 'Lord' already speaks. Alongside it Jesus Christ as 'the Kyrios' appears as a unique authority, i.e. the word of the living Lord as a divine person, who once taught as a human being but is now exalted to the right hand of God (36.5). Here nevertheless it is true that 'the citation formulae for the sayings of the Lord in I Clement stand out from the Old Testament sayings . . . by the fact that they are longer and more ceremonial'.[254] That may refer to the spoken word in preaching. In a similar way the sayings of the Lord in Acts 20.35 and Polycarp, Phil. 2.3 are introduced with an invitation to recall the words or the teaching of the Kyrios.[255] In 4.1 Polycarp invites his readers to walk according to 'the commandment of the Lord', and in 7.1, in a context which sounds Johannine, there is a warning against falsifying the 'Logia' of the Lord in accordance with one's own desires.[256]

In the sermon which has come down to us as II Clement, the speaker admonishes his audience not only to listen to the admonitions of 'the presbyters' in worship, 'but also, when we return home, we should remember the commandments of the Lord'.[257] In contrast to the Gospel writing, the 'word of the

Lord' can always be present in the memory. In other words, probably from earliest times the 'word of the Lord' was presented in worship, initially in free discourse, but later also in reading, and that is recalled time and time again. Here the concept of 'Gospel' initially played no essential role in this connection. Paul already designates concrete instructions and teachings of Jesus as word 'of the Kyrios', which as 'commandments' are certainly to be distinguished from the 'Gospel'.[258] Mark therefore no longer wanted primarily to produce a collection of mostly paraenetical sayings of the Lord but to relate the 'saving event', starting from the passion story. He quotes only relatively few 'sayings of Jesus' in a paradigmatic selection. Therefore he could give his work the designation εὐαγγέλιον. By contrast the 'sayings of the Lord' tended more in the direction of the 'commandments of the Lord' and at the same time towards Christ as a 'new lawgiver'.[259] The development was then furtherred above all by Matthew.[260]

In any case the teaching of Jesus was for a long time still popularly presented as a living 'word of the Lord', as λόγος κυρίου, the Lord who bestows salvation as God and coming judge.[261] Only gradually is this word of the Kyrios as presented by the Gospel writings – and here above all by Matthew – more and more regarded as being identical with the written 'Gospel' that contained the 'words' or 'commandments of the Lord'. But for a long time the 'abstract' Gospel did not yet have the same weight as the mention of the person of the Kyrios. However, in time the two became interchangeable. Later, the difference between the 'saving message' and the 'commandments of Christ' or the 'Kyrios', which is still clear for Mark (and Luke), was no longer seen so clearly. In some circumstances the two could therefore even be combined. Also, however, the opposition between the Gospel preached orally and the written account of Jesus which in fact was similarly presented and expounded by word of mouth in the reading in worship was not felt so sharply as we feel it. Moroever, as Papias, Basilides or Valentinus still show, there was an interest in old oral tradition about the Kyrios and its guarantors, although 'the Gospel' was already available in varying written form. Had Mark, after the preparation of Pauline (and in my view also Petrine) preaching, not introduced into his kerygmatic biography of Jesus the term 'Gospel' as a summary of the saving message grounded in the activity and passion of Jesus, and at the same time in 1.1 designated this 'Gospel of Jesus Christ', in other words, had he not given this new 'genre' its name, which then certainly also became established for the later Gospels, it would certainly never have been transferred in the second century to the 'Jesus writings' which governed the church. Presumably they would have been named 'Words' and 'Acts of the Lord' or something similar. And an attribution to a 'disciple of the apostle' would also have been avoided. Peter's name would have replaced that of Mark and Paul's that of Luke, as in the case of Marcion.[262]

These decades between the turn of the century and Justin were a time of perpetual transition, of missionary penetration into new social strata of education, and therefore also of intellectual experimentation and consolidation, in which the foundations of the later church first had to be formed, consolidated and established in a lengthy process. The foundations, which become increasingly clearly visible in the course of the second century, comprised the 'rule of faith', the monarchical episcopate and the 'collection of apostolic writings', Gospels, Acts and letters. All these works together were given the name 'New Testament'[263] only at a relatively late stage, by Clement and Tertullian. Talk of the *biblical* 'canon' is substantially later than that (see above, 10).

Thus in the sermon already quoted (presumably Roman), still one or two decades before Justin and Marcion, so-called II Clement, a quotation from the Gospel of Luke is introduced with the formula 'The Lord says in the Gospel.'[264] We find similar formulae in the Didache, which is of about the same date, and which comes from Syria.[265] However, such a reference to a Gospel writing still remains an exception.[266] Elsewhere a reference to the word of the Lord is enough. Even Hegesippus in connection with his account of the apostolic succession in

Rome can say that where the succession of the bishop was carried out in an orderly way, people acted 'as the Law, the Prophets and the *Lord* proclaim'.[267] He could also have said 'Gospel' here, but in this connection 'the Kyrios' still sounded more effective. This appeal to the word of the Lord by the use of introductory formulae like 'the Lord says' or 'commands', etc., also continues in quotations from the Gospels in the later fathers of the second and third centuries.

Sometimes it is also not easy to decide whether the reference is to a writing or to the living voice of the preaching of Christ. Thus the term εὐαγγέλιον appears three times in the Martyrdom of Polycarp, which probably presupposes a knowledge of all four Gospels, around 160 or 170. Twice it is a formula, at the beginning and at the end, in connection with the martyrdom,[268] and once in connection with the teaching.[269] In all three cases it can refer to the oral message of salvation handed down by the church and to the Gospel writings, which all contain clear paraenesis about martyrdom in the discipleship of Jesus. Here written 'Gospel' and oral message were not understood to be in opposition. The one 'Lord' stood behind both. However, at some points the written character emerges quite clearly, as in the Didache, which surely knew Matthew,[270] and also when in the Letter to the Smyrnaeans by Ignatius (around AD 110–114), the earliest champion of the monarchical episcopacy known to us, the Old Testament scriptures, i. e. Moses and the prophets, are set alongside 'the Gospel'.[271] In the Letter to the Philadelphians 8.2, 'the Gospel' is put in parallel with the 'community archives' (ἀρχεῖα) in which the Old Testament writings were stored. Here also a book of the Gospels is probably being referred to. Ignatius, too, knows Matthew and in my view John[272] – though not yet as an apostolic authority; and when the Didache speaks of the Gospel (of the Lord), it also probably means Matthew, i.e. the Gospel writing which was composed around AD 90 or 100 and established itself particularly quickly in the church because it contained what the growing church needed for its ethos and its order. That means that with it we are already brought very close to the time of the composition of the four Gospels between c. AD 70 and 100. What further information can we gain about that?

6. Papias' note about Mark and Matthew and the question of an original Aramaic Gospel

6.1. The note about Mark

The disputed note by Papias, the significance of which is often misunderstood, takes us over the threshold of the second century. Presumably in the time of Hadrian (117–138), like Basilides but probably somewhat earlier than him, the Bishop of Hierapolis[273] composed an 'Exegesis of the Sayings of the Lord' in five books, from which Eusebius quotes some small portions in his *Church History*.[274] It is striking that the author avoids the term 'Gospel' in the title of the work, nor does it occur in the few fragments which have come down to us, but this does not mean that he did not know it. The same is true of the term 'apostle'. He himself wanted to collect and probably also to comment on 'Logia', words (and deeds) of Jesus, not to write a new Gospel *or* a 'commentary on the Gospel' like Basilides. He writes in a very orderly style, which suggests a degree of rhetorical training, but he does not have the literary and philosophical training of Basilides. Papias is the first to speak of two Gospel authors, Mark and Matthew. He was intrinsically not so much interested in the earlier writings about Jesus as in the φωνὴ ζῶσα καὶ μένουσα, 'living and abiding oral tradition'.[275] Papias is writing at a time when oral tradition has become the problematical exception, and a written text has almost come to be taken for granted. Consequently he made enquiries of the 'elders', i.e. of the disciples of Jesus and their pupils, about their oral traditions; he mentions by name seven disciples of Jesus, whom we know through Mark, Matthew and Luke. In addition he refers to two outside those known to us from the Gospels and Acts: Aristion, and above all 'John the elder', 'the disciple of the Lord', whom he himself had heard and from whom he hands on numerous traditions about 'sayings of the Lord'. Among other things, he has received from this 'John the elder' the well-known and much-disputed report about Mark:

> This also the 'elder' says: Mark, who was the interpreter of Peter, wrote down carefully, but not in the right order, every-thing that he remembered, both what had been said by the Lord and also what had been done by him. For he had neither seen the Lord, nor had he followed him, but later (he followed) . . . Peter, who shaped his teachings to the needs (of the hearers), however, not in such a way that he gave an orderly account of the sayings of the Lord. So Mark did not make a mistake in writing down some things as he remem-bered them. For he had one concern, not to omit anything that he had heard or to falsify anything in it.[276]

The first important point is that this report is not, as is asserted time and again, the invention of Papias himself but oral infor-mation from the 'presbyter John, the disciple of the Lord', who died not too long after AD 100,[277] and therefore is a tradition going back to the last decades of the first century. Thus it comes near to the time when the Gospel of Mark was written, AD 69/70. The second point is even more important: contrary to the prevalent view, this is not an apologia for the Second Gospel, say even against some Gnostics,[278] but rather a moderate criticism, presumably – as already Bishop Lightfoot, E. Schwartz and others conjectured[279] – from the 'higher' standpoint of the Gospel of John. This has the right 'order', for example in the chronology of the activity of Jesus up to the day of his death and the resurrection appearances, and, unlike Peter's presenta-tion of Jesus' teaching, contains an 'ordered account of the discourses of the Lord'.[280] Nor was this Mark an eye-witness; he wrote down only 'some things' of Peter's preaching about Jesus, 'as he remembered them'. So the tone of the whole is more negative than positive. In other words, for Papias there are better accounts of Jesus. This restrained judgment on Mark, which indeed was not only the opinion of the 'presbyter John' but can also already explain the origin of Luke and Matthew as improved Gospel writings may, among other things, have contributed to the fact that despite the authority of Peter which stood behind it, Mark quickly lost importance in the second century, as the scanty early papyrus tradition shows. The 'better' Gospels largely suppressed Mark.

As I have shown in *The Johannine Question*,[281] the guarantor of this tradition, 'John the elder', is identical with the 'elder' of II and III John and probably also the author of I John and the Gospel. His name and very many details in the Fourth Gospel indicate that he comes from Jerusalem.[282] On the one hand the Fourth Gospel emphasizes the importance of Peter, but at the same time it also deals with him critically, gives prominence to other disciples like Philip and Thomas, and above all stresses the superiority of the enigmatic 'ideal' Beloved Disciple. The Beloved Disciple was later identified by second-century tradition in Asia Minor with a John, the 'disciple of the Lord', i.e., since Justin or the Valentinian Ptolemy and his enemy Irenaeus, the apostle and the son of Zebedee. Like the report of the 'elder John' about Mark referred to by Papias, the Fourth Gospel too shows a certain distance from the Petrine authority and tradition emphasized in Mark and in Luke which is dependent on it. That authority still prevails unbroken in Matthew. Therefore it is improbable that the editors of the Fourth Gospel (including Chapter 21) and of the letters also organized the first collection of four Gospels (see above, 167f.); the Johannine school and its head will hardly have treasured at least Matthew, despite certain structural parallels connected with the same time, and presumably the reverse was also the case. Moreover Matthew does not seem to have been used by the Fourth Gospel (see below, 78ff.). By contrast I Peter (5.13), 'She who is also elect (viz. the community)[283] in Babylon sends you greetings; and so does my son Mark', from the latter days of Domitian, confirms the link between Mark and Peter in Rome.[284] 'John the elder' is here handing on to Papias, who was probably a member of his wider circle of disciples, a mainly critical tradition which extends well back into the first century and which together with

I Peter 5.13 validates Irenaeus' indirect and Clement of Alexandria's direct report of the 'origin' of the Second Gospel with Mark, the disciple of Peter, in Rome. It also accords with the striking Latinisms in Mark (see below, 78 and n.318). I Peter 5.13 from the last years of Domitian (81–96) lies somewhere in time between Papias and Mark. Therefore the note is to be taken very seriously. Here the presbyter John is not handing on a secondary construction, but historical information which is of great value, about the origin of the earliest Gospel, combined with a more critical evaluation.

6.2. *The note about Matthew*

The enigmatic note about Matthew seems to deal even more critically with the Gospel circulating under this name:

> Matthew compiled the sayings (of the Lord) in the Hebrew language; but everyone translated them as he was able.[285]

It is impossible to refer this note to the canonical First Gospel, since that was originally written in Greek and was not translated from a Hebrew (i.e. Aramaic) original. The addition about the different translators is even more incomprehensible. Whom could Papias (or better the Elder) mean with the cryptic remark 'everyone translated them . . .'? Rather, the Greek Matthew was mainly based on the narrative of Mark, more than eighty per cent of which the author reproduces, in parts literally. Matthew adds the birth narrative to Mark and expands Mark with the five great discourse complexes which are theologically so impressive.[286] As a rule, the evangelist is supposed to have worked his rich special tradition and even more parts from the enigmatic Logia *Source (Q)* for the first Gospel into these five discourses. In my opinion this is a questionable hypothesis, because Q cannot really be reconstructed. Matthew could possibly have taken over directly from Luke the material which to a considerable degree he uses in common with him[287] (see below, 163ff.). In my view we must reckon with the possibility that he knew the Gospel of Luke, which was substantially earlier, and also used it in part, but in so doing valued the tendency of this 'Pauline' Gospel less than he did that of the 'Petrine' Mark, which gave him the whole course of the narrative and at the end the passion narrative as a soteriological climax. In my view the modern hypotheses about Q are largely built on sand. Here scholars have greatly exaggerated the possibilities of historical and philological argument. They are often based on the fashionable wish to have an 'unkerygmatic' Jesus and wisdom teacher who moralizes in his social thought, a figure who would fit better into our time. It is then easier to build a bridge from this utterly unmessianic construct to the Gnostic sayings collections.

A wish for a simply moral preacher of the kingdom of God already underlies Harnack's notable attempt at a reconstruction. Today the esoteric components are added.[288] Whereas it is clear where Luke and Matthew use Mark, we can no longer make an adequate reconstruction of the 'sources' of the Gospels before Mark and Luke. Here, as the ever new efforts constantly show, we all too easily lose ourselves in a jungle of hypotheses. At all events the history of the origin of the Gospels is far more complicated than we assume, and therefore can no longer really be surveyed in detail. What Harnack says of the Logia source, namely that everything still lies 'in the clouds of uncertainty',[289] is still all too true today, despite the tremendous amount of work that has been done since Harnack's book appeared ninety-two years ago. Scholars all too easily go round in circles, often without noticing it, and often arguments can be turned round effortlessly. The 'Logia source' cannot be arrived at simply by subtracting the material common to Luke and Matthew after previously excluding the passages taken over from Mark. As I have already emphasized, in principle we must reckon that the later Matthew knew the earlier Luke, took over parts which seemed to him appropriate, i.e. the content of which was promising, and in the process of course also altered his theological wishes accordingly. This is already indicated by the fact that as a rule the more original version is attributed to

Q-Luke as opposed to Q-Matthew. In addition – and here Papias can put us on the right road – there were certainly also one or more 'Logia collections'. But – as I have already said – we can no longer reconstruct these adequately, especially as we cannot know what the evangelists changed or omitted in the sources, unknown to us, which they probably had in more abundance than we suppose.[290] I shall go into this question at length in the last chapter (see below, 169ff.).

Schleiermacher had already conjectured that such a 'Logia source', which takes its name from the report in Papias (τὰ λόγια, i. e. words of God or words of revelation), could ulti- mately go back to an Aramaic sub-stratum connected with the person of the tax-collector Matthew, to whom the First Evangelist refers twice in his Gospel, against Mark, which he had before him.[291] A tax collector had to be able to write in an orderly way. That was not yet a matter of course in the group of twelve.[292] Of course, this too remains hypothetical, because the original Aramaic form of such an earlier Logia source remains an unprovable hypothesis that cannot be demonstrated clearly in any way. But the different translation mentioned by Papias in his remark that 'everyone translated it as he was able' can hardly be related directly to our Matthew and Luke, because the Greek wording of many of the texts common to Matthew and Luke, behind which the Logia Source is con- jectured, corresponds almost word for word. They therefore cannot rest on different translations. At best one can suppose translation variants in the case of some differing individual texts in both Gospels, which may refer to one (or several) source(s) of Jesus Logia (see below).

Probably this special information of Papias which is so diffi- cult to understand, like the note about Mark, also goes back to John the 'elder'. It seems that Eusebius is deliberately quoting 'Papias' in such an abbreviated form that it appears completely enigmatic to us. Perhaps his informant knew that there was once a collection of sayings of the Lord in Greek which already in Luke and Matthew (and possibly also in Mark) appears in differing versions, since 'each had translated them as he was able', and which was said to go back to an Aramaic original attributed to the apostle Matthew.[293] In the context, according to the Presbyter and Papias ἡρμήνευσεν is certainly to be understood as 'translating' and may not be toned down to mere rhetorical 'interpretation', since this was a text written in 'Hebrew' (i. e. Aramaic). Here Papias was certainly not referring to the 'semitizing' style of Matthew; this style is even more striking in Mark,[294] which is really nearer to a translation from the Aramaic. Irenaeus, or his source, the Roman archive, and the fathers after him will have misunderstood this enigmatic tradition and, to reinforce the authority of the Greek First Gospel, which 'pseudepigraphically' bore the name of the apostle Matthew, confused it with this much older Aramaic 'Collection of Sayings', in the meantime long since lost, assuming that there was an original Aramaic Gospel by the apostle.

Another comment on the name Matthew: apart from the First Gospel, to which he gives his name, Matthew plays no role in primitive Christianity. He appears only in the lists of apostles. He is only mentioned rather more frequently at a substantially later date in apocryphal writings on the basis of the unique success of the Gospel named after him. That makes it utterly improbable that the name of the apostle was attached to the Gospel only at a secondary stage, in the first decades of the second century, somewhere in the Roman empire, and that this essentially later nomenclature then established itself everywhere without opposition. How could people have arrived at this name for an anonymous Gospel in the second century, and how then would it have gained general recognition? With Kilpatrick and against Davies and Allison, in that case it would have to be argued that the work received its designation at the latest when it was disseminated in copies in other communities.[295]

As a result of this allegedly direct 'apostolic' origin from Matthew and the even more questionable claim to be the 'Hebrew' (i.e. Aramaic) Gospel and at the same time the oldest and original Gospel, the First Gospel already established itself quickly and tenaciously in the church at the beginning of the second century.[296]Another contributory factor in Matthew was its impressive depiction, shaped by precise and impressive theological reflection, of the teaching and activity of Jesus, beginning with his genealogy and miraculous birth up to the command of the Risen Christ to the eleven disciples to engage in mission and baptize: 'Go into all the world . . .' Thus at quite an early stage in the second century the Gospel became the most important church writing. As the unknown author of this Greek Matthew was a Jewish-Christian scribe with a rabbinic education,[297] it was long believed, indeed down to modern times, that the Gospel really had originally been written in Aramaic for Jewish Christians of Palestine and thus was the earliest. That it was the oldest Gospel still remained the view of great critics like D. F. Strauss and F. C. Baur and his school, and for conservatives like A. Schlatter or Theodor Zahn. However, there were considerable differences in the dating: this extended from the time of Claudius to that of Trajan, the latter date being that of F. C. Baur and his disciples. On the other hand, the majority of nineteenth-century exegetes still conjectured a time before 70, sometimes making a distinction between the alleged 'Hebrew' original – which in reality could not be proved – and the later Greek version.[298]

By contrast, the priority of Mark is quite modern; it only began to become established around 120–130 years ago.[299] In my view the First Gospel cannot have been composed before AD 90, and it can have been composed even later (between 90 and 100),[300] because it presupposes the powerful consolidation of Judaism in Jewish Palestine after the catastrophe of AD 70; moreover in its anti-Jewish polemic beyond question it knows the development of the rabbinate (see below, 186–205). The non-apostolic Gospels of Mark and Luke are around twenty and ten to fifteen years older respectively. In other words, Matthew was composed some time *after* Luke, who stands much closer to the catastrophe of the year 70, has precise knowledge of Jewish conditions before the Jewish War in his two-volume work, and does not yet presuppose the rising oppression of the church as this becomes visible in the later days of Domitian (AD 81–96). Matthew is already writing in a historical situation which has changed again from that of Mark and Luke, and which is similar to that of the Fourth Gospel.

6.3. *The riddle of a Jewish-Christian Aramaic Gospel and the tension between oral and written tradition*

Another possibility – completely hypothetical and therefore unprovable and irrefutable – would be that there really was such a thing as an original Aramaic Jewish-Christian Gospel which was at least in part akin to the later Greek Matthew in content, but in principle is to be distinguished from the latter, and that Papias, his informant John the Elder, and his successors attributed it to the apostle Matthew. For the trace of a Jewish-Christian Gospel (or even several) in Aramaic (and afterwards in Greek) runs through the whole of the early church, beginning with Papias, via Hegesippus,[301] who evidently knew two different such texts, Irenaeus (or his Roman source), Pantaenus and Clement of Alexandria, Origen, Eusebius and Epiphanius, to Jerome, who mentions such a Jewish-Christian work relatively frequently and wants to have it translated. The designation of the work can sometimes vary. There also seems to have been a Greek version of this 'Gospel according to the Hebrews'.[302] This is perhaps already attested by Papias and certainly by Hegesippus; according to Eusebius it is treasured by the Jewish Christians and only rejected by some (τίνες) contemporaries, although the first Christian literary historian immediately beforehand had himself confessed the 'holy number four' in the case of the Gospels – a sign of how influential this 'Gospel in the twilight' was even in the third and fourth centuries.[303] The testimonies to such texts extend to the Middle Ages. Understandably these apocryphal Gospels of Jewish-Christian origin in Aramaic and Greek were later subjected to considerable alterations and, as is shown by the few remains of them, sometimes ran wild. This contrasts with the four so-called canonical Gospels which, regardless of all discussions, were already largely recognized by the church in the first half of the second century. But in the tradition, time and again emphasis is put on the relative proximity of these Jewish-Christian writings to the Gospel of Matthew.[304] Yet another possibility cannot be ruled out but can just as little be proved: that the unknown author of the First Gospel, who surely was bilingual, also wrote a Gospel text in Aramaic. This would be comparable to Josephus who, before his Greek *Jewish War*, after AD 70 first wrote an Aramaic version for the Jewish Diaspora beyond the Euphrates in the East. However, we know nothing about its contents, and the Greek version of Josephus' *Jewish War* gives the impression of being totally independent.[305]

Starting from Papias' note about Matthew, which probably goes back to the presbyter John, this Jewish-Christian Gospel tradition is therefore one of the greatest unsolved riddles of Gospel writing. To mitigate the problem it has been conjectured that the Greek Matthew was later translated back into Aramaic and that Papias regarded this secondary translation as the original 'Hebrew' Matthew. But that is improbable on chronological grounds alone, for the Greek Matthew was written relatively late; moreover this would make the remarkable, disparaging remark of Papias 'and each translated it as he was able' quite incomprehensible, since in that case it would have had to have been directed in an abrupt critical way against our Greek Gospel of Matthew. For it probably means that various anonymous figures had translated the original collection of the 'Words of the Lord' by the apostle Matthew more or less badly into Greek. Zahn's conjecture that here again we have the 'oral interpretation' of individual discourses of Jesus from the originally Aramaic Matthew for the Greek-speaking communities of Asia Minor by *ad hoc* translators is even more improbable. Nowhere has anything been handed down to us about such a custom.[306] Be this as it may, Zahn also thought that 'the Greek Matthew was composed before the . . . end of the first century, say around 90', i.e. even he puts it relatively late and is thus historically correct; in addition he supposes that the Greek translator also used the Gospels of Mark and Luke.[307]

In reality the presbyter John, i.e. in my view the author who stands behind the Fourth Gospel and is the guarantor of Papias' tradition, did not have a particularly high opinion of Mark, and probably had an even lower one of the Greek Matthew, i.e. the whole of the 'Synoptic' tradition, since in content his own work is miles away from the Markan form of 'Jesus tradition'. The fragments of Papias in Eusebius have preserved his moderate but nevertheless critical judgment for us. In addition, Papias explicitly emphasizes that the oral tradition (especially that of his most influential tradent, the Elder John) is more important to him than the multiplicity of writings which were the fashion in his time. Of course he knew and used the Gospels, but in particular the progressive development of written documents intensified his interest in the 'tradition' from the 'unwritten tradition' and the 'voice which remains alive'.[308] Indeed the Pharisaic tradition similarly only found its first official written documentation in the Mishnah in the beginning of the third century after a tiresome progress and gradual preparation. By virtue of the Jewish-scribal origin of its author and its composition in geographical proximity to Jewish Palestine the First Gospel really was something like a connecting link between – earlier – Jewish Christianity and the church which had become Gentile Christian, although it is to be put relatively late and certain anti-Jewish features are unmistakable. People fought so vigorously because they were still basically so closely related. Indeed Aramaic-speaking Jewish Christianity in the motherland took quite for granted its possession of a rich Jesus tradition, fed by manifold reminiscences. Decimated by the catastrophe of 70 and forced aside, its tradition in turn was unfortunately overtaken and suppressed all too quickly by the writing of Gospels in the mainstream church. Here Matthew is still closest to it.[309] Unfortunately not even the slightest trace is left of the special Jewish-Palestinian Christians' Jesus tradition, which similarly assumed written form in Aramaic, unless – and here I do not completely give up hope – in the desert sand of Egypt or in Eastern libraries we find yet another text of a Jewish-Christian Gospel in Greek or Aramaic/Syriac.

Thus in reality the unresolved question of Aramaic (and Greek) Gospels among the Jewish Christians goes much deeper than the discussion which has again become fashionable today as a result of Crossan, Koester and others about the age and historical value of apocryphal Gospels like the Gospel of Thomas, the Gospel of Peter, or the dubious 'Secret Gospel of Mark' and individual indeterminable Gospel fragments on papyrus.[310] Those who want to investigate apocryphal Gospels which are really significant historically need first to take up the search for the Jewish-Christian texts. But presumably we shall not get very far. Too many sources have been lost, and therefore they can no longer be sure to lighten the darkness of Jewish-Christian Gospel-writing in Aramaic and Greek.

6.4. *The successful future of the First Gospel and its title*

Papias', or better the Presbyter's, enigmatic note did no harm to the First Gospel. The work by the Bishop of Hierapolis was not read a great deal, and sometimes it was read inaccurately. That may also apply to our most important source, Eusebius' *Church History*. The educated Origenist wrongly called Papias 'very weak-minded' because, like the Book of Revelation, the second-century tradition in Asia Minor, Justin and Irenaeus, he represented a chiliastic realism[311] which after the victory of Platonizing Origenistic theology in the East from the second half of the third century onwards could maintain itself only in the West; in the East the Revelation of John was suppressed until the sixth century.[312] The opposite is true of the effectiveness of the First Gospel. Of all the four Gospels – as I have already said – Matthew quickly gained the strongest influence on the church in the second century. For it emphasized that Jesus was not only the Redeemer but at the same time the messianic, even divine, lawgiver, whose authority surpasses by far that of Moses, a motif which above all Justin takes up. Origen and the later fathers can even speak quite unpolemically of the εὐαγγελικοὶ νόμοι, the 'Gospel laws',[313] which they found especially in Matthew. Only from the end of the second century, at least in Egypt, is it 'caught up with' by the Gospel of John, with its utterly christological and soteriological orientation, as what Clement of Alexandria calls the 'spiritual Gospel'.[314] This explains why among the pre-Constantine Gospel papyri in Egypt, John is most numerous but immediately followed by Matthew (see above, 42). A further reason why the First Gospel established itself so quickly was its allegedly direct apostolic origin. It was the first to make this claim. The unknown Jewish-Christian author, who at the same time was a member of the mainstream church, was presumably prompted to this by his knowledge of an old Aramaic collection of sayings of Jesus which was known under the name of Matthew. This put him at the head of all four evangelists and, as was later the case with John, gave him a greater authority than his forerunners Mark and Luke, who were regarded only as disciples of the apostles.

In all probability the unknown Jewish-Christian teacher from the borders of Syria/Palestine circulated his work, modelled on the earlier Mark, as εὐαγγέλιον κατὰ Μαθθαῖον. We must assume that copies of such significant works, concerning the whole church, were sent soon after their completion to the most important communities with covering letters. Presumably this happened through that community (or communities) in which he was a teacher and acknowledged authority, or through his disciples. Probably here too, as in the case of the Gospel of Mark, at least some previous liturgical usage lay behind his impressive work. One could speak of a degree of 'liturgical trial'. His version of the Lord's Prayer, which by comparison with the earlier Lukan version is an expanded one, was certainly also the prayer of that community (or those communites) with which he felt associated.[315] It was to become the prayer of the whole church. Contrary to a widespread view, the self-confident evangelist wrote his work not only for his communities in Southern Syria and Palestine, in which he must have been a great authority, but for the whole church; this is shown not only by the universal mission command to 'all nations' at the end of the Gospel, with its 'trinitarian' baptism formula (an additional reason for its quite late origin),[316] but also by the fundamental sentences 'You are the salt of the earth', 'You are the light of the world', in the introduction to the Sermon on the Mount.[317] The enigmatic tradition which appears in Papias (or, better, his informant) of the 'Hebrew' (i.e. Aramaic) collection of sayings of the Lord for the 'Hebrews' by the apostle Matthew, which then turned into the notion of a 'Hebrew' Ur-Matthew, at the same time secured the work pride of place among the Gospels as allegedly the oldest.

7. The Gospel according to Mark as the earliest Gospel and the title 'Gospel'

7.1. The evangelist Mark and the Peter tradition in Rome

In reality the Gospel of Mark is the earliest extant Gospel writing (that has come down to us). There has been a wide-ranging consensus among New Testament scholars about that since the second half of the nineteenth century. It is supported by all the serious exegetical historical and philological arguments. There is also a consensus that the Gospel was composed around AD 70. In my view it was written in Rome relatively shortly before the siege and conquest of Jerusalem (April–September 70), but after the murder of Nero (9 June 68), whose return as 'Antichrist' the evangelist expects in 13.14ff. The Roman origin is indicated by a broad ecclesiastical tradition, but also by an astonishing number of Latinisms, which are unique in Greek narrative prose and quite inexplicable if it originated in Syria, as is often conjectured.[318] The eschatological discourse (13.5–29) reflects the cruel experiences of the Neronian persecution in the past and the confusion of the Roman civil war which broke out after the death of Nero, whereas Mark is not informed about political and military events in Judaea and Syria. He draws a rather utopian picture of the Jewish War, which shows the geographical distance from which he writes. It begins with the desecration and destruction of the sanctuary by the eschatological enemy of God, and in the face of this calls for flight into the mountains without delay.[319]

The martyrdoms of the Neronian persecution in AD 64 also influence the decisive invitation to take up the cross and follow Jesus.[320] As far as we know, Nero was the first to have Christians crucified and burned as nocturnal torches.[321] Peter, too, is said to have been crucified at that time.[322] The fact that Mark 8.31–34 has Peter's confession followed by the announcement of the passion and the abrupt repudiation of Peter's objection, immediately followed by Jesus' invitation to the crowd and the disciples to 'take up the cross and follow' him, points to a very specific context. The crucifixion of Christians was still quite unusual in AD 70 and in the first century is attested only for Rome in AD 64 and later perhaps in Matt. 23.34. Here Mark is concerned with more than a voluntary, generalized invitation to be ready for suffering. We know of no Roman persecution of Christians in Syria in his or an earlier time.[323] All these connections make it probable that the earliest 'evangelist', Mark, really was a companion and interpreter of Peter, as 'the elder John' in Papias bears witness. That he knew Aramaic (with the right vocalization) and could also translate it properly into Greek is evident in several passages of his work, which cannot simply be attributed to an earlier written tradition.[324]

Foreign words and sentences in other languages are strikingly rare in Greek literary texts. The lexical Latinisms and Aramaisms thus point to the place where the work was composed and the origin of the author. He also writes a linguistically unobjectionable, though rhetorically simple, Koine Greek with a Semitizing stamp. On the other hand it is extremely improbable that the former fisherman from Lake Gennesaret spoke fluent and impeccable Greek. He could have needed a translator. Therefore it seems to me quite likely that the Greek-Palestinian John Mark, who has a (second) Latin name, from Jerusalem, the nephew of Barnabas,[325] who is mentioned in Acts, is to be seen as the author of the Gospel. He was acquainted with both Paul and Peter, but was obviously closer to Peter, as I Peter 5.13[326] and Acts 12.12–17 illustrate. After the death of the leading men of the first generation in earliest Christianity, James, Paul and Peter, between 62 and 64, this Mark must have had a special reputation in the communities; he also appears several times in the later letters of the New Testament, but loses his reputation in the later second century.[327]

On the other hand, it is interesting that his contemporary Luke can also openly report Mark's failure on the so-called 'first missionary journey'.[328] He criticizes John Mark in Acts discreetly and at the same time demonstrates his own superiority as author of a real 'Jesus biography' in the prologue of his Gospel. But Mark is still the most important author among the 'many' of Luke 1.1, for he was the first to give to his work the form of a historical narrative from John the Baptist to the passion and thus created the real Gospel form. Another argument is that this writing, quite novel in earliest Christianity, managed to establish itself in the communities and to be used extensively by such self-confident authors as Luke and the author of the First Gospel – in the case of Matthew around eighty per cent and of Luke more than sixty per cent[329] – only because a recognized authority and not an anonymous Gentile Christian,[330] i.e. a Mr Nobody in the church, stood behind it. It is correct to say that Mark is writing for a predominantly Gentile Christian community. Romans, written around AD 56/57, is already addressed to a community with a prevailing Gentile Christian stamp.

This tendency will have been further reinforced in Rome up to around AD 70. As a reading of both the letters of Paul and the Johannine corpus shows, earliest Christianity was bound by authority, beginning with the unique unsurpassed authority of Jesus, and this characteristic is continued up to the first decades of the second century. Martin Dibelius, the scholar with the clearest historical insight among the fathers of form criticism, expressly emphasized in connection with the collection of sayings of Jesus which served paraenesis 'the appreciation of tradition, of authenticity, and of authority'. 'The notion of authority was also a factor in their composition.'[331] Now this was true not only of paraenesis, where there was a firm emphasis on the fact that these were sayings of the Lord (and not just general Wisdom sayings), but also of the teaching and narrative tradition of the Gospels generally, including the mission preaching at the founding of communities. Moreover the trio of tradition, authenticity and authority was not just limited to the sayings of the Lord but applied – above all after the departure of the first generation in the time between 60 and 70 – to the 'apostolic preaching' generally. We already find the beginnings of that in the authentic letters of Paul, and it is evident after 70, e.g. in Acts, where there is emphasis on Peter and Paul, and in the second line John, James, Philip and Barnabas, and then also in I Peter, I Clement and the letters of Ignatius. Here with Polycarp, Papias, Justin or Irenaeus the second century continues what had already been becoming evident in the first century. Therefore nothing has led research into the Gospels so astray as the romantic superstition involving anonymous theologically creative community collectives, which are supposed to have drafted whole writings. In addition, the 'apostolic' authority of the men who were leading missionaries and teachers – leading in the full sense of the word – was excessively suppressed. Here scholars could already have learned better from Paul's appeal to his unique apostolic authority or the three 'pillars' in Jerusalem (Gal. 2.6–9).

This problem of authority arises most strongly in the earliest Gospel, which in fact represented a real innovation. That Simon Peter stands behind the Gospel of Mark, as people still knew very precisely throughout the second century, also follows from this Gospel itself, since he is given unparalleled significance in it. This cannot be explained by the completely vague and therefore inadequate term 'community tradition', a word which is particularly appropriate for disseminating obscurity. In a way, all information of the Gospels and indeed throughout the New Testament is 'community tradition', for Peter, Paul and the other influential missionaries were just as much a part of the community of Jesus Christ as their disciples and audience.

Moreover the same is true of the evangelists. Even the special 'theology' of the Gospel authors was already known in the communities from their preaching. Therefore this popular collective term cannot really explain the concrete textual and historical phenomena. The decisive question remains why a Gospel puts this particular tradition or opinion in the foreground (and no other), a question which as a rule is connected with the individuality and authority of the author, i.e. which has wholly personal reasons.

This in particular becomes visible in Mark. Thus in his work, Simon Peter is not only the first disciple to be called immediately after the public appearance of Jesus and at the same time to be named twice,[332] but also the one whose name appears last in the Gospel – quite unnecessarily. The young man in white garments, i.e. the angel at the tomb, gives the terrified women the instructions: 'But go and tell his disciples *and Peter* that he will go before you into Galilee.' The 'and Peter' disrupts the narrative and is completely superfluous. Peter is one of 'the disciples'. Matthew omits this unnecessary addition.[333] Here it is striking that in the numerous lists of disciples throughout the Gospel Simon or Peter elsewhere always comes at the beginning; only here does he follow at the end. In other words, this quite unusual τοῖς μαθηταῖς αὐτοῦ καὶ τῷ Πέτρῳ is a deliberate rhetorical *inclusio*: Simon Peter is as a disciple named first and last in the Gospel to show that it is based on his tradition and therefore on his authority. This argument cannot be dismissed with the assertion that here we have merely an indirect reference to the appearance of the Risen Christ to Peter first of all. It may be that Mark presupposes that his readers know this, and much else,[334] but this striking *inclusio* in any case shows the unique importance of the disciple Simon Peter in the Gospel itself, during the whole activity of Jesus and the passion between 1.17 and 16.7. In the 'rival' Gospel of John the focal points lie quite elsewhere. Here Peter is neither the first nor the last disciple to be mentioned and the Beloved Disciple is superior to him.[335] The resurrection appearances are not a topic in Mark's work; they are referred to only by the promise of the

Lord himself and the angel that in the future 'there in Galilee *you* (i.e. all disciples) will see him'. [336]

Another point is the predominantly Galilean character of his Gospel in comparison with John (and Luke). Peter was the spokesman of the Galilean disciples. All these facts speak for themselves. Mark mentions the 'disciples' of Jesus forty-three times in all, but at the same time he puts special emphasis on only one disciple, Simon/Peter. He is mentioned twenty-five times, i.e. as often as in Matthew, which is 70% longer, and where the term 'disciples' of Jesus appears around seventy times.[337] John and James, the sons of Zebedee, come a long way behind with only ten mentions each; with one exception both are always mentioned together, and apart from 10.35 and 10.41 always with Peter at their head, as the most intimate group around Jesus.[338] We meet Andrew, Peter's brother, four times, similarly always with Peter at the head;[339] alongside this the traitor Judas appears only three times.[340] Finally, all the disciples appear together in the catalogue of the Twelve in 3.16–19 with Simon Peter – as always – coming first. The 'Twelve' are mentioned in all only ten times. Going by the frequency of mentions, Peter is uniquely important for Mark as compared with the other Gospels.[341]

This unique accumulation of mentions of Peter in the substantially shorter Gospel calls for a meaningful historical explanation. Here the main question is not the significance of the Galilean fisherman Simon for the historical Jesus' circle of disciples – here we can be rather more restrained in our judgments – but first of all why the earliest Gospel puts such unique emphasis on him a bare forty years after the Passover at which Jesus died and around five years after his martyrdom. This question cannot simply be ignored or dismissed with cheap excuses: he stands at the head of all the lists of disciples, and he is the only one to be given the honorific title Πέτρος, 'Rock' (Aramaic *kēphā*), by Jesus.[342] As is shown by the letters of Paul, who eight times uses Κηφᾶς and twice Πέτρος, [343] and Acts, and already partially by the Gospels, this displaces his personal name *Shim'on*/Simon. With two exceptions,[344] in Mark he is the only disciple to appear as a personal conversation-partner of Jesus.[345] Only he is addressed by name personally by Jesus because of his failure in Gethsemane, and he is the only one to follow Jesus after his arrest to the palace of the high priest.[346] The event of his denial can only be based on his own action; we can reject as a complete aberration of typical German hyper-criticism the conjecture by Günter Klein and others that this is an unhistorical anti-Petrine invention.[347] In the first mention of the group of disciples (1.36), Mark speaks of 'Simon and those who were with him'.[348] By contrast, the 'disciples' are mentioned first only in 2.15. The very personal narrative about the healing of Peter's mother-in-law (1.29–31) is also unique; this presupposes that Peter was married, a fact which Paul confirms.[349] Moreover a survey of the mentions of Peter in Mark shows that they accumulate at key points in the Gospel: at the beginning of Jesus' activity (ch. 1), at the denouement (chs. 8 and 9) and in the passion narrative (ch.14).[350]

This surprisingly large number of mentions of Peter and the tradition associated with his name in Mark certainly cannot be sweepingly dismissed with the all too cheap catchphrase 'post-Easter tradition'. It was deliberately intended by the author from beginning to end. Certainly most of the mentions will come from 'old' tradition, but this was intentionally selected by Mark from the wealth of tradition in general and also shaped redactionally elsewhere, above all in the *inclusio* 1.16 and 16.7. If any figure in the Gospel is the decisive 'partner' of Jesus, it is Peter. Bultmann's sweeping verdict, 'The author is not interested in the disciples as historical persons or their relationship to Jesus,' does not apply to Peter at all. It corresponds, rather to the general hostility to real history which was the tendency of the Marburg scholar.[351] All this is certainly no coincidence; the author Mark must have had his reasons. Things may have looked somewhat different in the original group of disciples, and so John describes them in a different way. On the other hand, Luke and Matthew deliberately follow this emphasis on Peter, even if they tone it down somewhat in the overall framework of their larger Gospels. Matthew above all himself still has an interest in the further legendary elaboration of the Peter tradition.[352] At the same time it is striking that in all four Gospels James and the brothers either play a negative role or no role at all. This is best explained from the fact that the Synoptic Jesus tradition had already left Jewish Palestine behind and become independent before James took over complete control of the Jerusalem community in the forties and fifties.[353]

Only secondarily is it to be noted that the period of tradition between Jesus and the time of Mark is not more than forty years and the remembrance of the ministry of Jesus in Galilee and Jerusalem was still vivid. In other words, the fact that the name of Simon Peter has been quite deliberately and massively retained in his Gospel is grounded not only in the importance of Peter for the evangelist, but also in remembrance and historical reality. For Mark, the chronological distance from Jesus of about forty years could still be surveyed relatively easily,[354] and hardly more than five years separate him from the martyrdom of Peter, his teacher. Even if we did not have the reports of Irenaeus, the two Clements and Justin, the Papias note and I Peter 5.13, we would have to assume that the author of the Second Gospel is dependent upon Peter in a striking way, for historical, theological and quite personal reasons.

However, here his 'Gospel' does not appear as a simple historical report which is merely meant to satisfy the pro-sopographic curiosity of the reader. It always takes a model 'kerygmatic-missionary' form which is indebted to a concrete tradition tied to a person. The special feature of the earliest Gospel is that nothing is narrated here which is not intended as proclamation, and nowhere is there mere 'proclamation' without a concern to offer a dramatic narration of the 'story' and a selection of 'sayings' of Jesus. Here the narrator *also* remained aware throughout of the distance in time and in substance between him and the fundamental Jesus event. That is shown for example by the motif of the disciples' failure to understand Jesus before Easter, and also by the references to the time of the evangelist in the Little Apocalypse, Mark 13.5–17, and individual personal indications in the passion narrative.[355] Nevertheless, this unity of narrative and proclamation is never done away with. It is fundamental to Mark.

Here it stands in a powerful current of 'apostolic tradition' in the best sense, which combines missionary preaching and the telling of stories about Jesus very closely together. That many narratives seem to our modern understanding to have legendary elaboration should not disturb us. That is part of the primitive Christian style of thought, remembrance, narration and preaching. Mark the evangelist and the primitive community lived in a different world of ideas which we can no longer immediately share and understand. Is it not likely that precisely in this inseparable unity of story-telling and preaching he is dependent on the disciple of Jesus and later missionary, whom he mentions by far the most frequently in his Gospel? It was a mistake for wide circles in German New Testament scholarship in the post-war period to want to tear apart the two components of personal historical narration and 'kerygma' which are as it were amalgamated in Mark, and to play them off against each other. From the beginning the proclamation of Jesus Christ and narratives about him were inseparably associated. One could not 'preach' Jesus as the crucified Messiah and Son of God who had been raised and exalted by God without telling his history. Therefore against Rudolf Bultmann the Gospel of Mark too does not just serve as a 'supplement and illustration' of the 'Christian kerygma'; as narrative it is itself 'kerygma', i.e. saving message, and without the 'historical' experience that underlies it there would be no kerygma. The designation of the 'Christ kerygma' as a 'cult legend' and the Gospels as 'expanded cult legends' is also a mistake. Rather, from the beginning the proclamation of the 'history of Jesus Christ' which creates salvation is saving 'address' which calls for and brings about faith, and in terms of the phenomenology of religion cannot be put on the same level as the mythical *hieroi logoi* of the Greek myths which take place before history or even in a timeless world, like those of Eleusis or Dionysus. The unique thing about all these Synoptic reports is that they intentionally set out to tell the 'history' of a real 'historical' person who was active a few years previously in Galilee and was crucified at a Passover feast in Jerusalem. Mark, Luke and Matthew know that ultimately this history is grounded in living memory (Luke 1.1ff.) and that it is now proclaimed as God's action for the salvation of all human beings. The Synoptic Gospels also had a 'historical and biographical' interest in the *ancient* – not the modern – sense. However, one should not apply modern criteria for 'biography' or 'history' to these texts, in order in this way to discredit them *a priori* as a historical narrative in space and time.[356] Any historical source first requires an appropriate understanding in keeping with its character. Here slogans like 'cult legend' do not get us any further, because they contradict the self-understanding of the texts.

Now the bond between Mark and the Peter tradition does not mean that Mark simply hands on the Jesus tradition in the framework of the Petrine mission preaching. Mark, whose theological and literary capacities form criticism have failed to recognize, is far too sovereign an author for that. We can only say that Peter plays a central role in his Gospel, that with good reason we have to regard him as the decisive mediator of tradition, and that the report in the early church that he was a pupil of Peter and that his Gospel was presumably written in Rome five or six years after Peter's martyrdom also deserves a degree of historical trust. Furthermore, also on the basis of the letters of Paul and the later church tradition, we can conjecture that among the Twelve Peter played the most important role as a missionary in the West and there in a special way communicated the Jesus tradition as far as Rome. Perhaps the fact that in the Gospel of Mark the passion narrative and the vicarious atoning death of Jesus form the real focal point, whereas the ethical Jesus paraenesis, the 'words of the Lord', is only included in an eclectic way and refers not least to readiness to suffer as disciples of Jesus and to interpret the death of Jesus, is connected with this.

In that case here Mark would have handed on a tendency of 'Petrine' theology which is also to be found in I Peter; the same could also apply to the Markan son of God christology, which, while it is already unfolded in the miracle stories, here still hides behind the 'messianic secret'[357] and theologically reveals itself clearly and is consummated only in the passion. What is initially intimated in 'secret epiphanies' and misunderstood by the disciples becomes evident in the trial and death of Jesus.[358] In other words Mark no longer just wants, like others before him, to produce a collection of sayings of Jesus but *a priori* to present the Gospel in the form of a narrative which comes to a climax in the passion narrative. Here too he may be walking in the footsteps of his teacher, though we know extremely little of Peter's specific preaching (see below, 153ff.). In this case Peter would not indeed have been so far removed from the message of Paul as once the radical Tübingen school and its many disciples down to our day have claimed. I also think that numerous vivid episodes, which indeed seem archaic, could go back to the preaching of Peter, not least a series of almost 'offensive' miracle stories. The disciples, sent out by Jesus, indeed work in the consciousness of being able to do miracles themselves, but they also come up against limits here and there.[359] Here we should also not forget that in the last ten to twelve years of his life Peter was probably at least as much a 'missionary to the Gentiles' as he was to the Jews.[360] Only thus can we understand his influence in Corinth and in the West as far as Rome.

Behind the persistent refusal of the majority of New Testament scholars, despite all the historical arguments for the link between Mark and Peter in the early church, to accept any historical connection, there is probably also an unacknowledged modern apologetic interest, characteristic of Protestant theology after the Enlightenment, namely offence at the numerous miracle stories in the Gospel. Without any deeper examination, Bultmann, for example, attributes these stories, with very few exceptions, to the so-called 'Hellenistic community', which he claims to have depicted Jesus as a θεῖος ἄνθρωπος, a figure who has by now become very dubious.[361] Here surely he has the real 'historical-critical method' against him. Julius

Wellhausen already stated this modern aversion clearly: 'The miracle stories in the form in which they are presented in Mark are most resistant to being attributed to the most intimate disciples of Jesus'; therefore 'none of them may come from an eyewitness'.[362] This is contradicted by Eduard Meyer, the most significant ancient historian of his time (and like Goethe a 'decided non-Christian'): 'At all times, believers who are eye-witnesses narrate them in the same way as they are narrated in Mark, not only in the Middle Ages and in the East, and in the Greek world, . . . but similarly in the present in the case of pilgrimages, visions, etc.'[363]

The narrowness of our knowledge of sources and our 'enlightened' lack of understanding of elementary religious experience in a cultural world strange to us leads us to false historical conclusions. Eye-witnesses who are believers perceive things which are understandably closed to 'enlightened' sceptics. Nor should we overlook the fact that in the Second Gospel we do not have direct reports by Peter, but that of a disciple who naturally elaborates on his lively narrative and interprets it theologically in a midrashic way, following Old Testament models. Any 'historicist' interpretation which seeks only to reconstruct 'as it really was' misses his theological intention. This also applies to all 'biblicistic-fundamentalist rationalism'.[364] Paul himself can say almost as a matter of course that Christ worked through him with the aim of leading the Gentiles to the obedience of faith: 'with word and deed, with the power of wonders and signs, with the power of the Holy Spirit',[365] and 'the signs of an apostle were performed among you in all perseverance, with signs, wonders and acts of power'.[366] What will the Corinthians have imagined by that? The problem is that such 'miraculous' events of the past cannot be adequately 'analysed' with modern methods, that these are 'contingent' happenings or reports of such happenings which are difficult to follow, and that the 'facticity' of the event perceived can never be proved by such accounts. Origen already saw the problem of Christian miracles in his argument with Celsus, long before Lessing.[367]

7.2. *Mark's narrative about Jesus as 'Gospel'*

Because his work inseparably combines 'biographical stories' and 'proclamation' and the passion narrative, which is especially 'kerygmatic', with paradigmatic reports of Jesus' actions and teaching, Mark can call the whole of his narrative about Jesus from the appearance of John the Baptist up to the flight of the women from the empty tomb εὐαγγέλιον, 'saving message', in the full sense.[368] In other words, it is an account of Jesus' activity and vicarious death which brings about faith and thus salvation, extending to the testimony of the angel: 'You seek Jesus of Nazareth, the Crucified. He is risen; he is not here' (16.6). This last sentence sounds like a confession. For the author, the Gospel as a whole basically contains the whole message of salvation: baptism (in the form of the baptism of Jesus) and eucharist, the prophetic promises leading up to the messianic fulfilment and the future expectation. Jesus' preaching of the kingdom of God, his radicalization of the commandment, the depiction of the power of sin even over the disciples, Jesus' forgiveness of sins and call for faith, expiatory death and overcoming of death in his resurrection are mentioned here in the same way as the 'christological titles', the exaltation to the 'right hand of God', the parousia of Christ and the judgment. For the author as the 'Gospel of Jesus Christ' it therefore already meets the requirement of the sufficiency of Holy Scripture for salvation (*sufficientia sacrae scripturae ad salutem*) which old Protestant orthodoxy required of holy scripture as a whole, even if later Gospel authors want to expanded it, improve it and indeed – as in some circumstances with John – change it. In other words, the work as a whole is not merely 'the beginning of the Gospel', as scholars are fond of asserting today, but contains the *whole* offer of the message of salvation. The rival translation 'principle of the Gospel' does not make good sense; i.e. the beginning of the work in Mark 1.1 (and the title derived from it) describes the content of the whole book. It therefore also contains – from a theological perspective – more than mere λόγια κυρίου as these had already previously been disseminated in the communities both orally and in writing and was also used for a long time later as a favourite designation of predominantly paraenetic Jesus tradition (see above, 61ff.). The choice of the designation 'Gospel of Jesus Christ' was a deliberate theological decision.

The striking beginning, ἀρχὴ τοῦ εὐαγγελίου, has a parallel on the one hand at the beginning of the LXX book of Hosea, 'Beginning of the word of the Lord in Hosea';[369] we also find relatively frequently in Latin classical literature in many ways a reference to the beginning of a speech, a poem or historical conditions and events or simply mention of the *initium narrandi* or *sermonis*.[370] In the Latin manuscripts – though only of a later time – an *initium* or *incipit* often denotes the beginning of a book.[371] As a rule the Gospel manuscripts of the Vetus Latina have the simple title, but alongside it also *'initium (sancti) evangelii secundum Mattheum'* or simply *'Incipit cata Mattheum feliciter'*. In John we find only an *'Incipit evangelium secundum'* or a *'Initium'*. Only Mark has the simple title *'evangelium secundum Marcum'*, because there follows as *incipit* the *'initium evangelii Iesu Christi filii Dei'*. Accordingly a new sentence begins with *'sicut'*.[372] By contrast, in the Greek the direct combination of ἀρχή at the beginning of the book itself is very rare as opposed to the case with the Latin manuscripts.[373] It is an invention of theologians that ἀρχὴ τοῦ εὐαγγελίου refers to the whole writing. Accordingly only the narrative about John the Baptist and the baptism and temptation of Jesus is the 'beginning of the Gospel of Jesus Christ the Son of God'.[374] By contrast, the whole of Mark's work is to be the 'Gospel of Jesus Christ, the Son of God'. In this way, as has often rightly been emphasized, Mark created a new literary genre which ancient readers could certainly also regard as a biography, though one of an unprecedented kind. The story told in it calls hearers to belief in the person who is described in it, Jesus, the Messiah and Son of God, and thus to eternal life; in other words it seeks to be wholly and completely a message of salvation. Only for that reason is the designation εὐαγγέλιον Ἰησοῦ Χριστοῦ appropriate for it as a 'kerygmatic biography' of Jesus Christ, which in its narrative proclaims God's eschatological act of redemption and calls to faith. According to Mark, after the 'beginning', with John the Baptist, the baptism and temptation of the son of God, Jesus himself appears proclaiming a new message, 'the Gospel of God', about the fullness of time and the dawn of the kingdom of God, and calls for faith in this new message (πιστεύετε τῷ εὐαγγελίῳ).[375] This new message is first addressed to Jesus' hearers in Galilee but then time and again to those who hear the proclamation of his messengers and later, in the reading of the Gospel, those who take part in worship. For Mark (and his followers, the later evangelists) such faith is identical with radical conversion.

However, in contrast to all later Gospels, Mark uses the word relatively frequently: seven times in all. 8.35 speaks of giving one's life 'for my sake and the Gospel's', a formula which sounds like a hendiadys, since Jesus is the 'embodiment' of the Gospel in person. Here the evangelist may have in view *inter alia* the martyrs of the Neronian persecution, which happened only around five or six years earlier, and also included Peter (see above n.322). In 10.29, in answer to Peter's remark (10.28), Jesus speaks in an analogous way of the sacrifice of house and family 'for my sake and the Gospel's', and in 13.10 he says that 'first the Gospel must be proclaimed to all peoples'[376] before the end, i.e. the parousia of Christ. In this chapter he introduces hearers and readers to the sore trials of the church in the present, particularly in Rome, and directs attention to the parousia, which is still relatively near, though rejecting any enthusiastic imminent expectation.[377] This is a tendency which is further substantially reinforced in Luke between six and ten years later.

The last and most illuminating mention of εὐαγγέλιον is in 14.9; here Jesus sharply rejects the disciples' understandable indignation at the unknown woman who anoints him in Bethany with an incredibly expensive unguent (worth a year's wages to a labourer): 'Truly, I say to you, wherever the Gospel is preached in the whole world, what she has done will also be told in memory of her.' Here the preaching of the Gospel is

fused directly with the telling of a unique story. The unprecedented, offensive action of the woman is part of the Gospel. It
is strange that Matthew, who three times elsewhere expands
Mark's absolute τὸ εὐαγγέλιον into τὸ εὐαγγέλιον τῆς βασι-
λείας,[378] only here uses the word in the absolute, like Mark, and
further reinforces the reference by adding a demonstrative pro-
noun: 'wherever this Gospel is proclaimed . . .'[379] 'Proclaimed'
here could almost be interpreted as 'read out'. In other words,
presumably Matthew is thus already presupposing the reading
out of 'this – i.e. his written Gospel' in worship. He certainly
already knows the title of the Gospel of Mark, and correspondingly his work, too, is disseminated under a corresponding title,
albeit now apostolic. In Mark (and Matthew) Peter is evidently
the guarantor of this 'story-telling', for despite his defects and
his failure in the high-priestly palace he is the most important,
indeed for Mark (and Matthew) the one decisive, eye-witness to
Jesus' life and actions. Where he is absent, by the cross and at
the tomb, his place is taken by the women, who, like him, come
from Galilee.[380] In Mark his name stands at the beginning and
the end because in the unity of proclaimer and narrator he,
Peter, also is an essential part of the Gospel, far more so than
the unknown woman.

Apart from Mark 1.1, 'at the beginning', where εὐαγγέλιον
refers to the whole Gospel writing and ἀρχή, pointing to the
introduction before Jesus' public appearance, almost takes on
the character of the Latin '*incipit*' (a further proof that Mark is
writing in Rome), for the evangelist the word[381] still means the
orally proclaimed message that calls for and brings about the
faith of Jesus, which Peter heard and attested after Easter.
However, in the last instance (14.9) it becomes clear that this
proclamation is indissolubly bound up with the narration of
stories about Jesus. This narration also includes the strange
story of this woman, who anointed Jesus with extremely
precious unguent as an anticipation of his burial.

Here it is striking that Mark presupposes that such a story is
not an unimportant episode but is an essential part of the
Gospel which is preached and therefore also narrated 'in all the

world',[382] i.e. especially in all the widespread communities. Given the towering significance of Peter in the Gospel, we must see him after all as the most important 'narrator' of this saving message for the author, Mark. Like all the seven εὐαγγέλιον texts mentioned above, this last one (14.9), too, has deliberately been given its place by the evangelist. As in the penultimate text (13.10), it becomes clear here that in using the term Mark has in view the idea of 'world-wide mission',[383] which was unique for the ancient world and in the time of Mark still geographically somewhat unrealistic and amazing. In other words, his work expresses the experience of a purposeful, indeed 'enthusiastic', missionary in the footsteps of Peter and Paul. Therefore it cannot have been written only for the main community in Rome or the churches in Italy; as 13.10 and 14.9 indicate, it seeks, rather, to address the whole church, indeed, all humankind, about its salvation, as was later also the case with Matthew and John. In other words, the Gospel of Mark is to be read out, if possible, in all the communities at worship,[384] and for the author at the same time that means that it is preached. As εὐαγγέλιον, the word which is written, read out and interpreted takes its place alongside what has so far been the living voice of preaching: as spoken word and as scripture it is the 'saving message'. The Gospel writing, too, is meant to have a missionary effect; indeed it performs this function particularly emphatically by its fixed and thus abiding form – down to the present day: no literary work has had such an effect on the history of Europe, indeed of the world, as the collection of Gospels. This use of the term εὐαγγέλιον in the context of world-wide mission[385] forms the Markan climax to the story of the anointing, which in turn, framed by the decision to put Jesus to death (14.1f.) and the betrayal by Judas (14.10f.), introduces the decisive 'fifth act' of his dramatic narrative,[386] the passion story.

Here the 'Gospel of Jesus Christ the Son of God' (1.1) is first really completed and becomes the 'message of salvation' in the full sense for all humankind. When in a much-quoted phrase Martin Kähler called the Gospels 'passion narratives with an

disciples standing behind him, who also saw to the dissemination of the work. Just like Mark, his Gospel too was aimed at reading in worship, but at least as much also at intensive use in catechetical and ethical instruction in the Christian communities.

The situation with Luke-Acts, which was written about ten to twenty years earlier than 'the Gospel according to Matthew', probably between AD 75 and 80, is more difficult. In his 'Jesus biography', which is (and this too indicates a completely new step) the longest of all the Gospels[402] and more strongly adapted to the literary customs of his time, in contrast to Mark, the word 'Gospel' does not occur at all. However, the verb εὐαγγελίζεσθαι, 'proclaim the good news', taken over from the Septuagint (especially the prophets and psalms), is that much more frequent. The verb is completely absent from Mark, and in Matthew it appears only once.[403] Luke is particularly fond of this word and uses it more often than Paul,[404] whose travelling companion he was at a later period of Paul's life.[405] He thus shows that he too wants to be a 'theologian of the word'; one might almost describe this predilection for the proclaimed word of the message of salvation as a 'Pauline' trait.

Only in Acts does he speak twice of the missionary preaching of the '*Gospel*'. This happens once in the mouth of Peter, at the 'Apostolic Council', where with reference to the special case of Cornelius the leading apostle uses the term when referring to himself as the missionary to the Gentiles chosen by God: 'Brethren, you know that in bygone days God made the choice among you, that by my mouth the Gentiles should hear the word of *the Gospel* and believe',[406] while Paul says to the elders in Miletus that he 'received from the Lord Jesus the ministry to testify to the Gospel of the grace of God' (20.24). This last formulation, εὐαγγέλιον τῆς χάριτος, which has its closest parallels in Gal. 1.12,15f. and Rom. 1.1–5, shows that Luke was well aware of the special theological character of the Pauline mission preaching: the content of his message of salvation was 'God's grace'.[407] At the same time we may assume that Luke knew that the term εὐαγγέλιον also played a role in the

Petrine preaching as a summary of the saving message in the later period, when Peter among other things was *also* working as a missionary to the Gentiles like Paul and Mark was his companion (and interpreter). Is it a coincidence that the word appears not only in *all* the letters of Paul (including the Deutero-Paulines), Mark, Matthew and Acts but also in I Peter (4.17), which comes from the 'Petrine school', with the meaning 'God's message of salvation'?[408] Moreover, a little later, in I Peter 5.13, Mark is named as Peter's disciple and companion 'in Babylon', i.e. in Rome. Philemon 24 (and Col. 4.10, shortly before Luke, the 'beloved physician' 4.14) mentions Mark as a companion of Paul, presumably during his imprisonment in Rome between around 60 and 62. So in later years Mark could have formed a 'bridge' between Paul and Peter.

But back to Luke. For him – in a thoroughly Pauline way – εὐαγγέλιον in the mouth of Peter or Paul means the oral apostolic message of salvation after Easter, especially for the Gentiles, and not as in Mark[409] (and later in Matthew) as a term for the preaching of Jesus, or as in Mark 1.1 for a 'Gospel writing' and 'biographical' account of Jesus' activity and suffering.[410] Therefore despite his model, Mark, he does not use this word at all in his Gospel and contents himself with his favourite verb εὐαγγελίζεσθαι, which here already he uses ten times from the message of Gabriel to Zechariah up to the teaching of Jesus in the temple.[411]

Thus in the preface, with its dedication to Theophilus,[412] which falls outside the framework of earliest Christian literature of the first century, he says, not that the 'many' – among them first of all Mark, his main source, the unknown authors of his rich special material including the vague hypothetical 'Q-source(s)' and the independent tradition of his passion narrative[413] – had each composed a 'Gospel' before him, but that they had 'compiled *a narrative of the events which have been accomplished among us*'.[414] Here with διήγησις he chooses a theologically neutral historical-literary term which appears both in Jewish-Hellenistic literature and among Greek authors.[415] In so doing he shows himself – far ahead of his time

– to be the first Christian 'historian' and 'apologist'.[416] His brief preface corresponds to the prefaces in the specialist scientific writings of antiquity, not least those by doctors. This and other indications make it probable that he is identical with 'Luke, the beloved physician' of Colossians 4.14.[417] In Luke's view the 'Gospel according to Mark' – surely counted as first among the 'many' – which is too simple for him, is no longer adequate as reliable instruction for the 'noble Theophilus'. Therefore Luke wants to write for Theophilus a more complete and more precise 'historical' account of the life of Jesus and follows this up – presumably after an interval of a few years[418] – with a second 'report', similarly provided with a dedication, of the events from the resurrection to Paul's arrival in Rome around AD 60.[419]

Presumably both works were accompanied by a letter to the person thus honoured. We find such accompanying letters to literary works often in contemporary Roman literature.[420] In his two-volume work Luke proves himself to be a disciple of Paul not only by Pauline allusions but also by texts from his unique special material in the Gospel like Luke 15; 18.9–14 or 19.1–10, which express the unconditional acceptance of sinners by Jesus.[421] The 'profane' literary form, together with the preface and dedication, which are still quite unusual in the earliest Christian literature (significantly we do not find either in Jewish apocrypha and pseudepigrapha or in the earliest Christian writings[422]), should really have made a title like εὐαγγέλιον κατὰ Λουκᾶν impossible, especially as Luke presumably knew that the – predominantly – Pauline term for the 'message of salvation' preached by the missionary to the Gentiles did not directly fit the teaching of Jesus. Therefore in the Gospel he limits himself to either the verbs εὐαγγελίζεσθαι, διδάσκειν provided by the Old Testament or simply λέγειν and λόγος. Moreover, unlike Mark and Matthew, he probably did not write his two-volume work directly with all the communities of the mainstream church which formed gradually after AD 70 in view, but primarily for the 'noble' Theophilus and his circle of friends. In this point he initially differed considerably from the other evangelists Mark, Matthew and John. The 'profane' prologue, corresponding to more elevated literary customs, makes his two-volume work seem unique by comparison with the other primitive Christian writings, something about which cannot wonder too much in this early period.

Theophilus was perhaps an alias.[423] This 'friend of God' could very well have come from the highest circles of the Roman aristocracy (cf. Acts 23.16; 24.3; 26.25). He was certainly not an ordinary man. It is his rank in society that requires the preface, which is extremely strange for the earliest church.[424] Consequently, Luke's work took rather longer to become established in the church than the later successful Gospel according to Matthew. Mark and Matthew the 'Gospel' of a disciple of Peter, the most important witness for the Jesus tradition, and even more that of an 'apostle' from the group of the twelve, initially found it easier to gain recognition in the communities than the two-volume work of a later travelling companion of Paul, the 'thirteenth witness' and controversial apostle, who himself had not been an eye-witness. Only later, in the first decades of the second century, did it then overtake Mark, to which it was *a priori* superior by virtue of its greater volume of tradition. Although it was written earlier, it always had to fall back by comparison with the influence of Matthew.

Significantly, we find the first quotations of Luke in educated Christians like Basilides (AD 120/130) and Justin (AD 150). On the other hand, it is already presupposed in the secondary conclusion to Mark (16.9–21),[425] which was probably composed around 110–120, as it is already attested by Justin, the Epistula Apostolorum and Irenaeus (see above). Polycarp too (see above, 26f.) seems to have known Luke. Marcion (c. AD 144) took Luke over because it came from a disciple of Paul. However he had first to purge it of all Judaizing 'uncleannesses'.[426] All these Christian authors seem already to know it with the title εὐαγγέλιον κατὰ Λουκᾶν, for it is quite impossible that it should have been given this designation, which would have been quite inexplicable for a later time, only towards the middle of the second century (see above, 48ff.). Probably

Theophilus, the rich aristocrat, who was honoured and instructed by the work, then put it into circulation under this title, already following the example of the title of Mark,[427] by having it copied and sent to other communities, possibly especially those of Pauline origin. The title of the second work could also have come into existence as a result of the circulation brought about by Theophilus.[428] In that case the title of Luke's second work which was published a few years later, the plural πράξεις (τῶν) ἀποστόλων, 'Acts of the Apostles', would primarily refer to Peter and Paul. Towards the end of the first century and still in the first half of the second century they were by far the best-known apostles active as missionaries.[429] John the son of Zebedee came some way behind in third place – thus in the Acts of the Apostles themselves, but one could also refer to Gal. 2.6–9. Possibly Luke himself hoped in the end to disseminate his two writings with the help of this patron, since the process required quite considerable expense; moreover in his work he had in view not only the one person whom he addressed, Theophilus, and his circle, but at the same time especially the well-to-do and the better educated Christians, who in the 80s were still a comparatively small group in the church. Therefore in his two-volume work he is interested on the one hand in introducing individual dignitaries, but on the other in speaking to the conscience of the rich, to warn them against the danger of riches and point them urgently to the coming judgment.

This double strategy gives his work an apparently contradictory stamp.[430] A former godfearer, he is also not yet theologically so abruptly separated from the Judaism of his time as the later authors of the First or Fourth Gospels. Love of Judaism and its institutions, like the temple and the holy city, which he had come to know at first hand as a travelling companion of Paul,[431] keeps breaking through, despite the disappointment of the Greek Luke that the majority of God's people rejects his Messiah announced by the prophets. No Greek author before him has reported on Judaism in Palestine and the Diaspora in such a varied, informative and often also positive way, i.e. relatively objectively in terms of conditions in antiquity. Alongside Josephus and Philo's *Legatio ad Gaium*, his two-volume work is the most important source for the Palestinian Judaism of the first century AD.[432] There is not a trace in him of the antisemitism widespread in the educated Graeco-Roman world with its assertions and accusations which are often so senseless.[433] Israel is the people chosen by God, its God is the true God, and the holy scriptures inspired by him are also the divine word for the new messianic movement made up of Jews and Gentiles.[434] He knew that his most important source, Mark, was based on the tradition and authority of the apostle Peter, who for the West had been the decisive 'eye-witness and minister of the word' (Luke 1.2, cf. 24.47ff.; Acts 1.21f.) and therefore also gives Peter a central role in the Gospel, mentioning him twenty-eight times.[435] He also wanted through Peter to build a bridge from Jesus to Paul, the greatest missionary of the earliest church, with whom he had also been personally associated more than twenty years earlier. It is striking how much the two names of Peter and Paul dominate Acts; here of course Paul has the greater weight. The theological difference between Luke and Paul, which in my view was conditioned not least by the author's encounter with the Palestinian-Petrine Jesus tradition, together with its strong desire for harmonization, has not damaged this love of the 'apostle to the Gentiles'.[436] That despite all the differences he has learned from Paul is evident from his emphasis on radical grace towards sinners in the Gospel.[437]

Once the works of Mark, Luke and Matthew had been disseminated one after the other between 69/70 and 90/100 under this form of title εὐαγγέλιον κατὰ . . ., for later imitators this became something like a compulsory form of title. If an account of the teaching and activity of Jesus with a kerygmatic form wanted wider recognition in the communities, it had if possible to bear this superscription, which was becoming increasingly familiar to the communities.[438] At the same time the title indicated a unique content, 'the one saving message of Jesus' teaching and work' and the 'apostolic' authority standing behind it as author or tradition-bearer. Works without titles no longer had a chance of establishing themselves in the mainstream church. At best they reached esoteric circles as in the case of the Nag Hammadi texts. Where the name of the author was removed, as in the case of Hebrews and the Letter to Diognetus, at least the name of those to whom it was addressed (whether fictitious or authentic) was preserved. By their striking consistency in the manuscript tradition from Matthew to the book of Revelation, in particular the writings which later formed the 'New Testament' generally show that from the beginning, i.e. from the time they were produced or disseminated and circulated, they were associated with their original titles. In practice, therefore, these could no longer be changed. The few exceptions prove the rule. In contrast to this, both the titles and the textual tradition of the 'apocryphal' writings of the second century are often unstable. Essentially greater arbitrariness is predominant here. If the titles of the Gospels, the letters or the apocalypses had been changed or expanded, this would have left a record in the textual tradition, which is uniquely well attested for antiquity (see above, 26–31). Where there were uncertainties, for example with the Letter to the Ephesians,[439] discrepancies in the textual attestation indicate the fact.

The disciples of John who published the Fourth Gospel after the death of their teacher, probably not too long after AD 100, and in my view together with the three letters,[440] similarly chose the title which had become traditional in the last thirty years since Mark. They did so although, as I have already remarked, the word εὐαγγέλιον does not appear at all in the Johannine corpus, with its distinctive language.[441] Probably such a general term with a Pauline-Petrine stamp did not seem appropriate to the author, i.e. 'John the elder', to denote the unique 'testimony of the sending of the Son by the Father'.[442] For him, Jesus' preaching and activity could not be described by a single term; they could be conveyed appropriately only by their whole christological content. Mark in his christology, despite considerable differences, in a way stands closer to John than Luke and Matthew, who also as a result of the different prehistories in their accounts had a stronger 'biographical' character.[443]

It is almost a miracle that the church preserved the four earliest Gospels we have, so often differing in part, despite their striking discrepancies, indeed contradictions, and resisted any attempt at harmonization or radical selection along the lines of Marcion. On the one hand in so doing it created for itself a permanent cause of offence and theological controversy, indeed a direct occasion for contradiction by its opponents. The temptation to expand the series of four partially contradictory Gospels by constantly new narratives about Jesus and collections of sayings especially with additional revelations, like secret teachings from the risen Christ to his disciples,[444] was further increased by the plurality of these four which were already in existence shortly after AD 100. If one already had four such 'biographies', why not produce further 'more contemporary' or 'progressive' ones, if possible under other or even more famous – now only apostolic – names like Peter, Philip, Thomas or even Mary? On the other hand, precisely these four Gospels bore witness that the one truth in Jesus Christ could be, indeed had to be, seen in a variety of ways and always under different aspects. The fathers from Irenaeus through Origen and Eusebius to Augustine rightly emphasized this point, despite all their questionable harmonizing tendencies. The abundance of early Christian testimony about Jesus of Nazareth could never have developed like this in the course of church history and borne rich fruit had it been based only on one harmonizing Gospel in the style of Tatian's *Diatessaron* or one purified Gospel after the style of Marcion.

9. The Gospel as a message of salvation for the whole church

Contrary to a widespread view, none of the four Gospels was written only for one particular community; far less do they simply reproduce the views of one individual community. They give primarily the views of their authors. We cannot even say with certainty whether they ever came into being only in one community, for the missionaries of the early church travelled a great deal and could be authoritative teachers at different places. So we should stop talking automatically about 'the community of Mark', 'of Luke', 'of Matthew', 'of John' as the one really responsible for the composition of a Gospel writing and its theology. The four Gospels have nothing to do with 'letters' which were occasioned by a community. These are relatively rare in the New Testament and its environment.[445] Even more nonsensical is the term 'Q community', i. e. the community of the Logia source (we do not even really know in what forms this source [or these sources] existed).[446] The authors of these works do not represent the view of a collective community, but of an individual yet authoritative teacher of one or more communities (or a school), and in their quite different forms proclaim the one truth which should be binding on all believers. This is true regardless of the fact that of course authors were in constant dialogue with a community, or more frequently several communities, and with their disciples or school.

This situation already exists for Paul, whose first letter to the Corinthians cannot simply be identified with the views of the community in Ephesus and whose letter to the Romans cannot be attributed to Corinthian theology, although it was written in Corinth.[447] Indeed one could not derive Luther's work, either, from the Christians in Wittenberg, his disciples and friends. The authority of the first four Gospels known to us is, each in its own way, singular, and their claim fundamentally universal. Because of this claim that the truth contained in the Gospels was generally valid for the whole church, these writings were disseminated relatively soon after their composition, at least in the larger communities of the empire between AD 70 and around 110. For Mark and his followers the Roman empire means the greater part of the inhabited world. Therefore all four Gospels are also composed in Greek. A comparable Aramaic work remains in obscurity, and a Latin Gospel tradition was not yet necessary before the last decades of the second century. Universal statements about the preaching (and narration) of the Gospel like those in Mark 13.10 and 14.9 fundamentally refer to the area of Roman rule. In Rom. 15.19–24 Paul already has the whole of the empire including Spain in view, and the same is true of Luke with Acts 1.8.[448] For Mark, who is writing in Rome, like Luke, whose two-volume work ends with Paul's arrival and two-year stay in Rome, this perspective is important. The Roman historian Florus[449] could therefore say: 'So widely have (the Romans) extended their arms throughout the world, that those who read their affairs are learning history not of a single people, but of the human race.'

The exchange between the individual communities in the Empire by messengers with letters or whole delegations was lively from the start and corresponded to the new sect's universal, eschatological claim to the truth, which was valid for all men and women, Jews, Greeks, Romans, and barbarians.[450] At the same time this constant exchange was a basic condition for retaining its identity and the success of its dissemination. Only permanent contacts between the individual communities through letters and other writings and the messengers who brought them, who at the same time could have been the first 'exegetes' of such writings,[451] guaranteed the unity and missionary success of the church, which at the time of the composition of the four Gospels was not more than one or two generations old.[452] Before 70 Jerusalem and after 70 Rome stood at the centre of this travelling activity: 'it is the destination of most Christians whom we know as travellers.'[453] Thus the title 'message of salvation', εὐαγγέλιον, to be supplemented each time by Ἰησοῦ Χριστοῦ (Mark 1.1), with its universal meaning was quite appropriate for the new biographical-kerygmatic 'narratives about Jesus', beginning with Mark's work in Rome. This message written in the form of a story was therefore ultimately addressed to all communities; more clearly in Mark, Matthew, and John, rather less in Luke. But even in his case, as I have already remarked, the first addressee

Theophilus probably provided the distribution in the church, for both the author, Luke, and Theophilus, who was honoured by the dedication, were interested in the dissemination of the two-volume work.

The differences between the four Gospels according to Mark, Luke, Matthew and John, which could not be ignored or kept quiet about, were as a rule deliberately accepted in the communities, because it was known that the 'apostolic witness' had already had a variety of different forms, just as for a long time there had been 'Petrine', 'Pauline', later also 'Johannine' and then of course specifically 'Jewish-Christian' communities in connection with James, the brother of the Lord.[454] Possibly such 'doctrinal traditions' associated with individuals were even cherished and preserved in various 'house churches' in the same place.[455] The letters of Paul already indicate this multiplicity (and the tensions connected with it). Even the harmonizing Luke in Acts cannot completely remove the differences. How far the individual authors had special ties with particular communities and developed their 'Gospel' in possibly lengthy teaching activity, even in a kind of school, differed depending on their situation. The latter was certainly the case with John in Ephesus, but as III John shows, he also wrote to other communities, visited them, and was probably an authority in the whole of Asia Minor.[456] At any rate his Gospel, and the first letters – later called 'Catholic' – are for the whole church. The same may have been true of 'Matthew' in southern Syria/Palestine. Luke, the much-travelled 'beloved physician', who was certainly also versed in mission, could have composed his two-volume work for Theophilus in different places; here later church tradition mentions the province of Achaea,[457] but the work could also come from Rome. In disseminating it – presumably the task of Theophilus – people will primarily have counted on the special interest of the Pauline communities. Mark too, who as a disciple of Peter similarly wrote around AD 69/70 in or near Rome, where there were a number of 'house communities', certainly did not solely introduce the ideas of the contemporary Roman community (or communities), even if this now took on special significance as a result of its fiery trial in the Neronian persecution (AD 64) with its two apostolic martyrs.

The community of Roman house churches[458] became even more important a little later when with their flight to Pella on the outbreak of the Jewish War (AD 66), along with the threat of the destruction of Jerusalem, the Jewish Christians from Jerusalem who had hitherto set the tone lost their predominant influence.[459] But even more important for Mark than this specific Roman background was the recollection of the message preached and narrated (or recited in worship) by Peter and himself at many other places as well. The 'Gospel according to Mark' thus seems to be the first authoritative primitive Christian writing known to us, sent from Rome to the communities of the empire. Nevertheless it is not a forerunner of the utterly Roman I Clement. It was not at all typically 'Roman', but wholly orientated on the event associated with Jesus in Galilee and Jerusalem, and thus had an explicitly universal, one could even say 'ecumenical', claim – in this it was comparable to the Pauline Gospel which apparently was rather different. In its case the place of composition fades relatively into the background; the authority of the Roman community (or communities) as yet plays no role, in contrast to I Clement, the letter of Ignatius to the Romans or in Irenaeus. They were probably only in the process of recovering after the terrors of the persecution, around five years earlier.[460] The sole question is that of the saving word of the activity and death of Jesus. The author, who comes from Jerusalem, is also in fact only the second (or third)[461] New Testament author whose work we know. Only the authentic letters of Paul are certainly older. Probably more or less all the Gospels were written basically to be read out in many, if not all, communities of the expanding church. Their message concerned all Christians. Finally that is also true, with some qualifications, of Luke-Acts, which most falls out of the framework because of its literary form.

In all 'historical criticism' we should also not overlook the fact that all four Gospels are primarily writing about past events, lying four to seven decades back, set in Jewish Palestine between Galilee and Jerusalem. They do this with a great variety of information about the ideas, party groupings and opponents there, and at the same time of course the living faith of the evangelists, the guarantors of their tradition and their hearers (who sometimes changed) are also expressed in them. Only since the nineteenth century has there been a 'purely historical consciousness' and even today it is still basically a fiction to put the emphasis on the 'purely'. However, the strong reference to the present in the primitive Christian authors which is of course to be taken for granted in no way excludes the consciousness of chronological and geographical distance. Even John, who puts the most emphasis on the presence of salvation, is very well aware of this distance from the primal event which is the foundation of salvation and deliberately works with different levels of time.[462] One effort brings together all four evangelists: there is a concern to report a real past event which is the foundation for present (and future) salvation, and this is done by relating 'stories' which together refer to a unique 'history'. For this purpose Mark created a new 'kerygmatic-biographical' genre *sui generis*, which deliberately set out to proclaim the story/stories, understood as a real event, as a saving message.[463] In so doing he fused tradition and theological interpretation; one could even say historical reminiscence and 'fictitious' midrash-like elaboration. There was a firm basis for the designation 'apostolic' tradition for these new texts, in terms of both content and chronology, for these novel writings come from 'apostolic disciples' of the second and third generation and are based on authentic earlier 'apostolic' tradition. Here it makes little sense in a positivistic and apologetic way to insist one-sidedly on the thoroughgoing 'historicity' of these unique reports, but it seems hardly less one-sided, remote from history and dogmatistic to postulate on ideological grounds that they are purely fictional, as mere 'community formation' or an invention of the author.[464]

Very much as a matter of course, from the moment of their composition people in the communities were very interested in these novel texts, which supplemented the familiar reading of the Old Testament 'prophetic' writings, interpreted these writings point by point through the 'history of their fulfilment' and at the same time gave written form to the fundamental traditions of the oral 'Gospel' (see 128ff.). As 'additions' to the Old Testament texts they were predestined for reading in worship and went together almost seamlessly with oral teaching. That explains their relatively rapid and wide dissemination.

Thus, an astonishingly close 'networking'[465] of different communities between Rome and Syria becomes evident in the speed and intensity in which our earliest Gospel Mark (and probably already before him collections of logia and stories by other authors and from other places) was taken up and worked on, or how it was noted, 'interpreted' and supplemented by later evangelists like Luke and Matthew or even partially contradicted (above all by John). Luke and even more Matthew are in part very early 'commentaries' on Mark. The origin of the four earliest Gospels and other collections of the sayings of Jesus or later so-called 'apocryphal' Gospels, which as a rule were dependent on the former,[466] beginning with Mark (and earlier logia collections more or less unknown to us), thus presuppose a constant exchange between the communities. This is also typical of the second and third centuries. The Gospels after Mark therefore came into being to some degree through the 'scriptural exegesis' (and imitation) of earlier works. It was not least this exchange, the liveliness of which cannot be overestimated, which made it impossible later to reduce to one Gospel the multiplicity of Gospels that had come into being during one generation, whether in a single work abbreviated and made binding by 'purging' or in one work enriched by harmonizing.

It is therefore also improbable, as I have already mentioned (see above, 53ff.), that, as is often claimed, communities towards the end of the first century and in the first half of the second still as a rule had only a single anonymous Gospel book each. People were too curious not also to want to get to know other Gospel writings. Such curiosity was a thoroughly positive creative characteristic. In other words, people wanted to listen to other different 'apostolic' authors and tradents.[467] At most a community will have preferred one writing, say 'Matthew' or later 'John', to others. The collection of oral and written 'Jesus traditions' , as in Papias, or also 'new productions' of them, as in later apocryphal Gospels, was by no means an individual instance and can be understood all too well. People wanted to know more and more (in some circumstances too much). This is still true of the predilection for the Gospel of Peter in Syrian Rhossos, the discussion of the 'Matthias tradition' in Clement of Alexandria towards the end of the second century, or the long-drawn-out controversy over the 'Hebrew' Gospel of the Jewish Christians (see above, 12ff., 15ff.), which existed in various forms.

Lastly, the churches at the end of the first century and first decades of the second ultimately wanted a plurality of Gospels, just as they also refused to prescribe a stereotyped 'unitary theology'. Despite the strong awareness of the unity of the church, there was an amazing multiplicity of doctrinal views, which constantly led to differences, as Paul already shows. Early Jewish-Christian tradition built upon the teaching of Jesus, and the testimony of his disciples was rich from the beginning. Even if the 'reliable' Jesus tradition was strongly reduced – not least by the retreat of Palestinian Jewish Christianity after 70 – on the other hand the witnesses to the 'apostolic' preaching multiplied through the work of writers of the second and third generation. We already find its earliest version (including the controversies within the church) in the letters of Paul. Another, less clear area is the transmission of 'sayings of the Lord' with a christological and paraenetical orientation. The 'apostolic testimony' brought about by the Spirit was multiple and not without contradictions from the beginning. Here the theological multiplicity – despite the fundamental unity of the church through attestation of the person of Jesus Christ and the gift of the Holy Spirit – was certainly still substantially greater than what has been preserved for us in literary works of the early period up to the beginning of the second century. Thus, just as in the Gospels there is evidently a

Petrine (Mark), Pauline (Luke), Johannine and Jewish-Christian (Matthew) orientation, later in a corresponding way in the New Testament corpus of letters, despite the predominance of Pauline and Deutero-Pauline works we find analogous groupings: the two – very different – letters of Peter, the three letters of John and the Apocalypse, together with the letters of James and Jude. I Clement and the letters of Ignatius also have a quite distinctive theological stamp, although both already take the 'apostolic' tradition for granted. Here the question of the historically demonstrable authenticity of these writings does not play the decisive role, but their theological content, their use in paraenesis and church conflicts. These tendencies in writings continue in an almost confusing way in the 'apocryphal' works of the second century.

Especially between AD 70 and 150 the thought and teaching of the church developed in a very lively, indeed sometimes almost too lively way; there was more and more 'experimentation' and there were often vigorous arguments. In his preface, already between 75 and 80 Luke quite deliberately refers to the prior work of the 'many'. He wants to improve it; however, he does not reject this work but builds on it. Thus 'plurality' does not necessarily mean chaos nor – as often today – a dismissal of the question of truth. In the development of the second century, when the mainstream church was being more and more consolidated by the *regula fidei* and the *monarchical episcopate*, the progressive *multiplicity* of Gospel-like writings also brought with it the danger that the tradition would run wild, that there would be splits, and that special subjective, indeed false, teaching would arise. At that time this was countered not least by a concentration on what for us are the four earliest 'apostolic' Gospels and on the traditions which stood behind them or were prompted by them.

The Pastoral Epistles, written around the same time or shortly after those of Ignatius, are a typical example of this.[468] II Peter, the latest writing in the New Testament canon, can already refer to the Gospel and Matthew and the eye-witness or personal hearing of the alleged author.[469] Here it was believed that the 'apostolic testimony' of Jesus had been preserved 'unfalsified'. One essential reason for this 'consolidation' was the increasingly overabundant religious philosophical speculation of Christian 'Gnostics', who set out first to be more 'progressive thinkers' on a higher intellectual level, and who denied the reality of the humanity of Jesus, the saving significance of his death and the creation of the world as God's work, in favour of a Platonizing dualistic doctrine of souls and their redemption.[470] From a historical perspective the one-sided appeal to the entrusted apostolic 'deposit' of faith[471] is certainly open to attack, for there is no chemically pure divine, 'unfalsified tradition' in the strict sense. 'Tradition' is human work, and human tradition is always also shaped by those who hand it on and interpret it. The 'inspiration of a text' by God shows itself only by its 'spiritual' efficacy (*efficacia*, in the sense of the word in old Protestant dogmatics, which was understood as the work of the Holy Spirit in awakening and preserving faith, communicated by the word of God), i.e. by the way in which this word creates, strengthens and sustains living faith. It is here that the real mystery of our four Gospels lies. They exercised a unique influence in the history of the church, indeed of humankind. At the same time, according to all our historical knowledge and an impartial, sober comparison between the apocryphal Jesus traditions and the four Gospels, indeed the New Testament generally, the church of the second century could hardly have made a better choice. Here the Gospel of Mark, based on the authority of Peter, made a good beginning.

IV

'The Cross-Check': The Origin
of the Collection of the Four Gospels
and the Christian Book Cupboard –
An Attempt at a Reconstruction

1. Scripture reading in worship, the codex, and the community's book cupboard

The four Gospels were primarily written for liturgical reading and not so much for private interests or for the theological reading of individual prominent theological teachers, and – as I have already said several times – they made a claim to truth which applied to the whole church. That will even be the case for Luke, which was presumably read aloud in Theophilus's house community and disseminated by Theophilus in other communities. If we attempt to reconstruct the origin of the collection of four Gospels, we must therefore start from that text in which their role in worship is first described, a text which we already know and which I want once again to consider here briefly. It is the earliest description of a Christian service of the word and eucharist in the *First Apology* of Justin, which was written soon after AD 150 and depicts a form of worship which liturgically was already firmly fixed, evidently not only in Rome but, as Justin emphasizes, also in other parts of the Roman empire.[472]

The decisive factor is that the form of the liturgy of the word largely followed that of the synagogue, with the reading of a

particular section of the text and its exegesis in the following
sermon, as a rule with a strongly paraenetic character, framed
by prayers.[473] However, here Justin speaks only of the following prayer before the eucharist, though in ch.13 he does refer to
the many prayers and the praise of God in celebrations by the
community. This novel form of the pure liturgy of the word in
the 'house of prayer', the προσευχή, was an invention of
Judaism and corresponded more to the meetings of a school of
philosophers than to Greek worship with sacrificial processions
and the singing of hymns. This form, which Justin also presupposes already to be generally customary for the Christians,
must have come into being as early as the first century. The
Christians certainly did not take over this Jewish form of the
liturgy of the word later, decades after the separation from the
synagogue, but basically merely continued the traditional
Jewish form in the new eschatological community of salvation.
In Rome it could go back to the beginnings of the community
which was first founded there, and which had a marked Jewish-
Christian stamp, especially as the Gentile-Christians too were
predominantly former godfearers. Probably Christian worship
in Rome, corresponding to Roman notions of order, differed
considerably from the enthusiastic form described for Corinth
in I Cor. 14, though there too, according to Paul, edification
through the word and right order were to be central.[474]
Didactic writings like Romans, Hebrews and I Clement,[475] but
also Barnabas and II Clement, presuppose a regular reading of
the LXX in worship; otherwise the recipients would not have
been able to understand at all these letters which argued using
'scripture'. Had the writings of the Old Testament been unimportant for early Christian worship, it would not have been
possible to use them so intensively in arguments. The same is
true of catechetical instruction. Presumably those writings
which play an important role in quotations or allusions in the
New Testament were also predominantly used in worship.
They include the Pentateuch, above all Genesis, Exodus and
Deuteronomy; the Psalms, as probably the most important
early Christian text; and the Prophets, here primarily Isaiah,

but also the others, Jeremiah, Ezekiel, Daniel and the Twelve Prophets.

But where various Old Testament writings were regularly read aloud in worship, an equivalent to the Jewish Torah shrine was also needed,[476] a Christian book cupboard or community archive where the books used were kept in a relatively fixed order, ready to hand, and provided with titles.

There were no Old Testament writings without titles; here it was believed that the title usually referred to the author. As for order, the traditional Jewish 'historical' order was probably also followed: after the Pentateuch came Joshua, Judges, etc.; after Psalms the proverbs attributed to Solomon; and after Isaiah the later prophets. It must have been necessary to be able to find the biblical writings without difficulty – however, now as codices and no longer on scrolls. Codices were easier to use, to keep and to transport than the elegant but less practical scrolls. Nevertheless the codex was slow to establish itself in profane literature. That makes it all the more striking that Christian literature from the earliest second-century papyrus discoveries onwards was written almost entirely on codices. Great Christian communities, in the first line Rome, Antioch, Ephesus or Alexandria, will from the beginning have attached some importance to increasing the number of 'scriptures' available. I Clement and Justin show how extensive this collection could be. For example, I Clement contains the first reference to Judith of any kind and also already knows Esther,[477] Sirach and Wisdom.[478] In contrast to the Jewish scrolls in worship (to the present day), from the second half of the first century the Christian scriptures may already have been predominantly codices in which the names for God and Christ and the Holy Spirit were written as *nomina sacra* as distinct from the Jewish tetragrammaton.[479] At the same time these served as helps in reading. The revolutionary introduction of the codex and the *nomina sacra* cannot possibly be the result of a later 'redaction' of the four Gospels or other New Testament writings, as the numerous earliest LXX manuscripts from the first/second century in practice already similarly also contain this special form throughout.[480] That means that the introduction of the codex among Christians is essentially older than the origin of the four-Gospel codex. Indeed, it is a presupposition of this origin. In my view it could already derive from the separation between church and synagogue, which goes back in Antioch and Rome to the 40s. The transfer of the celebration of divine worship from the sabbath to the Lord's day, which is already demonstrable in Paul, is a partial analogy.[481] The Sunday celebration of the eucharist, the use of the codex instead of the scroll and the introduction of the *nomina sacra* indicate a concern to document the new character of the distinctive enthusiastic-eschatological movement over against the Jewish synagogue worship from which people had been quickly forced out as troublemakers. But there was also independence from pagan literary practice. Because the end was near and the 'Lord' was expected soon, Jewish and pagan literary conventions had become unimportant. In addition there were also practical pressures. A codex, initially as a rule only a signature or volume of folded leaves of parchment or papyrus which had been stitched together, was easier to make and use than an ordinary papyrus scroll. Moreover the scripture scrolls for synagogue worship with their calligraphy were very expensive and not easy to get hold of. They would hardly have been sold to the new 'heretics'. The early Christians therefore had to attempt to copy what were the most important holy synagogue texts for them, either in their entirety or in excerpts, as quickly as possible. Here the larger communities mentioned above showed the way for the smaller ones, which according to need provided themselves with copies from there.[482]

The whole question of the rise of the use of the codex in the Christian community is still discussed too much from the perspective of the collection of the four Gospels; here at the same time reference is made to the earliest literary evidence towards the end of the first century in Rome. In the process some of the fundamental insights of C. H. Roberts and T. C. Skeat, which we cannot go back beyond, are again being put in question.[483] The uniformity of early Christian book production, which is without analogy, must derive from 'apostolic times'. There are thus two reasons for the origin of the almost 'monopolistic' use of the codex, one 'theological and sociological' and the other practical. First, there was a concern to distinguish oneself from the use of scrolls in synagogue worship – something which initially was even a forced measure; secondly, the primitive Christian missionaries probably from the start took with them on their travels 'notebooks' made out of thin wooden tablets or 'parchment' which contained 'sayings of the Lord', important Septuagint texts, and also other notes, like the addresses of communities, itineraries, etc. The parchment codex and its use in the liturgy will have grown out of these notebooks. Possibly Paul already wrote his letters in such parchment volumes, especially as these were easier to transport than the sensitive and unwieldy scrolls. The mention of 'parchments' in II Tim. 4.13 could represent a recollection of earlier 'apostolic customs'.[484] The fact that the parchment notebook is a Roman invention does not contradict this conjecture. Practical objects of Roman origin were also not unknown in the Greek East.

The transition from the parchment notebook to the parchment codex took place in the second half of the first century. Martial writes his introduction to the second edition of his *Epigrams* c.84–85 and in it commends the books as a travelling companion: 'by which the parchment confines in small pages'. As a small codex fits into one hand, one can dispense with the shapeless book-covers which protect scrolls.[485] After Martial, larger works were also available in codex form on small parchment sheets, like Homer, Virgil, Cicero, Livy and Ovid's *Metamorphoses*. Even if we want to assume that these were sometimes extracts, it becomes clear that the parchment codices could contain far more text than the traditional scrolls in a relatively short space.[486] Aesthetic reasons and factors relating to the sociology of education explain why, despite its advantages, in the second and third centuries the codex was slow to establish itself in profane literary activity: 'the socially elevated, conservative classes of readers associated the new form of book too much with the notion of the codex as a notebook for jotting down everyday and transitory matters', and therefore saw 'the new book form as unworthy of demanding, classical litera- ture'.[487]

The few codices before the beginning of the third century comprise very few examples of classical 'high literature', and more works for school use, technical and medical works, or trivial literature. Here we encounter the same 'conservative' attitude in the pagan scriptoria and bookshops as we can observe – *mutatis mutandis* – with the Christian scribal customs of the second and the third centuries. It is also typical that the Jews have held on to the scroll for synagogue worship down to the present day.

Thus there are many reasons for the introduction and re- tention of the codex.[488] The main reason seems to be the demar- cation of the early, enthusiastic and eschatological worship from the traditional synagogue worship and the difficulty of getting hold of LXX manuscripts. Here the *nomina sacra* took the place of the tetragrammaton, which was still written with Hebrew characters; these *nomina sacra* were now also used for θεός, Χριστός, πνεῦμα and other central terms. In view of the imminent end, initially the old 'literary-liturgical' conventions had become unimportant. In addition there were purely practi- cal reasons: for travelling missionaries, handy notebooks on parchment were incomparably more useful than papyrus scrolls in a protective covering, and a distinctive 'book form' also set Christian literature clearly apart from pagan literature. What had proved itself in liturgical use, in scriptural discussion with Jewish opponents and in missionary work, was kept. It was also possibly by such external forms to show that one no longer belonged to this 'world which was passing away'.[489] It is not surprising that we have no written reports about this except in II Tim. 4.13. The earliest Christian texts say little or nothing about anything that could be taken for granted. That is true, for example, of reading the Old Testament in worship, which must simply be presupposed.[490] Once the large community in the imperial capital had become the focal point of the Christian communities after 70, the scriptorium there and the 'book cupboards' of the Roman house communities took on normative significance. Thus the codex form will have established itself firmly in parallel to the development which is visible in Martial from the book to the parchment codex (but independent of it), although there, in keeping with the Roman sense of order, the celebration of the liturgy will have been less enthusiastic than that in Paul's time in Corinth. Here initially the Christian scribes in Rome will have been less concerned for the dissemination of new Christian literature than for providing the house churches in Rome and the communities in Italy and in the West of the empire with 'prophetic', i.e. Old Testament, texts. Thus in my view the Gospel of Mark already came into being as a codex. It was necessary only, as in the case of schoolbooks, to fold a large number of parchment or papyrus sheets in the middle and to stitch them together.[491] As a rule the earliest Christian codices consisted only of one such signature, which could contain one Gospel.[492] Therefore initially the one-Gospel codex was the rule, and the four Gospels combined in one volume was an essentially later development, which in the time before Constantine must have been more the exception because of the great difference between the John and Matthew papyri and those of Luke and above all Mark.[493] The Christian scriptorium, the conservative scribal practices, the book cupboards of the house communities and liturgical needs must thus be regarded as being closely connected with the origin and dissemination of Christian literature and here in particular of the Gospels. Here the Roman community played a normative role because of its size and significance.

Christian writings gradually took their place alongside the most important writings of the LXX, like Mark and already before him individual letters of Paul which appeared in the 50s; of these, Corinthians, Romans and Philippians are already presupposed by Clement of Rome before AD 100. The same goes for Hebrews (see below, 128ff.). These Christian letters, too, were read out in worship; Paul already requires this in his earliest letter, I Thess. 5.27,[494] and this custom continues in the second century, not only with 'apostolic' writings but also with works like I Clement or the Shepherd of Hermas, episcopal letters and Acts of martyrs. However, Justin does not mention these, but only the 'reminiscences of the apostles', i.e. the four Gospels – and does so in first place. In other words, for him they are by far the most important;[495] only after this does he speak as an alternative reading of the 'writings of the prophets', by which he means the texts from the Old Testament which were important for the Christians. In other words, for him the reading of the Gospels must already have had some predominance, a development which – at least in Rome – may go back to the beginnings of the second century. Here we may infer from his own quotations of the Gospels that the Synoptics, i.e. above all Matthew and Luke, were more important than John (see above, 19f.).

But how far can we make inferences from Justin's description of the readings in worship in Rome (and elsewhere) to the situation at the time of the composition of the Gospel of Mark, two to three generations earlier?

Now the Roman community already had a well-filled 'book cupboard' at the time of I Clement, and I even believe that in the West this was a model for the other communities. Presumably it will have been built up again after the catastrophe of the Neronian persecution. As in later persecutions, at that time books in the possession of Christians will have been either confiscated or destroyed.[496] Five or six years after the persecution, the decimated community was probably in process of consolidating itself and building up a new collection (or new collections) of books. We can understand the intensive knowledge of scripture which Paul presupposes among the recipients of Romans only if he could assume that already around AD 57 interested Christians in Rome could study the most important books of the LXX, i.e. Isaiah, Psalms and the Torah, for themselves and that these scriptures were read in the presence of all members in worship. This was already necessary because of the controversy with the Jewish mother of the Christian communities, the synagogue. This means that these writings were already present in the mission churches in their entirety or in extracts and presumably at a very early stage in the simple and practical codex form. Probably the different house communities in the capital which are still to be presupposed in the letter to the Romans around AD 57,[497] and which in the circumstances also presented different types of teaching,[498] were brought more closely together as a unity after the catastrophe. In his letter to Corinth Clement represents the Roman community and its authority as a whole. The event of the Neronian persecution still leaves a direct stamp on the Gospel of Mark, with its urgent call to be ready for martyrdom and discipleship in suffering and its dramatic depiction of the eschatological distress to the point of saying, 'and you will be hated by all for my name's sake', which turns round the accusation of *odium humani generis* in Tacitus.[499]

Written for oral presentation in the community, it was certainly quickly included in the 'book cupboards' of the most important communities in the empire after the destruction of Jerusalem; after all, as the 'written' form of the 'Gospel of Jesus Christ' it represented something quite new, which the community urgently needed after the death of the great witnesses – James, Peter and Paul and probably most members of the first generation – [500] following the shattering experiences of the persecution in Rome, the beginning of the Jewish War and then the Civil War and the destruction of Jerusalem. Thus it probably came relatively quickly into the hands of Luke, who was particularly interested in the Jesus tradition, and then also into those of the unknown Christian scribe in southern Syria or the territory bordering Palestine to whom we owe the first Gospel. The 'elder' John in Ephesus and his school also took note of it. That – like the Apocalypse of John – it was written to be read aloud in worship is evident among other things from the peculiar remark in 13.14, ὁ ἀναγινώσκειν νοείτω, that the reader must pay attention and the hearer (or the reader) must remember what he has heard (or read).[501]

In my view, the solemn introduction Mark 1.1 already indicates public reading in worship; the Gospel of Jesus Christ does not primarily have individual private edification in view. Nor is the – new – title 'Gospel' enough, for already in the house communities in Rome and even more in the great city communities of Corinth, Ephesus, Antioch and Alexandria (though of course we have no early reports of them), around or shortly after 70 people had rather different – oral – expressions of the one 'saving message' and already even written collections of 'sayings of the Lord'. The term 'Gospel' was familiar to the communities through the Pauline mission, and probably also through Peter (see above, 61ff.), but only with reservations for narratives about Jesus and sayings of Jesus. For a long time a direct appeal to the word of the Kyrios still had greater weight (see above, III.5). Most of the inspired 'holy scriptures' of the prophets of the Old Testament already bore the names of their authors from Moses to Malachi and were sometimes also quoted with these names.[502] In the case of the letters of Paul in the archive, too, it was known from whom they came and to whom they were addressed; presumably people also knew about the 'Logia' of the Lord from the apostle Matthew, which according to John the elder, Papias' informant, were disseminated in versions of varying quality. Mark, too, could have known one such collection (or more) and used some of it, so that while he emphasizes Jesus' activity as teaching 'with authority',[503] he reports only select paradigmatic examples of this teaching, and is all the more concerned to put the acts and controversies of Jesus at the centre, above all the unique 'act' of his passion and resurrection, in which the whole work culminates and through which it first really becomes the 'saving message', the 'Gospel' in the full sense. Here Mark is comparable to John, despite all the great differences.

We can only conjecture what written sources Mark possessed. We only know that he was regarded as the vehicle of the Peter tradition and that this – from the beginning – gave his novel work a special authority. Perhaps he had notes written by himself or someone else, say, on chapter 4, the parable chapter, the miracle stories, the little apocalypse Mark 13, or the passion narrative. In this area all considerations remain hypothetical. However, on the basis of the arguments presented so far I think it extremely improbable that his work was put into the book cupboards of Rome (there may have been several 'community libraries' in the metropolis) and the other communities without a title and anonymously. Two statements are misleading in the workbook by H. Conzelmann and A. Lindemann, a text widely used in Germany, namely that 'Mark does not give the name of any author and is thus an anonymous work', and the application of this also to Matthew.[504] As a rule all Gospel manuscripts mention the names of the authors as *superscriptio* and *subscriptio* alongside the usual indication of genre and content, in the two cases mentioned, Mark and Matthew. In the first case there is no reason not to see Mark as the author; in the second case we have an assignation to a pseud-epigraphical author: the reference – as I have often pointed out – is to the disciple who is from the group of the Twelve and an apostle.

This information about authorship was quite sufficient for the community of the time. Everyone knew who the person was, because they knew these names. With the same reason the editors of the workbook could also say that I Clement[505] or Barnabas were also anonymous. In the case of I Clement there is no adequate reason for doubting the authorship; in the case of Barnabas we again have a writing which was pseudepi-graphical from the beginning (see above, 131ff.). The fact that the name of the author does not appear directly in Mark and Matthew[506] is connected with the genre 'Gospel of Jesus Christ': Jesus Christ is the real 'author' of this history as a message of salvation. But that does not exclude the mention of the author in the title. There were in fact already different forms of the oral and later of the written 'Gospel'. People had to know from the beginning what authority stood behind this special form of the 'message' of salvation. Paul already can speak of '*his* Gospel'.[507] Presumably the Roman 'community scribes' disseminated Mark's work relatively quickly in copies in the most important other churches; Theophilus will have had the same thing done with Luke's work.[508] In the case of Matthew it may have been the communities in southern Syria in which he was active; in the case of John his disciples after the death of the elder, in my view together with the letters.

After the letters of Paul we find the custom of sending letters, reports and copies to other communities in many forms, thus in the seven letters of the Apocalypse, the letters of John, the letters of Ignatius, in Polycarp, Dionysius of Corinth and the reports of martyrs. We probably have circular letters to various communities in James and I John, and as a pseudepigraphon in I Peter. There is a striking report in the Shepherd of Hermas, where the seer is given the task of making two copies of a letter from heaven which is revealed to him, i.e. of the new doctrine of penance, and giving one of them to Clement. Clement is 'then to send them to the cities outside, for that is his task'. Presumably Clement was also responsible for the scriptorium of the community in Rome. Grapte is to receive the other copy and 'admonish the widows and orphans. You yourself are to read it out in this city (together) with the presbyters who lead the church.'[509] If the new penitential doctrine which was revealed to Hermas was disseminated so energetically and purposefully in Rome itself and from Rome to other communities, will not something similar already have been done in the case of the Gospel of Mark, whose content was far more sensational? As people outside Rome wanted to know from whom this new, one might almost say revolutionary, text, came or what authority stood behind it, in accordance with the introduction ἀρχὴ τοῦ εὐαγγελίου Ἰησοῦ Χριστοῦ this will presumably have been sent under the title εὐαγγέλιον (Ἰησοῦ Χριστοῦ) κατὰ Μᾶρκον to the communities in question with an accompanying letter. This Mark was evidently no unknown figure, but a personality known and acknowledged not only in Rome, but in widespread parts of the church between Judaea and the capital. As a matter of course his work was also put into the community libraries in Rome for liturgical use, after the 'scriptures of the Old Covenant', of which there were already a larger number of copies.

2. Written and oral tradition in Clement of Rome

Clement of Rome is the first to indicate the existence of such a 'Jewish-Christian' collection of writings. However, like the copies of the letters of Paul which were available to him but not yet in a fixed collection,[510] and like the letter to the Hebrews,[511] Mark and the later Gospels were not yet understood as 'Holy Scripture', i.e. as γραφή in the strict sense, and quoted with corresponding introductory formulae like γέγραπται and γεγραμμένος. This term remains limited to Old Testament texts,[512] i.e. those which were assumed to belong to the past time of the revelation to Israel. On the other hand, the invitation to 'remember the Word of the Lord' also has a clear authoritative ring.[513] Clement's request to his readers to 'pick up' the letter of the 'blessed apostle Paul' written around forty-five years beforehand[514] is the first explicit and concrete reference to the use of an *earlier* Christian writing of another author which was kept in a community – presumably for liturgical reading.[515] Here Clement of course presupposes that in both Rome and in Corinth the letter is still extant and is also known from readings. He refers to it because now almost five decades later there are again divisions and unrest in the Corinthian community. Among other things, the intervention of Rome is a typical example of the intensive exchange among the communities.

However, Clement does not yet quote the text of a Gospel literally, because he feels bound up with the teaching of Jesus through the living oral tradition.[516] Therefore he calls on the recipients of the letter to 'remember' the 'words of the Lord Jesus' and follows this up with a free compilation of logia which are closely based on Matthew's Sermon on the Mount and Luke's Sermon on the Plain. Probably the Roman community also had a collection (or several collections) of sayings of the Lord with a catechetical orientation in its book cupboard, which it could later dispense with because of the major Gospels.[517] I would even conjecture that Clement, around or shortly after AD 100, knew all three Synoptic Gospels but deliberately quoted them freely because he did not want yet to tie 'the word of the Lord Jesus to a fixed wording' but to allow it to have an indirect effect. The fact that it was there in different versions gave him the freedom to shape his own. The written text which he knew was only an aid to memory. Thus he says at a second point: 'Remember the words of Jesus our Lord! For he said:[518] Woe to that man (who rebels against the body of Christ V.7): it would be better for him not to have been born . . .'[519] With this saying, which in Mark, Matthew and in part in Luke is connected with the unmasking of the traitor Judas at the last supper, Clement associates a free version of the saying about causing offence: ' . . . than to cause offence to one of my elect. It would be better for him to have a millstone hung around his neck and be cast into the sea than to lead astray one of my elect.'[520] The person who splits the body of Christ by 'revolt' and dispute can be compared with the traitor Judas, and Jesus' threat about the one who causes offence to his elect and leads them astray in the faith applies to him. Here Clement has reshaped two sayings of Jesus from different contexts in relation to the situation in Corinth. There could be a knowledge of all three Synoptics at precisely this point.

Clement also presupposes Synoptic texts at some other points, like 24.5,[521] where he presupposes the parable of the sower. Further possible allusions are 23.4, which with the 'image of the gradual process of ripening' recalls Mark 4.28;[522] I Clement 27.5 has points of contact with Matt. 5.18 (Luke 16.17), but in 15.2 the quotation from Isa.28.13 clearly assimilates Mark 7.6 against the LXX.[523] The word could possibly come from a collection of testimonia which in turn is influenced by Mark. There is perhaps a similar instance in 4.10 in the quotations from Ex.2.14, where it is assumed that a κρίτην which has found its way in from Luke 12.14 suppressed the ἄρχοντα of the LXX.[524] All in all, the influence of Synoptic tradition in Clement does not seem to be all that great. The wide-ranging synagogue closing prayer[525] and still Justin's liturgy of the word around fifty years later show that around AD 100, despite Paul, the Roman community was still largely in the shadow of Judaism (see above, 117f.). Already for that reason the use of the LXX in Clement is still by far the most predominant. But the relatively few quotations and allusions to sayings of Jesus suggest the probability that the Gospel texts are not unknown to him, even if he does not refer to them, but reminds the Corinthians of the words of the Lord.

Already in his time, in the last years of the first century and in part at the beginning of the second, the three Synoptic Gospels were thus present in the book cupboards of the community in Rome, but were not yet thought of as being on the same footing as the 'prophetic writings', as 'scripture'. Presumably Mark was the first 'written' Gospel, which was also used in worship in Rome; around ten to fifteen years later Luke,[526] and a further ten to fifteen years later the first 'apostolic' Gospel 'according to Matthew', followed. The Roman community will have been among the first communities to be sent this Gospel from places in Syria-Palestine with its high theological claim. That Matthew also soon found recognition in Rome, as throughout the church, can hardly be surprising. It brought what people needed. With Luke and even more with Matthew, the teaching of Jesus was now also available in extended written form; the earlier collections of logia were gradually suppressed, and therefore apart from Mark, none of the sources of Luke remain; moreover after the appearance of a Gospel in the name of the apostle Matthew, interest was lost in earlier collections of sayings of Jesus in his name. Mark alone was preserved only as a result of the towering authority of Peter which went with it and its composition in Rome. It is one of the miracles of the Gospel tradition that it, too, was not lost. Presumably in the second century it was soon present only in the book cupboards of larger communities. Here the disproportionate representation in the tradition of the early Gospel papyri speaks for itself.[527]

3. The development before Justin: Barnabas and II Clement

Justin's report, about fifty years after Clement, which first mentions the 'reminiscences of the apostles' as Jesus writings read in worship, then indicates the end of this lengthy development, which already came to a conclusion some time before him. In Justin the Gospels have full, unlimited authority as apostolic testimony. The act of violence on the part of his opponent Marcion, who somewhat earlier, around 140, attempted to get the one true 'apostolic Gospel' from the work of Luke by rigorous literary criticism, rejecting all the other Gospel writings, is also an indication of this development. That talk of the 'word of the Lord Jesus' was more popular than quoting the Gospel writings well into the second, indeed into the third century, is not only an expression of a bond to the divine authority of the Exalted Christ (see above, 61), but also a reference to the 'conservative' character of primitive Christian worship from the end of the first century to the second half of the second: people liked to preserve old established custom, in a way quite comparable to the usage of the synagogue. Liturgical usage tends to keep its weight and to last for a long time. That was also why it was so late, and with some reluctance, that people came to talk of the 'Gospels' in the plural. The designation of the Gospels as 'scripture' and the use of quotation formulae like 'it is written' (γέγραπται) in citing the Gospel texts can be demonstrated only at a relatively late date and hesitantly. First of all these formulae were in a peculiar state of suspension. Initially 'Gospel' was not yet a fixed literary term like 'law and prophets'; to begin with, the meaning of (oral) 'message of salvation' still predominated. As scripture, too, 'the Gospel' or 'the Gospels' was to recall the word of the Lord and testify as a narration to the saving work of his death and his resurrection. Quotation of it, as I Clement already shows, was not yet strictly tied to the wording of scripture, so that in the case of the words of the Lord there is often argument as to whether what we have is 'oral tradition', a non-canonical source or – and initially this is the most probable – a free quotation from or an allusion to the Gospels. But gradual 'progress' is in fact visible.

We find the formula 'as it is written' for a Gospel quotation for the first time in Barnabas 4.14: 'Many are called, but few are chosen.'[528] That Barnabas knows the Gospel tradition is quite evident from Barn.5.8–10, where following the Gospels he first mentions Jesus' preaching and miracles towards Israel, and then the election of the (twelve) apostles for the purpose of the future preaching of the Gospel.[529] The subsequent, almost offensive, formulation that the apostles chosen by Jesus himself 'were lawless beyond any sin so that he could show that he had not come to call the righteous, but sinners',[530] is based on a heightened interpretation of the failure of the disciples to the point of Peter's denial and their doubt in the face of the Risen Christ in the Gospels. The knowledge of John's baptism (Barn.11.1f.) and above all the passion narrative of all the Gospels is presupposed in Barnabas and illuminated and shaped in the light of Old Testament texts. Between AD 70 and 180 there was no opposition between the Gospel preached by word of mouth and the Gospel set down in writing. A text from the Acts of Peter shows with what naivety towards the end of the second century or in the third century the Gospel writings and living apostolic preaching are still seen as a unity: as Peter enters the triclinium in the house of Marcellus in Rome, he sees that the Gospel is being read aloud. He rolls it up and begins to explain 'how the Holy Scripture of our Lord should be preached', which 'we (the apostles) have written down according to his grace as far as we understand it'. Then he explains the story of the transfiguration which 'had just been read out to him'.[531] The scriptural form appears as an aid to recalling the Gospel of the forgiveness of sins preached by the apostles – and that is already true for I Clement and even more for Barnabas.[532]

Here it is to be noted that in the case of Barnabas as an alleged early 'apostolic' writing sketched out from the beginning as a pseudepigraphon there was no room for clear quotations from the 'later' Gospel writings.[533] Rather, the unknown author is exclusively interested in a rigorous and largely anti-Jewish exegesis of the 'prophetic texts', primarily from Genesis, Psalms and Isaiah, and the salvation communicated by it.[534]

That around AD 130 the step from a Gospel writing to 'Holy Scripture' was no longer a large one is shown by II Clement, which is roughly contemporary. There the same saying of Jesus appears as in Barn.5.9, but now explicitly introduced as a word of scripture. 'But another word of scripture says, "I have not come to call righteous, but sinners."' This is the explanation of why Jesus 'must save the lost'.[535] In 2.1, Isa. 54.1 is cited and interpreted as the first quotation from this presumably Roman sermon. The saying of Jesus takes this up. The quotations from Isaiah predominate, immediately followed by Mark or Luke; here Christ speaks 'about how one must think about God and about the judge of the living and the dead' (II Clem. 1.1), through the Old Testament prophets *and* through the Gospel. Accordingly – as I have already indicated – the formula 'for the Lord says in the Gospel' also appears once (II Clem. 8.5, see above, n.264). There are several reasons why II Clement sometimes quotes literally, but also uses Matthew and Luke in a harmonizing way and introduces individual 'apocryphal' quotations.[536] Thus although over two generations 'the Gospel' now exists in various written forms, the oral tradition used in catechesis still lives on; indeed, as the example of Papias, Basilides and Valentinus shows, this is once again artificially enlivened by a deliberate search for tradents (see above, 65ff.). The report in the fragment of the earliest Christian apologist Quadratus, in the time of Hadrian, that some of those healed or raised from the dead by Jesus had lived down to his time, belongs in this context (see above, 273, n.416).[537] That too presupposes a knowledge of the collection of several Gospels.

A 'Peter renaissance ' also begins, which is indicated by new Petrine writings. These include II Peter, in which Peter immediately before his martyrdom[538] not only describes himself in the first person plural as a missionary narrator of the activity of Jesus,[539] but also as an eye-witness quotes the voice of God at the transfiguration in a form which varies slightly from the

Matthaean version[540] and at the end warns against the false interpretations of 'our beloved brother Paul' who is sometimes difficult to understand.[541] As long as he still 'lives in this body', he wants to keep the readers 'awake through remembrance',[542] so that even after his martyrdom they remember his message.[543] These writings also include the *Kerygma Petri* and other works written in the first person like the Gospel of Peter, the Apocalypse of Peter and about a generation later the first Acts of Peter, but also the original document of the Pseudo-Clementines, in which Peter is the central figure. These are last attempts at a *direct* appeal to the prince of the apostles: people were not content just with disciples of apostles or second-rank figures from the group of Twelve, and attempted in an artificial way, by pseudepigrapha, to hold on to the oral tradition which had been lost. The knowledge of the four Gospels with the decisive role of Peter is a natural precondition of this.

However, appeal to the 'word of the Lord' always made a better impression, referring directly to a pre-existent, incarnate and exalted Kyrios rather than to a mere writing, especially as this one Kyrios had already spoken as a divine authority in the prophetic writings of the Old Covenant and inspired the prophets, and only last of all had appeared as incarnate Son of God and teacher. It was in the nature of things for his words still to be quoted relatively freely from memory, whether they now came from 'Gospel writings', from some 'Logia collections' made for catechetical purposes and still there in church book cupboards, or from 'oral tradition' learnt by heart. 'Scholarly' interest was still slight. From 70 to around 130 the written Gospels tended to be there for the community rather as constant 'aids to memory' and not yet as 'Holy Scripture' in the strict sense, even if they were read aloud in worship. That is also evident, among other things, from the secondary conclusion to Mark in 16.9–20, around 120, in which all four Gospels are used, but there are also echoes of oral tradition (see above, 102). That the title εὐαγγέλιον was nevertheless also known for these writings is shown – as I have already said (see above, 48ff.) – by Ignatius, the Didache and the εὐγγελικαὶ γραφαί of the earliest Apologist, Aristides (see above, nn.241, 247), Marcion and at this particular point II Clement as 'the earliest sermon to a Christian community which has been preserved in its entirety'.[544] It was possibly preceded by the reading of an Isaiah text, but the relationship between the text read out and the preaching is not clear.[545] II Timothy 4.13 already points to the connection between scriptural reading and paraenetic-didactic preaching.[546]

With Barnabas, II Clement and Marcion we are no longer all that far from Justin's *Apology* and his *Dialogue*, in which he presupposes the knowledge of all four Gospels and their authors and at the same time – completely as a matter of course, in general terms and over a broad period – the reading of the Gospels along with a sermon in the worship of the Roman community and other communities. Here – and this is the last step – the Gospels are mentioned as 'Reminiscences of the Apostles' in the plural and before the 'prophetic writings', i.e. the Old Testament. This new predominance of the Gospels may be connected, among other things, with the controversies over the devaluation of the writings of the Old Testament and their image of God in gnosticizing circles. That is said to be the reason why Marcion was expelled from the Roman community in AD 144. His teacher Cerdo had already put forward similar views in Rome in the time of Hadrian.[547] As it made little sense to use the Old Testament as a basis for argument in the dispute with these teachers, the Gospels along with the letters of Paul took on even greater significance.

The decisive years for the composition, the dissemination and the establishment of the four Gospels lie between 70 and around 140, a period in which we have little information about the church and from which not many writings have been preserved either. Therefore I have been able to make only a hypo-thetical attempt in conclusion at sketching out the development of the collection of the four Gospels. However, I think that this cross-check is historically plausible and explains the disputed phenomenon of the collection of the Gospels better than earlier hypotheses.

4. *The significance of the Roman book cupboard*

As I have already said on several occasions, the question is concentrated on the content of the liturgical 'book cupboard' of a few larger and leading communities (and the work of the *scriptoria* and copyists standing behind them), which shaped the opinion of the smaller communities around them, and above all here the church of Rome, which not only shaped the whole of the West but also in many way had an influence on the East, especially in the time before Alexandria took over a leading role.[548]

Presumably – as I have said – the Gospel of Mark with a title was disseminated from the Roman community among the most important churches of the eastern Mediterranean and of course was also put in the 'book cupboard' of the Roman community (or in the cupboards of the various house communities) after the writings of the Old Testament (and not as yet on the same level as them) for liturgical usage. Some years later the Gospel of Luke followed, and after a shorter space of time the Acts of the Apostles. Probably people in Rome in particular were proud of both works, as they came from the disciples of the two first and greatest Roman martyrs and because the first work had been written in Rome, whereas the two-volume work ended in Rome. The first 'apostolic' Gospel according to Matthew quickly assumed first place on the basis of its content and the apostolic authorship attributed to it, and as the allegedly oldest, originally 'Hebrew', Gospel forced the works of disciples of the apostles, which seemed less authoritative, into second and third place. As the Gospel stamped most strongly by the Old Testament, with its beginning which recalled Gen. 2.4 and 5.1[549] and the subsequent royal genealogy beginning with Abraham, it followed on from the Old Testament writings which were already in the 'book cupboard' almost seamlessly. Because it put the logia tradition in a literary order and offered a theological interpretation (as the Gospel of Luke, on which it is partially dependent [see below, 169ff.] had already done, but in an even more impressive way), in the long run it suppressed earlier collections of logia,[550] some of which had already been associated with the name of Matthew. Since it loved self-discipline and a strict ethic, it may already have pleased a Roman presbyter like Clement, although he does not yet quote it literally: around AD 100 it was still too young for that.[551] It increasingly became the normative source of the 'words of the Lord' which had been neglected in Mark, even if these words were still offered for a long time in a relatively free and at the same time harmonizing way in accordance with particular paraenetic aims. All in all, as is very well shown by I Clement, attitudes towards the tradition in Rome were more conservative, yet simply because of the size of the city it was tolerant of 'experiments'. Only Marcion's attack on the well-tried Jewish-Christian tradition seemed intolerable. By contrast, Valentinus could hope to become presbyter (or even bishop?) in Rome. In the time of Irenaeus his disciple Florinus was still a respected presbyter against whom Irenaeus had to protest energetically.[552]

Precisely because between 70 and 200 the community in Rome was still relatively 'pluralistic', it could exercise a relatively far-reaching influence on the other churches of the empire and was attractive to travelling Christian teachers with quite different tendencies, who founded schools there.

This split attitude – conservative in external forms, but tolerant, indeed even pluralistic – at first made it difficult for the Fourth Gospel really to establish itself completely in Rome. It certainly came to Rome soon after its composition, presumably together with the Johannine epistles, and then probably found its place in the Roman 'book cupboard' (or cupboards), but for a long time it was not regarded as 'on the same level' as the other Gospels. That still has an effect even in Justin, who knows it as an apostolic Gospel, but in the quotations from the 'reminiscences of the apostles' prefers Matthaean and Lukan texts, often in a harmonizing way. His disciple Tatian, however, quotes the prologue and bases the Diatessaron on the Johannine framework, but he was accused of having Valentinian-Encratite tendencies (see above, 24ff.). Valentinus probably treasured it, and that is even more true of his disciples:

Ptolemy quoted it as a writing of the apostle John in his *Letter to Flora* and he or his disciples produced an exposition of its prologue; Heracleon wrote a learned commentary on it, probably before Irenaeus. But their opponent Irenaeus is also particularly fond of it and at the same time shows that it could be used as a sharp weapon against the flood of Gnostic speculations. On the other hand, in his time the Roman presbyter Gaius was its embittered opponent and denounced it together with the Apocalypse as an impudent forgery by Cerinthus, the opponent of John.[553] Thus still in the second half of the second century in particular the 'great church' of Rome must also have been theologically quite an interesting city: on this point it was hardly inferior to Alexandria, which flourished a little later. It had presbyters like the gnosticizing Florinus in office[554] and the ultra-conservative Gaius, not to mention the numerous 'heretical' schools and teachers. We could therefore regard the 'book cupboards' there from very different perspectives.

Given all this, it seems to me very probable that Irenaeus has his 'historical' order of the Gospels and also the brief accounts of their origin from there. The collection of the four Gospels and their ordering according to the historical sequence of composition goes back to the 'Roman book cupboard'. It was probably also Rome's most valuable gift to the church coming into being in the second century. At any event Rome – before the rise of Alexandria with its catechetical school and above all the formation of the library of Origen and Pamphilus in Caesarea in Palestine – was the most important theological and literary centre. Asia Minor – stamped by John the elder and his school, by the Apocalypse of John which came from the school, Papias, Polycarp, Apollinaris of Hierapolis, Melito, Miltiades and Irenaeus who came from Asia Minor – was theologically more one-sided and therefore more fruitful than the relatively broad-minded Rome. Simply because of its link to the strong Johannine tradition and the letters of Paul, Asia Minor certainly did not produce the collection of four Gospels and then introduce it into the church. Indeed at a later stage Asia Minor could not assert itself in the dispute over Easter either; however, given the close contact between Asia Minor and Rome in the course of the first half of the second century it could have helped to further the development towards the collection of the four Gospels, as the churches of Asia Minor must have been particularly interested in the recognition of the Johannine corpus in the church. But this recognition was possible only in connection with the three other Gospels, the authority of which was older. There was no way round Rome in this connection.

So in my view the order Matthew, Mark, Luke, John, Acts, apostolic letters (above all those of Paul) and the Apocalypse in Irenaeus and then in the book cupboards of important communities emanated from Rome during this period and gradually established itself as the predominant order, perhaps with the support of the communities in Western Asia Minor. Certain variants in the order of the Acts of the Apostles and the Catholic epistles or the so-called 'Western' order were all too understandable in this slow, gradual process. According to all we know, by contrast Alexandria and the Egyptian communities dependent on it had no normative influence on the composition of the collection of the Gospels in the first half of the second century. The church of Egypt first had to recover from the catastrophic consequences of the Jewish revolt in 115–117, which probably also destroyed many of the communities with a Jewish-Christian stamp. The Gnostic currents did the rest; nevertheless basically already Clement of Alexandria, who treasures Irenaeus and quotes him, observes that clear strict order of 'apostolic' writings which the Bishop of Lyons defends on the basis of earlier tradition from Rome and Asia Minor and which Tertullian in Carthage then already took quite for granted. However, because of the cultural situation in Alexandria Clement deals more 'generously' with 'apocryphal texts'. The order here is one which cannot be the result of an act of force by an individual teacher, a church group or community, say, in the form of a deliberate recension; rather, it grew gradually in connection with practical use in worship. Of course the authority of leading communities, above all Rome, and perhaps also Ephesus, stood behind it. The uncertainty of

Bishop Serapion of Antioch about the Gospel of Peter and the apparent generosity of the scholar Clement of Alexandria show that people were still quite flexible on this point. Here the West and Asia Minor were ahead of the East. So presumably we owe the origin of the collection of four Gospels primarily to the 'Roman book cupboard'. Irenaeus in Gaul already presupposes this 'perfect result' and defends it powerfully against last doubts. To emphasize the point once again: in its selection and ordering the church of the second century showed historical and theological understanding. I would like to repeat emphatically here the remark made above (33): the church really could not have made a better choice.

V

The Gospel as Kerygma *and* Narrative

Now, after these long deliberations about the second question (see above, 6f.), we can finally answer the first question raised right at the beginning, how the saving message of Jesus Christ, preached by word of mouth, which the earliest Christian literary witness that we know, Paul, calls 'the' or 'my Gospel', but also 'Gospel of God' or 'of Christ',[555] could become a 'biographical' writing which narrates Jesus' saving activity in words and actions and at the end, as its goal, his passion.

1. *The history of Jesus and the eye-witnesses*

Luke, the first Christian 'historian', is the only evangelist to speak explicitly in his prologue about the tradents of the Gospel tradition. The 'many' (πολλοί) before him, among whom we are to include above all Mark, 'compiled a narrative of the things which have been accomplished among us, just as they were delivered to us by those who from the beginning were eye-witnesses and ministers of the word'. In other words, he knows that Mark, the material that most scholars today ascribe to the problematical Logia source(s) and the rich special traditions which he collected, largely in written form,[556] rests on the oral tradition of eye-witnesses who had also been the first Christian missionaries. As the emphatic 'just as they were delivered *to us*' shows,[557] between Jesus and the earliest 'literary sources' about him (including Luke, the author himself) stand only those who had been direct eye-witnesses of the activity of Jesus from the beginning, i.e. the disciples whom, according to Luke's understanding, the Risen Christ called as 'apostles' and who as such became 'ministers of the word'.[558] Luke was an author at the end of the second generation, not of the third or even fourth, as the old Tübingen school supposed. It is very probable that in using the special term 'eye-witness' he is thinking specifically of Peter (cf. n. 557), the informant behind the Gospel of Mark, and perhaps also of Matthew as the authority behind the enigmatic 'Logia source'. He will also have known by name other literary and oral mediators of the tradition, possibly including women. The 'many' who 'composed a narrative' need not have been authors of whole collections like Gospels; they can have also brought Luke partial collections, like the original of his stories about the birth and childhood of Jesus, the special source of his account of the passion, the decisive parts of his special material and even passages which scholars are fond of assigning to Q, like the Sermon on the Plain or parts of the tradition about John the Baptist which are not dependent on Mark. As he used a firm hand in shaping his narrative material stylistically, above all in the transitions, in practice it is often impossible to separate 'tradition' and 'redaction' with some degree of certainty.[559] We should certainly not overestimate all too much our literary-critical possibilities in the reconstruction of 'sources'. However, this applies even more to the Acts of the Apostles than to the Jesus tradition proper of the Gospel, which Luke is more concerned to hand down unchanged. According to Jeremias, what is striking is 'Luke's restraint in making redactional interventions into the sayings of Jesus'. Finally I ask myself whether Luke did not already summarize the non-Markan material as a unity before he incorporated the predominantly narrative Markan material into which he made rather more marked interventions than did Matthew later.[560] The work on the Gospels and Acts may possibly have been extended over a number of years. In other words, in the sphere of dividing out Luke's sources, which are of the utmost significance for the Jesus tradition, apart from Mark we can no longer gain any real clarity, but only express conjectures with more or less of a basis.

However, Luke was not the only one in the first century to

speak of eye-witnesses.[561] The letter to the Hebrews, which is roughly contemporaneous with Luke-Acts, speaks of the message that brings salvation, which 'began with the preaching of the Lord (i.e. Jesus himself) and was then attested to us *by those who heard him*, while God also bore witness by signs and wonders . . .'[562] Here also the author belongs to the second generation. Even two generations later, Papias, Basilides and Valentinus were looking for earlier tradents who were to pass on to them traditions of the oral history of Jesus and the apostles.[563] That Luke partly detached himself from parts of the theology of his mentor Paul[564] may be connected – quite apart from his tendency to harmonize[565] – with the impact made on him by the Jerusalem Jesus tradition (and here probably not least that of Peter) in connection with the apostle's last journey to Jerusalem.[566] Basically, we owe his Gospel to the stimuli which he received from concrete contacts with Jesus tradition, not least in Jewish Palestine itself. At various points Mark, too, indicates 'eye-witnesses' which were still known to him or to the Roman community, above all before and in the passion narrative.[567] This personal link of the Jesus tradition with particular tradents, or more precisely their memory and missionary preaching, on which more or less emphasis is put, is historically undeniable. From the beginning, the recollection of the 'words (and actions) of the Lord' played a role. It refutes the purely form-critical approach to the Jesus tradition which for around two generations has been dominant in Germany in an almost scholastic way and has long since become sterile. Only now is a U-turn beginning, not least on the basis of books about Jesus from authors who have in part fundamentally changed their opinion on this point.[568]

According to the old form-critical approach, the tradition 'circulated' quite anonymously, atomized, i.e. carved up, into the tiniest of units, in the communities, which are viewed as pure collectives. Here it has become too easy to forget that from the beginning not only the personal authority of Jesus but also that of the teacher and the bearer of the tradition was fundamental.[569] In these collectives the Synoptic tradition was largely invented, say by spinning sayings of Jesus, anecdotes and narrative details out of Old Testament texts or by taking over alien Jewish or pagan material. The use of this method, for example by Rudolf Bultmann himself, shows that judgments about authenticity are all too often not based on real form-critical observations but are largely negative historical assessments which correspond to a generally anti-historical tendency: the more radical the better. That has little to do with a pertinent historical method. Cautious weighing up of the evidence, the attempt at a gradual approach with the help of pertinent analogies and plausible arguments, but not 'radical criticism', would be the only right way here. In his two reviews of Bultmann's *History of the Synoptic Tradition,* Dibelius already criticized this one-sidedness, although he himself was an energetic advocate of the form-critical approach (though at the same time he had a greater historical understanding).[570]Above all he emphasizes how 'conservative' is the treatment of tradition in the Synoptic Gospels and how little the typical theologoumena of the Hellenistic community like 'belief in the Kyrios and sacramental theology' become visible in them. It is here perhaps that the deepest difference from the Gospel of John lies. It can be said of the latter that 'christology' has largely (though not wholly) absorbed 'history', so that here too in particular unresolved questions remain, above all the question, which probably cannot be solved with the means of positivistic historiography, of the 'self-understanding' of Jesus.[571] At best we see his 'assertion of being sent' i.e. the effect that he had on others. The 'inner life of Jesus' remains closed to us. In the case of Bultmann, however, a gulf opens up between his Jesus book, which though one-sided, is nevertheless an attractive literary approach, and his hyper-critical and destructive *History of the Synoptic Tradition.*

The conservative character of the Synoptic tradition is connected with the fact that the authoritative bearers of the tradition down to (John) Mark himself were guarantors of the tradition who had close ties with the mother country of Jewish Palestine. However, this in no way means a 'slavish' preservation and use of the tradition. All three authors, Mark, Luke and above all Matthew – the last-mentioned most of all – were far too prominent theological thinkers and authors, who for all their faithfulness to the tradition shaped the material in terms of the goal of preaching which was their concern. Therefore we have no uninterrupted, direct access to the Jesus tradition, the *ipsissima verba* or historical events. Given the state of the sources it is no longer possible to reconstruct a 'life of Jesus'. We can always only approximate to this, as far as is possible. The disciples of Jesus and first eye-witnesses did not have our historical interest. That also applies to Peter, the most important among them. Nevertheless, their testimony gives us very clear contours of the activity of Jesus and his passion. Such attempts at an approximation which take the sources seriously are therefore meaningful and theologically necessary, so that christology, i.e. the heart of Christian theology, does not succumb to a modern docetism and volatilize the man Jesus along with his unique history, the 'Logos *made flesh*', so that it becomes a mere Christ idea.[572]

2. *The Gospel as 'kerygma', I Cor. 15.1–11 and 'Jesus narrative' in Paul*

But what is the cause of the apparently fundamental difference between the understanding of the Gospel as a didactic message about *christology and soteriology* in an anthropological context that has been thought about thoroughly, which is so characteristic of Paul in his letters, and the Gospel as a narrative of Jesus' activity in a quite fixed biographical, chronological and geographical framework between Galilee and Jerusalem and from the appearance of John the Baptist up to his passion and resurrection?

Paul certainly confesses to the Galatians that he received his Gospel 'through a revelation of Jesus Christ' and not 'from a human being', i.e. in connection with his Damascus experience, which radically overturned the life of the Pharisaic scribe and persecutor of Christians. But even in Damascus he makes contact with the Christians there and is baptized, before – probably already as a missionary – he sets out for a lengthy stay in Nabataean Arabia.[573] He also returns to Damascus around two years later and spends some time in the community there. Already in the earliest period, between three and six years after the Passover at which Jesus died, he must also have become familiar with the basic facts of the Jesus tradition. Otherwise he could not have preached the crucified Jew Jesus as Messiah, Son of God and saving Lord.[574]

Therefore it is not surprising that we have on the other hand quite a different text from him, in which he describes the content of the Gospel in brief, stereotyped sentences that can only be based on traditions which he himself has received from others and which go back to the primitive community in Jerusalem. This 'Gospel' was one of the first things that he communicated to the Corinthians on founding their community about 49/50, and at the end he even cites eye-witnesses, from Cephas/Peter through 'the Twelve' to himself. After all, he expressly emphasizes that this Gospel has been preached by the eye-witnesses mentioned and that the Corinthians also accepted it in faith.[575] Now in the utmost brevity, and in the form of a catechism or confession, this 'Gospel' contains 'facts' which had to be narrated if they were to be comprehensible to the hearers; at the same time their fundamental significance for the faith was always interpreted. Thus – as in the Gospel narrative – they combine the event reported with its 'theological' interpretation in an inseparable unity. In this summary of the Gospel the apostle wants to remind the forgetful Corinthians of the foundation of their faith. This runs:

> *That Christ died* for our sins in accordance with the scriptures, *that he was buried, that he was raised on the third day* in accordance with the scriptures, and *that he appeared to Cephas, then to the twelve* . . .[576]

What is narrated is a unique, once-for-all, event in time and space, the fact of the death of Christ. Elsewhere Paul stresses on numerous occasions that Christ was crucified; indeed with the utmost brevity he can even present 'Christ crucified' to the Corinthians as the embodiment of his Gospel.[577] Apart from the frequent mentions in Paul, with few exceptions we find this emphasis on the crucifixion of Jesus as a historical fact only in the passion narratives of the Gospels (and in Acts). Thus for example the angel at the tomb speaks to the women of 'Jesus . . . the crucified'.[578] Alongside this, in Paul there are also a number of formulae which emphasize the dying of Christ 'for us/you' and the resurrection of Jesus by God. These catechetical formulae, which are the earliest 'creed', do not form the original starting point of the earliest Christian 'message of salvation',[579] but are merely a confessional abbreviation of the real saving event – which is certainly necessary –, the 'fact' of Jesus' death and resurrection. Before it could be believed in and confessed in the Pauline mission communities, this saving event had to be narrated and interpreted so that it could be understood by the communities which had been newly founded by the apostle. Basically, the same thing is already true for the pre-Pauline mission preaching in Palestine by the eye-witnesses. Without a narrative of these concrete, datable events, the meaning of the numerous christological formulae quoted by Paul in the letters would have been quite inaccessible to the first hearers. Without the Gospel reports, we today would also have no understanding whatsoever of Paul's talk of the 'crucified Christ'.[580] The same is true of his listing of the witnesses to the resurrection. This cannot advance a stringent 'proof' of the resurrection of Jesus as God's miracle for ancient or modern sceptics, nor does it seek to do so; rather, it 'bears witness' to the experience of an encounter with the Risen Lord.

Rudolf Bultmann, who wants to beat Paul here with the cudgel of content-criticism (*Sachkritik*), misses the point. Paul is well aware that the resurrection appearances of the disciples of Jesus, the brother of the Lord and 'all the apostles', like his own experience before Damascus to an even greater degree, are utterly ambivalent in the eyes of unbelievers.[581] However, that was the case at the beginning even with the disciples themselves,[582] just as the empty tomb could also be interpreted in different ways, for example as a theft of the body by the disciples in order to deceive. The appearances of Jesus were later interpreted by enemies as necromancy and as a magical illusion, or as the manifestation of an executed criminal who has become a ghost whose soul could find no rest because of his violent death.[583] So Celsus later objected: 'Who has seen this? A crazy woman, you say, and perhaps another victim of the same bewitching.'[584] A similar objection could already have been made to Paul. In particular, the 'objective' events behind these catechetical confessional formulae in I Cor. 15.3f. had to be narrated with reference to the testimony of the disciples if the formulae were to be understood as a 'saving message' by Paul's first hearers in Corinth. They also had to be explained – for example in relation to 'the scriptures' and the death of Christ 'for our sins'. These two things together, narrative and scriptural argumentation, were already fundamental to the proclamation of the Pauline Gospel. That Paul really narrated the story of the passion in Corinth follows from his reference to the institution of the Lord's supper in I Cor. 11.23–26: 'For I received from the Lord what I also delivered to you, that the Lord Jesus, on the night when he was betrayed (or delivered up), took bread, and when he had given thanks, he broke it, and said, "This is my body for you." In the same way also the cup, after supper, saying: "This cup is the new covenant in my blood. Do this, as often as you drink it, in remembrance of me."'

Here too, historical recollection of a concrete event, i.e. a 'fact', during the meal on the last night of Jesus' life, in Jerusalem, before his crucifixion on the following day, is inseparably fused with the interpretation of the faith on a scriptural background. There is no point in wanting to separate the two, event and faith, strictly in detail in order to make an adequate reconstruction of what really happened at the last supper by a comparison with Mark's account based on Peter tradition, which is similar but diverges in details. Here, for the historian at best the approximation which has already been mentioned is possible.[585] Paul several times cites other 'words of the Lord',[586] and even where he does not do this literally, allusions to the Jesus tradition can often be seen in his writings, especially in the paraenesis.[587] He makes direct quotations in his letters relatively rarely because in the letters he is always addressing concrete, usually controversial, problems, in which the Jesus tradition did not play a central role – leaving aside the abuse of the Lord's supper in Corinth, the problem of divorce, the material support for the apostle by the community or the question of the parousia and the resurrection from the dead. However, the narration of Jesus' activity and death, his crucifixion and resurrection, was fundamental in the foundation of a community,[588] which as a rule took place over a lengthy period of time.

The same is true of the Petrine mission preaching, which came to be recorded late in Mark's account of the passion, in I Peter and in a form shaped by Luke – in Peter's mission speeches in Acts. The problem is that we do not know the content of Paul's mission preaching when he founded new communities – which was certainly rich. Among other things it included turning away from the idols to the true God and the rejection of pagan vices, things to which he alludes only occasionally. The seven authentic letters are predominantly concerned with concrete conflicts in the communities, conflicts with both a theological-soteriological and a pastoral-ethical character; the two cannot be sharply separated. Only in the letter to the Romans does he develop particular fundamental, yet controversial aspects of his Gospel (one could also say his theology) in systematic form. Jesus' teaching and activity, the fact of his atoning death and his resurrection,[589] his exaltation to the right hand of God and his parousia, were not put in question in the communities.

This is also the case with his dignity as Messiah of Israel. Conzelmann's emphasis in connection with Schoeps 'that Paul never uses a scriptural argument to show that Jesus is Messiah (contrast Luke)',[590] is quite simply connected with the fact that this question belonged to the phase of the founding of the community, where it was decided in the affirmative and was not in question again in the letters. It was no longer doubted but universally recognized. Indeed, in Paul 'Christ' had already long since become a proper name. In the founding of the community, where Paul initially was still discussing with the synagogues,[591] the problem of the crucified Messiah certainly stood at the centre, and Paul will have discussed this basic question with Jewish opponents and sympathizers, also in the form of a scriptural argument. He, the former scribe, knew that Χριστὸς Ἰησοῦς was originally a confessional formula, like κύριος Ἰησοῦς, and initially had the meaning 'the anointed is Jesus!'[592] The same also goes for the significance of the narrative about Jesus and the words of Jesus at the founding of new communities by the missionary Paul. Some of this is also still visible in the letters. The young communities knew from Paul himself that Jesus was a Jew who lived 'under the Law'; that he was born of a Jewish woman, i.e. Mary;[593] that as Messiah he was descended from David;[594] that he had brothers who were married, of whom James, the most important, was well known.[595] Further, they were informed about Jesus' 'messianic service' towards his people.[596] His communities knew the Aramaic name Cephas and that this meant Petros, rock;[597] probably also that it was given to him by Jesus. And they knew who the 'Twelve', James or 'all the apostles' were. They received further information from him about his Jewish past as a Pharisee and persecutor, the event at Damascus, his visits to Jerusalem, the Apostolic Council, and so on. If Paul could report so much about the earliest community, its beginnings and his personal biography when it seemed necessary, would he have been persistently silent about Jesus himself? What he reports in his letters about Jesus and the past twenty or thirty years of the quite young Christian community as a whole is indeed only a tiny and to a large extent chance fragment of what he had to relate when founding communities. In his missionary travels in Syria, Cyprus and in the province of Galatia he was also accompanied by the former disciple Barnabas, who came from Jerusalem; later in Macedonia and Achaea by Silas/ Silvanus from the same city. Both of them probably possessed more tradition about Jesus than he did, since he only received his call before Damascus around three years after Easter, as a persecutor of the Hellenists in Jerusalem.[598]

There is no question that in respect of oral Jesus tradition Paul was by far inferior to Peter, the Twelve and the brothers of Jesus. Nor is there any doubt that the emphasis of his message lay on the atoning death of Jesus: on the cross and his resurrection and their soteriological and anthropological consequences, on being 'in Christ', belonging to the 'body of Christ', and the presence of the Spirit with his gifts in the community and in the individual believer. Here, however, we should not forget that already for Paul a basic presupposition of the saving event was the sending of the pre-existent Son of God into the world, i.e. his real incarnation.[599] Already for him the eternal Son of God had become a real man in space and time, in Judaea, and only a few years previously. This is a quite incredible and revolutionary message, without analogy in the ancient world! He *must* have told of this man Jesus when founding communities, not least because he would have been constantly asked anew about this strange and truly unprecedented story by his astounded hearers. He would also have been asked about this crucified Messiah Jesus in Judaea, who could not have been preached without a vivid and concrete account, simply because his hearers would have had a healthy curiosity, the curiosity of growing faith, curiosity which had been brought about by the Holy Spirit himself! The Gospels, with their narrative about Jesus, would not have come into being without this Spirit-given 'healthy curiosity'. As Luke recalls,[600] Paul preached in the form of free conversation, which was interrupted by questions. Here his Jewish conversation-partners were certainly interested in scriptural exegesis and scriptural proof; but even more, both Jews and Gentiles were interested in the concrete person of Jesus himself – not just in the exalted Christ alone.

What is typical of Paul and the whole of primitive Christianity is that – in contrast to the Enlightenment christology since the end of the eighteenth century – one cannot tear apart the earthly and exalted Lord; this is the same identical person. The human Jesus cannot yet be played off against the exalted heavenly Christ. That then happens first with the Gnosticizing docetists, who in a way were forerunners of some modern christologies. Without the concrete report about the Palestinian Jew Jesus, the exalted Christ would bear no real personal features. People could not have believed in him as a real person, in the incarnate Son of God who died for all on the cross. Paul was anything but a docetist. Today once again, behind the prohibition of investigating the human Jesus with the help of historical and philological methods, which keeps appearing and is dogmatically motivated, there basically stands a concealed docetism which is hostile to history. Some theologians do not want to perceive the *vere homo* and others – who are in the majority – deny the *vere deus*. For a third group, basically there is no longer either the one nor the other, but only a shadow, the 'Christ idea', which can no longer be identified. Fundamentally they all take offence at the real 'kenosis', the incarnation of the Son of God which is completed on the cross. It is remarkable how much the motif of the 'exaltation to the right hand of God' and any speculative apocalyptic elaboration of his heavenly glory fades into the background in Paul;[601] in the foreground is the crucified, i.e. human Jesus, 'who paradoxically – as "God incarnate" – became obedient to death, death on the cross'.[602] 'Though he was rich, yet for our sake he became poor, so that by his poverty you might become rich.'[603] In other words, Paul surely also narrated Jesus' way to the cross. The incarnate Son of God could have avoided arrest (I Cor. 11.23) and crucifixion. The 'he humbled himself, being obedient to death', in the Philippians hymn includes the whole history of Jesus. We cannot say that Paul 'is not interested' in this 'history',[604] which is of course not identical with our modern 'enlightened' secular and critical understanding of history *quasi deus non daretur*.[605] The 'history of Jesus' is presupposed in his letters, and the recipients knew it, at least in its main features. Paul never speaks of the death of Jesus without thinking of this man in space and time. Only one man, Jesus the Son of God, sent by the Father, could be crucified and die as an atoning victim for the salvation of all. We should not make Paul the first docetist. When he writes in Rom. 15.8, 'For I tell you that Christ became a servant to the circumcised to show God's truthfulness, in order to confirm the promises given to the patriarchs,'[606] he means Jesus' 'messianic service' to his own people, the Jews. In other words, even in Paul the narrating of the story of Jesus, especially the passion narrative, belongs to the fundamental preaching of the Gospel with which he founded his communities.

3. Peter and the 'narrated Gospel'

We now have every reason to assume that the narration of Jesus' teaching and healing, his death and the appearances of the risen Christ, was much more at the centre of the missionary preaching of direct disciples of Jesus, and above all of Peter himself, than it was with Paul. After the persecution by Herod Agrippa,[607] Peter increasingly undertook missionary journeys outside Palestine[608] until he was executed in AD 64 in connection with the Neronian persecution. Peter's growing travels in the Diaspora during the 50s basically once again did away with the division of the mission spheres between Jews and Gentiles which had been established at the 'Apostolic Council' in AD 48/49 and are reported by Paul in Gal. 2.7f. For later, sometimes in the footsteps of Paul, Peter also visited predominantly 'Gentile-Christian' communities like Antioch, Corinth and Rome;[609] in other words, in practice he too carried on a mission to the Gentiles.[610] In the passage just mentioned, Paul says that the pillars 'entrusted me with the Gospel to the Gentiles, just as Peter had been entrusted with the Gospel to the Jews. For he who worked through Peter for the sending (ἀποστολήν) to the Jews also worked through me for the Gentiles'.[611] Here Peter is assigned 'the Gospel for the Jews'; in other words he is entrusted with the same 'message of salvation' as Paul,[612] as far as the christological and soteriological content is concerned. This one 'Gospel' forms the foundation of the unity of the church. According to I Cor. 15.11 it is also proclaimed by the other witnesses to the resurrection. The main difference is that Peter is to preach it (above all) to the Jews, whereas Paul fulfils the same task towards the Gentiles. Peter and the Jewish Christians also 'know that a man is not justified by works of the law but through faith in Jesus Christ'.[613] However, this division could not be strictly maintained, especially as the 'mission to the Jews' carried on by Peter (and other apostles) was not as successful as Paul's 'Gentile mission'.

The division of tasks described in Gal. 2.7 was difficult to maintain in practice. Towards the end of his letter to the Romans Paul calls himself 'apostle to the Gentiles', yet in the same breath he can say that through his 'Gentile mission' he wants to make his fellow-Jews 'jealous, and thus save some of them' (Rom. 11.13f.).[614] This is connected not least with the fact that the 'Gentiles' of the Pauline mission, at least in the first century but in part also later, were quite predominantly 'god-fearers', i.e. pagan sympathizers with Jewish belief in God. Therefore in new places of mission Paul first of all visited the synagogue(s) there, where he met Gentile sympathizers and Jews. Together with a few Jewish Christians these former 'god-fearers' formed the core of the newly-founded Pauline communities. It was never possible to draw a neat division between mission to the Gentiles and mission to the Jews in the church.[615] Conversely, things can hardly have been otherwise with Peter; indeed we may assume that since his 'mission to the Jews' was not particularly successful, in the later years between the Apostolic Council and his martyrdom (c.AD 49–64), he increasingly turned also to the non-Jews, which in reality meant (as already in the case of Paul) especially 'Godfearers' and pagan sympathizers with the synagogue. Since the New Testament term εὐαγγελίζεθαι, which in its Aramaic equivalent possibly appears already on the lips of Jesus,[616] goes back to the Hebrew *biśśar* in Deutero-Isaiah and the Psalms, we may assume that the corresponding noun corresponds to the Aramaic *beśōrā* (*tābā*), 'good news'.[617] Thus it seems very likely that the term εὐαγγέλιον in the sense of a message of salvation, or its Aramaic equivalent, already played a not unimportant role in the earliest

Jerusalem community, again with Peter, but that there its content and proclamation was shaped very much more strongly by the Jesus tradition, i.e. the words and actions of Jesus, including the story of his passion, than it is in the letters of Paul; though even Paul could not dispense with telling stories about Jesus when founding his communities.

We should not doubt that the mission preaching of Peter (and his followers)[618] between Syria and Rome had a tremendous influence on the earliest church and is the main source for the mediating of Jesus tradition, but we do not have any of it directly. We possess only the indirect allusions in the letters which Paul has left us, and these show that the influence of Cephas/Peter was quite considerable, also in the communities close to Paul. Indeed it is by no means a matter of course that in Corinth, a community founded by Paul, a 'Cephas/Peter party' came into being which caused Paul difficulties, and that the Jewish Christians in Antioch, including Paul's trusted missionary colleague Barnabas, followed Peter's behaviour, although Paul had been very closely associated with this community for many years.[619] We also find the same thing in Acts, in the first half of which, chs. 1–15, Peter plays an extremely prominent role, and then has to disappear from the scene. We find hints of Peter's preaching in the speeches which Luke attributes to him, for example in the sketch of the activity of Jesus given to the Roman centurion and 'godfearer' Cornelius and his house in Acts 10.36–43. In Acts 2–5, by contrast, we get examples of Peter's preaching to convert the Jews, even if their colouring is more Lukan than originally Petrine. Luke, who in fact gives what is theologically quite an apt portrait of Paul in Acts 13.38f. and the Miletus speech (20.18–35), may also have had some tradition about Peter's preaching after all. Here it is significant that he puts the term 'Gospel' into the mouth of both Paul *and* Peter.[620] Indeed we get the impression that with his speech at the Apostolic Council, where Peter says that 'the Gentiles should hear the word of the Gospel', Peter too is approved as a missionary to the Gentiles. He also says that God has chosen him to preach the Gospel among the Gentiles and that as God has also 'purified their hearts through faith',[621] they should not have the burden of the law laid upon them, since 'we believe' that Jews and Gentiles 'will be saved by the grace of the Lord Jesus'.[622] These are the last words that Luke has Peter say. None of this is chance. It sounds almost like a future programme, and comes relatively near to what Paul presents to Peter as his own view in the dispute in Antioch mentioned in Gal. 2.14–18. The πιστεύομεν of Peter in Acts 15.11 is matched by the ἐπιστεύσαμεν of Paul in Gal. 2.16, which includes Peter.

In my view, the connection between the term 'Gospel' and Jesus' ministry, preaching and passion as a narration of Jesus, which appears clearly for the first time in Mark, goes back to the Petrine origin of his work, because Peter, the leading 'eyewitness' (I Cor. 15.5), and the communities which he founded and influenced, could already sum up in the word 'Gospel', 'saving message', the messianic activity of Jesus in words and actions, which was completed in his passion. Like the verb εὐαγγελίζεσθαι/*bissar,* the noun εὐαγγέλιον/*besōrā* (*tābā'*) has something of an Old Testament/Jewish background. Through its special form and content, this Petrine terminology partially differs from the meaning of the word customary in Paul, who received his Gospel through a personal 'revelation of Jesus Christ' and fought for the truth of this Gospel in Jerusalem and Antioch.[623] However, as I Cor. 15.1–11 and 11.23ff. show, even Paul knows that the narration of the passion and the 'resurrection events' is an elementary part of the proclamation of this 'Gospel' and that this one 'saving message' binds all those who proclaim Jesus, from Peter and James through the 'Twelve' and 'all the apostles' to himself. The significance of I Cor. 15.11, a passage which is all too easily forgotten in New Testament theology (see above, 145ff.), cannot be estimated highly enough. Among other things, despite all the difficulties (which are sometimes great), indeed tensions and fights, it is the basis for the final unity of the primitive Christian proclamation of Christ; one could also say on the basis of I Cor. 15.1–11 that it is the basis of the christological unity of the Gospel. This is true regardless of the fact that Paul probably in part explained and developed the content of the Gospel revealed to him in a different way from that in which Peter presented the message that he preached. At their memorable fourteen-day meeting in Jerusalem according to Gal. 1.18 they will certainly have exchanged views on the 'Gospel' that they preached.[624] On the other hand, after the interlude in Antioch a gulf opened up between them – at least for a decade – of which Luke was probably also aware. Therefore despite his efforts at harmonization, Luke may in principle avoid the word εὐαγγέλιον in his 'kerygmatic biography' of Jesus because in Paul the word did not have this fundamental significance of 'Jesus narrative'.

VI

Conclusion: Torah and Gospel as Narratives of Two Different Saving Events

1. *Moses and the Exodus event in Mark*

There may be an additional, deeper reason why by contrast in Mark, and therefore in the Petrine tradition which underlies it, the narrated story of Jesus' words and actions, including the miracle stories which cause so much offence today, could be called a 'message of salvation'. Judaism, too, knew an elemental saving event in history that had to be narrated: the account of the exodus, i.e. the miraculous liberation of Israel from slavery in Egypt by the God of the fathers, YHWH, under the leadership of Moses; the giving of the Torah to Israel on Sinai through him as a sign of its election and therefore as the climax of this saving event and the forty years journey through the wilderness – here one could speak of the time of Israel's testing and passion (brought on by its own fault) – up to the death of Moses at the gates of the Promised Land. In the celebration on Passover night the whole Jewish people commemorated this 'saving event', with the son asking questions and the father of the house telling the family community the stories of this miraculous liberation. On a wider scale the whole Torah from Exodus to the end of Deuteronomy comprised the 'biography' of Moses, the unique liberator and lawgiver of God and the greatest prophet and miracle-worker in Israel.[625] And in Deuteronomy 18 the Torah points to the eschatological promise of a 'prophet' like Moses, which in Judaism was bound

158

up with the expectation of the return of Elijah in accordance with Mal. 3.23. Moses, the first redeemer, was the type of the final eschatological redeemer, and Elijah the manifestation of the 'Moses *redivivus*'.[626]

The Gospel of Mark in particular is strikingly stamped with a Moses-Elijah typology. For Mark and for the whole of primitive Christianity, John the Baptist is the 'Elijah *redivivus*',[627] and, like Israel, Jesus is tempted in the wilderness. His temptation lasts forty days; Moses stays the same time on Mount Sinai; Elijah walks forty days to the mountain of God in the desert, being refreshed by an angel.

Whereas Israel received the manna as the food of angels but nevertheless failed, the angels served Jesus in (or after) that time of victory over temptation.[628] According to Ex. 14.31, 'Israel saw the great act[629] which the Lord . . . had done and the people were afraid and *believed in him and in his servant Moses*.'[630] In the Song of Moses (15.18) which immediately follows, the people recognizes *God's kingly rule*.[631] Both together recall Jesus' proclamation of the dawn of the kingdom of God in Mark 1.15: 'The time is fulfilled and *the kingdom of God is at hand*; repent and *believe in the message of salvation*.'[632] The Moses typology reappears in individual miracle stories, above all in the double story of the feeding of the 5,000 and the 4,000 which – as was the case with Israel in the wilderness – could not dissipate the disciples' failure to understand (Mark 8.14ff.). However, their climax is the transfiguration of Jesus, at which Elijah and Moses appear.[633] By contrast, in the passion, at the Passover meal with the sacrifice of the new covenant which works universal atonement, in the judgment on the shepherd of Israel,[634] and in the cry of godforsakenness, it takes on the features of an antitype. Elijah, the helper in the time of distress in ancient Judaism, did not appear to save the crucified Messiah (15.35f.). Jesus died miserably, with a wordless cry, the death of a cursed one.[635] In contrast, according to the widespread legend, Moses was either transported to heaven without dying or God himself took the soul from the mouth of this friend of God (Ex.33.11) without the pangs of death, 'as with a kiss'.[636]

The gulf between the Jewish legends of the end of Moses and the death of Jesus could not be deeper here. Furthermore, Moses' attempt to ask forgiveness for his people after the sin of the Golden Calf, throwing his own life into the balance,[637] is rejected, whereas Jesus gives his life as 'a ransom for the many'.[638] Jesus as the eschatological messianic teacher first rightly brings God's holy will in the Torah into effect by the twofold commandment to love God and one's neighbour which had already been required by Moses, and in so doing approvingly quotes the Jewish 'confession of faith', the *Shema Yisrael*.[639] The scribe who has to preserve the legacy of Moses[640] assents to this with his whole heart. And indeed previously Jesus argues for the resurrection from the dead – completely in the Pharisaic sense – against the doubts of the Sadducees. According to the Pharisaic-rabbinic view the resurrection of the dead is already based in the Torah through Deut. 32.39, 'I can kill and make alive.' Jesus also appeals to the Torah as an answer to the Sadducean doubts; not, however, to a passage of text but fundamentally to God's revelation to Moses by the burning bush, where God appears as the 'God of Abraham, Isaac and Jacob',[641] i.e. as the 'God of the fathers', who is 'not a God of the dead, but of the living'.[642] On the other hand Jesus himself appears as 'Lord of the Torah', who interprets the sabbath commandment in an extremely distinctive way,[643] puts in question the commandments relating to purity and the right to divorce, shares meals with sinners, and never wants to pour old wine into new skins.

Most of these features, which demonstrate the eschatological distance from the old, are taken over from the Markan tradition by Matthew and Luke.[644] In Mark the Pauline (and Johannine) contrast between Moses, the lawgiver to Israel, and Christ, the universal eschatological saviour and Son of God, is matched by the typological relation and at the same time antitypical contrast between the two in the framework of a new historical narrative as definite, final – eschatological – saving event. Here the prophet Isaiah (more precisely, Deutero-Isaiah) and his servant songs take on fundamental significance for the eschatological interpretation of the Jesus story.[645] The old saving event of the exodus and the time in the wilderness are taken up in quite a new way on a prophetic basis and in view of the messianic end-time that has dawned in Jesus and is thus reinterpreted. Here in my view is an essential root of the Markan(-Petrine) use of εὐαγγέλιον in the sense of the radically new eschatological message of salvation which has to be narrated.[646] Matthew has continued this dialectical relationship and expressed it in heightened form in the antitheses of the Sermon on the Mount. Here Jesus teaches the disciples and the people from the Mount, as God himself gave the law from Mount Sinai, the new 'Torah of the Messiah', which begins with the Beatitudes. Similarly, at the end of the Gospel, from the mount of revelation in Galilee the Risen Christ commands the eleven disciples to teach the observance of his commandments to all peoples and at the same time gives the promise – as once in the case of Israel when it went through the wilderness – always to be present in his community.[647] Here the older evangelist Mark is offering a hand to the younger one, who writes in the name of Matthew; like Mark he is a 'theological teacher' of high authority and at the same time (still more than Luke) his real 'exegete'. Independently of this, in a logion of Jesus which has usually so far been attributed to Q, Luke expresses the salvation-historical tension between the old and the new eschatological message: 'The law and the prophets were until John; since then the good news of the kingdom of God is preached, and everyone enters it violently.'[648]

2. The priority of the 'Gospel reading' over that of 'the prophets'

It was only consistent for this twofold relation between Moses (and the prophets) and Jesus, which was positive but at the same time even more antithetical, also to find expression in worship. We receive from Justin the first clear information about the structure of an ordered Christian Sunday service, at which the eucharist followed a part concerned with the word, the form of which is completely stamped by synagogue worship with the reading of scripture, preaching and prayer. I have already referred to this fundamental text from various aspects. It has a key function for the significance of the collection of the Gospel and its connection with Christian worship in the first half of the second century. The decisive passage runs:

> And at a particular time there is a long reading from the reminiscences of the apostles or the writings of the prophets. When the reader stops, the president in a discourse gives an admonition and invitation to imitate these good (teachings).

There follows the prayer which leads into the eucharist. This form of worship is certainly not an innovation; in Rome it may go back to the beginning of the second century or possibly into the first. What is decisive for us is the statement that the reading is either from the reminiscences of the apostles (note the plural) or from the writings of the Old Testament, which in primitive Christianity and thus in Justin were all understood as 'prophetic writings' pointing towards Christ.[649] In other words, the reading of the Gospels had come to have a place alongside that from the 'prophets', i.e. the 'Old Testament'.[650] Here the 'particular time' probably refers to sections of a fixed length, i.e. to a kind of pericope. In other words, this reading of the Gospels or the 'prophetic writings' (and possibly also the two together) took the place of the reading of the 'Torah', obligatory in Judaism, as the climax of the ministry of the word; however, the Torah reading itself was not abandoned, but integrated into the presentation of the prophetic promises. The Jewish threefold division into Torah, Prophets and Writings was replaced by the early Christian understanding of the whole of the 'Old Testament' as a prophetic collection of writings which finds its fulfilment in the Gospel of Jesus Christ as an eschatological message of salvation.[651]

As I have already said, this form of the liturgy of the Word, in which the reading and exposition of 'Gospels', or better 'the Gospels', occupies a place before and alongside that of the 'prophetic writings', goes back a long time before Justin, since for him it is already recognized Christian usage. It may have been the case at least for Asia Minor, Rome and the rest of the West (see above, 116f.). Here the 'Jesus story', as it had been handed down in written form as the 'Reminiscences of the Apostles', i.e. as 'Gospel', takes on the dominant role in worship over against what had previously been 'Holy Scripture', the Septuagint. The Old Testament, now mentioned only in second place, appears no longer in the sense of an *a parte potiori* as the law of Moses but as saving testimony to the acts and work of Jesus. In particular, this dialectical relationship of 'old' and 'new' accounts, old and new 'salvation history', and at the same time 'old and new covenant' (see below, n. 321), is also expressed in the reading of scripture and in the preaching of early Christian worship. We find this twofold relationship, partly typological and partly anti-typical, from the end of the first century in various forms in John, the letter to the Hebrews, Barnabas, Justin, Melito of Sardes and Irenaeus. However, the substance itself is older and is ultimately grounded in the behaviour of Jesus. It was only consistent that this theologically tense relationship in the terminology of the παλαία and καινὴ διαθήκη, the 'Old and New Testament', which nevertheless emphasize the positive unity, should find a record,[652] a terminology which in fact appears for the first time in Paul, but not yet applied to a corpus of writings. Today for the sake of the truth of the Christian faith we should not simply want to dispense with it and speak, say, of the 'first' and 'second' Testaments.[653] Jesus and primitive Christianity were not concerned with a numerical enumeration but with the promises to the fathers and the prophets and their messianic fulfilment in God's saving presence.

The tense relationship between 'law and Gospel' was therefore not exclusively Pauline; it had very different forms and nuances and was fundamental to the relationship between the 'Jewish mother' and 'Christian daughter', the synagogue and the church, from the beginning.[654] It is also grounded in a community tradition which, no less than Paul, thought in terms of typology and salvation history. Here it could base itself above all on the Jesus tradition, which in the awareness of the messianic fulfilment in the present through the activity of Jesus already had a quite 'dialectical' relationship to the tradition laid down in the Torah of Moses, since Jesus already had understood himself as the messianic plenipotentiary who proclaimed the true eschatological will of God.[655] That is already shown by the antitheses of the Sermon on the Mount in Matt. 5.20–48 and 'messianic sayings' like those in Mark 2,[656] but also in the concentration of the Torah on the twofold commandment to love.[657] Probably this understanding of Jesus tradition in its dialectical relation to the Torah is also not least connected with Peter's preaching, which has already found some record in the Gospel of Mark.

3. Unity in multiplicity

If the Pauline 'Gospel' concentrated on the saving significance of the death of Jesus on the cross and his resurrection – i.e., as I Cor. 15.1–8 shows, an event which similarly had to be narrated – the Petrine-Markan form includes more markedly the whole saving 'messianic' activity of Jesus in word and deed, an activity which, however, Paul also indicates in Rom. 15.8 with the formula 'that Christ became a servant to the circumcised to show God's truthfulness, in order to confirm the promises given to the patriarchs'. However, particularly through Mark, the tradition of the sayings of Jesus which already existed in logia collections was included only in a paradigmatic and eclectic way. In Mark, too, the climax and goal of his work also lies in the passion narrative, which tells of that unique event which is the basis of the salvation of all believers (including the uncomprehending disciples). The Pauline and Petrine versions of the Gospels evidently do not differ fundamentally in this basic certainty: Mark had also had personal ties with Paul. The Synoptic Gospels and the letters of Paul do not stand in irreconcilable opposition to each other in the saving message of the justification of the sinner before God by the death of the Son of God on the cross which they contain, despite all the differences in detail. Both were and are necessary for the church and Christian theology.

Here the old Tübingen school – led astray by the sharp polemic of the letters of Paul and the real battles which lie behind them – very one-sidedly read a false opposition into the primitive Christian texts. Only the letter of James falls outside this framework, as does the Gospel of Matthew – though only partially; the verdict depends on its interpretation as a whole. The latter in my view in fact also owes its decisive element, its soteriology, to the 'Petrine' Gospel of Mark on which it is based.[658] It is perhaps also no coincidence that even a former companion of Paul, Luke, probably a Greek and former God-fearer, could write a 'Synoptic' Gospel, i.e. a Gospel dependent on Mark and his Petrine tradition, whereas a Jewish-Christian authority, John, who presumably came from Jerusalem, composed a Gospel which in essentials, say in its fully developed christology of pre-existence and mission, the 'by faith alone' and the radical view of the attainment of salvation solely from grace and the doctrine of predestination based on it, was closely associated with Paul. Here too the theological lines of development overlap. John and the unknown author of the Gospel of Matthew, who is not insignificantly different in his theology, are the dominant theological thinkers of primitive Christianity at the end of the first century and the beginning of the second. The theology of the New Testament writings rests primarily on 'three pillars', two late and one early: first of all on Paul, whose letters were written around 50 and 60, and at the end, between 90 and 100, on Matthew and John. Between them as mediators stand the great 'narrators' Mark and Luke. Despite all the sometimes considerable differences and tensions, these authors all point back to the one centre, the person of Christ, the foundation stone,[659] the Son of God incarnate of John 1.14 and the salvation brought about by him. Basically they are at one with Paul in the one confession I Cor. 15.11, which brings together such opposed people as Peter, the Twelve, James the brother of the Lord, all the apostles and outsiders and the thirteenth witness: 'So we preach and so you believed.'[660] They are all basically witnesses to the one Gospel.

The significance of the unity of the church which we already find in the community in Corinth that has just been founded and in Paul's battle over the communities in Galatia (I Cor. 1.10–16; 11.18; Gal. 1.6–9; 3.1ff.; 5.15 etc.) continues in the second century, at the precise time when the four-Gospel collection had received its fixed, unalterable form. In this connection, here is a passage from a recent history of dogma:

> Without doubt from the middle of the second century the church found itself in the most serious crisis of its history. Hated and persecuted on all sides, but at the same time undermined by emancipatory Gnostic groups and anti-churches of all kinds, itself still without binding norms, it seemed only a matter of time before the church went under in the maelstrom of increasing Christian pluralism and the unity which had been preserved externally changed into syncretistic phenomena of dissolution . . . We must have in view this situation with all this confusion and danger to understand what it meant for the church to find the strength in the midst of the persistent crisis of its existence to develop the fundamental norms of its faith, indeed literally to elevate these norms – their origin is almost anonymous – in the face of the teeming Christian plurality by safeguarding the historical identity of the revelation and to define as the foundation of what is Christian the rule of faith, the holy scripture of the Old and New Testaments and the continuity of the church tradition in connection with 'ministry' and 'succession'.[661]

Already at the beginning of the second century, threat and counter-movement became visible and alongside the continuous use of Old Testament texts in worship it was above all the collection of the four Gospels as writings to be read in liturgy which worked against the decay of the church and despite, indeed because of, their difference, set up new signposts pointing towards the future.

The early church could therefore endure and make fruitful

the offence which was caused by its four very different Gospels and which continually threatened to be a stumbling block, because it knew that despite all the differences, indeed manifest contradictions, these four reports were grounded in the one Lord and his work of salvation for God's lost creatures and because beyond all the contradictions, this 'plurality' pointed to a wealth of theological thought and narrative which first fully developed this work of salvation in its various perspectives. The work of Christ and the message which goes out from it cannot adequately be summarized in the theological outline of a single Christian teacher. From the beginning the difference between the Gospels was necessary and was not only tolerated by the church but willed in this form. Therefore in the great communities, in the first place probably in Rome, the four Gospels were collected gradually, used in readings in the liturgy and deliberately preserved.

The forms of the one 'saving message' of Jesus which are so different have not weakened the church on its tense way through history, but precisely through their creative multiplicity have strengthened its identity and its missionary power.

The 'multiplicity' of the Gospels may sometimes seem an aporia to us today and perplex us, but in reality – contrary to all false attempts at harmonization – they became an inexhaustible source of power, the power which created true faith, love and hope. We should reflect on that positively, not least in the ecumenical dialogue between the different confessions which split the one church, in my view in the end above all externally. Looking back on the history of the church which is now almost two thousand years old we must say that, thank God, the real unity of the churches does not lie in our different, indeed controversial human convictions and efforts, but in the one Lord, the 'head', i.e. 'God incarnate', the judge who himself took judgment upon himself, who, 'obedient to death on the cross', became the redeemer of all; whose body is the church, despite all the failure, selfishness and self-righteousness of its members,[662] because he alone can pronounce us 'godless' righteous. By the will of God we have the one – unique – 'good news', the one Gospel which stands at the beginning of the church, in sometimes very different and human forms. Yet all four Gospels proclaim solely the one Lord of the church and the one salvation brought about by him.

VII

Postscript: Reflections on the Logia Source and the Gospels of Luke and Matthew

1. The riddle of 'Q' and the possibility of a dependence of Matthew on Luke

We came to the conclusion that the titles of the Gospels are original and not a later addition, that they basically go back to Mark 1.1, 'the beginning of the Gospel of Jesus Christ', i.e. to the earliest Gospel, which – probably immediately after its composition – was given the title 'Gospel according to Mark' on its dissemination in the communities, and that the later Gospel writings were successively likewise given an analogous title, 'Gospel according to' plus the name of the evangelist in the accusative when they were published or disseminated. Consequently, relatively quickly a kind of 'compulsory title' developed, which then continued even with the later 'apocryphal Gospels' composed in the second century. Furthermore, a comparison of titles shows that the 'non-apostolic' titles must be older than the 'apostolic' titles. Once the names of apostles had come to be used in titles to give a work additional authority, it was hardly possible to choose authors with lesser authority. In the second century the Gospel of Mark would presumably have been named after Peter and that of Luke after Paul; in addition the Kyrios would have been included in the title (see above, 61ff.). Moreover the completely unitary form of title together with the name of the author would be inexplicable in the case of a later secondary addition. Once dissemination had taken place, this would necessarily have led to a multiplicity of titles. Later, there was no longer an institution which could have imposed this form so rigorously that in the uniquely broad tradition, any divergent form of the title has been so completely suppressed that it left no further trace. Moreover, since the Gospel writings were used in worship, from the beginning it would have been quite indispensable to have a designation for the writing that was being read out; that already followed from the use of Old Testament texts in readings.

Furthermore *all* New Testament book titles and not just those of the Gospels display a considerably 'conservative' capacity for persistence. Here the earliest textual tradition knows virtually no basic variants. Although this tradition was still relatively variable in the first half of the second century, by comparison with later 'apocryphal' texts the protection of liturgical usage nevertheless kept it relatively constant, more constant than the text of the essentially older Septuagint, which had run wild as a result of numerous Jewish and Christian recensions. This constancy is true not only of the text and especially of the titles but also of the new external form of the codex (as opposed to the scroll), and is connected with the persistence of the early Christian writers or *scriptoria*. Only in the very much later manuscripts, like the minuscules, did the titles have to be expanded by decorative elaborations and learned additions.

The order of the origin of the Gospels which arises from this, Mark c.69/70, Luke c.75–80, Matthew c.90–100, John c.100–105, also explains the literary dependencies, for example that of Luke and Matthew on Mark and similarly the knowledge of Mark and Luke in John. In this case ought we not to also leave open a partial dependence of Matthew, which is considerably later, on Luke, at least as a possibility? As a rule, however, this is not thought of at all. Only in very rare cases has a possible dependence of Matthew on Luke been considered, for example by C. G. Wilke, one of the first champions of the priority of Mark.[663] Zahn at any rate thought that Mark and Luke were also used by the Greek translation of the originally Hebrew

Matthew which was made around 90.[664] H. P. West conjectured that in addition to Mark, Matthew was dependent on a 'primitive Luke', which in turn had been adopted by Marcion, but the completely unprovable hypothesis of a 'Proto-Luke', adopted by John Knox, perverted his observations, some of which were correct. They too were hardly noted by scholars.[665] The reflections by R. V. Huggins, *Matthean Posteriority: A Preliminary Proposal,* which should also be taken seriously, suffered a similar fate.[666] Huggins emphasized, as Wilke had already recognized, that Luke is 'more primitive' than Matthew by comparison in the redactional elaboration of the text, and that the problem of the 'minor agreements', which gave rise to unprovable critical hypotheses, fall away, that the argument about the order of the material loses its significance if Luke is prior to Matthew, and with few exceptions Matthew fundamentally follows the narrative thread of his main source Mark. The argument from the order of the material also makes a dependence of Luke on Matthew extremely improbable.[667] Matthew deliberately chose Mark as a primary source for theological reasons and takes over 110 of the 128 Markan pericopes. Luke has only the character of a secondary source, from which Matthew selects what fits his ideas as a redactor; one could also say the theological stamp of his portrait of Jesus.[668] In the case of the infancy narratives and accounts of the resurrection Matthew knows Luke's report but does not follow it.[669] The only problem with Huggins is that he does not consider whether Matthew has yet other sources with discourse material at his disposal alongside Mark and Luke, sources which Luke too could have used, perhaps in a rather different form. Certainly the existence of 'Q', whatever is to be understood by that, cannot be ruled out from the start. Even if we can be certain that Matthew as a rule follows Mark and has largely used him, and we conjecture with good reason that he also took over material from Luke, the sum total of his sources remains as unknown to us as the πολλοί in Luke 1.1.

However, such self-critical considerations are rarely engaged in by scholars. Rather, almost exclusively a single logia source

('Q') common to Matthew and Luke is introduced to explain the numerous verbal parallels. An attempt is made to arrive at this by extracting from the remaining text of Matthew and Luke – after removing all the Markan material common to the two Gospels – what is still a considerable number of agreements of greater or lesser extent in passages, clauses and terms which are similar in wording.[670] This procedure results in a not inconsiderable but very heterogeneous body of text in which, moreover, one can also partially note an order which is analogous in Matthew and Luke.[671] Whereas of the total of 11,708 words in Mark, 8,555 recur in Matthew and 6,737 in Luke, over and above that Matthew and Luke have common material of around 4000 words, but this only partially corresponds word for word.[672] The 'Logia source' arrived at in this way forms the basis for a whole branch of scholarship; here scholars are not only concerned with an attempt to restore 'Q' but also seek to establish different strata of redaction and secondary additions and theological changes in the reconstructed text. Wider hypotheses are then developed on this very uncertain foundation which relate not only to the history of the Jesus tradition but to that of primitive Christianity and its theological development, indeed ultimately to the person and preaching of Jesus generally. Among other things there is talk of the Galilean 'Q' communities which are said to have had quite a different 'kerygma' from the rest of the primitive community, or of a special theology of 'Q' with its distinctive stamp, which after the excision of 'secondary' elements takes on an utterly unapocalyptic and unmessianic character. On this basis a quite new, contemporary picture of Jesus can be constructed, in accordance with modern political, religious and theological wishes. The main champion of 'Q', Adolf von Harnack, was already interested in such an undogmatic, primarily ethical, picture of Jesus.[673]

I do not want to get lost here in the abysses of 'Q' research, which is extending on every side and digging deeper and deeper, far less to give any kind of definitive answer in this realm which has become impossible to survey. I simply want to ask a series of questions which are meant to make us reflect on what can be shown to be probable by means of historical philology. That means that I do not dispute the existence of 'Q', but only the possibility of demonstrating its unity and reconstructing it in any way which is at all reliable, since a whole series of indications suggest that the later Matthew used the earlier Luke. Here Matthew, too, could have one or more logia sources at his disposal.

1. Is not the origin of the Gospels of Luke and Matthew essentially more complicated in terms of literary criticism and tradition history than we generally imagine on the basis of the predominant two- (Mark, 'Q') or four- (Mark, 'Q', Lukan special material, Matthaean special material) source theory? The mere fact that today a distinction is also usually made between 'Q'-Luke and 'Q'-Matthew and that in the case of 'Q' some scholars speak of a source which can no longer be fixed clearly, but sometimes prefer to speak of strata of tradition, should make us cautious here. Precisely if, building hypothesis on hypothesis, one wants to work out various strata of redaction in 'Q' (even in quite different communities),[674] the unity of the 'Q source' flows between one's fingers and with almost the same justification one can assume various 'sources'. Does not the undaunted confidence of some scholars here rest on a self-confidence for which there is no substantive justification? Ought we not rather to reckon that in the early period of the Gospel tradition, the roughly forty years up to the composition of the Gospel of Mark, the weight of the authority of the eye-witnesses was still very tangible and that oral tradition initially predominated, i.e. that in this stratum of the tradition we come very close to the remains of the preaching of Jesus himself? That means that much that is attributed to the theological tendency of 'Q' could in general go back to Jesus himself or to the description of his preaching in the primitive community in Jewish Palestine.

2. The priority of Mark is now recognized almost universally, and rightly so. But doesn't this already raise problems? Thus on the basis of Streeter's so-called 'minor agreements' it is assumed, for example, that the form of text which Luke and

Matthew had before them had a somewhat different form from the one that has come down to us, so there is sometimes a concern to construct an 'Ur-Mark'.[675] In this way it is then possible to solve the offensive problem of Mark 1.1 by declaring this introduction to be a secondary addition, despite the relatively uniform textual tradition.[676] But the καθώς at the beginning of v.2 presupposes a protasis, and Matt. 3.3 corrects the defective quotation of prophets in Mark 1.2 by omitting Mal. 3.1 and changing Isa. 40.3 LXX into a fulfilment quotation. As the textual tradition of Mark 1.1–3 (except υἱοῦ θεοῦ in 1.1, omitted by homoioteleuton) is on the whole relatively uniform, it certainly may not be eliminated with the claim that it is secondary, as Lachmann does. Could we not easily dispense with the hypothesis of an 'Ur-Mark' or a 'Deutero-Mark', which is difficult to explain, if we break with the dogma that Luke and Matthew came into existence completely independently of one another? Matthew would then have taken over such 'minor agreements', i.e. agreements between him and Luke in the sphere of the Markan original, from the text of Luke. I believe that all the 'minor agreements' are thus best explained without complicated and unverifiable literary-critical hypotheses. As a rule one can demonstrate why Matthew here is borrowing from Luke over against or in addition to Mark.[677]

3. The existence of a 'Logia source' (or probably more than one) is quite plausible. However, it cannot be proved that merely one 'Logia source' existed. To claim that it was a unity is to beg the question. Luke and Matthew are said already to have had 'Q' in very different forms. That then applies even more to the less numerous passages which are common to Mark and 'Q'. The collection of logia in the early period presupposes open forms which are therefore different in their various expressions. First of all these may have been notes for personal use. In this way the parchment notebook will have prepared the way for the later Christian codex (see above, 116ff.). Anyone who is expecting the end of the old age in the imminent future was initially hardly interested in larger literary production in traditional forms. On the other hand, written

aide-memoires were helpful, indeed necessary, for the missionaries. The prologue to the Gospel of Luke already makes it improbable that the Synoptists worked only with oral tradition over and above Mark, their literary basis. The 'many' who 'composed an account of the things that have taken place among us' at least predominantly indicate written sources, even if we cannot exclude the possibility that Luke also goes back to oral narratives which he was then himself the first to write down.[678]

But can we discover how many (more or less) different 'reports' Luke took account of and at least to a considerable degree also used for his work? Is it enough to read the three sources Mark, 'Q' and the special material into the 'many'? 'Q' does not form a real entity, far less the special material. Luke can have come across quite different, partly overlapping 'logia collections' which he then used, along with other material, in his relatively extensive[679] 'special material'.[680] How do we know that the material that he has in common with Matthew and against Mark between Luke 3.7b and Luke 19.26 is based on a unitary source? Could there not have been several sources which the first Christian 'historian' Luke in his own judgment collected and used 'thoroughly and precisely' (ἄνωθεν and ἀκριβῶς: 1.3)? The argument based on order, that 'Q' begins with the appearance of John the Baptist and ends before the passion narrative, which is omitted, and is predominantly limited to Jesus' preaching of the word with parousia discourses and parables, does not say much. Here, for example, Matthew could have been critically selective and although on the whole as a rule he follows the Markan narrative, he could have nevertheless sometimes taken note of the thrust of Luke's text, changing it round here and there as he looked it through.[681] Moreover the remarkable fact that the 'Q' fragments are composed in a better, less Semitizing Greek than Mark, and that therefore less of a translation from the Aramaic can be detected, could most easily be explained by the fact that here the practised stylist Luke has had a hand in the matter, and for all his efforts to preserve the wording of the Jesus tradition from an unknown source could have kept intervening to smoothe out the text and to correct it. As Jeremias has shown, the evangelist's hand is clear above all in the introductions and the transitions.[682] But perhaps the unknown translator (or translators) from the Aramaic already had a better command of Greek than Mark with his simple *koine* Greek.[683] Even the problem of the doublets in Matthew and Luke which were derived from Mark and 'Q' as a double tradition could be much better explained by a specific use of Luke by Matthew (alongside Mark and other sources). The larger the number of sources used, the easier it is for doublets of all kinds to arise. In fact in contrast to Luke, Matthew loves duplicating persons and sometimes also texts. Therefore these accumulate in Matthew.[684]

The widespread and certainly justified opinion that on the whole Luke has preserved the order of the 'Q' material and also its linguistic form better than Matthew, who for theological and narrative reasons shaped his discourse material with considerably more energy, could at least partly be explained by the fact that from time to time he deliberately changed Luke, who did not always suit him, not least also in order to smoothe and to abbreviate it, as he also did when using Mark. Quite certainly at the same time we can see in him a more marked theological concern to reshape. His five great discourse complexes are predominantly fashioned by this. Luke has little to set over against this overarching skill in composiiton.[685] He has brought together his 'special material' and the so-called 'Q' material almost entirely into two blocks comprising the so-called 'lesser' (6.20–8.3) and 'greater insertion' (9.51–18.14), and simply inserted it into the narrative thread of Mark after 3.19 and at the beginning of Mark 10. Could not Matthew have shaped his artistic discourses – among other things – also by drawing critically on this great reservoir? Luke's 'Sermon on the Plain' is itself a mere 'shadow' of the Sermon on the Mount. Therefore it is utterly improbable that, for example, Luke reshaped a Matthaean original. He would not have torn apart discourses which have been worked out so masterfully, but integrated them into his work. One could make a Sermon on the Mount out of the Sermon on the Plain, but not vice versa. Therefore Luke cannot be dependent on Matthew, as is constantly asserted.[686] It is frequently – not to say as a rule – evident even from investigations of details that Luke has the earlier tradition and form of description. In no way may he be made the destroyer of such a grandiose work as that of Matthew, by claiming that he copied out Matthew and in so doing – in overweening vanity – destroyed the grandiose architecture of the work along with its impressive theology. Others may attribute that to Luke, I do not.

4. That there was a logia source (or better sources) which Luke *and* also Matthew could have used is already suggested, in my view, by Papias' much- misunderstood and enigmatic note about Matthew: it is to be taken quite seriously, word for word. It is presumably about an original Aramaic collection of sayings of the Lord which was attributed to the apostle Matthew and translated into Greek in very different ways or, as Papias (or the presbyter) says in a somewhat disparaging way, 'as each was able'. Consequently Luke and Matthew, and indeed presumably already Mark,[687] had it each in a quite divergent form, so that we must ask the fundamental question whether we may still speak of one 'Q' source. That the author of the First Gospel had some interest in this apostle is shown by the renaming of the tax-farmer Levi, son of Alphaeus, as Matthew,[688] and the addition ὁ τελώνης, 'the tax-farmer', in the catalogue of disciples in Matt. 10.3.[689] It is surely striking that this disciple of Jesus, who elsewhere in the New Testament is utterly unimportant, becomes the 'apostolic author' of a Gospel. Why should the author of the First Gospel have emphasized this particular peripheral figure so discreetly?

It is utterly improbable that these two little references should first have helped the Gospel to get its name essentially later and at a quite secondary stage. Presumably the evangelist, who deliberately inserted it into his work against Mark, on which he was basing himself, wanted in this way to refer to the apostle Matthew as the guarantor of the tradition and also to disseminate his Gospel under this apostolic name (see above, 71), although for him too – following Mark, whom he prized highly – Peter was far more important. His own authority as a teacher of the third generation after the 'apostolic disciples' Mark and Luke was too slight really to give emphasis to the new work, so he gave it the name of an 'apostolic' source and in this way provided additional help towards establishing his work, which is theologically so impressive, in the communities (see above, 71).

That would mean that the sources of the evangelist probably also included a collection of 'logia of the Lord' which according to Papias was attributed to Matthew. Towards the end of the first century this apostle gave his name to the whole work of this highly-gifted theologian, who wanted to remain anonymous, because he lacked 'apostolic' authority, and assured its success.[690] Papias' note about Matthew, which probably goes back to the presbyter John, could thus refer to a historically meaningful context and at the same time explain the pseudepigraphical title of the first Gospel, together with the fact that it then soon came to be regarded as the oldest.

5. The only problem is that this logia source (or sources) can now no longer be reconstructed in any way, especially as it had no single form in Greek, but evidently circulated in different forms of language and probably also with different extents. As long as the oral tradition of the word was still fluid and lively (and not only the Synoptic Gospels with their considerable differences but also the 'sayings of the Lord' in individual 'Apostolic Fathers'[691] and possible prior stages of the Gospel of Thomas are clear witnesses to this), we can hardly already presuppose a *fixed* and closed form for such sources.[692] Mark is the first to give this to the Gospel tradition with his 'biographical' Jesus narrative extending from the appearance of the Baptist to the passion, under the key work 'Gospel'. He is therefore indicating a certain break. From his work onwards it was necessary to decide to give the whole 'Jesus story' including the sayings tradition a more definitive form. That is precisely what Luke attempts to do by including the sayings tradition, prefacing it with the birth narrative and at the end reporting the resurrec-

tion appearances; the First Evangelist does the same thing even more markedly and with greater theological reflection.

We can conjecture that such a logia collection (or collections) came to be used already by Mark, but certainly by Luke, Matthew and in part also by later works like the Gospel of Thomas together with the Synoptic tradition[693] (see above, 169ff.), but then as complexes of tradition with a greater or lesser degree of disorder were gradually displaced by the Gospels.[694] If we want to investigate the influence on Luke and Matthew, this influence must at the earliest begin where the linguistic differences are quite considerable, so that one is almost tempted to speak of translation variants. We also find a larger number of such parallel texts with considerable differences – alongside texts which largely coincide word for word – in the Logia source conjectured for Luke and Matthew, and they cause the 'Q' hypothesis some difficulties, since because of them such differences must be assumed between Q^{Luke} and $Q^{Matthew}$. These put in question the unity of this 'source' as a whole, though it must still be retained, because alongside this there are passages which resemble each other almost word for word. Therefore scholars so far have at most conjectured a clear dependence on 'Q' where there are the closest verbal agreements between Luke and Matthew.[695] However, since we cannot exclude in principle a partial use of Lukan passages by Matthew, indeed in my view this is in fact highly probable, we would have to adopt precisely the opposite procedure: *specifically in cases of word-for-word agreement we have to reckon with a use of the earlier Luke by the later Matthew, whereas in the case of great differences in wording, different translation variants deriving from divergent logia sources can be conjectured.*[696]

These markedly divergent texts include some parables:[697] Luke 19.12–27, the parable of the pounds = Matt. 25.14–30, the parable of the talents; Luke 15.4–7 = Matt. 18.12–14, the parable of the lost sheep, which stands in a completely different theological context in each Gospel; the parable of the great supper, Luke 14.16–24, which is matched in Matt. 22.2–10 by a wedding feast; the similitude of the narrow gate, Luke 13.23f., which in Matthew 7.13f. appears substantially expanded as a double parable of the narrow and the wide gates and the corresponding twofold way. Further examples are the logia about (fire and) division which Jesus brings, Luke 12.49–53 and its abbreviated parallel Matt. 10.34–36, the similitude of the expected weather, Luke 12.54–56 = Matt. 16.2f., or the invitation to reconciliation in Luke 12.57–59 and Matt. 5.25f. It would be easy to continue this series further. What has been said also applies, for example, to large parts of the Sermon on the Mount, in which the order indicates a common source which, however, the two evangelists had in a different form (cf. e.g. Luke 6.20–36 with Matt. 5.1–12, 39–42, 44, 48 and the concluding parable Luke 6.46–49 with Matt. 7.24–27).[698] However, we cannot arrive at any certainty about the 'Q' original in this way, especially as we must reckon in Matthew with doublets not only from Mark and Luke but also from the logia source(s), which for us have become an unknown factor.[699] All three could have influenced the text of Matthew at the same time. So in individual cases it is quite conceivable that Matthew takes over a logion direct from 'Q' and scorns the Lukan version, or allows himself to be influenced by both versions at the same time. Above all, in the last resort we remain very much in the dark about the sources of Luke, a Gospel earlier than Matthew, which go beyond Mark; here we can hardly get beyond conjectures for which there is a greater or less degree of substantiation. On the question of the Pre-Markan sources there is a blatant disproportion between the efforts of scholarship and the yield that can be said to be probable. For that very reason, ought we not to become more modest, particularly in research into the Synoptics?

One could assume, for example that Luke's Sermon on the Plain already existed in one of his discourse sources, and that Matthew also had a similar source, which as a self-confident teacher he then expanded into the Sermon on the Mount by traditional material which he used in teaching. In the process, however, he also used passages from Lukan texts outside the

Sermon on the Plain, indeed he even drew them in a quite indi-
vidualistic way from Mark.[700] Here, as throughout the Gospel,
we should not underestimate the influence of his personal theological thinking. Even if with Bergemann (see above, n. 671) we
assume such a 'basic document' independently of 'Q', we do
not know whether it did not as yet contain quite different pieces
of tradition, and there is no way of reconstructing its wording.[701] *As we know, we cannot solve equations with several
unknowns.*[702] Now the 'Q' hypothesis, like the sources of Luke
(apart from Mark), contains numerous unknowns. That is
already true of the Sermon on the Mount. As I have emphasized
many times before, the conditions of the composition of all
three Synoptic Gospels – leaving aside the basis in Mark which
they share – are far more complicated and full of variations
than we imagine. We have long exaggerated the possibilities of
literary criticism, the favourite toy of New Testament study.
Here we need more continence. At best we will be able to say
with a certain degree of probability that most of those texts in
which the agreement between Luke and Matthew is greatest
have been taken over by Matthew from Luke, or at least have
also been essentially influenced by him. Basically we can establish only the agreements in wording and content or judge their
extent and examine the probability of redactional interventions
of the evangelists on the basis of stylistic or theological analogies. The real form of the 'Logia source' (or 'sources') thus
escapes our grasp, as does the origin and form of the other
sources of Luke, the so-called 'special material', especially as
Luke is a master of restyling. On the other hand, he treats the
tradition of the sayings of Jesus in a relatively conservative way.
Because of his origin, Luke is probably the better Greek stylist,
and like Mark, he is a gifted story-teller. By contrast, Matthew
has a greater ambition in the theological and redactional shaping of his material. These uncertainties also apply to Matthew's
lesser special material. In the case of all the evangelists, the
direct influence of a still living oral tradition remains uncon-
trollable.

  6. First let us look at those texts which fit no 'Logia source'

simply by virtue of their genre. Here I conjecture a dependence of Matthew on Luke in the tradition about John the Baptist in Luke 3.7–9,16b = Matt. 3.7–12.[703] It is understandable that instructions to the soldiers and tax-collectors in Luke 3.12–14 arouse his disapproval: these are no longer professions for Christians in his time.[704] The temptation narrative, Luke 4.1–13 = Matt. 4.1–11, which as a rule the First Evangelist tightens up and makes theologically more precise, according to his salvation-historical scheme putting the fall from the pinnacle of the temple in the 'holy city' at the centre of the story, contrary to Luke.[705] The tempter requires a miracle to legitimate him in the face of Israel to prove that he is the Son of God.[706] By comparison, what for Matthew is the decisive closing scene, the view from a 'very high mountain' over all the kingdoms of the world, forms the negative counterpart to the sending of the eleven disciples 'to all peoples' (28.16–20). At the same time the diabolical authority over all kingdoms and 'their glory' is there set over against the universal authority of the Risen One.[707] The Matthaean version of the centurion of Capernaum, a narrative which by its form and content alone falls completely outside the 'Q hypothesis', and which like most of his miracle stories is tighter and clearly more theological than the original on which its based, will be dependent on the more circumstantial Lukan narrative, into which Matthew has inserted the threat of Luke 13.28–30 in a reversed form in 8.11–12, in a way which fits the content well. Matthew must have been particularly fond of the word of judgment in 8.12b, 'There will be wailing and gnashing of teeth'; in addition to this passage, where he is dependent on Luke, he adds it five times in other contexts.[708]

At the same time it becomes clear how Matthew has come to differ from Luke, the disciple of Paul. Among other things, he too was a theologian of the threat of judgment. It is no coincidence that the discourses of Jesus before the passion end with three fulminating parables of judgment in Matt. 25. Another healing which does not fit well in 'Q' is the exorcism in Matt. 9.32–34, which he takes over from Luke 11.14 and with which he concludes the series of miracle stories in chapters 8 and 9. Here this last healing makes an effective contrast to the subsequent question from the Pharisees about Beelzebul,[709] which is dependent on Mark 3.22, through the amazed remark of the people, 'Such a thing has never before happened in Israel.' In Matt. 12.22, where as an introduction to the subsequent complex about an alliance with the devil[710] it leads to a doublet to 9.32–34 with a rather freer formulation, he makes the crowd raise the question about the Son of David, which is particularly important for him. Here the εἶπον and the ἐν (τῷ) Βεελζεβούλ associates him with Luke against Mark. The whole passage shows how complicated the identification of Synoptic sources is.

On the other hand, texts relating to God's unconditional forgiveness like Luke 15.11–32 about the prodigal son, Luke 18.1–14 about the Pharisee and tax-collector or 19.1–10 about the chief tax-collector Zacchaeus, who remains in his profession and only promises compensation, hardly fit Matthew's theological scheme. He did not want to take over other Lukan passages because like the parable of the unjust steward, Luke 16.1–8, the importunate widow, 17.1–8, or the nocturnal request, 11.5–8, they could almost appear morally offensive or inappropriate. By contrast, the function of the parable of the lost sheep, Luke 15.1–7 = Matt. 18.12–14, is completely transformed, and he can completely dispense with the narrative of the lost coin in Luke 15.8–10. Possibly the parable of the two sons in Matt. 21.21–31 is a Matthaean adaptation of the story of the prodigal son in Luke. He also felt the version of the Our Father in Luke 11.2–4 to be theologically defective by comparison with the liturgical version which was familiar to him. In contrast to his use of the Markan material, behind which stood the authority of Peter, whom he also revered, Matthew dealt more eclectically, i.e. critically, with Luke. After all, Luke had been a disciple of Paul, and Matthew had not been too fond of Paul.[711] No wonder that in a series of points the Letter of James, which in my view is earlier, stands very close to his Gospel and against Pauline thought and behaviour.[712]

This critical attitude towards Luke also applies, among other things, to the texts about Samaritans in Luke 9.52–56; 10.30–36; 17.11–19. According to Matthew, as 10.5 shows, Jesus' sending out of the disciples did not as yet include Samaria. Therefore he has no room for such traditions. Understandably he also rejects the second sending out of the seventy-two in Luke 10.1f. and contents himself with the sending out of the Twelve which he finds in Mark 6.7–13 (and prepares for the definitive sending out of the eleven in 28.18ff.). This he supplements with words from Luke 10 and from other sources. For indeed Jesus' activity is first of all limited to the people of the twelve tribes; the seventy-two Gentile nations, which are indirectly indicated by the seventy-two messengers in Luke 10.1, do not fit into his christological scheme. The Twelve are not to 'go the way to the Gentiles'; indeed, they are not even to enter a 'city of the Samaritans' (10.5).[713] The exception which proves the rule is the second healing story, 8.5–13, about the Gentile centurion in Galilean Capernaum, which with nine verses by comparison with its abbreviation in Luke 9.1–10, including the added threat, is the longest in the Gospel; like the third temptation (4.8), it again points to the mission at the end of the Gospel, 28.18–20. In this way, the theological and literary interweaving of the individual pericopes is reflected far more strongly throughout Matthew than in Luke. Like the account of John the Baptist and the temptation story, the centurion of Capernaum – as I have already said – seems to be a foreign body within 'Q'. Here, also on the basis of the note on Papias, the real starting point should be a collection of 'sayings of the Lord'. Similarly, John the Baptist's question and the following discourse of Jesus in 11.7–11 could be taken over from Luke 7.18–28. Here, as so often elsewhere, Luke's version gives the impression of being more original than that of Matthew. The same is true of his comparison with John the Baptist in Luke 7.31–35 and Matt. 11.16–19.

It is not my concern here to give a detailed demonstration of whether and where Matthew is not dependent on 'Q' but on Luke – that would call for a lengthy monograph, though it would be worth while. I want to indicate that given the common textual material this *need* not always be the case and that time and again with good reasons Matthew *could* be going back to the earlier Luke. Indeed, a comparison of the texts shows that this twofold dependence is more probable than the hypothesis of one single common source which on closer, (self-)critical examination cannot be worked out precisely. It could also be put another way: in the question of the sources of Luke and Matthew, are we not asking more of the 'Q' hypothesis than it can bear, because in the form in which it is usually put forward this hypothesis is so convenient? For a long time I too presupposed almost as a matter of course that it is the simplest and worked with it. However, as I actually came to investigate the problems of the Gospels I became more and more doubtful. The question of the 'sources' of the three Synoptic Gospels cannot be answered in a straightforward way: apart from the priority of Mark, in the end it seems to be insoluble. As I have already said, we move more or less in the realm of hypotheses: Matthew *can* also be dependent on Luke and 'Q' probably existed in the form of one or – as seems to me to be more likely – several 'sources'; however, we can no longer really reconstruct these. Moreover, above all we should no longer attempt to invent the existence of strata of redaction or 'Q' communities and theologies to match, building further hypotheses about the history of primitive Christianity on them.

7. The objection that where Matthew follows the Markan narrative the influence of further sources is hardly detectable does not tell against his adoption of passages of text from Luke either. For the work of Peter's disciple Mark already had a unique authority for the unknown Christian scribe in southern Syria or in non-Jewish Greek-speaking Palestine: his account of Jesus takes over more than eighty per cent of Mark,[714] and Mark gives the first Gospel its inner narrative structure and to a large degree governs its construction. This is true above all for the second part of the Gospel from 12.46 and Mark 3.31 on and comes to completion in the passion narrative, where apart from certain legendary expansions, Matthew follows Mark's

account completely and with Mark, over against Luke, who here partially uses an independent source, deliberately avoids any more profound corrections – for example a more marked stylization as the account of a martyrdom. We see this above all in the nucleus of the Markan narrative, the account of the crucifixion in Matt. 27.26–56 = Mark 15.15–41.

That Matthew takes over from Mark almost word for word the passages in the Golgotha narrative which Luke and John find offensive is part of his *theologia crucis*. In other words, as a rule Luke (or 'Q') is important for him only where he has no basis in Mark. For Matthew, Mark remains the fundamental authority, because he knows that Peter stands behind it. Nevertheless we do have a series of lesser parallels of Luke and Matthew against Mark, the 'minor agreements' which have already been mentioned.[715] That Matthew here allowed himself to be influenced by Luke in small details of narrative, language and style – as furthermore John too is influenced by Mark and Luke – seems to me to be a more plausible solution than the unprovable hypothesis of a Proto- or Deutero-Mark. This seems as improbable as the much-discussed Semeia source of the Fourth Gospel or the conjecture of a 'Proto-John' which is often put forward. In taking over the text of Mark, Matthew here and there also took a look at Luke and sometimes allowed himself to be influenced by Luke.[716] The relatively uniform textual tradition should make us more mistrustful about an often deeper-reaching secondary revision of the text of the Gospels that we have. That applies even to John 21. I do not believe that the original Gospel of John came into circulation without this 'additional chapter'.

2. *The chronological priority of the Gospel of Luke over the Gospel of Matthew*

1. All these considerations lead to the concluding question: can it really be proved adequately that Luke is essentially earlier than Matthew? Only if this is possible can we presuppose that Matthew knew not only Mark and one or more logia sources,

but also Luke and – as I believe – also in part used them. In my view there are so many good reasons for this that I would almost speak of a stringent proof.

This example indicates that chronological questions play an important role in the New Testament and can have theological consequences, even if some theologically narrow exegetes look down on such problems with a degree of contempt. Not a few false trails could have been avoided had these questions, which also include the origin of the Gospel through specific persons in space and time, had been taken more seriously. I am thinking, for example of the mind-boggling hypothesis of a 'pre-Christian' Gnosticism, the still virulent thesis of a chronologically 'pre-Pauline' 'Hellenistic' community, a Luke to whom anti-Marcionite tendencies were imputed and who was put close to the apocryphal Acts of apostles and Gospels, or a John whose work is reduced to a conglomerate of different sources and levels of redaction and who is put either around 170, as under the influence of Valentinians and Montanists, or – as an alleged source for Mark and Luke – before the Synoptics, around 50.

2. Two errors came together in the false dating of Luke and Matthew, one 'conservative' and one 'critical'. First of all the 'conservative' error. That the 'Hebrew' Matthew is the earliest Gospel has been the common view of the church since Irenaeus. Despite their sharp criticism of the Gospels, even F. C. Baur and the Tübingen school maintained this, though because of their notorious late and wrong dating of all the Gospels they put Matthew as the earliest Gospel after 100.[717] Conservative theologians like Schlatter and Zahn defended the priority of Matthew perceptively and tenaciously well into the twentieth century. W.R.Farmer and his friends still do so today. The first reason was the Jewish-Christian nature of this Gospel, which must be particularly striking to experts in rabbinic literature. Here the first volume of Billerbeck's commentary, 1,055 pages long, speaks for itself; the second, containing Mark, Luke, John and Acts, is only 853 pages long.[718] A second reason was the significance of this 'apostolic' Gospel for the church and its

pregnant theology by comparison with its 'non-apostolic rivals' which – in my view – were in reality its forerunners.

Granted, in the last third of the nineteenth century the priority of Mark largely became established, but the tendency to put Matthew, with its distinctive 'Jewish' and theological profile, too early has remained. After brief reflection Ulrich Luz conjectures: 'We may not put the Gospel of Matthew long after the year 80.'[719] The commentary by W. D. Davies and D. C. Allison goes into the problem at greater length. It gives a survey of the different opinions, which range from AD 40 (Hugo Grotius) to after AD 100 (F. C. Baur, O. Pfleiderer, H. J. Holtzmann, H. von Soden), and itself arrives at a period 'in all probability between AD 80 and 95'.[720] However, U. Schnelle, who in his *Introduction* usually follows the 'consensus', refers to AD 110 as the *terminus ad quem* because of the use of Matthew by Ignatius, but then puts it without any further reason in the period 'around AD 90'.[721]

3. By contrast, F. C. Baur and his pupils (A. Schwegler, E. Zeller, G. Volkmar) and other critical spirits ultimately dependent on the Tübingen school put the Gospel of Luke in the second century, well after Matthew.[722] More recent authors are more reasonable. Howard Marshall conjectures 'a date not far off AD 70'. He rightly refers to the striking interest in the destruction of Jerusalem, which, he thinks, presupposes 'a knowledge of and an interest in a recent event'.[723]

Along with others, J. A. Fitzmyer sees as the best solution 'to adopt the date for Luke-Acts that is used by many today, c.AD 80–85'.[724] Schnelle thinks on the one hand that 'the date of composition of Luke-Acts can only be defined vaguely'. Like Matthew it presupposes the destruction of Jerusalem, but it is decisive that Luke is writing 'from the perspective of the third primitive Christian generation'.[725] However, that is bound up with the chronological definition of what is meant by the 'third generation'. The decisive question is whether he was a disciple of Paul, a question which I would without reservation answer in the affirmative.[726] The Acts of the Apostles could not have been written at a great chronological distance from Paul; as a comparison with the letters of Paul shows, it contains far too many pieces of valuable historical information for that. The author knows conditions in Judaea before AD 66 from his own experience. Moreover his Gospel is still relatively close to the original event. That is evident from a comparison with the works attributed to the later apostles, beginning with Matthew and John and extending to the apocryphal Gospels like those of Peter and Thomas. I myself would therefore conjecture a date more like 75–80 for the Gospel and a date around two to five years later for Acts. In the 'events which have been fulfilled among us' the prologue to the Gospel includes the period up to the eye-witness of the author in the last part of the Acts of the Apostles, i.e. there is an intrinsic connection between the 'things which have been accomplished among *us* in Luke 1.1' and the 'we'-passages in Acts.[727] On the other hand, the striking difference, indeed contradiction, between the end of the Gospel (24.43–52) and the beginning of Acts (1.1–11 and here especially 13) does presuppose a certain chronological distance between the two works.

4. Numerous historical details in Luke-Acts which do not allow an essentially later beginning in time support this approach. One of the reasons for this dating of Luke's work is his proximity to the capture of Jerusalem. It is striking that this Gospel, by comparison with all the other New Testament writings, goes into the catastrophe in a unique way. Luke still seems to be deeply moved by it; in other words, it did not lie all too far in the past.

After describing the entry into Jerusalem Luke introduces as special material an episode which he has shaped effectively:

And when he drew near and saw the city he wept over it, saying, 'Would that even today you knew the things that make for peace! But now they are hid from your eyes. For the days shall come upon you, when your enemies will cast up a bank about you and surround you, and hem you in on every side, and dash you to the ground, you and your children within you, and they will not leave one stone upon another in you, because you did not know the time of your visitation.'[728]

This is a realistic description of the siege and capture of the city formulated in the language of the LXX, of a kind that we do not find elsewhere in the New Testament. The preceding scene 19.39f., in which the Pharisees in the crowd ask Jesus to tell his many disciples who are acclaiming him to be silent, and Jesus' answer, 'If these are silent the stones will cry out', refers to the destruction: the 'stones crying out' are the ruins of the city which is completely destroyed. Because in 19.44 with the 'and they will leave no stone on another' he has anticipated Mark 13.2, in 21.6 Luke needs only to improve Mark's style and describe the event announced as still lying in the distant future, in imitation of prophetic language.[729]

We find a further realistic reference which is abundantly clear and at the same time historical a little later in Luke 21.20 and 21, where in contrast to Mark 13.14 the auctor *ad Theophilum* does not speak of the 'abomination of desolation' in Jerusalem after Daniel,[730] but says that the encirclement of Jerusalem by the Roman army announces its imminent devastation.[731] The next sentence, about the inhabitants of Judaea fleeing into the hills, the population of the city leaving it and the inhabitants of the flat land not having to take refuge in it,[732] depicts in a very concrete way the real situation in the Jewish mother country immediately before the siege and capture of Jerusalem, as opposed to the apocalyptic-utopian description by Mark, who was writing in Rome a few years earlier. In a utopian way Mark envisages the 'Nero *redivivus*' who is expected soon as an eschatological enemy of God, i.e. the anti-Christ. Here Luke provides a vivid short commentary on Josephus' account in the Jewish War, of how on the approach of the Romans many fled from the open country into the city to seek protection there and then later were either killed or sold as slaves.[733] Josephus' *Jewish War* was written at around the same time as the Gospel of Luke.[734] The catastrophe which breaks in on Judaea and Jerusalem is for Luke 'days of vengeance, to fulfil all that is written . . . For great distress shall be upon the earth[735] and wrath against this people; they will fall by the edge of the sword, and be led captive among all nations;[736] and Jerusalem will be trodden down by the Gentiles, until the times of the Gentiles are fulfilled.'[737]

With this radical change over against the Markan pattern, which historically is relatively indeterminate and which for the evangelist, too, is related to the apocalyptic time of distress that is still to come, Luke is still completely under the impact of the most recent past, whereas for Matthew after about twenty years this lies so far in the past that he can take over Mark 13.19f. without commentary, and with slight abbreviations and changes. Whereas Luke looks back to the realistic experience of the time of 'wrath upon this people', still during the course of the war Mark looks ahead, as does Matthew much later, to the future of the Danielic eschatological 'tribulation such as has not been from the beginning of the creation . . . till now, and never will be'. This Mark and Matthew expect in the approaching future.[738]

The 'trampling of Jerusalem by the Gentiles' in Luke probably refers to the camp of the Tenth Legion; the καιρὸς ἐθνῶν is meant to be the last interval before the parousia, i.e. the time in which the author is writing his two-volume work, which for him is at the same time the last interval for the Gentile mission, an interval which did not begin all that much earlier and which will still last for a certain period.[739] Only after the conclusion of these 'years of the Gentiles' will the cosmic signs of the real end time come, which 'bring fear on earth over the Gentiles' and point to the imminent appearance of the Son of man (21.25ff.).

Luke's gaze in the Gospel can focus so strikingly on the Jewish War, the destruction of Jerusalem and the fearful consequences for the Jewish people, and in so doing radically change his Markan original and even go into historical details, because this event does not lie too far back in the past: it shook him personally. With few exceptions, Matthew passes over it because between twenty and thirty years have passed and in the meantime Judaism in Palestine and Syria had risen again under the spiritual leadership of the rabbinate, which was in process of formation. This had largely overcome the crisis of the destruction of the temple.

That is also evident from other texts, thus the remarkable conclusion of the parable of the unmerciful servant in Luke 19.27 with the reference to the enemies who 'do not want me to rule over them' and who are to be executed, and also the logion Luke 13.34f. which is usually attributed to the Logia source and which in a lament over Jerusalem with a wisdom stamp[740] indicates: 'Look, your house will be abandoned (to doom).'[741] God will forsake the temple which protects the city[742] and thus give the city over to judgment.[743] This will be an original saying of Jesus which Luke adds to a saying about the fate of Jesus in Jerusalem, whereas Matthew makes an effective composition by putting it at the end of the great discourse against the scribes and Pharisees and immediately before the prophecy of the destruction of the temple 24.1f. and the discourse about the parousia.[744] Luke already understood 13.35a as a reference to the destruction of the temple, followed – after a lengthy interval, as is shown by 21.24–28 – by the parousia, to which there is a reference with the quotation from Ps.118.26. Matthew adds an ἔρημος to the ὁ οἶκος ὑμῶν and refers it to the permanent destruction of the sanctuary, which has already for some time been lying as a heap of ruins. Matthew could have taken this saying over from Luke and very skilfully have placed it at the end of chapter 23.[745]

Jesus' admonition to the weeping women who followed him on the way to the cross, 'You daughters of Jerusalem, do not weep for me, weep rather for yourselves and your children,' indicates how shaken Luke is by the catastrophe. These are tones of compassion of the kind that one does not hear in the other Gospels.[746]

The evangelist seems to have experienced this time himself. Probably his particular detachment from an enthusiastic expectation of an imminent end[747] is connected with the fact that at that time he himself experienced the eschatological exuberance in the Christian communities (cf. Mark 13.7f. = Matt. 24.6–8. Luke therefore omits the ἀρχὴ ὠδίνων ταῦτα in 21.11 but adds the invitation to ὑπομονή in 21.19). It is remarkable that Luke, the non-Palestinian Greek, makes the most impressive reference among all the New Testament authors to the conquest of Jerusalem and its cruel consequences, whereas the Jewish Christian and former scribe who composed the First Gospel and was close to Palestine, makes only peripheral mention of this fearful event which deeply shook not only Judaism but the whole of the eastern Roman empire – as a judgment. Among other things, that indicates that Luke is relatively close to the events, whereas Matthew (and John) are at some distance in time. In Mark – in Rome – interest can be detected in the Jewish War; however, he is still very badly informed about the real events, and for him the catastrophe of the city as an eschato-logical event associated with the anti-Christ already lies in a relatively near future.[748] His work is intended to prepare and strengthen the communities in the face of the severe tribulations that the enemy of God will soon bring by inviting them to take up discipleship of the cross.

By contrast, particularly in redactional passages, sometimes clearly changing Mark which he had before him, Luke speaks in a very concrete way of the fearful event of the most recent past, not only because he himself is still moved by it but because those whom he is addressing, Theophilus and his circle of friends, are affected by it. He does not do this polemically in self-righteous *Schadenfreude* at the well-deserved punishments of the Jews.[749] However, we detect in him – as we do not in the First and Fourth Evangelists – the shock, indeed the mourning, above all in the gripping scene before the crucifixion of Jesus in Luke 23.27–31. We should not be over-hasty in making Luke, the Greek and former God-fearer, who of all the Gentile authors informs us most objectively about Jewish affairs, who loves the temple and the holy city so that he makes his Gospel begin with a scene of sacrifice in the temple and end with the praise of the disciples in the temple,[750] an anti-Judaist, as has sometimes become the fashion today.[751] To explain this unique phenomenon it is necessary to put his Gospel relatively early, say between 75 and 80. Numerous coins were still circulating in the empire with the inscription *Iudaea capta* (or *delicta*) and the lamenting Jewish woman under a palm tree or a Roman trophy; the Colosseum was still being built in Rome with the help of the monstrous plunder of war. It was completed in 80 and the last *Iudaea capta* coins were minted under Titus in 79–81.[752] In my view not only Josephus' *Jewish War* but also the Third Gospel will have been written at this time.

5. With Matthew things are quite different. With two exceptions he alludes to the Jewish War and its consequences only where the motif is provided for him by Mark.[753] First there is the insertion Matt. 22.6f., which disrupts the parabolic narrative of the great supper; in v.6 this is dependent on Mark 12.6, and in 22.7 it depicts the angry reaction of the king who issues the invitation: 'and he sent his armies, destroyed those murderers and burned their city.' It may come from the evangelist, who saw the destruction of Jerusalem as God's just punishment. But we cannot also exclude the possibility that he already found it in a source. The same goes for the Jews' curse upon themselves in 27.25, which had such a pernicious effect down their history;[754] this points to the fearful bloodbath during the Jewish War. If Matthew is writing in one of the cities of Phoenicia or southern Syria near the border with Jewish Palestine, he could have still been envisaging the grisly mass killings which Josephus describes.[755] In other words, in contrast to Luke, but in a similar way to John,[756] who in his rigorism is in some respects closer to him than is thought, the First Evangelist keeps a considerable distance from the Jewish War and its immediate fearful consequence; at the same time both he and John are engaged in sharp controversy with the synagogue which regained strength after the catastrophe, John in Asia Minor[757] and Matthew in geographical proximity to Jewish Palestine. In contrast to Luke, Matthew no longer directs his gaze backwards to the destruction of city and temple; for him both are worth mentioning only as a divine act of judgment. He no longer makes any mention of a lament of Jesus over

Jerusalem; rather, he strictly and firmly points to the coming judgment of the Son of man (ch.25).

6. This changed attitude is connected with the fact that the Gospel was composed substantially later and the historical situation had changed: at least ten and perhaps even twenty years may lie between it and Luke. In keeping with this, Matthew's picture of Judaism is rather different from that of Luke or Mark. In the meantime the absolute religious predominance of scribes in the Pharisaic tradition has developed, those figures who are later designated 'Tannaites' and to whom we owe the origin of the Mishnah and the early rabbinic tradition. This revival of Palestinian Judaism, which is presupposed in Matthew (and at a greater geographical distance also in John), and which also had a relatively rapid effect on the nearer Diaspora in southern Syria or Phoenicia, may have taken around twenty years after the catastrophe.

The new situation can be detected throughout the First Gospel, above all in Matthew 23, where the evangelist introduces the hearers and readers of his work to his own time and to the situation of those communities in which he was active as a teacher and a Christian scribe.[758]

Conversely, we could also say that Matthew transposes the Jewish opponents of his time back into the time of Jesus. That was not sufficiently seen by earlier scholars, for example Schlatter and Zahn, who precisely because of the 'rabbinic character' of Matthew followed the tradition of the early church in still regarding it as the earliest Gospel.

This change is evident in Matt. 23, for example, in the stereotyped sevenfold use of the formula 'scribes and Pharisees',[759] six times in the accusatory cry of woe, 'Woe to you, *Scribes and Pharisees*, (you) hypocrites.' For Matthew both terms form a unity, one could almost speak of a hendiadys.[760]

With one exception the 'scribes' as the spiritual leaders stand in first place in the double formula; only in Matt. 15.2 has the evangelist significantly abbreviated the text of Mark 7.1, which in contrast to Matthew still clearly distinguishes between the two groups: 'The Pharisees and some of the scribes who had come from Jerusalem gathered around him.' Matthew's version is: 'At that time Pharisees and scribes came to Jesus from Jerusalem.'[761]

In other words, Matthew can both use the double formula and also speak only of the Pharisees or scribes; the same opponents are always meant, whereas Mark and sometimes also Luke still differentiate more clearly here.[762]

For Mark, in keeping with history, the scribes are at home above all in the Holy City, where together with the chief priests and elders they form the governing body, the Sanhedrin.[763]

In Luke, too, the Pharisees appear for the last time at the entry into Jerusalem (19.39); after Jesus' arrival in the city above all the scribes and chief priests appear as his opponents.[764]

In John, on the other hand, the scribes have to some degree been 'absorbed' by the Pharisees. Three times we encounter 'chief priests and Pharisees' as the real adversaries of Jesus (11.47, 57; 18.3). The way to this simplification is already prepared for by Matthew.[765]

There will be a direct dependence of Matthew on Luke in Matt. 22.35, where in the introduction to the pericope about the greatest commandment instead of Mark's εἷς τῶν γραμματέων Matthew has a Pharisaic 'expert in the Law' (νομικός)[766] put to Jesus the question which tempts him (πειράζων αὐτόν). Only here does Matthew have the rare term νομικός. This is a typical 'minor agreement' which in my view can most sensibly be explained by the dependence of Matthew on Luke. In my view he has taken this over, including the address διδάσκαλε, from the Lukan version, which stands in quite a different context.[767] The occasion, too, is obvious. He wanted to avoid Mark's positive judgment on the scribe which culminates in Jesus praise 'You are not far from the kingdom of God', and instead chose the more negative introduction in Luke; he also limits himself to the introduction by Jesus and gives this a version which sounds completely rabbinic.[768]

The real key to fixing the historical context of Matt. 23 and thus of the whole Gospel, and its dating, lies in the introduction to this chapter, 23.1–12, which is artistically shaped by the evangelist, above all from the Lukan logia tradition.[769] The starting point, which is decisive for the understanding the whole and for the situation of the First Evangelist, is Jesus' instruction in 23.2f.: 'The scribes and the Pharisees sit on Moses' seat; so practise and observe whatever they tell you, but not what they do . . . '

Here I simply want to refer to the clear verdict of an expert[770] on the 'time and context of Matt. 23.2':

After the destruction of Jerusalem a period of transition followed, during which the authority of the chakhamim, i.e. the 'wise men', the self-designation of the rabbinic scribes in the cities, became increasingly established. In the course of this development, which first reached a provisional culmination under the presidency of Rabban Gamli'el in the Bet Din in Jabneh (c.AD 85–115), a distinctive understanding of office on the part of the chakhamim developed. The ordination of the chakham – initially by his own teacher, then by the Bet Din in Jabneh – becomes the recognized sign of his authentication in the office of teacher and judge. In officially exercising this office the chakham stands in the succession of Moses. On a cathedra – in Palestine designated ספסל – the authorized chakham held office in his official function as judge and teacher . . . The statement in Matt. 23.2 is best explained against the background of an established and largely-accepted rabbinic self-understanding during the time of the presidency of Rabban Gamli'el in the great Bet Din.'[771]

Presumably the programmatic introduction in Matt. 23.1–3, in connection with Mark 12.37b-38 and Luke 20.45f.,[772] comes from the evangelist himself. Here we trace his redactional hand, as in the introduction to the antitheses of the Sermon on the Mount in 5.20.

Becker's investigation of Matt. 23 confirms the dating of the First Gospel which has already been argued for several times here, between 90 and 100, i.e. in the last decade of the first century. If we consider the contemporary context more precisely, an earlier date is hardly possible.[773] This brings Matthew relatively close in time to John, the final redaction of which, however, is to be put a bit later, shortly after AD 100. John knew him and took account of him least – if at all – by comparison with Mark and Luke. The difference in time from the editing of the Fourth Gospel might amount to less than ten years. In content they can sometimes come close together, for example in texts which transfigure Peter like Matt. 16.16–19 (cf. Matt. 18.18 and John 20.23); John 6.68f.; 21.15–17.[774] I Clement 5.4, with the special emphasis on Peter (cf. John 21.18) and Paul as Roman martyrs, falls around the same time. Both evangelists stand at the 'exit' of the New Testament period as congenial theologians, and in their works, which externally and theologically are so different, in a special way embody all the inner tensions and the wealth which mark out all four Gospels and the letters.

Matthew 23.8, in which the institutionalized use of the honorific title 'rabbi' for ordained scholars is already presupposed, is probably redactional. In contrast to the form of address 'rabbi' (or once in an elevated form 'rabbouni') used to Jesus in Mark and John,[775] Matthew puts this original honorific form of address only in the mouth of the traitor Judas, in a disparaging way.[776] That is certainly no coincidence and indicates what I see as the unmistakable change in Judaism after 70. In the meantime 'rabbi' had become the fixed title of ordained scribes; thus it could no longer be used by the real disciples of Jesus. By contrast, the Greek Luke completely avoids this form of address in his work and replaces it rightly by the equivalent διδάσκαλε or κύριε. In accordance with ancient literary custom, Luke generally removes Aramaic words. In this way, at his later time Matthew is probably also rejecting Christian claims to honorific titles in communities, say in connection with the rise of the monarchical episcopate, which probably stemmed from the leading role of James the brother of the Lord in Jerusalem and which, as Ignatius shows, first became established in Syria and then in Asia Minor. The community in Greece (Philippi and

Corinth) and also in Rome was still for some time governed by a college of presbyters. The new situation in Matthew is also evident from the fact that he is the only evangelist to put the post-Easter term ἐκκλησία twice on the lips of Jesus in the sense of 'church' and actively to call for 'church discipline' (16.18; 18.17).

In contrast to Matthew and John, in Mark and Luke we do not yet find any comparable controversies relating to 'church law' in connection with a monarchical government of the community or the question of 'church discipline'.[777]

7. Another piece of evidence for a relatively late dating of the First Gospel is the trinitarian baptismal formula which – independently of Matthew – we find in the early Christian period elsewhere only later in the Didache and then again in Justin.[778] By contrast Luke – who is earlier – still exclusively, like Paul, has a one-member baptismal formula.[779] But 'trinitarian' formulae with no reference to baptism often occur almost at the same time as Matthew in I Peter 1.2; I Clement and around fifteen years later still in Ignatius[780] – a further indication of the late origin of Matthew. The widespread hypothesis of a secondary insertion is nevertheless resolutely to be rejected, as the attestation of the text is completely uniform.[781]

8. Finally, apart from John, the First Gospel presupposes the most developed polemic between Jews and Christians. At the time of the two latest Gospels towards the end of the first century the two parties had already grown wide apart. This is particularly evident in connection with the Palestinian/Jewish-Christian character of the First Gospel. This Matthew contains isolated references to a Jewish polemic against Jesus which we find again in an essentially stronger form in the Jewish informant of Celsus, the opponent of Christianity towards the end of the second century, and which there assumes almost the character of a Jewish anti-Gospel. A little later, Tertullian seems to know such an 'anti-Gospel'.[782]

Whereas Mark 6.3 mentions Jesus 'the carpenter and son of Mary' and does not mention the name of his father Joseph anywhere in the Gospel, Matthew replaces this by the question 'Is this not the son of the carpenter (and) is not his mother named Mary?' (13.55).[783] In so doing he avoids a double scandal: offence was presumably caused both by the profession of Jesus as a simple carpenter and also by the mere mention of his mother, without a father. Luke, who passes over Mark 6.1–6 in favour of a special tradition which has been shaped redactionally, has only the question of the people of Nazareth, 'Is this not the son of Joseph?' (4.16–30[22]); he makes no mention at all of carpenter.[784] Such a detail did not fit into a work dedicated to the 'most excellent Theophilus'. Taking this with the Christian assertion of the virgin birth, Jewish opponents could refashion Jesus' profession and the mention only of his mother into a sign of a complete lack of education and the charge of a dishonourable birth. Celsus' Jew relates that Jesus' mother came from the most wretched circumstances and had been rejected by her betrothed, a carpenter, because of her adultery with a Roman soldier Panthera.[785]

Matthew, who in 13.55 makes Jesus the 'carpenter's son' and thus like Luke evades the profession of Jesus himself, and mentions his mother only after his father, seems to have known comparable accusations. Therefore he emphasizes the just conduct of Joseph over Mary's pregnancy and emphasizes – in my view in deliberate opposition to Luke, who quite one-sidedly emphasizes Jesus' mother as the recipient of revelation and the main agent and gives the father the role of an extra[786] – no less one-sidedly the role of Joseph as the one who obediently follows the divine instructions, whereas Mary is depicted in a completely passive way. This looks like a deliberate counterpart to Luke's account, which Matthew finds offensive,[787] and by which he seeks to reject Jewish calumnies. The same is true of the accusation against Jesus as one who leads the people astray and against the disciples as deceivers[788] in connection with the charge that the disciples stole the body of Jesus.[789]

The concluding sentence, 'and this story has been spread among the Jews to this day', points to the development of an anti-Christian Jewish tradition about Jesus to which on the Christian side was opposed the legend of the guards on the tomb and their bribery; this had the further advantage of making the guards witnesses of the resurrection.[790]

The motif of leading the people astray also appears in John and is then taken up again by Celsus,[791] along with the conjecture that the body has been removed by someone unknown.[792]

The heightened polemical situation of Matthew is also evident in the duplication of the accusation of an alliance with Beelzebul;[793] this corresponds to the defaming of Jesus in John 8.48, to the effect that he is a Samaritan possessed by a demon. This heightened controversy with a caricature of Jesus among opponents explains the intensification of the polemic against the Jews in the two late Gospels which today is rightly complained about: this is typical of the tribulations of the church on the threshold of the second century. The lack of understanding, indeed the hatred, had intensified in a pernicious way *on both sides* in the 'family dispute'. Here the Jews were in a safer legal position than the 'vagrant' Christians, who during the later reign of Domitian and then under Trajan constantly had to reckon with accusations before the Roman courts.

Not only in the apologetic elaboration of the infancy narrative and the polemic expansion of the resurrection narrative does Matthew prove to be essentially later than Luke, but also in a comparison of the genealogies. While the truly 'royal' genealogy of Jesus in Matthew, constructed in an artistic rather than a 'historically exact' way, with its series of three times fourteen names between Abraham and Christ and the four Gentile women Tamar, Rahab, Ruth and Bathsheba, seems impressive,[794] Luke's genealogy, which goes back from Jesus to Adam, indeed to God himself, seems enigmatic.[795] So we can understand all too well why Matthew replaced the special Lukan genealogy with a 'more scriptural' one.

9. Conversely, above all in Acts Luke shows a strikingly good knowledge of Jewish conditions in Palestine before 70; this proves that – as was already demonstrated in respect of the Jewish War – he still stands personally close to this time. Here we can see the effect of his visit to Palestine as a travelling companion of Paul, probably at the Feast of Weeks in AD 57. At that

time he will have got to know the Jewish metropolis which he loved; in the autumn of 59 he will probably have set off with Paul on the journey from Caesarea to Rome.[796] His connection with the first generation of the 'eye-witnesses and ministers of the Word' (1.2) seems to have been substantially stronger than that of Matthew, who is wholly a member of the third generation. So Luke knows not only the view of the two great traditional parties and the oppositions between them (Acts 23.6–10) but also the special hostility of the high-priestly party of the Sadducees to the Christians,[797] whom they persecuted from the beginning. He is informed that one of the twelve apostles bore the surname 'the Zealot', which appears only in contemporary Jewish sources,[798] that 'Sicarii' planned revolts against Rome,[799] that figures like Judas the Galilean, Theudas[800] or the anonymous Egyptian[801] emerged as instigators of unrest with a prophetic or even 'messianic' claim; he knows the procurator Felix and his venality, and he also knows that Felix was married to Drusilla, a Jewish princess – she was the daughter of Agrippa I – with a doubtful past.[802] Felix's successor Festus, who was of a rather different stamp, is aptly characterized; here the scene with Paul, Festus, King Agrippa II and his sister Berenice who was all too well known in Rome in the 70s as the substantially older mistress of Titus, is unique.[803] Luke experienced Paul's fate in Rome, his trial in Caesarea and the journey to Rome as his travelling companion and as a contemporary witness,[804] as later – albeit at a greater distance – he witnessed the fall of Jerusalem, which he set down in the Gospel in such a varied way. Like Josephus in the *Jewish War*, in the second part of Acts he writes his own view of Christian (and at the same time Jewish) '*contemporary* history'. In this genre he was a century or two ahead of this time. Despite all his tendency towards harmonization, hagiographic idealization and the miraculous, his historical sense already found expression in the Gospel. Thus we owe to him the chronological location of the activity of both Jesus and of the apostle Paul in world history.[805]

We can therefore hardly put Luke-Acts much later than 75/80 or at the latest 85. This is also supported by Luke's picture of Roman rule, represented by individuals, and also the varied and sometimes directly positive picture of its dispensation of justice. He can still hope that at a time when Jerusalem 'is trampled on by the Gentiles' (see above, 191), reasonable Roman magistrates will treat the new Jewish-universal eschatological movement correctly and assess it appropriately, indeed that individual representatives, beginning with centurions and extending as far as governors like Sergius Paulus, will show a positive interest in it and turn to it, or at least, as in the case of Gallio, will treat it justly in the face of Jewish charges. Even a person like Agrippa II, who knew all too well the Jewish groups of his time, shows such interest in the new Jewish sect, though this is somewhat distanced. Paul's wish that a man in such a high position as Agrippa might be converted is the wish of the author Luke. Around three years after this memorable encounter with Paul, the great-nephew of Herod removed from high-priestly office the high priest Annas II, son of the Annas of the passion narrative,[806] because he had executed James the brother of the Lord and other Jewish Christians in Jerusalem.

This attitude of Luke's towards Roman rule fits admirably into the early Flavian period under Vespasian (68–24 June 79), Titus (to 13 September 81) and the early Domitian, but hardly into his later period or into that of Trajan, when there were again more pogroms of Christians. Christian apologetic with a philosophical stamp which addressed the educated and is directed towards the organs of state, the emperor and the senate, only begins under the milder regimes of Hadrian or Antoninus Pius. Luke, whom we can regard as a quite independent earliest Christian 'historian' and 'apologist' of a special kind, composed Luke-Acts in a better political milieu than that under the late Domitian and Trajan. He could still hope that the reprieve given by God could become a time of unhindered preaching of the gospel, and although he was very well aware of the Neronian persecution and the martyrdom of Paul (and Peter) and did not conceal the suffering of the Christians, he could end with the hopeful sentence about the prisoner Paul: 'preaching the kingdom of God and teaching about the Lord

Jesus Christ quite openly and unhindered' (28.31). This ἀκωλύτως sounds like a legacy in keeping with his time, to some degree as a heartfelt wish and a task combined. In the First Gospel,[807] I Peter, the Apocalypse and the Johannine corpus, I Clement or even the Shepherd of Hermas, the horizon has clouded over again.

10. As a last argument for the dating, to which I have already referred on numerous occasions, I would like to point out that the 'non-apostolic' Gospels according to Mark and Luke in my view certainly came into being before those regarded as 'apostolic', since after one Gospel had been provided with the name of an apostle all the other later ones had to be 'apostolic'.

All these factors taken together virtually compel us to conclude that Luke must have been composed considerably earlier than Matthew.

Now if Luke is to be put at least ten and more likely fifteen, indeed perhaps even twenty, years before Matthew, it seems to me quite impossible that the cautious, theologically creative scriptural scholar on the borders of Jewish Palestine did not know the work of Paul's disciple Luke. Matthew hardly used fewer sources than the 'beloved physician'. In my view he used both Mark *and* Luke, and in addition probably more collections of logia than just one. These sources could also have overlapped. The logia collections may have been derived in the communities from an originally Aramaic collection made by the disciple Matthew. This gave his Gospel the 'apostolic' name.

The task of writing a 'better Gospel' than previous comparable works, which in the same way was to take the 'apostolic' Jesus tradition of the disciples quite seriously as well as to make visible his own theological notions as a message for the assailed church of his time, required preliminary work and thorough information. Matthew certainly was no less sparing in this respect than the *auctor ad Theophilum*. In so doing he stands on an equal footing alongside the elder John of Ephesus, though the distinctive and impressive character of the latter reshaped the tradition far more strongly than in the case of Matthew, who fortunately reproduces all his sources very much more faithfully.

It follows from all this that we can no longer be so self-confident and so inventive in hypotheses in a search for 'Q', or even in reconstructing this source (or sources), as scholars have been over the last century.

3. *Summary*

In conclusion, the following results of our reflections should be noted.

1. Matthew presupposes Mark and Luke as sources which are fixed in writing and are clearly attainable for us. As the primary source, Mark, whose theology he also treasured theologically, gave him the narrative thread; he used Luke eclectically as a secondary source.

2. We can only conjecture what further sources he used in addition to this. Probably he knew one (or, better, several) collection(s) of 'Logia of Jesus' from which he likewise selected what seemed promising. Perhaps here an Aramaic original is identical with the collection made by Matthew which is mentioned by the presbyter John in Papias. He and already Luke, indeed even Mark, seems to have had different versions of this, since 'everyone translated it as he was able'. In addition there was special material which in part could also derive from oral tradition and frequently had legendary character. But in all this we can do no more than conjecture.

3. Thus we are to assume that he had similar, indeed possibly almost identical, traditions from the logia tradition and at the same time from Luke. Therefore we cannot ever define precisely either his dependence on some forms of logia collection or on Luke. Where his text corresponds almost word for word with that of Luke, dependence on Luke is likely, whereas where in the same material the differences between Luke and Matthew are considerable and considerably redactional reworking by Luke and Matthew does not seem probable, it is possible to

conjecture a common 'Logia source' for Luke and Matthew with different versions. In other words, the tradition of the sayings of all three Synoptic Gospels is essentially more complicated than has been assumed hitherto, and the process of tradition can be traced only with many reservations and in a largely hypothetical way.

4. On the other hand, the question of the striking 'minor agreements' is solved. Here Matthew, who as a rule follows Mark's narrative version even down to the wording, is at points influenced by Luke's reworking of Mark. All the complicated conjectures of an Ur-Mark or a Deutero-Mark are therefore unnecessary. And the fact that Matthew and Luke sometimes interrupt the thread of Mark at the same point to insert logia material is best explained by this dependence of Matthew on Luke, whose narrative thread he could see just as clearly as that of Mark.

5. On this basis, all attempts to reconstruct a single self-contained logia source along with the conjectures about the strata of its redaction, its different theologies and communities seem questionable. The collections of sayings of Jesus which were certainly used by Luke and Matthew evade our attempts at reconstruction; the composition of the two Gospels presupposes too many possibilities which we can no longer see through sufficiently clearly. There is no way in which we can make a direct reconstruction of 'Q', which previously seemed possible, after excluding all the common Mark material by subtracting the texts in both Matthew and Luke which corresponded with each other. This material could too often have been taken over by Matthew from Luke, and it could also come from a variety of logia collections (or different versions of a collection) which both had at their disposal.

6. The focus of the historical investigation into Jesus shifts even more than before to the two earliest – 'non-apostolic' – Gospels Mark and Luke and the question of their 'sources'. Here even more restraint is called for in all attempts to reconstruct written sources, as we can no longer make synoptic comparisons and here too there are too many possibilities which we

can no longer fathom. But because Mark is based on the authority of Peter, which probably also means that it is based on Petrine tradition, and Luke as the first Christian historian used a larger number of evidently very different sources yet was extremely careful in the tradition of the sayings of Jesus, a historical approximation to the person of Jesus of Nazareth, his activity and his passion, is both meaningful and possible. Here the figure of Jesus takes on very clear contours. Elements of Matthew's special tradition, for example in parables, and even from the Fourth Gospel, can make a contribution here.

7. If the logia tradition nevertheless shows some corresponding tendencies, this is connected with the preaching of Jesus and of the earliest Palestinian primitive community. Indeed it would be exceptional if through the process of tradition which now extended over some decades, despite all the changes the 'sayings of the Lord' had not to a large degree taken on the inimitable character of the language and teaching of Jesus. This still emerges abundantly clearly in the Synoptic Jesus tradition, in comparison, say, with John and the Gospel of Thomas.

8. Anyone who wants to maintain the existence of 'Q' in the form that has been conjectured hitherto must produce stringent proof that in principle Matthew cannot be dependent on Luke, say because Luke was composed later or at best at the same time. I doubt whether this will be possible. However, in all these questions we are not helped by merely literary-critical hypotheses. We have had more than enough of those. Only convincing historical and philological arguments will take us further.

Chronological Table

Passover AD 30	Death of Jesus
c. 50	I Thessalonians, the earliest Christian literary testimony
54–68	Nero
to 57 or 62	The seven authentic letters of Paul: I Thessalonians; I Corinthians; II Corinthians; Galatians; Romans (winter 56/57); Philippians and Philemon either 55/56 or 58–62
62	Martyrdom of James in Jerusalem
64	Persecution by Nero; martyrdom of Peter and Paul in Rome
69–79	Vespasian
66–70(74)	Jewish War
69–70	Gospel of Mark in Rome
c. 75–85	Gospel of Luke and Acts
79–81	Titus
81–96	Domitian
c. 90–100	Matthew in Syria/Palestine; I Peter in Rome
96–98	Nerva
98–117	Trajan
c. 96–100	I Clement in Rome
c. 95–105	The 'elder' John in Ephesus; Cerinthus
c. 100–110	Editing of the Johannine corpus
c. 110–114	Martyrdom of Ignatius
c. 115	Letter of Polycarp (c. 70/80–156/167)
115–117	Jewish rebellion in Cyrene and Egypt
117–138	Hadrian
c. 120–130	Mark 16.9–20; II Peter; Papias of Hierapolis: Five Books about the Logia of the Lord
c. 130	Letter of Barnabas; II Clement; Conversion of Justin in Ephesus

Chronological Table

c. 130–140	Basilides in Alexandria; Shepherd of Hermas; Gospel of Peter; Apologies of Quadratus and Aristides
138–151	Antoninus Pius
c. 135–150	Valentinus in Rome
144	Excommunication of Marcion in Rome
after 150	Justin's *Apology* in Rome; Ptolemy, pupil of Valentinus; Polycarp, bishop of Smyrna, visits Rome
c. 160	Justin's *Dialogue with Trypho*; Melito of Sardes (*Homily on the Pasch*); Heracleon, First commentary on John?
161–180	Marcus Aurelius
c. 170/180	Celsus: first literary enemy of the Christians; Hegesippus: Five books of *Hypomnemata*
177	Persecution in Lyons: Irenaeus (c. 125–200) becomes bishop there
180–192	Commodus
c. 180	Irenaeus, *Adversus haereses*; martyrs of Scili (North Africa); Vetus Latina; Theophilus of Antioch; Pantaenus in Alexandria
193–211	Septimius Severus
c. 200	Clement of Alexandria (c. 150–220); Tertullian in Carthage (c. 160–220)
c. 220	Hippolytus in Rome (c. 170–235), pupil of Irenaeus
c. 246/48	Origen, *Contra Celsum*

Notes

1. For the order of the LXX see M. Hengel, 'Die Septuaginta als christliche Schriftensammlung . . .', in M. Hengel and A. M. Schwemer, *Die Septuaginta zwischen Judentum und Christentum*, WUNT 72, Tübingen 1994, 221f. However, the order in the LXX manuscripts was not so uniform as that in the NT.
2. Thus Josephus in his Preface to the *Antiquities* 1, 13; cf. *c. Ap.* 1, 1.
3. If they write about later events, for example about the destruction of Jerusalem (see above, 72, 74), they do so in the form of 'prophecy', i.e. as a rule as *vaticinia ex eventu.*
4. Jesus: 1.14f.; church: 13.10; 14.9; Christ as the content of the Gospel, 8.35; 10.29, see above, 61ff.
5. Cf. in the secondary conclusion 16.9–20 the additional mention in 16.15, which links 13.10 and 14.9 with the end of Matt. 28.18–20.
6. Gal. 1.12, 16.
7. See J. Schniewind, *Euangelion. Ursprung und erste Gestalt des Begriffs Evangelium*, BFCTh 2.R. 13/27, Gütersloh 1927/31; P. Stuhlmacher, *Das paulinische Evangelium I. Vorgeschichte*, FRLANT 95, Göttingen 1968, 153–206, is still a basic work; see also, with sometimes very questionable arguments and conclusions, J. Frankemölle, *Evangelium – Begriff und Gattung. Ein Forschungsbericht*, SBB 15, Stuttgart ²1994, bibliography. The formula εὐαγγέλια θύειν, thank-offering for good news, is relatively frequent in Greek sources. The significance of the term for the ruler cult is sometimes excessively exaggerated on the basis of the inscription from Priene (see V. Ehrenberg and A. H. M. Jones, *Documents illustrating the Reigns of Augustus and Tiberius*, Oxford ²1967, nos 98, 38, 41 cf. nos 99, 14 and also A. Deissmann, *Light from the Ancient East*, London 1929, 366f.). The ruler cult had no influence on the formation of New Testament terms. For the use of the term in the singular and the plural in Irenaeus see n. 30 below.
8. Acts 4.12; Gal. 1.12; I Cor. 2.2. Cf. I Cor. 1.23; Gal. 3.1; Rom.1.16, etc.
9. Plural εὐαγγέλια: II Kingdoms (Sam.) 18.22 (with the meaning 'reward for a messenger', perhaps also feminine singular); 18.25 for

bᵉśōrāh; feminine singular εὐαγγελία: 18.20, 22(?), 27 similarly for
bᵉśōrāh; 27: εὐαγγελία ἀγαθή: *bᵉśōrāh tōbāh*. Cf. still IV Kingdoms
7.9 feminine singular. For the verb *biśśar* see II Kingdoms 18.19f.,
27(26), 31; also I Kingdoms 31.9; II Kingdoms 4.10; III Kingdoms
1.42: ἀγαθὰ εὐαγγέλισθαι; cf. Isa. 52.7. The meaning of 'proclaim
news of a victory or of peace, i.e. "good news"', still comes through
in Deutero-Isaiah and in the Psalms: in addition to Isa. 52.7 (2x) see
also 40.9; 60.6; 61.1 (essentially for Jesus – see Luke 4.18; 7.22 =
Matt. 11.5); Ps. 39(40).10; 67(68).12; 95(96).2; cf. Joel 2.32(3.5);
Nah 1.5(2.1). For the Old Testament-Jewish terminology of verb
(*biśśar*) and noun (*bᵉśōrāh tōbāh*) see Stuhlmacher, *Evangelium* (n.
7), 109–53. Megillat Taanith 12 is important: On the 28th of the
month Adar the good news (*bᵉśōrtā tābā*) came for the Jews that they
did not need to deviate from the law (ibid., 130f.), also Targ. Isa. 5.1,
where 'who has believed our report (*lišmu-ʿatēnū*)' is translated
libsortānā. Is it probable that the root of the primitive Christian
terminology of *bᵉśōrāh*/εὐαγγέλιον lies in this 'message'. For this see
also M. Hengel and A. M. Schwemer, *Paulus zwischen Damaskus
und Antiochien*, WUNT 108, Tübingen 1998, 154f. *Paul between
Damascus and Antioch*, London 1997, 92f. (the German edition is a
much expanded version of the English, so in what follows, there are
references to the German only where there is no equivalent in the
English translation).

10. I, 66, 3 on the account of the eucharist in the Gospels see M. Hengel,
Studies in the Gospel of Mark, London 1985, 64–88. In the account
of Basilides and his school by Hippolytus, *Refut.* 7, 22, 4, cf. 7, 27, 8,
the plural comes from Hippolytus, see below, n. 234. For the rareness
of the plural even in Irenaeus see Yves-Marie Blanchard, *Aux sources
du Canon, le témoignage d'Irénée*, Paris 1993, 151–64.

11. Above all accumulated in the context of his exegesis of Ps.22 in the
Dialogue with Trypho, where he produces a larger number of Gospel
quotations from Matthew, Luke and Mark: *Dial.* 99–107 (100, 4;
101, 3; 102, 5; 103, 6; 104, 1; 105, 6; 106, 1.4); elsewhere, apart
from *Apol.* 66, 3, in 67, 3; but cf. his pupil Tatian, *Or* 21, 1f., who
invites the Greeks to compare their myths (1) and ἀπομνημονεύματα
(2) with 'our reports' (τοῖς ἡμετέροις διηγήμασιν). The rigorist Tatian
avoids the pagan term for the genre.

12. On this see T. Zahn, *Geschichte des neutestamentlichen Kanons* I, 2,
Erlangen/Leipzig 1889, 471–6: 'The name was admirably chosen and
very appropriate for giving pagans with a literary education a correct
notion of the nature of the Gospels' (471). For more recent discussion
see T. K. Heckel, *Vom Evangelium des Markus zum viergestaltigen
Evangelium*, WUNT 120, Tübingen 1999, 313ff.

13. *Apol.* 2, 11, 3ff. = Xenophon, *Memorab.* 2, 1, 21ff. For the significance cf. the verb, *Apol.* I, 33, 5: οἱ ἀπομνημονεύσαντες πάντα περὶ
τοῦ σωτῆρος ἡμῶν Ἰησοῦ Χριστοῦ ἐδίδαξαν. I believe that the dependence on the 'Reminiscences of Socrates' is important for him and
that here he is not simply following the diffuse literary understanding
of his time. He mentions Socrates positively nine times in all in the
first and second *Apology*; he quotes Plato's *Dialogues* fourteen
times, five of them the *Republic*. For the term see M.Hengel, *Studies
in the Gospel of Mark* (n. 10), 68 and 165 n. 25. For the genre of
apomnemoneumata as well as Zahn (n. 12) see the description by
E. Schwartz, *PW* II, 1, 1895, 170f.: 'Reports about actions, remarkable details, especially sayings, which merely rest or seek to rest on
personal reminiscence of the things themselves or the oral tradition
about them.' – 'The sense of the title still lives on in the consciousness
of the second-century Apologists when they call the accounts of the
evangelists ἀπομνημονεύματα in contrast to the lying myths of the
pagans' (171). In addition to the *Memorabilia* of Socrates cf. also
those of Zeno on his teacher Crates, Diogenes Laertius 7, 4 and the
Reminiscences of Stilpo and Zeno, Athenaeus IV 162b, those of
Callisthenes, *Athen.* VIII 350d = FGrHist 124 F 5: ἐκ τῶν Καλλισθένου
. . . Ἀπομνημονεύματα; Pollux, *Onom.* 9, 93 = F 4 by contrast speaks
of *apophthegmata*. Stobaeus (*Flor* III, 6, 57–60; 29, 84) several times
quotes fragments of Epictetus, four times under *apomnemoneumata*;
by contrast Arrian speaks in terms of reminiscences of λόγοι and
ὑπομνήματα of Epictetus in the introductory letter to the Diatribes,
see ed. Schenkl p. 5.465–7, cf. M. Spanneut, 'Epiktet', *RAC* 5, 662.
Marcus Aurelius I, 7 also speaks of *hypomnemata* of Epictetus which
were given to him to read as a young man by his philosophical teacher
Rusticus. The term was not clearly fixed. Justin follows this older
philosophical genre. Favorinus, the contemporary of Justin und
Epictetus, by contrast writes *apomnemoneumata* in the sense of fruits
of reading; see E. Mensching, *Favorin von Arelate* I, Berlin 1963,
27ff., on the Fragments see 65–99. According to Origen, *c. Celsum* 6,
41, a Moiragenes wrote out *apomnemoneumata* on the magician and
philosopher Apollonius of Tyana. According to Eusebius, *HE* 5, 8, 8,
Irenaeus quotes from the '*apomnemoneumata* of an apostolic presbyter' (see *Adv.Haer.* 4, 23, 1f., cf. 4, 28, 1; 30, 1; 31, 1; 32, 1), without giving the name; Eusebius, *Dem. evang.* 3, 6, 2 (GCS p. 132, 10
ed. Heikel), speaks of written *apomnemoneumata* of the disciples of
Jesus; Clement of Alexandria, *Strom.* 2, 118, 3 (GCS p. 117, 3), uses
it for an alleged statement of Nicolaus from Acts 6.5 disseminated by
his followers. The term is not used all that frequently. For the key
word 'reminiscence' in Xenophon, *Memorabilia*, see 4, 8, 2. This is

also important for Justin.

14. *Chronicon Paschale*, ed. Dindorf, Bonn 1832, I, 13f. in his writing on the Passover; see also O. Perler (ed.), *Meliton de Sardes, Sur la Pâque*, SC 123, 1966, 244ff.

15. *Tr. in Ioh* 36, 1, CChr.SL 63, 8 p. 323.

16. Cf. Matt. 4.23.

17. A.von Harnack, *What is Christianity?*, reissued New York 1957, 70 (fourth lecture: I am grateful to Dr R. Deines for this reference).

18. A. von Harnack, *Dogmengeschichte* [4]I (Darmstadt reprint), 81; cf. id., *What is Christianity?* (n. 17), 144.

19. Ibid., 102; cf. *What is Christianity?* (n. 17), 180: 'Paul transformed the Gospel without doing violence to its essential features . . . into a universal religion.'

20. Id., *What is Christianity?* (n. 17), 184.

21. Id., *Dogmengeschichte* I (n. 18), 108.

22. See e.g. J. D. Crossan, *The Historical Jesus*, San Francisco 1991, 421: 'The historical Jesus was, then, a peasant Jewish Cynic.' 422: 'His strategy . . . was the combination of *free* healing and *common* eating, a religious and economic egalitarianism . . . He announced . . . the brokerless kingdom of God'; see also the even more radical naiveté of B. L. Mack in his two interconnected books *A Myth of Innocence. Mark and Christian Origins*, Philadelphia 1988, and *The Lost Gospel. The Book of Q and Christian Origins*, San Francisco 1993. The problem is that the logia source Q has itself become a modern pseudo-scientific 'myth' and scholars, who regard themselves as being so critical, have rarely perceived this even now. Here I prefer the old myths of the primitive Christian community. See the brief but telling review by K. Berger in the *Frankfurter Allgemeine Zeitung* 120 of 24 May 1995, 13: 'Jesus a Cynic in the wood: Galilee lies in the heart of the United States. Burton L. Mack explains about the New Testament': 'Thus, in Christianity as in the United States the slogan is to be, "Away with the myth of the strong man, in with a new social programme." The shocked reader discovers that such a simple truth might probably be only to be found among the theologians.' *The Five Gospels. The Search for the Authentic Words of Jesus. New Translation and Commentary*, by R. W. Funk, R. W. Hoover and the Jesus Seminar, San Francisco 1993, publicized at great expense, blows the same shrill trumpet. See the collected blurbs on the first page, 'Praise for the Five Gospels', and also R. W. Funk, *Honest to Jesus. Jesus for a New Millennium*, San Francisco 1996. To be honest, after all the ideological experiences with the misuse of political terms like 'community of the people', 'solidarity' and 'socialism' in the so progressive twentieth century which lies behind us, I find this 'new

Jesus' and his 'contemporary message', associated with much 'political correctness', dismayingly boring. It is really not worth bothering about it. The Gospel is not suited to political and ideological demagogy. The real Gospel of Jesus Christ is above all about ethics which, thank God, certainly has something to say about a new basis for our whole life. Basically Jesus preaches the 'justification of the godless' and 'peace with God'. That was the message that he brought to the 'poor in spirit', the 'tax-collectors and sinners'.

23. I am intrinsically quite critical of this still young theological discipline, which is also mine. The (hyper-)specialization in a book of 680 pages has not done us a service; rather, labyrinths of hypotheses have been erected from which it is often difficult to find a way out. Intrinsically all regular theologians, systematic theologians, Old Testament scholars, church historians and practical theologians need also to be New Testament scholars. See M.Hengel, 'The Tasks of New Testament Scholarship', *Bulletin for Biblical Research* 6, 1996, 1–20.

24. 145 years after the Hijra, which would correspond roughly to the time of Irenaeus, c. AD 180. For Ibn-Hisham's biography of Muhammad, *Sirat Muhammad*; see A. Guillaume, *The Life of Muhammad*, London 1955. See also W. Montgomery Watt and Alford T. Welch, *Der Islam, I. Mohammed und die Frühzeit. Islamisches Recht – Religiöses Leben*, RM 25, 1, Stuttgart etc. 1980. The study of the biographical tradition on Muhammad could be very stimulating for New Testament scholars. The rich, often special, tradition of Jesus agrapha in Muslim authors is also completely neglected, see M. Asin et Palacios, 'Logia et Agrapha Domini Jesu apud moslemicos scriptores, asceticos praesertim, unitata', in R. Graffin and F. Nau (eds), *Patrologia Orientalis*, XIII, Paris 1919, 330–431, 529–624. This material would at least be interesting for form-critical studies and in part is probably of Jewish-Christian origin.

25. Cf. Acts 1.1.

26. 408 pages to 271. However, we should not forget that the narrative literature in the NT in turn largely consists of 'speeches'; in Acts they comprise one third.

27. See M. Hengel and A. M. Schwemer, *Paul* (n. 9): in Gal. 1.10–2.18 Paul is writing 'acts of the apostles in a nutshell'.

28. See now the masterly new commentaries on Acts by C. K. Barrett, *The Acts of the Apostles*, I, Edinburgh 1994, and J. Jervell, *Die Apostelgeschichte*, KEK 3, 17(1), 1998. They will change the face of research into Acts, which for so long had been constricted by F. C. Baur, his pupil E. Zeller, *Die Apostelgeschichte nach ihrem Inhalt und Ursprung kritisch untersucht*, Stuttgart 1854, and their followers.

29. More recently, the leading papyrus expert T. C. Skeat has often

pointed out the age of this collection and associated it with the origin of the codex of four Gospels; see *ZPE* 102, 1994, 263–68; *NT* 34, 1992, 194–9; *NTS* 43, 1997, 1–34: 31f. The literature on the four-Gospel collection is overwhelming. Here I shall mention only a few titles which seem to me to be significant: H. v. Campenhausen, *The Formation of the Christian Bible*, Philadelphia and London 1972, 155ff., 170ff., 195ff.; P. Vielhauer, *Geschichte der urchristlichen Literatur,* Berlin and New York 1975, 781–6; H.-J. Schulz, *Die apostolische Herkunft der Evangelien,* QD 145, Freiburg ²1994, ch.I. The presidential address by G. N. Stanton, 'The Fourfold Gospel', *NTS* 43, 1997, 317–46 (on Irenaeus 319–22) is also important; see also above, 35 (n. 144), C. J. Thornton in his critical discussion of the questionable theses of P. Vielhauer. For the whole problem see now also Heckel, *Evangelium* (n. 12), passim; especially on Irenaeus 350–3 and below n. 144.

30. See Blanchard, *Sources* (n. 10), 157; see already Zahn, *Kanon* (n. 12), I, 162f.

31. *Adv.Haer.* 2, 22, 3–5. Underlying this is the notion of an activity of Jesus lasting many years, which was read out of John. In his extended report on the Gospels in *HE* 3, 24, 3–15, Eusebius tries to balance out the opposition between the Johannine and the Synoptic chronology with a compromise.

32. Irenaeus, *Adv.Haer.* 3, 11, 7. For the term see Heckel, *Evangelium* (n. 12), 351 n. 468; cf. n. 41 below, on Muratorian Canon 17.

33. Irenaeus, *Adv.Haer.* , 3, 11, 3; see also the testimony of the evangelists on the one God, 3, 9–11, 6.

34. Irenaeus, *Adv.Haer.* 3, 11, 7.

35. Irenaeus, *Adv.Haer.* 3, 11, 8 end: with Noah, Abraham, Moses and the fourth covenant, 'of the Gospel through our Lord Jesus Christ'.

36. Cf. *Adv.Haer.* 3, 1, 1; 11, 8.

37. The attributions of the four beings by the throne of God change often, see later Augustine, *De cons. evang.* 1, 6, 9 CSEL 33, ed. Weihrich, 1904, 9f.; see also U. Nilgen, *Lexikon der christlichen Ikonographie* I, 1968, 696ff. T. C. Skeat, *NT* 34, 1992, 194–9, conjectures with a convincing argument that Irenaeus' association of the four Gospels with the four beasts which he cites in the order given in Rev. 4.7 goes back to an earlier source which is orientated on the order in Ezek. 1.10. Transferred to the Gospels this would then produce the 'Western' order Matthew, John, Luke, which in turn refers back to a four-Gospel codex around 170. In my view this tradition could come from Asia Minor, where there was an interest in placing the late Gospel of John before the 'non-apostolic Gospels' (cf. above, 40, 109).

38. Irenaeus, A*dv.Haer.* 3, 11, 8: ὁ τῶν ἁπάντων τεχνίτης λόγος, ὁ

καθήμενος ἐπὶ τῶν Χερουβὶμ καὶ συνέχων τὰ πάντα, φανερωθεὶς τοῖς ἀνθρώποις ἔδωκεν ἡμῖν τετράμορφον τὸ εὐαγγέλιον. τὰ εὐαγγέλια οὖν τούτοις σύμφωνα, ἐν οἷς ἐγκαθέζεται Χριστός: the four beings which support God's throne and the four Gospels correspond: τετράμορφα γὰρ τὰ ζῷα, τετράμορφον καὶ τὸ εὐαγγέλιον.

39. 3.11.8: φανερωθεὶς (ὁ λόγος) ἔδωκεν ἡμῖν τετράμορφον τὸ εὐαγγέλιον, ἑνὶ δὲ Πνεύματι συνεχόμενον. In these manifold arguments for the number four from the form of the world, salvation history and the four beings around the throne of God we must not overlook the fact that for his main opponents, the disciples of Valentinus, the 'fourness' (τετράς, τετρακτύς, *quaternatio*) was a fundamental ontological entity, as already with the Pythagoreans, against which he constantly writes polemic. On this see the Irenaeus index by B. Reynders, CSCO 142 (Subsidia), Vol. II, 265f., s.v. *quaternatio* = τετράς, τετρακτύς. He therefore avoids applying this term to the Gospels. See below n. 47.

40. O. Cullmann, 'Die Pluralität der Evangelien als theologisches Problem im Altertum', in *Vorträge und Aufsätze Tübingen 1925–1962*, ed. K. Fröhlich, Tübingen 1966, 548–5: 562ff. Against this see rightly Stanton, 'Gospel' (n. 29), 319f.

41. Muratorian Canon lines 16–20, see E. Preuschen, *Analecta. II. Zur Kanonsgeschichte*, Bern [2]1990, 28; translation by H. Merkel, 'Pluralität' (n. 97), 10ff.: 'though also in the individual Gospel writings different beginnings [with corresponding tendencies or basic notions, see Merkel, n. 6] may be taught, that is not important for the faith of the believers, for to them the one and guiding Spirit has been made known in all (*licet varia singulis evangeliorum libris principia doceantur nihil tamen differt credendium fidei cum uno ac principali spiritu declarata sint in omnibus omnia*); cf. n. 32 above. For more details on the Muratorian Canon see Stanton, 'Gospel' (n. 29), 318, 322–25 and Heckel, *Evangelium* (n. 12), 340–2, who with good arguments defend the early dating against the late dating in the fourth century argued for by G. M. Hahnemann, *The Muratorian Fragment and the Development of the Canon*, Oxford 1992 and A. C. Sundberg, *HTR* 66, 1973, 1–41; see also already the review by E. Ferguson, *JTS* NS 44, 1993, 694–7. The Muratorian Canon does not so much have the character of the later canonical lists as that of the earlier Gospel prologues or the early church 'library lists' on which Irenaeus' information about the four Gospels is also based. One is also reminded of the brief 'historical' information in Clement's *Hypotyposes*. I regard the text as being later than Irenaeus; in favour of this is, among other things, its critical but historically well-informed judgment on Hermas which in the second century was still very much treasured, as Clement of Alexandria shows. Numerous

details point to an origin in the West, thus the reference to Bishop Pius, the brother of Hermas, the absence of the letter to the Hebrews, which was problematical in the West, the indication that Luke omits the martyrdom of Peter and Paul's journey to Spain (37–38) and the positive emphasis on the letter to the Romans with Christ as the *principium scripturarum* (44f.). The extended description of the origin and importance of John could be directed against Gaius and the Roman Alogoi. That Basilides is made to come from Asia Minor and be 'founder of the Kataphrygians' (84f.) indicates a certain distance in space and time. I still think that the attribution to Hippolytus (or his circle) in J. B. Lightfoot, *The Apostolic Fathers I, 2 Clement of Rome*, reprint of the 1890 edition, Hildesheim and New York 1973, 405–3, and his attempt at a retro-translation in metre into Greek are worth considering. It would fit the circle around the eccentric Hippolytus. The problem is that the abominably bad translation into Latin has completely mutilated the text. For this question see also Campenhausen, *Bible* (n. 29), 254; B. M. Metzger, *The Canon of the New Testament*, Oxford 1987, 191–201, and above all the thorough and comprehensive study by P. Henne, 'La Datation de Canon Muratori', *RB* 100, 1993, 54–75.

42. For Marcion see above, 31–33 and n. 151. He regarded his Gospel of Luke as the one that Paul describes in Rom. 2.16 as his Gospel: κατὰ τὸ εὐαγγέλιον μου διὰ Ἰησοῦ Χριστοῦ.

43. Irenaeus resolutely rejects Tatian, although he is a disciple of Justin, because of his later ascetic encratism and his dualistic tendencies, see 1, 28, 1 and 3, 23, 8. It remains unclear whether he already knew the Diatessaron. It is mentioned for the first time only by Eusebius.

44. Cf. 3, 11, 9, the polemic against those who with the Fourth Gospel at the same time also reject the promise of the Paraclete (i.e. against Gaius and his followers) and immediately after that the attack on the Valentinian Gospel of Truth.

45. *Comm. in Joh* 5, 5 (MPG 14, 193D); cf. 10, 3 (MPG 14, 312B).

46. *HE* 3, 25, 1: τὴν ἁγίαν τῶν εὐαγγελίων τετρακύν.

47. He had already previously reported at greater length about the first three Gospels (3, 24, 5–15) and in so doing presented his theory of the Gospels. In this context he uses the Greek word τετρακτύς, which already among the Pythagoreans and the Valentinians expressed the divine basic number of being, without taking offence at it, as does Irenaeus, who deliberately avoids it for the Gospels. Further examples in G. W. H. Lampe, *A Patristic Greek Lexicon*, Oxford 1987, 1390. See above n. 39.

48. Eusebius, *HE* 6, 12, 2–6. According to Jerome, the predecessor of

Serapion, the apologist and bishop Theophilus, had already composed something like a Gospel harmony; he also already quotes the Gospel of John, see nn. 229 and 521 below.

49. ψευδεπίγραφα: the rare word appears here for the first time in Christian literature.

50. For the Gospel of Peter see M.G.Mara, *Évangile de Pierre*, SC 201, 1973; *NTApoc* I, 216–27. The fragment from the passion and resurrection narrative, a parchment manuscript from the eighth/ninth century, was found in the tomb of a monk in Akhmim in Upper Egypt. Because of the Johannine references Mara, 215–18, conjectures that it was composed in Asia Minor in the middle of the second century. For this see now Heckel, *Evangelium* (n. 12), 288–300. For the wrong historical dating see the fantastic claims by J. D. Crossan, *The Cross that Spoke*, San Francisco 1988 (see e.g the Index, 435f.). The fragment POx 2949 published by D. Lührmann, 'EvPt 3–5 in einer Handschrift des 2./3. Jahrhunderts', *ZNW* 72, 1981, 216–26, only partially corresponds with the Akhmim version. The Akhmim text contains an altered text. However, I very much doubt whether Lührmann's reconstruction of POx 4009, *NT* 35, 1993, 390–410, comes from the Gospel of Peter. His reference to II Clem. 5.2–4 is also more than questionable. Far less may the new text resembling a Coptic Gospel which has been translated by H. M. Schenke, 'Das sogenannte "Unbekannte Berliner Evangelium"', *Zeitschrift für antikes Christentum*, 1998, 199–213, which presupposes all four Gospels, be identified with the Gospel of Peter. See also the truly miraculous multiplication of the sources in Crossan, *Jesus* (n. 22), 427–9, including the 'Cross Gospel', 'now embedded in the Gospel of Peter'. It is said to have been composed around AD 50 in Sepphoris in Galilee. One needs this many new sensational views to become a successful author of Jesus literature. Cf. H. Koester, *Ancient Christian Gospels. Their History and Development*, London 1991, 220–40, who not only maintains the complete independence of the Gospel of Peter from the four Gospels but thinks that it contains quite ancient fragments which 'were employed' by Mark and Matthew 'in a different context'. In reality, the Gospel of Peter offers free novellistic elaborations of an earlier Gospel tradition from the collection of the four Gospels.

51. For the Irenaeus papyrus, POx 405, end of the second and beginning of the third century BC. It was discovered around 250 miles south of Alexandria. For this see A. Rousseau and L. Doutreleau, *Irenée de Lyon. Contre les héresies* III, 1, SC 210, 1974, 126–31. Clement mentions Irenaeus by name in his work 'On the Pasch'; see Eusebius, *HE* 6, 13, 9. He already quotes Irenaeus' work in 1, 148 (= *Haer.* 3,

21, 2 = Eusebius, *HE* 5, 8, 11–15); 7, 108, 2f. = *Haer.* 5, 8, 2; cf. *Protr.* 1, 42 = *Haer.* 4, 7, 2, etc. For Tertullian see *Adv. Val.* 5, 1: '*Irenaeus omnium doctrinarum doctissimus explorator*'; cf. 7, 3ff.

52. Heckel, *Evangelium* (n. 12), 350 n. 463: Irenaeus, *adv.Haer.* 1, 20, 2; 2, 24, 3 (cf. II Clem. 8.5) and also the chiliastic Papias logion 5, 33, 3f. Similarly, 5, 36, 2 seems to go back to the tradition of the presbyter in Asia Minor and could possibly likewise come from Papias, see 5, 36, 1 end and 5, 33, 4. That means that Irenaeus is not quoting any 'apocryphal' Gospels, but 'orthodox' tradition from Asia Minor deriving from the 'presbyters' and here above all from the work of Papias. See also the tradition on the age of Jesus, *Adv.Haer.* 2, 22, 3–5. All these traditions could have the character of 'interpretations' of sayings of the Lord.

53. *The Didascalia Apostolorum in Syriac*, CSCO 402 and 408, translated by A. Vööbus, I/II, 1979, 191 n. 118, 199 nn. 224–6: Gospel of Peter; cf. also 157 n. 18 on the role of the women who followed Jesus as 'deaconesses' and the logion 110 n.123, the agraphon, which also appears in Clement of Alexandria, *Strom.* I, 177, 2: 'Be trusted money-changers.' Cf. also Vööbus' introduction to divergent Gospel traditions (I, 52*-55*).

54. Ibid., I, 38.

55. See H. Kutter, *Clemens Alexandrinus und das Neue Testament*, Giessen 1897; J. Ruwet SJ, 'Clément d'Alexandrie: Canon des écritures et apocryphes', Biblica 29, 1948, 77–99, 240–68, 391–408 (for the apocrypha see 396–401); E. Molland, *The Conception of the Gospel in the Alexandrian Theology*, SNVAO. HF 1938, 2, 14–16; H. v. Campenhausen, *Formation* (n. 29), 293–307; M. Mees, *Die Zitate aus dem Neuen Testament bei Clemens von Alexandrien*, Bari 1970, with a list of the 203 quotations from Matthew in Clement, 17 from Mark, 90 from Luke, 93 from John and a reference to 'apparent quotations' from Matthew, Luke and John, which according to Mees are to be attributed to 'influences from homiletics, catechetics and liturgy' (ibid., 190ff.); A. Mehat, *TRE* 8, 1981, 101–113: 105f.

56. Campenhausen, *Formation* (n. 29), 293.

57. Mehat, *TRE* 8 (n. 55), 337.

58. Ibid.

59. Kutter, *Clemens* (n. 55), 31–45: 42.

60. Ibid., 44: 'His way of not looking at scripture but simply applying it hastily (however, this criticism is only partially correct, MH), suggests an authority of scripture which is already established before Clement considers it.'

61. Quoted in Eusebius, *HE* 6, 14, 5–7. By the 'elder' he may have meant above all his teacher Pantaenus. Cf. also the report on Mark in

Eusebius, *HE* 2, 15, 1f. For Mark in Rome and the order of the Gospels in Irenaeus see above, 34–38.

62. See above, 26ff.

63. Clement, *Strom.* 1, 147, 5 (GCS [Stählin] 2, 91, 27f.): ἐν δὲ τῷ κατὰ Ματθαῖον εὐαγγελίῳ, there follows the genealogy of Jesus in Matt. 1.1–16; *Strom* 1, 145, 2 (GCS 2, 90, 6): ἐν τῷ εὐαγγελίῳ τῷ κατὰ Λουκᾶν γέγραπται οὕτως there follows the date in Luke 3.1f.; *Paed.* 1, 38, 2 (GCS 1, 112, 29): ὁ κύριος ἐν τῷ κατὰ 'Ιωάννην εὐαγγελίῳ [λέγει]; 1, 80, 1 (GCS 1, 136, 31f.): κἂν τῷ εὐαγγελίῳ διὰ 'Ιωάννου [λέγει].

64. Clement, *Quis dives* 5, 1 (GCS 3, 163, 13): ταῦτα μὲν ἐν τῷ κατὰ Μᾶρκον εὐαγγελίῳ γέγραπται.

65. Ibid.: τὴν αὐτὴν τῆς γνώμης συμφωνίαν.

66. Ibid.: cf. Matt. 19.16–30; Luke 18.18–30.

67. Clement, *Strom.* 3, 92 and 3, 93, 1 (GCS 2, 238, 27f.): ἐν τοῖς παραδεδομένοις ἡμῖν τέτταρσιν εὐαγγελίοις οὐκ ἔχομεν τὸ ῥητόν, ἀλλ' ἐν τῷ κατ' Αἰγυπτίους.

68. Clement, *Strom.* 3, 45, 4 (GCS 2, 217, 5ff.): here first of all quoted anonymously; 3, 63, 1 (GCS 2, 225, 3f.): for the first time, still uncertainly, with title: φέρεται δέ, οἶμαι, ἐν τῷ κατ' Αἰγυπτίους εὐαγγελίῳ. There follows an extended exposition: Salome is right in her question (64, 1) and the Lord did not lie in his answer (63.3). For the Gospel of the Egyptians see E. Preuschen, *Antilegomena*, Giessen 1905, 1–3; A. Resch, *Agrapha*, ²1906, reprinted Darmstadt 1967, 252–57, nos 34–38, cf. no.37 on the title; Hippolytus, *Refut.* 5, 7, 9 for the Naassenes: ἐν τῷ ἐπιγραφομένων κατ' Αἰγυπτίους εὐαγγελίῳ. See also *NTApoc* 1, 209–15.

69. Clement, *Strom.* 2, 45, 4f. (GCS 2, 137, 1f.): ὡς Πλάτων ἐν Θεαιτήτῳ λέγει, καὶ Ματθίας ἐν ταῖς Παραδόσεσι . . . ἢ κἂν τῷ καθ' 'Εβραίους εὐαγγελίῳ . . . For the Matthias traditions see *NTApoc* I, 382–5; for the Gospel of the Hebrews, 172–8.

70. Clement, *Strom.* 5, 96, 2–4 (GCS 2, 389). The second quotation touches *inter alia* on Gospel of Thomas 2 = POx 654 see *NTApoc* I, 117, 4a/b and 98.

71. Clement, *Strom.* 5, 63, 7 (GCS 2, 368, 26ff.): παρήγγειλεν ὁ κύριος ἔν τινι εὐαγγελίῳ; for this see A. Resch, *Agrapha*, ²1906, 108f.: Agraphon 84.

72. Clement, *Strom.* 4, 41, 2 (GCS 2, 266, 25f.): ἢ ὥς τινες τῶν μετατιθέντων τὰ εὐαγγέλια; cf. also 7, 96, 3f. (GCS 3, 68, 16f.): 'The truth will not be found by changing the meaning [of the scriptural passages].'

73. Clement, *Strom.* 3, 26, 3 (GCS 2, 208, 7ff.); 7, 82, 1 (GCS 3, 58, 20ff.); *NTApoc* I, 306.

74. Hippolytus, *Refut.* 7, 20, 1, cf. 20, 5.

75. Clement, *Strom* 7, 108, 1 (GCS 3, 76, 20ff.); *NTApoc* I, 383.

76. See the index in O. Stählin, *Clemens Alexandrinus* IV, 1, ²1980, 26, where 28 texts included in Resch, *Agrapha* (n. 68), are listed, and also the index in Resch, 419. Here I shall limit myself to texts in which Clement named the author or a Gospel. However, by comparison with the constant quotations and allusions from the four Gospels, this number is small. Sometimes it is unclear whether he is quoting an oral tradition or has a primitive Christian source. Thus *Strom.* 7, 93, 7 (GCS 2, 66, 22ff.) on the virginity of Mary after her birth, which could refer to *Protevangelium of James 19* (38–40).

77. From *Hypotyposes*, Book 7, according to Eusebius, *HE* 2, 1, 4; see von Campenhausen, *Formation* (n. 29), 301 n. 189.

78. See Molland, *Conception* (n. 55), 14–16.

79. See the index in Stählin, GCS 4, 2, 429ff., on εὐαγγέλιον and ibid., 534 on κύριος.

80. Clement, *Strom.* 3, 8, 5 (GCS 2, 199, 17f.); almost synonymously 3, 76, 1 (GCS 2, 230, 1f.): here there is also ἀπόστολος followed by the formula ἐν τῷ εὐαγγελίῳ γεγραμμένον; cf. 3, 70, 3 (GCS 2, 228, 3); 4, 91, 1 (GCS 2, 288, 10); 6, 88, 5 (GCS 2, 476, 10): the connection (συμφωνία) of law, prophet and apostle with the Gospel.

81. This applies even more than in the case of the Gospel tradition to Old Testament pseudepigrapha and apocryphal apostolic writings like the Kerygma Petri, the apocalypses of Peter, Zephaniah and Elijah, Hermas, the Didache, I Clement, Barnabas, etc. See the index in Stählin IV, 1 (n. 79).

82. One need only think of the topic of Jesus and the Essenes from the Enlightenment to the discoveries of Qumran or the controversies over the Turin shroud. The formation of legends is part of historical reality.

83. Justin, *Dialogue* 103, 8. Heckel, *Evangelium* (n. 12), 92, puts forward the view that in this formulation Justin is dependent on the prologue of Luke and thinks that Luke 1.3 refers the παρηκολουθηκότι ἄνωθεν πᾶσιν . . . to all the apostles. But we should not impute such simplicity to Justin, as if he did not know the many meanings of this verb. In Justin the formulation is a general one which is connected with Papias' terminology: the apostles had disciples who followed them. Around 150 it was known from the Acts of the Apostles that Luke was a disciple of the apostle Paul. Παρακολουθεῖν is one of Justin's favourite words: he uses it nine times in all in various contexts and forms, see also Arndt/Gingrich/Bauer, *Lexicon*, ad loc. συντάσσειν (as opposed to the Lukan ἀνατάσσειν) is another of Justin's favourite words. See also above, 65ff., for the terminology of

Papias, who is around a generation earlier.

84. Stanton, *Gospel* (n. 29), 330, referring to an 1867 edition of the Muratorian Canon by S. Tregelles. 'Radical criticism' all too easily overlooks this fact.

85. For Mark see *Dialogue* 106, 3, where he speaks of the 'Reminiscences of Peter' and refers to Mark 3.16f.; i. e. he knows that Mark goes back to a Petrine tradition: see C.-J. Thornton, 'Justin und das Markusevangelium', *ZNW* 84, 1993, 93–100; M. Hengel, *Die Johanneische Frage*, WUNT 67, 1993, 67 = *The Johannine Question*, London and Philadelphia 1989. 13f. (the German edition is a much expanded version of the English, so in what follows, there are references to the German only where there is no equivalent in the English translation); id., *Studies in Mark* (n. 10), 68f., 75f. In *Dial.* 81, 4 he mentions the 'apostle' John as author of the Apocalypse. For Justin and the Gospels see the still fundamental reflections by Zahn, *Kanon* (n. 12), I, 463–560; A. J. Bellinzoni, *The Sayings of Jesus in the Writings of Justinus Martyr*, NT.S 17, 1967 rightly and firmly rejects the claim that Justin uses non-canonical Gospels (139f.). See now also Heckel, *Evangelium* (n. 12), 310–29. On 326f. he lists the few agrapha and 'apocryphal motifs' and comes to the conclusion: 'Therefore it is not very probable that Justin used a further apocryphal "Gospel" from which he could draw such information.'

86. Hengel, *Johanneische Frage* (n. 85), 26f. = *Johannine Question*, 5; see also the index under Gnosis; von Campenhausen, *Formation* (n. 29), 234–40: 238. For Irenaeus see 3, 11, 9.

87. Irenaeus, *Adv.Haer.* 3, 2, 1: '. . . *in accusationem convertuntur ipsarum scripturarum, quasi non recte habeant neque sint ex auctoritate, et quia varie sint dictae, et quia non possit ex his inveniri veritas ab his quis nesciant traditiones*'. For the *traditio, quae est ab apostolis* see 3, 2, 2.

88. Irenaeus, *Adv.Haer.* 3, 11, 7.

89. Hengel, *Johanneische Frage* (n. 85), 28 n. 48, cf. 49f. = *The Johannine Question*, 142 n. 23. For his knowledge of the Gospels see now Heckel, *Evangelium* (n. 12), 336–9: 'Celsus argues against a collection of Gospels which he finds among the Christians.' For the polemic against the Christian apologies see 2, 44: ἀτόπους ἀπολογίας εὑρίσκοντες.

90. Origen, *Contra Celsum* 2, 27. For Celsus and the New Testament see G. Rinaldi, *Biblia Gentium*, Rome 1989, 55–64: 63f., 702ff., 729ff.; H. Merkel, *Die Widersprüche zwischen den Evangelien*, WUNT 13, Tübingen 1971, 8–13.

91. The charge of 'falsification' of the original message or the 'scriptures' was raised in early Christian polemic in many ways. Thus from Justin

onwards in respect of the LXX against the Jews, in the case of
Marcion against the original apostles, in the case of Irenaeus,
Tertullian and Clement against Marcion and the real Gnostics. On
this see A. Bludau, *Die Schriftfälschungen der Häretiker*, NTA XI, 5,
Münster 1925, and on the other side B. Ehrman, *The Orthodox
Corruption of Scripture. The Effect of Early Christological
Controversies on the Text of the New Testament*, New York and
Oxford 1993.

92. See the fundamental work by Merkel, *Widersprüche* (n. 90).
93. 2, 12, 29: *omnem . . . falsitatem abesse ab evangelistis decet*. Cf.
   above, 4f., n. 15.
94. Merkel, *Widersprüche* (n. 90), 259–61; see D. Wünsch, 'Evangelienharmonien', *TRE* 10, 1982, 631–5. Osiander's Gospel Harmony
   appeared in 1537 in Basel under the title *Harmoniae evangelicae
   libri IV graece et latine*. It found numerous revisers and imitators.
   The term 'Gospel harmony' probably comes from him (quotations
   in Wünsch, 632).
95. Wünsch, *Evangelienharmonien* (n. 94), 632.
96. See the extensive harmonizing accounts of the writing of the Gospels
   in Eusebius, *HE*, 3, 24.
97. See Merkel, *Widersprüche* (n. 90), and id., *Die Pluralität der
   Evangelien als theologisches und exegetisches Problem in der Alten
   Kirche*, TC 3, 1978.
98. Origen, *Comm. in Joh.* 10, 14 (SC 157, 1920, II, 390), speaks of the
   κατὰ τὴν ἱστορίαν ἀσυμφωνία of the four Gospels, which he seeks to
   overcome through spiritual, i.e. allegorical, interpretation.
99. See e.g. the attempt by the learned Julius Africanus, later librarian of
   the emperor Alexander Severus, to reconcile the genealogies of Jesus
   in *Ep.ad Aristidem*; text and translation in Merkel, *Pluralität* (n.
   97), 50ff. (cf. Eusebius, *HE* 1, 7). Julius Africanus is opposing a
   widespread theological construction which wanted to see in the contradictory genealogies a reference to the kingly and priestly office of
   Christ, which scorned the historical truth and gave the impression
   that 'the evangelists had lied and not offered the truth, but (only) a
   supposed praise' (51). However, his 'historical solution' by means of
   a levirate marriage is no less artificial. Tatian omitted the genealogies from the Diatessaron because they could not be reconciled, see
   below, 223.
100. Eusebius, *HE* 4, 29, 6: τὸ διὰ τεσσάρων τοῦτο προσωνόμασεν.
   Epiphanius (*Pan* 46, 1, 8f.) and Theodoret of Cyrrhus (MPG 83,
   372) call it εὐαγγέλιον, see W.L.Petersen, *Tatian's Diatessaron. Its
   Creation, Dissemination, Significance and History of Scholarship*,
   SVigChr 25, 1994, 39–42. In my view the designation might go back

to the author himself. See now with good observations, C. D. Allert, 'The State of the New Testament Canon in the Second Century', *Bulletin for Biblical Research* 9, 1999, 1–18.

101. He is already mentioned as an Encratite by Irenaeus, *Adv.Haer.* 3, 23, 8; 1, 28, 1. After the martyrdom of Justin he separated from the church and founded his own school, similar to the school of Valentinus. Irenaeus probably knows him only from hearsay, but his bitterness against his 'apostasy' can still clearly be detected. Clement, *Strom.* 3, 92, associates him with the Encratite Julius Cassian (see above, n. 66) and counts him in the school of Valentinus. On the other hand he cites with approval his apologetic *Oratio ad Graecos,* in which Tatian depicts 'Hebrew philosophy' as the earliest wisdom.

102. See Hengel, *Johanneische Frage* (n. 85), 41–5.

103. See now Petersen, *Diatessaron* (n. 100).

104. Cf. Petersen, *Diatessaron* (n. 100), 76–83, 378f., and Allert, 'Canon' (n. 100), 4–6. For the destruction of more than 200 Diatessaron manuscripts by Bishop Theodoret of Cyrrhus (423–457) see Petersen, 41ff.; B. M. Metzger, *The Early Versions of the New Testament,* Oxford 1977, 10–36. For the Encratite changes and interpolations see 33–6. However, he did not use an apocryphal Gospel: 'On the whole . . . the amount of extra-canonical material that seems to have been present in Tatian's Diatessaron hardly justifies the opinion . . . that Tatian made extensive use of a fifth apocryphal Gospel', cf. 28f. The 'Five-Gospel' enthusiasm is a modern invention. Cf. below n. 107 on the designation *diapente* in Victor of Capua.

105. See L. Leloir, *Ephrem de Nisibe. Commentaire de l'Evangile concordant ou Diatessaron, traduit de syriaque et d'Arménien. Introduction, traduction et notes,* SC 121, 1966.

106. The most important Greek fragment is a parchment scroll from Dura Europos; see Aland, *Synopsis,* [15]1996, 493. It shows the scrupulous work of Tatian, who put the text of all four Gospels together again like a mosaic. As the Roman fortress at Dura Europos on the Euphrates was destroyed by the Persians in the winter of 256/7 and the fragment was found near a Christian house church founded between 222 and 235, the parchment fragment seems to come from a scroll from the first decades of the third century; see Petersen (n. 100), 196–203. The use of a parchment *scroll* could derive from Jewish-Christian influence.

107. Thus between 541 and 546 Bishop Victor of Capua made a similar harmony on the basis of the Old Latin translation of the Diatessaron and the Vulgate text. This is contained in the Codex Fuldensis. He

gave it the designation *diapente* because it was based on the Diatessaron and the four Gospels.

108. Justin, *Dial.* 88, 3; cf. Gospel of the Ebionites and Epiphanius, *Panarion* 30, 7f.; see Aland, *Synopsis*, 27; and the detailed evidence in Petersen (n. 106), 14–21.

109. E.g. Justin, *Dial.* 35, 36; 47, 5 and 61, 4 = John 3, 3.5, cf. Bellinzoni, *Sayings* (n. 85), 101f., 130–8. See already W. Bousset, *Die Evangelienzitate Justins des Märtyrers in ihrem Wert für die Evangelienkritik*, Göttingen 1891, and the detailed review by E. Schürer, *ThLZ* 1891, 62–67; at length, W. D. Köhler, *Die Rezeption des Matthäusevangeliums in der Zeit vor Irenäus*, WUNT II/24, Tübingen 1987, 161–264, esp. 254: Justin uses no other written sources for the Gospel material which he includes than the canonical Gospels (256). See now Heckel, *Evangelium* (n. 12). 315ff., for Justin's free way of dealing with New Testament traditions, in a critical discussion of Bellinzoni, 324ff. He says of Justin's way of harmonizing: 'The very way in which he combines material from Matthew and Luke shows how his thought is orientated on issues' (325). For the 'apocryphal' Jesus tradition see 325f. and above, n. 85.

110. See G. Zuntz, *Lukian von Antiochien und der Text der Evangelien*, AHAW.PH 1995, 2, 29–36.

111. W. F. Wisselink, *Assimilation as a Criterium for the Establishment of the Text. A Comparative Study of the Basis of Passages from Matthew, Mark and Luke*, Kampen 1989; Heckel, *Evangelium* (n. 12), 348ff. The harmonizing parallel influences begin early and presuppose a collection of four Gospels which is not yet fixed in one codex. They are connected above all with the liturgical use of the different texts.

112. Thus alongside Mark 16.9–21 see the pericope about the woman taken in adultery in John 7.53–8.11, which is absent from the old tradition and is also put elsewhere by individual late witnesses to the text, e.g. all by itself in Luke after 21.38 or 24.53; the addition in the Old Latin translation at the baptism of Jesus in Matt. 3.15 (a: fourth century; [g¹], having probably found its way in from the Diatessaron, cf. already Justin, *Dial.* 88, 3); the logion Luke 6.4 D; also the enigmatic 'Western non-interpolations' in Luke, which perhaps derive from the influence of Marcion's purged text of the Gospels.

113. Mark 16.9–21, the addition 16.8b and the Freer-Logion in 16.14.

114. Hengel, *Johanneische Frage* (n. 85), 57; K. Aland, *Neutestamentliche Entwürfe*, ThB 63, 1979, 246–82, on the different endings to Mark and the text-critical problem; also Heckel, *Evangelium* (n.

12), 281–6: 'The author takes over almost all motifs of canonical tradition' (283). Heckel rightly sees in this early expansion an indication that the collection of four Gospels came into being before Marcion. See now also the thorough University of Chicago dissertation of J. A. Kelhoffer, *The Authentication of Missionaries and their Message in the Longer Ending of Mark/Mark 16.9–20*, WUNT II/112, 2000.

115. See D. A. Koch, *Die Schrift als Zeuge des Evangeliums. Untersuchungen zur Verwendung und zum Verständnis der Schrift bei Paulus*, BHTh 69, 1986, 186: 'Of 93 different texts which Paul cites in his letters, 52 have been altered by Paul, 37 texts have remained unchanged and in 4 cases the origin of the textual deviation cannot be assessed with certainty.' That also applies to the quotations in Justin, Irenaeus and Clement of Alexandria. Only Justin in the *Dialogue with Trypho* must work rather more carefully with the LXX text, but even he does not always do this (see below, n. 120).

116. See Hengel, 'Septuaginta' (n. 1), 182–284. See above, p. 1. The collection of articles by E. Tov, *The Greek and the Hebrew Bible. Collected Essays on the Septuagint*, VT.S 72, 1999, offers important insights.

117. See R. Harris, *Testimonies*, I and II, Cambridge 1919 and 1920; P. Prigent, *Les testimonia dans le Christianisme primitif. L'épître de Barnabe I–XVI et ses sources*, Paris 1961; O. Skarsaune, *The Proof from Prophecy. A Study in Justin Martyr's Proof-Text Tradition . . .*, NT.S 56, Leiden 1987. According to the letter to Onesimus (Eusebius, *HE* 4, 26, 13), Melito composed 'extracts from the Law and the Prophets about our redeemer and our whole faith'. Extracts from the Prophets have also been handed down by Clement of Alexandria (GCS 2.A., 3, 136–155).

118. For the problem see H. Y. Gamble, *Books and Readers in the Early Church*, New Haven 1995, 1–41: *Literacy and Literary Culture in Early Christianity*, which in turn takes up the work of William Harris, *Ancient Literacy*, Cambridge, Mass. 1989. However, I believe that Gamble underestimates somewhat the knowledge of reading in the communities. This was probably above the average among the people and will have been at a similar level to that in Jewish communities. For Jews and Christians knowledge of the 'Holy Scriptures' was equally important in order to maintain their identity in a hostile world. After all, it was necessary to be able to appeal to the written word in the face of pagan pressure. Cf. the reference to reading the scripture, study and teaching in I Tim. 4.13; II Tim. 3.15f. and the towering significance of the argumentation in

Hebrews, 1 Clement, Barnabas and later in Justin based on the scriptures and – at a 'higher philosophical level' – in Clement of Alexandria. Even in the third century, the Syrian Didascalia still requires reading to be limited entirely to the biblical writings, and strictly rejects the pagan writings (CSCO 402, 1979, translated A. Vööbus, I, 14): 'However, avoid all books of the heathen, because you have to do with strange sayings or laws or prophecies, those which also turn away the young from the faith . . . For what is lacking for you is the word of God, that you should cast yourselves upon these tales of the heathen? If you wish to read narratives or stories, you have the Book of Kings; but if wise men and philosophers, you have the prophets. And if you desire songs, you have the Psalms of David . . . Abstain completely therefore from strange [writings] those which are contrary [to these].' For the Didascalia see above n. 53; J. J. C. Cox, 'Prolegomena to a Study of the Dominical *Logoi* as cited in the *Didascalia Apostolorum*', in *Andrews University Seminary Studies* 13, 1975, 23–9, 249–59; id., 'Note on the Title of the *Didascalia Apostolorum*', in *Andrews University Seminary Studies* 13, 1975, 30–3; further on the Latin versions see E. Tidner, *Didascaliae apostolorum canonum ecclesiasticorum traditionis apostolicae versiones Latinae*, Texte und Untersuchungen zur Geschichte der altchristlichen Literatur 75, Berlin 1963.

119. For its dating see Hengel, *Johanneische Frage* (n. 85), 59ff.

120. Skarsaune, *Proof* (n. 117); Hengel, 'Die Septuaginta als von den Christen beanspruchte Schriftensammlung bei Justin und den Vätern vor Origenes', in *Jews and Christians. The Partings of the Ways AD 60–135*, WUNT 66, Tübingen 1992, 39–84: 51–67 = *Judaica, Hellenistica et Christiana, Kleine Schriften* II, WUNT 109, 1998, 335–80.

121. Its self-confidence is already evident in Rom. 16.22, cf. I Peter 5.12; Hengel, *Evangelienüberschriften* (n. 10), 43ff.

122. See the list in Nestle/Aland [27], 684–9, and the new list of papyri in *Bericht der Hermann-Kunst-Stiftung zur Förderung der neutestamentlichen Textforschung für die Jahre 1995–1998*, 14f.: P 103, second/third century: Matthew; P 104, second century: Matthew; P 101, third century: Matthew; P 106–109, third century: John; P 111, third century: Luke. See now in more detail J. K. Elliott, 'Six New Papyri of Matthew's Gospel', *NT* 41, 1999, 105–7, and 'Five New Papyri of the New Testament', ibid., 205–13. The first series of six new papyri of Matthew, five of them from the second and third centuries, have been published by J. D. Thomas, *POx* LXIV, 1997, 1–11, nos 4401–4 (= P 101–104); 4405 (= an additional fragment of a codex page from P 77); 4406 (= P 105) was used as an amulet

from the fifth/sixth century. P 104 is dated to the second century, P 104 and P 77 to the late second or early third century. All come from codices. The four new John papyri from the beginning or the middle of the third century have been edited by W. E. H. Cockle, *POx* LXV, 1998, 10–20, nos. 4445–8 (= P 106–109). Interesting features of the large Fragment 4445, 20 (P 106) = John 1.34 are the probable reading [ἐ]κλεκ[τὸς τοῦ θεοῦ], which here reinforces the originality of this *lectio difficilior,* and Fragment 4448 (P 109), from John 21.18–20, 23–25, the end of the Gospel, which together with Tertullian, *De anima* 50, 5, suggests that this chapter belonged to the form of the Gospel as originally disseminated. See also the edition of all twenty-three Johannine papyri between P 2 and P 95 by W. S. Elliott and D. C. Parker, *The New Testament in Greek* IV. *The Gospel according to St John*, NTTS 20, Leiden etc. 1995, with eleven papyri from the second to the end of the third century or the beginning of the fourth. This number has increased to sixteen as a result of the new finds.

123. See e.g. P 4 Luke; P 5 John; P 45 Matthew-Acts; P 64, 67, 4, Matthew and Luke (second century); P 66 John; P 70 (about 200) Matthew; P 75 Luke/John.

124. K. Aland, *Studien zur Überlieferung des Neuen Testaments und seines Textes*, ANT 2, 1967, 35–57.

125. For the composition of the Gospel of Mark, the minor agreements and the newer Deutero-Mark hypotheses see the numerous studies of A. Fuchs, beginning with his thesis *Sprachliche Untersuchungen in Matthäus und Lukas. Ein Beitrag zur Quellenkritik*, Rome 1971, AnBib 1971, and now A. Ennulat, *Die 'Minor Agreements'*, WUNT II/62, 1994. See 444 for a presentation of the investigations of A. Fuchs. See also Hengel, *Mark* (n. 10), 1–30. The problem of the minor agreements disappears if one assumes that Matthew used Luke, which seems to me to be fairly certain: see above, 169ff.

126. For Codex D and the so-called 'Western' text see K. and B. Aland, *Der Text des Neuen Testaments*, ²1989, 60f., 63f., 68f., 118f., see also Index, 370; for Luke see J. A. Fitzmyer, *The Gospel according to Luke I–IX*, AB 28, 1981, 128–33 (bibliography: see there especially the investigations by A. F. J. Klijn); for Acts see C. K. Barrett (n. 28), 2–30: 5f., 21–9. The Codex Bezae text of Acts is certainly a secondary revision; by virtue of its tendency it fits admirably into the middle to second half of the second century.

127. This tendency can sometimes be found in Anglo-Saxon textual criticism, see Ehrman, *Corruption* (n. 91). Here I miss a clear definition of 'orthodox' or 'proto-orthodox'. From the later post-Nicene standpoint, all the christologies of the second century were 'hetero-

dox'. Of course there have always been tendentious alterations in the copying of New Testament texts, and the various groups have bandied accusations to this effect, but one hardly does justice to this complex situation with the phrase 'orthodox corruption'. Did not the influence of Marcion's text have a 'corrupting' effect on the church's textual tradition (see below)? Because later they almost all seemed more or less 'heterodox', in complete contrast to the New Testament as a rule the pre-Nicene fathers have been preserved almost by chance in very few manuscripts, sometimes only in one. D. C. Parker, *The Living Text of the Gospels*, Cambridge 1997, goes in the same direction as Ehrman and picks out a few inconspicuous examples from the wealth of the textual tradition. It was not so much deliberate 'falsification of the text' as the negligence of many copyists and their tendency to harmonize which led the text to 'run wild', see J. R. Roys, 'Scribal Tendencies in the Transmission of the Text of the New Testament', in *The Text of the New Testament in Contemporary Research. A Volume in Honor of Bruce M. Metzger*, ed. B. D. Ehrman and M. W. Holmes, Grand Rapids 1995, 239–52, with a comparison of the misquotations of the most important Gospel papyri which, on the basis of the investigations of E. C. Colwell and E. W. Tune, show the considerable differences in quality between P 45 and P 46, which are full of mistakes, and P 66 and P 75, which are of comparatively high value. His conclusion is also worth noting: 'The papyri do not contribute many new readings that are tempting. What they do, is usually to provide additional, typically earlier, support for readings already known.'

128. K. and B. Aland, *Text* (n. 126), 284f.: twelve basic rules for textual criticism.

129. Ibid., 300 (English edition, 297).

130. Against E. J. Epp, 'The Multivalence of the Term "Original Text" in New Testament Textual Criticism', *HTR* 92, 1999, 245–81 (with bibliography), above all in connection with the various hypotheses put forward by H. Koester, especialy in id., *Gospels* (n. 50). A deterrent example of this 'method' is given by P. Sellew, 'Secret Mark and the History of Canonical Mark', in *The Future of Early Christianity. Essays in Honor of Helmut Koester*, Minneapolis 1991, 242–7. For criticism of these fantastic conjectures see Metzger, *Canon* (n. 41), 133 n. 41. For the 'Secret Gospel of Mark' see also below, n. 184. For criticism of Koester's conjectures see also Heckel, *Evangelium* (n. 12), 269–73.

131. A. von Harnack, *Marcion. Neue Studien zu Marcion*, reprinted Darmstadt 1960; he is followed by von Campenhausen, *Formation* (n. 29), 148ff. However, I cannot go with his still popular thesis:

'The idea and reality of a Christian Bible were created by Marcion,
and the church, which rejected his work, did not precede him here
but – from a formal point of view – followed his example.' Here a
complicated process is over-simplified. The collection of the Gospels
and apostolic letters was already 'in the making' before Marcion,
and even without him it would hardly have taken shape in another
form as we find it later in Irenaeus. See now, however, Heckel,
Evangelium (n. 12), 267–69. For Marcion and the canon generally
see Metzger, *Canon* (n. 41), 90–9; B. Aland, 'Marcion/Marcioniten',
TRE 22, 1992, 89–101; cf. Ulrich Schmid, *Marcion und sein
Apostolos*, ANT 25, 1995. The assumption which goes back to F. C.
Baur and is made by J. Knox, *Marcion and the New Testament. An
Essay in the Early History of the Canon*, Chicago 1942, that
Marcion used a 'Proto-Luke' which has been expanded by the
church for the purpose of anti-Marcionite polemic not only com-
pletely fails to recognize the historical context of the Third Gospel
but also comes to grief on its stylistic and theological unity.
Moreover there is no manuscript evidence for such a hypothesis.
Such a manipulation of the text would have had to find a record
around 150; moreover it would no longer really have been generally
recognized.

132. Hengel, *Johanneische Frage* (n. 85), 139, 155ff., 202.

133. See Hengel and Schwemer, *Paul* (n. 9), 6–11, 18–21. Presumably
Acts was written some years after the Gospel, see above, 99ff. The
title could be original, see below n. 103.

134. As a true Docetist he rejected the birth and youth of Jesus. In Christ
the good God himself appears as a preacher in Galilee, provided
with a pseudo-body, see von Harnack, *Marcion* (n. 131), 123ff. and
Tertullian, *De carne Christi*. By contrast the Marcionites still seem
later to have accepted the baptism of Jesus by John, ibid., 114, 174,
357.

135. Thus e.g. E. Hirsch, *Das Alte Testament und die Predigt des
Evangeliums*, Tübingen 1936, and the new edition of this along with
other of Hirsch's works on the Old Testament by Hans Martin
Müller, Tübingen 1986, see there, 129f., the rejection of Marcion's
dualism; however Hirsch puts forward the view 'that Old Testament
belief in God, although authentic religious concern and true knowledge about the divine mystery are alive in it, has been done away
as false faith and worship in faith in Jesus Christ'. Cf. 133: 'that we
must regard the Old Testament in principle as a document of universal religious history and that it is to be subjected formally to the
dialectic of the terms truth and untruth, revelation and human
vanity in the same sense as any other non-Christian religion'. See the

even more questionable remarks on 137. Cf. also the first articles in
E. Haenchen, *Die Bibel und Wir*, Tübingen 1968, 4ff., 26f., 50–72
(written in the year of the 'Reichspogromnacht', 1938), 88f. Here,
as in Hirsch, we still have the strange mixture of antisemitism and
modern 'progressive' theology.

136. Perhaps Melito of Sardes is a theological predecessor. But too little
of his work has been preserved. For the collection of the four
Gospels before Irenaeus see above, 50ff.

137. Irenaeus, *Adv.Haer.* 1, 27, 2: *secundum Lucam evangelium circum-
cidens; non evangelium, sed particulam evangelii tradens eis*; 3, 12,
12: *secundum Lucam . . . evangelium et epistolas Pauli decurtantes*;
cf. Tert., *Praescript. Haer.* 38: *machaera non stylo usus est*: Marcion
did not use the stylus but the knife.

138. Modern scholars have been particularly interested in Irenaeus as an
anti-Gnostic author; he has been neglected as the first interpreter of
the New Testament. But see now R. Noormann, *Irenäus als
Paulusinterpret*, WUNT II/66, Tübingen 1994. A dissertation about
Irenaeus as exegete of John by B. Mutschler is in preparation. See
also J. Hoh, *Die Lehre des hl. Irenäus über das Neue Testament*,
NTA VII, 4.5, Münster 1919; Campenhausen, *Formation* (n. 29),
182ff.

139. He quotes only I and II John, but probably saw the whole as a unity;
see Hengel, *Johanneische Frage* (n. 85), 19f., 101f., 151.

140. Irenaeus, *Adv.Haer.* 3, 11, 9; 4, 34, 1, etc. However, the singular is
still by far the most frequent. See above n. 79; for similar terminology in Clement of Alexandria see above, n. 79.

141. Irenaeus, *Adv.Haer.*3, 1, 1: *qui quidem et omnes pariter et singuli
eorum habentes Evangelium Dei.*

142. Ibid. See Eusebius, *HE* 5, 8, 2–4.

143. E. Schwartz, *Gesammelte Schriften* V, Berlin 1963, 175f., speaks of
'refined untruthfulness' in connection with Irenaeus and the
Johannine tradition, see Hengel, *Johanneische Frage* (n. 85), 13 n.
10 = *Johannine Question*, 137 n. 4.

144. C. J. Thornton, *Der Zeuge des Zeugen*, WUNT 56, Tübingen 1991,
10–54. For the community libraries generally see Hengel, *Studies
in the Gospel of Mark* (n. 10), 77f. For a critical discussion of the
erroneous assertion by Vielhauer, *Geschichte* (n. 29), 783 (and
many other authors), that 'a demarcated collection of Gospels exists
from the time of Irenaeus, who seeks to provide theological
justification for the canon of four Gospels and precisely in so doing
proves its novelty', see Thornton, *Zeuge* (n. 144), 55ff. and 59f. and
the no less questionable conjectures by H. Koester about the final
redaction or origin of the 'canonical' Gospels and their insignifi-

145. cance in the first half of the second century. See also above, n. 29.

146. It could be connected with the enigmatic information in Acts 12.17c, see n. 353.

146. Irenaeus, *Adv.Haer.* 3, 3, 2: 'So we will present only the apostolic tradition and the preaching in faith of the greatest and oldest church which is universally known, which was founded and built by the most illustrious apostles Peter and Paul in Rome.' For the problem see the study by H. Lietzmann, *Petrus und Paulus in Rom*, AKG 1, ²1927, especially 226–47, which has not yet been superseded; R. Pesch, *Simon Petrus*, PuP 15, Stuttgart 1980, 109–134; Hengel and Schwemer, *Paulus* (n. 9), 382, 388, 391f., 435, above all on the earlier stay of Peter in Rome under Claudius. It may be that I Peter was written in Rome shortly before AD 100, in order to provide some counterbalance to the collection of Paul's letters which had then likewise been completed and to emphasize the significance of Rome over against Asia Minor, as I Clement later does over against the community in Corinth.

147. See above, 65–73.

148. Irenaeus, *Adv.Haer.* 5, 33, 4, cf. Eusebius, *HE* 3, 99. According to him, Papias belongs to the 'presbyters who had seen John, the disciple of the Lord', and whom he instructed about the miraculous fertility of the millennium (5, 33, 3, where he quotes from the work of Papias).

149. Hengel, 'Septuaginta' (n. 1), 273.

150. For the community libraries and the Fourth Gospel see Hengel, *Studies in the Gospel of Mark* (n. 10), 77ff.; id., *Johanneische Frage* (n. 85) 68, 154f., 208. For Justin see Hengel, *Kleine Schriften* II (n. 120), 342–47; *Johanneische Frage* (n. 85), 61–7 = *Johannine Question*, 12–14.

151. In addition to Irenaeus, *Adv.Haer.* 3, 1, 1 see also 3, 14, 1: '*is Lucas inseparabilis fuit a Paulo, et cooperarius eius in Evangelio*' and '*qui semper cum Paulo praedicavit et dilectus ab eo est dictus* (Col. 4.11), *et cum eo evangelisavit, et creditus est referre nobis Evangelium . . .*'. Here the relationship between Paul and Luke is elaborated in a 'hagiographical' way. Similarly also Muratorian Canon 3–5, which in my view comes from Rome: he composed his Gospel under his own name in accordance with the views of Paul. For the Muratorian Canon see n. 41 above. For the relationship between Luke and Paul see above, 99–104. In my view Marcion presupposes basically the same scheme and can therefore declare the purged Luke to be the Gospel preached by Paul, see above, n. 42; Hengel and Schwemer, *Paulus* (n. 9), 9–26 = *Paul*, 6–11; Jervell, *Apostelgeschichte* (n. 28), 79–86.

152. Therefore Paul soon appeared as the author of the Letter to the Hebrews.
153. Justin, *Apology* I, 67, 2.
154. Cf. also Rev. 1.3 in Asia Minor and I Tim. 4.13, cf. Hengel, *Studies in Mark* (n. 10), 75ff.; J. C. Salzmann, *Lehren und Ermahnen*, WUNT II 59, Tübingen 1994, index 534: 'Schriftlesung'.
155. Irenaeus, *Adv.Haer.* 3, 2f. = Eusebius, *HE* 5, 6. Cf. Thornton, *Zeuge* (n. 144), 32ff., 45ff.
156. Eusebius, *HE* 5, 4, 1f.
157. Irenaeus, *Adv.Haer.* 3, 3, 2: 'Every church must agree with this church because of its special pre-eminence.' This did not exclude his criticizing Bishop Victor for his indolence over the presbyter Florinus, who had a tendency towards Valentinianism; see the fragment of a Syriac letter no. XXVIII in W. W. Harvey, *Sancti Irenaei Libros quinque adversus haereses*, 1857, II, 457; cf. Eusebius, *HE* 5, 20, 1–6 and 5, 15 and also his letter of protest to Victor of Rome because of the latter's intolerance in the dispute over Easter in the name of the churches in Gaul: Eusebius, *HE* 5, 24, 10–17.
158. Significantly, in Romans Paul does not speak of a 'community' in Rome, but in 1.6f. only of the 'beloved of God and called Gentiles' there; in Rom. 16.5 he speaks of the 'house community' of Prisca and Aquila; Acts 28.15 speaks only of brothers; see also P. Lampe, *Die stadtrömischen Christen in den ersten beiden Jahrhunderten*, WUNT II/18, ²1989, 67ff. In I Clement 42.4f., Clement of Rome uses 'bishops' together with 'deacons' only in the plural.
159. This term εὐαγγελιστής for the author of a Gospel writing does not yet appear in Irenaeus; it was first used by Hippolytus and then frequently by Origen, see Lampe, *Lexicon* (n. 47), ad vocem. See also above, 48–56, the superscriptions of the Gospels.
160. Whether it ever existed is a matter of dispute; however, our Greek Matthew certainly cannot be identified with it.
161. Preuschen, *Analecta* (n. 41), 27; corrected text in Aland, *Synopsis*, 538: '*Tertium evangelii librum secundum Lucam. Lucas iste medicus . . . conscripsit.*' Cf. *NTApoc* I, 34ff.; for the age, above n. 41. For Luke the Physician see above, 101, 109 and below, n. 678.
162. Text in Aland, *Synopsis*, 549; see A. von Harnack, *Die ältesten Evangelienprologe und die Bildung des neuen Testaments*, SBA 1928, 322–41: 324, who wants to put them between 160 and 180, still before Irenaeus, and with the first editor, Dom de Bruyne, regards them as anti-Marcionite texts which come from Rome. This enigmatic and partly mutilated text deserves a new investigation, since while the critical analysis by J. Regul, *Die antimarcionitischen*

Evangelienprologe, AGLB 6, 1969, illuminates the complicated textual history, its historical positioning of the texts remains unsatisfactory. See his split verdict: 'How is one to give the prologue a meaningful setting? By way of anticipation, it should be said that this question cannot be resolved satisfactorily. The prologues do not give us enough points of contact for a precise placing' (94). Unfortunately he then goes on to make an unfounded assertion which is one of the clichés of present-day 'critical research'. 'Rather, we must begin by assuming that the Gospels do not intrinsically justify their attribution to the apostles and disciples of apostles, but these attributions are deliberate actions on the part of the orthodox church in the process of formation'. This image of the 'orthodox church in the process of formation' which freely invented the names of the authors of the Gospels in the second century is built up on an unhistorical bogeyman which to the present day confuses the brains of exegetes and which does no justice either to the witnesses of the second century or to the origin of the collection of the Gospels.

163. According to the tradition of the elders in the *Hypotyposes,* see Eusebius, *HE* 6, 14, 5, before the report about Mark. For Clement of Alexandria and the Gospels see above, 15–19.

164. K. Berger, *Im Anfang war Johannes. Datierung und Theologie des vierten Evangeliums,* Stuttgart 1997; W. Schmithals, *Johannesevangelium und Johannesbriefe. Forschungsgeschichte und Analyse,* BZNW 64, 1992. Both sweep aside the information from the second century and accordingly arrive at quite different results.

165. The Neronian persecution is not mentioned because everyone knew about it. The whole of Irenaeus' work, written between 180 and 190, also shows virtually no evidence of the cruel persecution in Lyons and Vienne, where he had become bishop in 177.

166. The prologue to the Gospel of Mark, already mentioned, confirms these statements: Mark wrote his Gospel in Italy after the death of Peter. See Aland, *Synopsis,* 548; Harnack, *Evangelienprologe* (n. 162), 324; Regul, *Evangelienprologe* (n. 162), 29: *post excessionem ipsius Petri descripsit idem hoc in partibus Italiae evangelium.*

167. Eusebius, *HE* 3, 39, 3: ἅ τε Ἀριστίων καὶ ὁ πρεσβύτερος Ἰωάννης, τοῦ κυρίου μαθηταί, λέγουσιν. Cf. also II and III John and Hengel, *Johanneische Frage* (n. 85), 96–119 = *Johannine Question,* 24–34.

168. Ibid., 224ff., 264–74 = 102–8.

169. Cf. the earlier 'anti-Marcionite' prologue which has already been mentioned; see Aland, *Synopsis,* 549; Regul, *Evangelienprologe* (n. 162), 16.30ff.: Luke is said to have come from Antioch and to have died in Thebes at the age of eighty-four (cf. Luke 2.37). He is said to have written his Gospel in Achaea (cf. II Cor. 8.18). This

information can no longer be verified. Its origin could lie in the lost *Hypotyposes* of Clement of Alexandria or the *Hypomnemata* of Hegesippus.

170. The name could be an evocative cover. See below, n. 423.

171. See below, n. 460.

172. Both according to the sixth book of the *Hypotyposes,* Eusebius, *HE* 6, 14, 6f.; 2, 15, 1f.; according to the Latin translation of the *Hypotyposes* by John Cassian on I Peter 5.13 he had been asked by 'knights at the imperial court'; cf. Jerome, *Vir.Ill.* 8. Here the legendary transformation of a tradition can be followed in the same author. Texts in Aland, *Synopsis*, 555f., 562.

173. This evaluation corresponds to the find of Gospel papyri in Egypt (see above, 42f.).

174. The division was probably necessary because a codex with all four Gospels would have been too unwieldy. In the case of P 75, T. C. Skeat arrives at a 'one-quire codex' of 72 leaves. He conjectures that this was sewn together with a second codex which contained Mark and Matthew: see 'The Origin of the Christian Codex', *ZPE* 102, 1994, 263–8; Stanton, *Gospel* (n. 29), 326f. See also below, n. 216.

175. Augustine, *De cons. ev.* 1, 1, 3 (ed. Weihrauch, 3 = Merkel, 'Pluralität' [n. 97], 41), explicitly emphasizes that the order of the Gospels also represents the chronological order of their origin: *hoc ordine scripsisse perhibentur (viz., quattuor euangelistae): primus Mattheus, deinde Marcus, tertio Lucas, ultimo Iohannes.* The most important, Matthew and John, who were chosen by the Lord as disciples, stand at the beginning and at the end; they put the mere disciples of the apostles 'as it were . . . in the middle' so that they 'are supported from both sides, like children who need their parents' arms'. There is a true theological insight here, but historically things are quite different.

176. See the short survey in *Nestle's Einführung in das Griechische Neue Testament*, revised edition by E. v. Dobschütz, [4]1923, 9; E. Preuschen, *Analecta. Kürzere Texte zur Geschichte der Alten Kirche und des Kanons*, II, *Kanonsgeschichte*, Tübingen [2]1910, 43, 49: 39th Easter festal letter of Athanasius; 54: *Decretum Gelasianum*; 63: Stichometry of Nicephorus; 74: Eusebius, *HE* 6, 25, 4–6. T. C. Skeat, 'The Oldest Manuscript of the Four Gospels', *NTS* 43, 1997, 1–34, reconstructs from the papyrus fragments P 64- 67 (Matthew) and P 4 (Luke) an early codex, which can still belong to the late second century (30). Unfortunately it is no longer possible to establish the order of the Gospels ('canonical' or 'Western' order); however, there does seem to have been yet another Gospel between Matthew and Luke (18f.). This would then be the earliest known

codex of four Gospels. Cf. J. K. Elliott, 'Manuscripts, the Codex and the Canon', *JSNT* 63, 1996, 105–23. For P 75, see n. 174 above.

177. In the newly-published POx 4445 (n. 122) = P 106, ed. W. E. H. Cockle, from the first half of the third century (11), the remnants of the pagination (columns γ and δ), as in P 66, indicate that 'this copy of St. John's Gospel was also the first item in the codex or stood by itself'. The latter is more probable.

178. After the attempted reconstruction by T. C. Skeat.

179. Tertullian, *Adv. Marc.* 4, 2, 5, knows an order John, Matthew, Mark, Luke; the Old Latin Vetus-Latina manuscript k has John, Luke, Mark, Matthew; Irenaeus, *Adv.Haer.* 3, 11, 8 in the order of the symbols of the evangelists from Rev. 4.7: lion = John; bull = Luke; human being = Matthew; eagle = Mark. But see 1.10: human being = Matthew; lion = John; bull = Luke; eagle = Mark, for which T. C. Skeat, *NT* 34, 1992, 194–9, conjectures Irenaeus' source and to which a codex in the Western order would correspond. By contrast, the list of the canon in Codex Claromontanus has Matthew, John, Mark, Luke, see Preuschen (n. 41), 41.

180. See the explanation by Augustine, above n. 15.

181. Augustine, *De cons. ev.* 1, 2, 4, CSEL 43, 4, makes him the mere 'follower' and 'epitomator' *(pedisequus et breuiator)* of Matthew. This fundamental error continued to have an effect down to the second half of the nineteenth century. Cf. also von Campenhausen, *Formation* (n. 29), 171. I would doubt whether we are to understand its preservation merely as an answer to Marcion's reduction: 'In the effort to sacrifice none of the old and "authentic" sources, it was once again brought out and taken up.' Already before Marcion it must have been a fixed part of a collection of three or four Gospels in major communities. People were aware of its age and authority and therefore preserved it. For the relative insignificance of Mark see also 80 and n. 327. This suppression by the larger Gospels also makes it extremely improbable that Mark underwent several revisions in the second century. It would have been too insignificant for that. The only – necessary – expansion was the addition of the extra conclusion after the offensive ending in 16.8; see above, n. 114. There is no trace in the second-century textual tradition of one or more far-reaching recensions of Mark. By contrast, it is only too understandable that time and again it should have been expanded in a harmonizing way with Matthaean and Lukan parallels.

However, there should be no talk here of a 'recension'. There is insufficient attestation in the elaborations of the textual tradition for this.

182. That of Mark only in the framework of P 45, the great Chester

Beatty Papyrus. Apart from this one papyrus from the third century for Mark we have only P 88 from the fourth century and P 84 from the sixth century.

183. In the view of the editor, J. D. Thomas, of these twelve fragments of Matthew, around nine come from a time no later than the middle of the third century; two, P 104 and P 64, 67, 4 (the last three as fragments of a manuscript, see T. C. Skeat, 'The Oldest Manuscript of the Four Gospels', *NTS* 43, 1997, 1–34), presumably still belong to the second century: see J. K. Elliott, 'Six New Papyri of Matthew's Gospel', *NT* 44, 1999, 105–7. Cf. also D. E. Aune, *The Early Reception of Matthew's Gospel: New Evidence from Papyri?*, forthcoming 2000. For the papyri see also n.122.

184. Eusebius, *HE* 2, 16, 1: 'Mark is said to have been the first to have been sent to Egypt, to have preached the Gospel composed by him, and to have founded churches in Alexandria'; 2, 24; Jerome, *Vir.ill.* 8; further examples in Morton Smith, *Clement of Alexandria and a Secret Gospel of Mark*, Cambridge, Mass. 1973, 31, 33f., 279ff. A later tradition has the Gospel of Mark even written in Egypt (31). However, I regard the fragment of a letter of Clement with the 'Secret Gospel of Mark' discovered by M. Smith as a refined forgery. For the speculations based on it see Epp, 'Multivalence' (n. 130), 256f., and his reference to Koester, *Gospels* (n. 50), 293–303 (especially 301f.).

185. According to the *Hypotyposes* in Eusebius, *HE* 6, 14, 7. See above, n.61.

186. C. H. Roberts, *Manuscript, Society and Belief in Early Christian Egypt*, Schweich Lectures 1977, London 1979. Presumably there are still numerous small fragments of papyri of the Gospels in the great papyrus collections in Oxford, London, Paris, Berlin, Vienna, Florence and Cairo. A more intensive search here is needed.

187. See Metzger, *Versions* (n. 104), 36–8. We find the same unique order in the so-called Mommsen list of the canon, see Preuschen (n. 41), 37, after Codex Cheltenhamensis. By contrast, Codex Sangallensis has the more Western order Matthew, John, Mark, Luke, see above n.37 and 179. For other rare possibilities of the order see Zahn, *Kanon* (n. 12), 364–75.

188. We shall constantly be returning to this point in the course of our investigation: see above, 38ff., 50ff., 78ff.

189. Justin, *Dialogue with Trypho*, 106, 3.

190. Constantine introduced the first, not to say splendid, parchment codex into the church, after countless copies of manuscripts had been destroyed in the Diocletian persecutions. This is what we have in the form of Codex Vaticanus und Codex Sinaiticus, see now T. C.

Skeat, 'The Codex Sinaiticus et Vaticanus et Constantine', *HTR* 100, 1999.

191. Heckel, *Evangelium* (n. 12), 158–218.

192. Eusebius, *HE* 3, 24, 7. See Heckel, who follows Harnack's interpretation, namely that this tradition still belongs in the second century, more precisely in the time before the appearance of the Alogoi, indeed, with C. E. Hill, 'What Papias said about John (and Luke)', *JTS* 49, 1998, 582–629, he conjectures that this text could come from Papias. In reality this leads to the particularly high esteem for the Fourth Gospel, say, in Clement of Alexandria, and could come from his *Hypotyposes* or from an unknown third-century source from the library in Caesarea (see above, 219f. n. 61). Here the significance of the 'Alogoi' is overestimated by Harnack; in the East initially they played no role. Dionysius of Alexandria is the first to be interested in them, to devalue the Apocalypse. Then of course comes Epiphanius, who is probably the first to invent the designation 'Alogoi' for heretics; previously people talked about Gaius and his circle. A legitimation of the earlier Synoptics by John is typical of Alexandrian theology and the leading role of the Fourth Gospel in Egypt. At the same time, the conflict which is here becoming evident in Irenaeus, between the one-year activity of Jesus in the Synoptics and the several years in John, is resolved. The concluding sentence comes from Eusebius, who can base his own harmonizing theory on the contradictory chronology in John and the Synoptics on this tradition; see his subsequent solution of the problem in *HE* 3, 24, 8–13 (see n. 31 above).

193. See above, 38ff.

194. Regul, *Evangelienprologe* (n. 162), 45.

195. In the revised twenty-seventh edition, 719ff., the *variae lectiones minores* which tend to be overlooked and more evidence about the titles are noted. For misleading information see e.g. W. D. Davies and D. C. Allison, *The Gospel according to Saint Matthew*, ICC 1988, 129, who emphasize that 'this textual tradition supplies more than one superscription'. However, they fail to note that the expanded titles are all *very* late and that in B and partially in Sin the short form κατὰ Μαθθαῖον is in part the consequence of the existence of a large codex in which all four Gospels are combined under the heading τὸ εὐαγγέλιον, so that the individual writings are designated only by κατὰ plus the author's name, see Hengel, *Studies in the Gospel of Mark* (n. 10), 65ff. See n. 5 there for the earlier literature. Gamble, *Books* (n. 118), deals with the problem all too briefly and unfortunately once again repeats the old theses about anonymous Gospels without titles. No thought is given to how these sometimes quite improbable titles were arrived at later and how different

anonymous Gospels were used in the service.

196. Hengel, *Studies in the Gospel of Mark* (n. 10), 65–72.

197. Ibid., 74f., 172f. nn. 6off. Presumably the original form was Πέτρου ἐπιστολή α: a v (P 72, third/fourth century, A, Sin, K, 33, 69). As usual, B has the short form alone with the name in the genitive; later manuscripts expand it. The same is true of II Peter, James, Jude and probably also the Johannine letters, see Aland[27], 1993, including the *variae lectiones minores,* 743ff. The larger number of variants is striking. From the beginning the title of the Gospel was stable. Cf. some contemporary examples from Greek literature: Διοδόρου τοῦ Σικελίωτου βιβλιοθήκης ἱστορικῆς βίβλος πρώτη; Πλουτάρχου βίοι παράλληλοι; Φιλοστράτου βίοι σοφιστῶν or ἐς τὸν Τυανέα Ἀπολλώνιον; Ἀλκινόου διδασκαλικὸς τῶν Πλάτωνος δογμάτων. One could continue the series indefinitely.

198. See for example the different titles of Josephus' *Jewish War,* Περὶ τοῦ Ἰουδαϊκοῦ πολέμου (πρὸς Ῥωμαίους) or Περὶ ἁλώσεως, in H. St. J. Thackeray, Josephus II, *The Jewish War* I–III, LCL 1927, viif. Even individual dialogues of Plato sometimes had a double title: on the one hand they were named after the conversation partner, and on the other after the content. Thus: Φαίδων – περὶ ψυχῆς or Φαῖδρος – περὶ καλοῦ. Great authors like Aristotle or later Galen could in some circumstances quote their own works by different titles. Often the titles were also established by the editors, thus in the case of the writings of Plotinus by his pupil Porphyry, or in the libraries. That is why so many works of pre-Socratics have the uniform title περὶ φύσεως; see Hengel, *Studies in the Gospel of Mark* (n. 10), 173 n. 65.

199. On this point even Marcion's view was not too far removed from the usual conviction of the church.

200. In classical Greek, κατὰ appears in quotations or assertions, κατὰ Ἀισχύλον, Aristophanes *Thesmophoriazusai,* 134 (from the Lycurgy); Plato, *Phaedrus* 227b: κατὰ Πίνδαρον (*Isthmians* 1, 2); Diogenes Laertius 2, 11: according to Favorinus, Anaxagoras is said to have asserted in his 'mixed histories' . . . (καθ' ἅ φησι Φαβωρῖνος): here we have the meaning 'after the version of'. Cf. also II Macc 2.13: ἐν ταῖς ἀναγραφαῖς καὶ ἐν τοῖς ὑπομνηματισμοῖς τοῖς κατὰ τὸν Νεεμίαν. For this see E. Schwyzer, *Griechische Grammatik* II, *Syntax und syntaktische Stilistik,* HAW, Munich 1950, 479, 'according to the assertion of' (in quotations). The title κατά with the accusative and the name of the author is not simply a replacement for the genitive, this Arndt/Gingrich/Bauer, *Lexicon,* ad loc.; the instance from John Lydus cited there is very late and is influenced by Christian terminology; see further in Hengel, *Studies in the Gospel of Mark* (n. 10), 65f.

201. Thus e.g. the *subscriptio* of the Daniel text of minuscule 88 according to J. Ziegler (ed.), *Susanna. Daniel. Bel et Draco,* Göttinger LXX XVI, 2, 1954, 8, 223: Δανιὴλ κατὰ τοῦς Ἑβδομήκοντα. Cf. Hengel, *Studies in the Gospel of Mark* (n. 10), 65f.

202. Hengel, 'Septuaginta' (n. 1), 182–284: 187f., 236–41.

203. See Hengel, *Studies in the Gospel of Mark* (n. 10), 65f.

204. See C. H. Roberts and T. C. Skeat, *The Birth of the Codex,* London 1983, and the review by C. P. Bammel, *JTS.*NS 38, 1987, 516–19; C. H. Roberts, *Manuscript* (n. 186), 86, index s.v. Codex and Scroll. Further see above, 116ff.

205. See K. Aland, *Repertorium der griechischen christlichen Papyri,* I, *Christliche Papyri,* PTS 18, Berlin 1976. Cf. now e.g. in the new volume *POx 65,* 1998, no. 4442, 1ff., the Christian Exodus papyrus codex from the early third century and the Jewish LXX Esther scroll from the first or (beginning of) the second century AD, no.4443, 4ff.

206. See the plural in Justin, above, 20.

207. The only rare exception, justified by the content, was the combination of Gospels and Acts in P 45 und P 53, both third century. But they do belong closely together in content.

208. See Aland, *Repertorium* (n. 205), 7. Such later mixed texts are, for example the odes of the Old Testament with Luke 1.54f.; 2.29ff.; see 160–4, or amulets, 147–9.

209. Cf. II Thessalonians, Ephesians, Pastorals.

210. Cf. I Peter; a further wave of Petrine writings arises around 120/130: II Peter, Gospel of Peter, Kerygma Petri, Apocalypse of Peter, see above, 133f.

211. Tertullian, *De pud.* 20, 2f.

212. Thus already Pantaenus, the teacher of Clement of Alexandria. He made the bold conjecture that Luke translated the 'Hebrew' letter of Paul into Greek (*Hypotyposes,* according to Eusebius, *HE* 6, 14, 2f.). He says that Paul omitted the prescript to the letter with the apostle's name out of humility in order not to provoke aversion to him among the recipients in the Holy Land. Origen thought (according to Eusebius, *HE* 6, 25, 11–13) in a critical philological way that the elegant style of the letter indicated rather Clement of Rome or Luke as the author and that the letter contained 'teachings of the master' which had been retained in the memory. It is nonsensical to regard the conclusion of the letter, 13, 22–25, as a forgery pointing to Paul. A forger would simply have put a prescript with the name of Paul at the beginning. The Letter to the Hebrews in particular shows how restrained people were even over the title in secondary interventions and how conservative they were in retaining a title which was difficult to understand, and which in the case of Hebrews comes

at the latest from the collection of the letters of Paul around AD 100. Presumably in Hebrews and I John, for reading in worship an original prescript which was thought to be inappropriate was removed, since it was initially known from whom the writing came. In the Johannine letters the author was known through the title; in the case of Hebrews the information about the recipients, in analogy to the other letters of Paul, may come from the editor of the Pauline corpus. It is interesting that a title for it was indispensable. That applies to all the writings read out in worship and kept in community libraries. However, in this special case it was possible to dispense with details about an author, because the fact that it was part of the corpus indirectly indicated a Pauline origin. The editor may already have supposed it to be by Paul. Nevertheless, this was initially doubted, at least in the West. For the prescript of Hebrews see the acute observations by E. Bickerman, *Studies in Jewish and Christian History*, III, 1986, AGAJU 9, Leiden 1986, 336–49: 348: 'Note that the Alexandrian editor [of P 46, but that also applies to the editor of the collection of Paul's letters, MH], although firmly believing in the Pauline authenticity of the letter, refrained from naming the apostle in the colophon.'

213. Only at a very late date does the name of Paul then appear on a minuscule (81).

214. Hengel, *Studies in the Gospel of Mark* (n. 10), 72f.

215. Eusebius, *HE* 5, 16, 10.16; 5, 19, 3f. For the earliest synods see É. Junod, 'Naissance de la pratique synodale et unité de l'Église au IIe siècle', in *Einheit der Kirche in vorkonstantinischer Zeit*, ed F. v. Lilienfeld and A. M. Ritter, Erlangen 1989, 19–34, and I. A. Fischer and A. Lumpe, *Die Synoden von den Anfängen der Kirche bis zum Vorabend des Nicaenums,* Konzilsgeschichte A 16, Paderborn, etc. 1997. Before the Montanist disputes we have only references to authoritative letters from communities or bishops and to local differences of doctrine or even episcopal visits to other communities, but no synods extending beyond communities or provinces.

216. The conjectures by Heckel, *Evangelium* (n. 12), 217–18 and index s.v. 'Evangelium' and 'Überschriften', point in this direction. He again wants to associate the superscriptions with the single act of a collection of the four Gospels. However, his argument is completely unconvincing. The origin of the uniform superscriptions cannot be explained by an ecclesiastical act of force by the Johannine school in Asia Minor in connection with John 21, nor is it possible to explain in this way the various authors' names, above all those of Mark, Luke and Matthew, or the corresponding 'historical' order. It also remains completely inexplicable how the disciples of John came

upon the title εὐαγγέλιον, which plays an important role only in Mark (see above, 90ff.), already fades into the background in Matthew and Luke (see above, 50ff.) and does not appear at all in the Johannine corpus and the fragments of Papias. Moreover John 21 is *sui generis* and has no *direct* literary dependence on the three Synoptic Gospels. Nor does it contain any direct reference to their special authority, far less did it serve to establish a collection of four Gospels. The Johannine school wanted to disseminate and establish its own writings in the church. It hardly had any reason to make a special plea for the Synoptic Gospels, from which its own writings were substantially different and which they often contradicted. An anonymity of the earlier Gospels is also extremely improbable. It also remains inexplicable that *nowhere* do we find a trace of earlier variant titles. Had the codex of four Gospels and the titles associated with them originated between 110 and 140, these would not have been able to establish themselves throughout the church in such a uniform way; that is illustrated a little later by the inauthentic conclusion to Mark, 16.9–20 (see above, n.114). No connection can be demonstrated between the later 'additional conclusions' and the titles of the Gospels. The titles must be substantially older. Here the whole of Heckel's attempted explanation rests on an ahistorical construction. It is regrettable that too little attention is paid to the question of reading in worship and so decisive a text as Justin, *Apol* I, 66, 3. At any rate, between 110 and 140 the Gospel of Mark was already between forty and seventy years old and formed the basis for the whole of later Gospel writing. With such a later emergence the 'compulsion towards titles' in the case of the 'apocryphal' Gospels would no longer have arisen. *The roots of the title of the Gospel are to be sought solely in Mark.* As the later Gospels (Luke, Matthew) use Mark or at least presuppose it and know it, it seems likely that the title of Mark has been taken over (see above, 48ff. and 53ff.). The conjecture by T. C. Skeat, 'The Origin of the Christian Codex', *ZPE* 102, 1994, 263–8: 263, takes a similar direction to Heckel. He assumes that the origin of the four-Gospel-codex is connected with a crisis which broke out in the church in connection with the composition of the Fourth Gospel which then led to a first exchange between the most important communities. But we do not know anything about such a 'crisis' either. Nor do I find convincing the conjecture of D. Trobisch, *Die Endredaktion des Neuen Testaments*, NTOA 31, 1996, who connects the introduction of the *nomina sacra* and the codex with the redaction of the four-Gospel canon, and indeed the New Testament generally with the overcoming of the difficulties which had been caused by Marcion, the various dates for

Easter, etc. (138ff.). Trobisch argues that there was a concern to overcome these tensions by harmonization along the lines of the later letter from Irenaeus to Bishop Victor of Rome (Eusebius, *HE* 5, 24, 13) and this found a receptive readership. But when, where and by whom is this tremendous work of redaction supposed to have been carried out and established in such a uniform way? Furthermore, the uniformity of the four-Gospel collection has quite a different character from the other texts of the New Testament. Although Trobisch's volume is instructive in many ways, it falls far too short on historical grounding and setting. The same is true of the decisive motive force, liturgical reading in worship. Thus the whole attempt proves to be a construction which contradicts the historical realities. See the criticism of Stanton, *Gospel* (n. 29), 338: 'Both theories [of Skeat and Trobisch, MH] require a much higher level of structure and centralized organization within early second-century Christianity than I think is likely.'

217. Ibid. (n. 29), 340: 'I prefer a theory of gradual development to a "big bang" theory.' This gradual growth of the collection has been argued for in many ways since Zahn; see the evidence in Heckel, *Evangelium* (n. 12), 209 n. 434; cf. also Stanton, *Gospel* (n. 29), 336ff., who connects the origin of the collection of four Gospels with the rise of the codex. However, in my view the Christian codex is older, see above, 116ff.

218. For Papias see Eusebius, *HE* 3, 39, 4. Cf. also the letter of Bishop Serapion of Antioch to the community of Rhossos with the negative judgment on 'pseudepigrapha' like the Gospel of Peter, Eusebius, *HE* 6, 12, 2–6; see above, n. 49.

219. For Polycarp see already the comparison of the prescript with I Clement and numerous parallels in letters; for Dionysius see Eusebius, *HE* 4, 22, 2; 23, 11. The letter was probably already known to Irenaeus and was probably also used in Lyons, *Adv.Haer.* 3, 3, 3 = Eusebius, *HE* 5, 6, 3, as it contains 'the tradition which he [Clement] had received most recently from the apostles'. Clement of Alexandria calls him an apostle in *Strom.*4, 105, 1 and uses it extraordinarily frequently. The letter appears in the Codex Alexandrinus. Cf. further the *Apostolic Constitutions*, which make Clement the mediator of apostolic doctrine to the church (6, 18, 11; cf. 8, 46, 13 and 47, 85). We meet him as an apostolic disciple of the first order in the Pseudo-Clementine romance. Only Eusebius, *HE* 6, 13, 6, puts the letter along with Wisdom, Sirach, Hebrews and the letters of Barnabas and Jude among the 'Antilegomena', i.e. the writings which have not been recognized everywhere in the church, presumably because they were not directly recognized as apostolic. In his

survey of the canon in 3, 25, 1–7 Eusebius does not mention I Clement at all, but in 3.16 he emphasizes that 'as formerly, so also now it is still in public use in most churches'. For the whole question see at length H. L. Lona, *Der erste Clemensbrief*, KAV 2, Göttingen 1998, 89–110.

220. See Eusebius, *HE* 4, 23.

221. Eusebius, *HE* 6, 25, 3, still uses the word in a relatively vague way for the four Gospels in the sense of a 'church norm'. For the development of the concept see T. Zahn, *Grundriss der Geschichte des Neutestamentlichen Kanons*, Leipzig ²1904, 1ff. The term appears for 'a collection of holy scriptures recognized as normative in the church around the middle of the fourth century' (1). Athanasius is the first to be able to say that Hermas 'does not belong to the canon (μὴ ὄν ἐκ τοῦ κανόνος, ibid., 8 = *Decr. syn. Nic.* 18, MPG 25, 448a).

222. See Hengel, *Studies in the Gospel of Mark* (n. 10), 64–84, and above, 53ff. Cf. von Campenhausen, *Formation* (n. 29), 173 n. 123: 'these ancient and original designations were already long established, as Papias indicates and indeed presumably Justin as well, and could no longer be altered arbitrarily.'

223. The Old Latin translation of the Gospels, which was presumably made in Carthage before 180 (see the Scillitan martyrs, who already had the letters of Paul and other books in Latin – probably the Gospels – for worship) naturally presupposes the well-known Greek form of the title εὐαγγέλιον κατὰ, see Hengel, *Studies in the Gospel of Mark* (n. 10), 66 n.17. A single papyrus sheet connected with P 4, 64 contains the mere superscription ΕΥΑΓΓΕΛΙΟΝ ΚΑΤΑ ΜΑΘΘΑΙΟΝ, but is later than the papyrus (see above, nn. 176, 183) and may be assigned to the early third century. T. C. Skeat, *NTS* 43, 1997, 18 conjectures that 'the fragment comes from a fly-leaf at the beginning of the manuscript'.

224. See Hengel, *Johanneische Frage* (n. 85), 13–67 = *Johannine Question*, 2–13, on John; Köhler, *Matthäusevangelium* (n. 109) on Matthew and É. Massaux, *Influence de l'Évangile de Saint Matthieu sur la littérature chrétienne avant saint Irénée*, Louvain 1950 = *The Influence of the Gospel of Saint Matthew on Christian Literature before Saint Irenaeus*, Vols I–III, translated by N. J. Beval and S. Hecht, edited with an introduction and additions by A. J. Bellinzoni, Macon and Leuven 1990, on all the Gospels and Acts.

225. I am indebted for this reference to C. Markschies, who calculated this figure on the basis of Harnack's *Geschichte der altchristlichen Literatur bis Eusebius*.

226. Typical of this situation is the utterly unsatisfactory treatment of the problem in Vielhauer, *Geschichte* (n. 29), 252–8, and the defence of

his position without any substantive argument in *NTApoc* I, 78f.: 'The age of the κατά titles is probably scarcely to be determined exactly' (79): rather too convenient a verdict. Similarly G. Strecker, *Literaturgeschichte des Neuen Testaments*, 1992, UTB 1682, 126, who merely refers to the disputing of 'the constancy of the tradition of the *inscriptio* and *subscriptio*' by F. Bovon, 'The Synoptic Gospels and the Non-Canonical Acts of the Apostles', *HTR* 81, 1988, 19–32. But Bovon, who sees in the introduction of these titles 'the result of an effort of stabilization' over against the excessively powerful apocryphal literature and decrees without further argument that 'they are therefore secondary' (23), does not go at all into the basic problems: the inexplicable unity, the origin of the names which is difficult to explain, the early attestation and the necessity of giving a title in the liturgical use of scriptures. Where, when and by whom is this 'effort of stabilization' supposed to have taken place, and how can it have been carried through so uniformly and without contradiction? It is also unsound method to challenge the uniformity of the titles of the Gospels on the basis of the *complete* instability of the apostolic Acts and their designations, which is easy to explain, and to assert freely with no reference to any source that 'the Gospel of Matthew could have been called "Beginnings" (γένεσις) or "Life" (βίος) just as Luke-Acts could have borne the title "Narrative" (διήγησις), or Mark that of "Memoirs" (ὑπομνήματα)'. Here the fundamental difference between the unique title and the relatively popular general designations of genres is overlooked and room given to fantastic conjectures. Would it not have been more appropriate here to speak of a now untenable modern historical hyper-criticism instead of an 'effort of stabilization'?

227. Irenaeus, *Adv.Haer.* 3, 11, 8; see above, 236.

228. Which is not identical with a codex of four Gospels, but only means collection in an ordered sequence in important Christian community libraries, in analogy to the book cupboard in large Jewish synagogue communities, see above, 116ff.

229. According to *Vir. ill.* 25 Jerome had read a Gospel commentary under the name of Theophilus. *Epistles* 121, 6 shows that this must have been a kind of harmony: *Theophilus Antiochenae ecclesiae septimus post Petrum apostolum episcopus, qui quattor euangelistarum in unum opus dicta compingeret* ... Perhaps this attempt was a reaction to Tatian's Harmony. The two were contemporaries. Cf. above, 57f. on Basilides before Marcion.

230. See C. Markschies, 'Heracleon', in S. Döpp and W. Geerlings, *Lexikon der antiken christlichen Literatur* (with bibliography). Text in J. A. Robinson, *Text and Studies, No. 4 The Fragments of*

Heracleon, Cambridge 1891; W. Völker, 'Quellen zur Geschichte der christlichen Gnosis', *SQS* NF 5, 1932, 63–86; see also J.-M. Poffet, *La méthode exégétique d'Heracléon et d'Origène*, Paradosis 28, Fribourg 1985.

231. Hengel, *Johanneische Frage* (n. 85), 37–40 = *Johannine Question*, 8–10; W. A. Löhr, 'Ptolemaeus, Gnostiker', *Lexikon der antiken christlichen Literatur* (n. 230), 527f.; for John 1 see Irenaeus, *Adv.Haer.* 1, 8, 5; *Letter to Flora*: see Epiphanius, *Panarion* 33, 3–8. The exposition of the prologue criticized by Irenaeus could also come only from a pupil of Ptolemy. The reference to him as author (1, 8, 5), which has been preserved only in the Latin text, would then be a gloss.

232. Eusebius, *HE* 4, 7, 7 according to Agrippa Castor: εἰς . . . τὸ εὐαγγέλιον τέσσαρα πρὸς τοῖς εἴκοσι . . . βίβλια, see W. A. Löhr, *Basilides und seine Schule*, WUNT 83, Tübingen 1996, 4–14.

233. Perhaps περὶ τοῦ εὐαγγελίου. The title recalls the λογίων κυριακῶν ἐξήγησις of Papias.

234. Löhr, *Basilides* (n.232), 12. In the case of the texts handed down by Hippolytus it is difficult to distinguish between Basilides himself and his school. Cf. e.g. Hippolytus, *Ref.* 7, 21, 3 = Matt. 13.31 (Mark 4.30ff.; Luke 13.18f.); 7.22 = John 1.9 (introduced by the formula ἐστι τὸ λεγόμενον ἐν τοῖς εὐαγγελίοις, which probably comes from Hippolytus); 7, 26, 9 = Luke 1.35; 7, 27, 5 = John 2.4 and Matt. 2.1f. Cf. also Hegemonius, *Acta Archelai* 76, 5 = Luke 16.19ff., and Clement of Alexandria, *Strom.* 7, 106, 4 and 1, 146, 1ff., which presuppose Luke 2.1 and 3.1ff.; further *Strom.* 3, 1, 1f. = Matt. 19.8. The same is true of Ptolemy and his pupils.

235. Löhr, *Basilides* (n.232), 3–4; Origen, *Comm in Luc.*1 and the relatively free translation by Jerome.

236. Cf. also the protest of Irenaeus against this opinion of the Valentinians, *Adv.Haer.* 2, 22, 3–5, see above, n. 31.

237. Hippolytus, *Ref.* 7, 27, 8. Cf. Hengel, *Studies in the Gospel of Mark* (n. 10), 71, 167 n.46.

238. Hippolytus, *Haer.* 7, 20, 1; cf. Clement of Alexandria, *Strom.* 7, 108, 1 (above nn. 69 and 75); see also Löhr, *Basilides* (n. 232), 15ff., 24ff.

239. Valentinus, the 'rival' Christian philosopher of religion in Rome and founder of the Gnostic school which later became influential, will have received the traditions from Theodas, a disciple of Paul, Clement of Alexandria, *Strom.* 7, 106, 4; cf. C. Markschies, *Valentinus Gnosticus*, WUNT 65, 1992, 299ff. Like his pupil Ptolemy, probably Valentinus already criticized Marcion, the 'hyper-Paulinist'. This Theodas was to give his teaching greater

authority in the face of Marcion and the more conservative main-stream church. Analogous 'orthodox' lines of tradition are: the apostles (above all John), Polycarp, Irenaeus and other hearers of Polycarp, or: the apostles, the Presbyter John and Aristion, Papias, Irenaeus, or in the letter of Polycrates, Bishop of Ephesus, to Victor of Rome about the Easter dispute: the apostle Philip and his daughters, the disciple John, Polycarp, Melito and others. See Hengel, *Johanneische Frage* (n. 85), 33ff., 71ff. This information must not be banished sweepingly to the realm of legend. In the face of such historically disputed chains of tradition associated with persons, Marcion concentrated solely on concrete writings.

240. NHG I, 48, 6–13; cf. Mark 9.4: καὶ ὤφθη αὐτοῖς Ἡλίας σὺν Μωϋσει; for the key word φαντασία cf. Mark 6.49; for the failure to under-stand what resurrection means see Mark 9.10 (special material). Translation by M. L. Peel, *Nag Hammadi Library*, ³1988, 56. For the historical context see Markschies, *Valentinus* (n. 239), 356–61. The first editors had attributed the text to Valentinus. This has been abandoned. But this author of a gnosis which sets out deliberately to be a church gnosis should not be put too late.

241. Cf. also Justin, *Dial.* 10; Aristides, *Apol.* 2 (p. 9f. ed. Hennecke, TU 4, 1893), the invitation to the emperor to read the εὐαγγελικὴ γραφή himself, = 15, 1 (Goodspeed, p.19).

242. Irenaeus, *Adv.Haer.* 1, 31, 1. Cf. Epiphanius, *Panarion* 38, 1, 5: among the Cainites.

243. Presumably the Protevangelium of James from the middle of the second century.

244. *NT Apoc* I, 374–82.

245. *Decretum Gelasianum*, see Preuschen, *Analecta* (n. 41), 59. Gospel of Mary: see W. C. Till and H.-M. Schenke, *Die Gnostischen Schriften des Papyrus Berolinensis 8562*, TU 60², 1972, 24–79. Besides the Coptic manuscript of the early fifth century we have a Greek papyrus fragment from the beginning of the third century (25). Here Mary Magdalene appears as a revealer over against the disciples and provokes contradiction from Andrew and Peter. For the title see n. 251 below.

246. Epiphanius, *Panarion* 26, 2, 6.

247. H. Koester, *NTS* 35, 1989, 373 n. 2, 376f. Cf. also F. Bovon, *HTR* 81, 1988, 19–36. Koester stands things on their head. Of course Marcion also knew the other Gospels Mark, Matthew and John, and Justin and the mainstream church certainly did not take over from their fiercest opponent the titles, which are clearly attested for the Gospels from the middle of the second century. εὐαγγέλιον (κατά . . .) had long been recognized as a book title in the Christian

communities around 144 and was used in worship. If we had alternatives to this, there would necessarily have been variant titles in the Gospel tradition. But these do not appear anywhere. Which authority would also have given these titles, in imitation of Marcion, such general dissemination and recognition so late? Furthermore the term εὐαγγέλιον for a writing occurs at the time of Marcion or before him in II Clem. 8.5; Didache 8.2; 15.3f.; Aristides (see above, n. 241) εὐαγγελικὴ γραφή (see below) explains the unusual word εὐαγγέλιον to pagan readers as a 'form of literature'. Cf. Justin, *Apol.* 66, 3; 67.3, who there refers to a collection of scriptures in worship which has long been introduced and which for him is already traditional (see above, 19); further Basilides (see above, 57), Ignatius, Smyrnaeans 5.2 and 7.3; Didache 8.2; 15.3f. and as the decisive starting point Mark 1.1 (see above, 48ff., 90ff.). W. Schmithals, *Das Evangelium nach Markus*, ÖTK NT 2, 1, 1979, 73f. sees in Mark 1.1 'the reference by a copyist', who in a composite work was 'explicitly referring his readers . . . to the beginning of a following work'. In reality this must have been the very first copyist of all, otherwise we would have had corresponding variants in the written tradition, as in the case of the secondary ending to Mark. And this 'first copyist' would already have had to understand the present writing as a 'Gospel', otherwise the sentence is quite incomprehensible. In reality, the sentence comes from the evangelist, who thus at the beginning of his work characterizes the content 'theologically'. Koester, 370, regards Schmithals' conjecture as 'not impossible', although Schmithals assumes that the designation 'Gospel' for 'a written document . . . arose *at the latest* in the first half of the second century', which Koester wants to deny (my italics). Koester is ready to accept the views of R. H. Gundry, 'EUANGELION: How Soon a Book?', *JBL* 115, 1996, 321–5, without going into the question of titles. It is all too understandable that according to our very fragmentary knowledge Marcion himself does not mention the name of Luke. In so doing he would have unmasked himself as a forger. The only question is precisely how he arrives at this Gospel, which is hardly suitable for him. John and Mark would have been more appropriate.

248. Other 'Gospels' were named after Christian groups, for example 'the Hebrews' (see above, 17), 'Nazareans' or 'Ebionites', i. e. after the Jewish Christians. A Gospel of Barnabas influenced by Islam probably comes from the beginning of the sixteenth century, see *NTApoc* I, 85 n. 1.

249. See Hengel, *Studies in the Gospel of Mark* (n. 10), 70f. n.39f. The Gospel of Thomas has only a *subscriptio* ΠΕΥΑΓΓΕΛΙΟΝ ΠΚΑΤΑ

ΘΩΜΑΣ. The *inscriptio* clearly displays a historicizing secondary character by comparison with the Synoptic Gospels: POx 654, 1–5: οὗτι οἱ λόγοι οἱ [ἀπόκρυφοι οὓς ἐλά]λησεν Ἰη(σοῦ)ς ὁ ζῶν κ[αὶ ἔγραψεν Ἰούδα ὁ] καὶ Θωμᾶ . . . 'These are the hidden words which the living Jesus spoke. And Judas who is also Thomas wrote them down.' Such detailed information about content and author is quite unthinkable in the earlier Gospels. It gives the impression that Judas Thomas already wrote down the sayings of Jesus during his lifetime, to some degree by dictation. A wide gulf separates the original Gospel superscriptions and introductions from this. This introduction, which is impossible for the first century, already indicates the secondary character of the earlier Greek version of the Gospel of Thomas. The same goes for the Encratite and Gnosticizing tendencies of many logia. We can only make almost unverifiable hypotheses about earlier prior forms of this strange text.

250. The Gospel of Truth (NHL I 16, 31–43, 24) has neither *inscriptio* nor *subscriptio;* it merely begins with the statement, 'The Gospel of truth is joy . . .'; whether it is connected with the *veritatis evangelium* mentioned by Irenaeus, *Adv.Haer.* 3, 11, 9, is disputed. For the whole question see the commentary by J.-E. Ménard, *L'évangile de vérite*, Leiden 1972, 71ff. Cf. also 34, 34ff.: 'This is the word of the Gospel of the discovery of the Pleroma.' It consists in the discovery of the pneumatic origin of the Gnostic. It uses all four Gospels, but above all John, see Hengel, *Johanneische Frage* (n. 85), 43f. The introduction in the so-called 'Gospel of the Egyptians' (NHL III 40, 12–69, 17; cf. the parallel version NHL IV 80, 1–81, 3) runs: 'the holy book of the [Egyptians] of the great invisible spirit.' Only in the colophon 3, 69, 6 does the designation 'the Gospel of the Egyptians, the holy, secret book written by God', appear: see A. Böhlig, *Das Ägypterevangelium von Nag Hammadi*, Göttinger Orientforschungen VI/1, Wiesbaden 1974, 29, on the concept of the Gospel. In addition to the 'Gospel of Eve' Epiphanius also mentions a 'Gospel of Perfection' in *Panarion* 26, 2, 5: εὐαγγέλιον τελειώσεως, cf. Filastrius, *Haer.* 33, 7, CSEL 38, 18, 18: *evangelium consummationis*.

251. Like the Gospel of Thomas, the Gospel of Philip has the designation ΠΕΥΑΓΓΕΛΙΟΝ ΠΚΑΤΑ ΦΙΛΙΠΠΟΣ only as a *subscriptio* (NHL II 51, 29–86, 19). That is also true of the 'Gospel according to Mary', [ΠΕΥ]ΑΓΓΕΛΙΟΝ ΚΑΤΑ ΜΑΡΙΑΜ, which is a revelation of the Risen Christ to the disciples, whom he sends out 'to preach the Gospel of the kingdom of the Son' (9, 9f.; cf. 8, 22; 18, 19). This too is wholly dominated by Gnostic cosmology and anthropology, see Till and Schenke (n. 245), 62–79.

252. 'Take the letter of the blessed apostle Paul. What did he write to you

first at the beginning (of the proclamation) of the Gospel?' Cf. Phil. 4.15; I Cor. 15.1f.

253. 13.1f.; cf. Luke 6.31, 36–38; Matt. 5.7; 6.12, 14; 7.1, 12: it is a catechetical compilation of sayings of the Lord from the Sermon on the Plain and the Sermon on the Mount which need not necessarily be dependent on a written Gospel and which also appear in later catechetical tradition. However, we cannot rule out a written exemplar in the form of a collection of 'sayings of the Lord'. Indeed, Clement presupposes that these 'sayings of the Lord' are also known in Corinth, cf. I Clem. 46.7f., 'remember the words of Jesus our Lord', and also Mark 14.21; Luke 17.1, 2; Matt. 26.24 and 18.6f. Here there could perhaps be an indirect dependence on Mark. See *The New Testament in the Apostolic Fathers*, Oxford 1905, 58–62; H. Koester, *Synoptische Überlieferung bei den Apostolischen Vätern*, TU 65, 1957, 4–23. See also below, n. 530.

254. Koester, *Synoptische Überlieferung* (n. 253), 5.

255. 'Remember the words of the Lord Jesus that he said . . .' and 'Remembering what the Lord said teaching'. There follow sayings of the Lord which he has compiled from Matthew's Sermon on the Mount in a free rhythmic and catechetical form (Matt. 7.1f.; 5.3, 10); here in the formulation Polycarp is probably partially dependent on I Clem. 13.1f.

256. Cf. Hengel, *Johanneische Frage* (n. 85), 72f. Here Polycarp, Phil. 7.1a will clearly be referring to I John 4.2f.; II John 7. There follows, again as a statement of the Kyrios, in 7.2b a combination of quotations from Matt. 6.13a (Luke 11.4c) and Matt. 26.41 (Mark 14.38). Here Polycarp in any case presupposes Matthew but perhaps also the Synoptics generally. Massaux, *Influence* (n. 224), 2, 28–45 emphasizes the influence of Matthew too one-sidedly. We cannot rule out knowledge of Mark and above all of Luke. Polycarp also presupposes Acts, the letters of Paul, I Peter, I John and I Clement. The letter will hardly have been written after 120 and at all events may not be put too late; see J. B. Bauer, *Die Polykarpbriefe*, KAV 5, Göttingen 1995, 21f. One factor in favour of an early date is that the community in Philippi evidently does not as yet know a monarchical episcopate.

257. II Clem. 3.13.

258. Cf. I Cor. 7.10, cf.12; 9.14. Here the word of the Lord is a concrete individual commandment, the Gospel the message which must be proclaimed. In I Thess. 4.15 the 'word of the Lord' is an apocalyptic saying about parousia and resurrection.

259. Paul speaks in I Cor. 14.37 of the 'commandment of the Lord' and in Gal.6.2 of the 'law of Christ'. Cf. also I Cor. 7.25 and 7.10. Here

we already have a fixed terminology in the Pauline communities. In addition, the terminology of the commandment occurs both in the Gospel of John and in I John: in John 13.34 it means the commandment to love, and in 14.15, 21 it refers to the invitation to have faith. In I John 2.3f.; 3.22ff.; 4.21; 5.2f. it is about the true faith and the commandment to love. Cf. also Ignatius, Eph. 9.2; Trall. 3.1; Polycarp, Phil 2.2; 4.1; 5.1; see also Papias in Eusebius, *HE* 3, 39, 3.

260. Matt. 28.20: 'teaching them to observe all that I have commanded you'. For the new law with an anti-Jewish tendency cf. Barn.2.6: 'new law of our Lord Jesus Christ'; Justin, *Dial.* 11, 4; 12, 3; cf. 122, 50, who is fond of combining new law and new covenant. In abrupt opposition to the 'old law' see Melito, *Homily on the Pasch*, 3f., 45f., Christ as the 'new lawgiver', see Justin, *Dial.* 18, 3. Cf. also Kerygma Petri in Clement of Alexandria, *Strom.* 1, 182; 2, 68, 2, where the κύριος is called νόμος καὶ λόγος. See also Arndt/Gingrich/Bauer, *Lexicon*, ad loc, no.5, above all Hermas on the identification of Gospel and Law.

261. II Clement 1.1: 'Brothers, we must think thus of Jesus Christ as of God, as of the judge of living and dead. And we must not think little of our salvation.'

262. On this see A. von Harnack, *Die Entstehung des Neuen Testaments und die wichtigsten Folgen der neuen Schöpfung*, Leipzig 1914, 47 n. 1: had the collection of the four Gospels been made late, presumably 'care would already have been taken in the superscription for the Gospel of Mark to appear as that of Peter and the Gospel of Luke as that of Paul'.

263. See Zahn, *Kanon* (n. 12), 1888, 1, 1, 103–13; Irenaeus, *Adv.Haer.* 3, 12, 12 (*differentiae utriusque Testamenti . . . causas*) still means the two covenants in the Pauline sense of II Cor. 3. The anonymous anti-Montanist in Eusebius, *HE* 5, 16, 3 (around 200) can say that one may not enlarge or add anything to the 'word of the new covenant of the Gospel' if one is resolved 'to live by the Gospel itself'. Here Gospel, new covenant and immutable right way of living are interconnected.

264. II Clement 8.5. There follows a quotation from Luke 16.11 with slight variations and a literal quotation of Luke 16.10a, see Hengel, *Studies in the Gospel of Mark* (n. 10), 167 n. 42.

265. 8.2; 15.3, 4; see below.

266. See above, 55, 73, and below, n. 301.

267. Eusebius, *HE* 4, 22, 3.

268. 1.1: 'So that the Lord may show us from above what is according to the Gospel' , cf. 19.1.

269. 4: 'This is not how the Gospel teaches.' This is directed against the urge for martyrdom, which, as the example of a Phrygian shows, leads to apostasy: presumably a polemic against budding Montanism. For the Martyrdom of Polycarp, the Gospels and Montanism see G. Buschmann, *Das Martyrium des Polykarp*, KAV 6, Göttingen 1998, 49–58: 'The author probably referred back to all four Gospels and possibly also to traditions outside the New Testament' (49a). Features of the imitation of Christ in accordance with the passion story can clearly be recognized.

270. 8.2: 'as the Lord commanded in his Gospel', followed by a reference to the Our Father in Matt. 6.9–13 and preceded by a reference to Matt. 6.5: here the 'Gospel of the Kyrios' is that of Matthew. Cf. Didache 15.3; this could refer to Matt. 5.22–26 and 15.4, which refers to 6.7ff. and 6.16ff. In the Didache εὐαγγέλιον no longer means only oral teaching; there can even be a reference to Matt. 10.40–42 in 11.3.

271. Smyrn 5.1; cf. 7.2. Cf. Hengel, *Studies in the Gospel of Mark* (n. 10), 71.

272. Hengel, *Johanneische Frage* (n. 85), 68ff. = *Johannine Question*, 14f. See below, n. 551.

273. Eusebius twice calls him bishop of Hierapolis in Phrygia (see 2, 15, 2; 3, 36, 2 = Irenaeus), a further friend of Polycarp, at the same time bishop in Smyrna, and hearer of John, very probably the elder John, see Hengel, *Johannine Question* (n. 85), 16ff., 24ff. As is shown by the letters of Ignatius, c. AD 110–114, the monarchical episcopate had just come into being in Asia Minor. In Syria it had been already acknowledged; in Rome it was only established with Anicetus around AD 140/150. There is no good reason to doubt these remarks of the first church historian, who had read the work of Papias. Probably the precursor of the monarchical episcopate was James, the brother of the Lord, in Jerusalem. It began in the East and moved to the West, see Hengel, 'Jakobus der Herrenbruder – der erste Papst', in *Glaube und Eschatologie, Festschrift für W.G. Kümmel zum 80. Geburtstag*, Tübingen 1985, 71–104: 103f. For Papias see U. H. J. Körtner, *Papias von Hierapolis*, FRLANT 133, 1983 and 'Papias', *TRE* 25, 1995, 641–4 (with bibliography). His discussion of the texts about Matthew and Mark in his monograph, 203–20, is the least satisfactory part of the work. In dating (88–94, 97ff., 225f.) he arrives at an early date around 110 instead of the time of Hadrian, 117–138, inferred on the basis of Philip Sidetes (Fragment 11, Funk-Biehlmeyer; 10, Körtner, 63; 16, Kürzinger). According to him, the reference to the 'days of Hadrian' rests on a confusion with the Quadratus fragment in Eusebius, *HE* 4, 3, 2f. Particularly given

his early dating, it is remarkable that he passes such a negative verdict on the notes about Mark and Matthew. Now Heckel, *Evangelium* (n. 12), 219–65, also goes into Papias' work at length and positively; from a fragment he wants to infer a collection of four Gospels between 110 and 120. His thorough investigation sometimes comes to interesting conclusions, but he reads rather too much out of the few fragments.

274. Eusebius, *HE* 3, 39, 1. Cf. above, nn. 232 and 233, for the titles of Basilides' work.

275. For a higher estimation of oral tradition see Loveday Alexander, 'The Living Voice. Scepticism towards Written Word in Early Christian and in Greco-Roman Texts', in *The Bible in Three Dimensions*, ed. D. J. A. Clines et al., JSOT.S 87, 1990, 221–47 (242ff. on Papias und Clement of Alexandria). Heckel, *Evangelium* (n. 12), 244, gives examples from the second century; he rightly emphasizes that Papias of course also used written sources, as Eusebius, *HE* 3, 39, 7 reports at the end of his account where he mentions 'witnesses' from I John and I Peter.

276. Eusebius, *HE* 3, 39, 15.

277. According to Irenaeus, *Adv.Haer.* 2, 22, 5; 3, 3, 4 = Eusebius, *HE* 2, 73, 3, John lived until the days of Trajan (98–117).

278. According to Irenaeus, *Adv.Haer.* 3, 11, 7, the reference to Mark 14.34 was made by some Docetic Gnostics who separated Jesus from Christ and said that the Christ who had come from heaven remained incapable of suffering: only the man Jesus suffered. See on this also the Gospel of Peter, which makes Jesus call out, 'My power, my power, you have forsaken me' (Aland, *Synopsis*, 489); cf. I John; see Hengel, *Johanneische Frage* (n. 85), 129ff. As Irenaeus explicitly emphasizes, the Gospels were not fundamentally put in question by the Gnostics, but rather confirmed (see above, 11f., 34f.). Marcion is an exception here.

279. Hengel, *Studies in the Gospel of Mark* (n. 10), 18; R. Bauckham, 'Papias and Polycrates on the Origins of the Fourth Gospel', *JTS* 44, 1993, 24–69: 50. See now at length Heckel, *Evangelium* (n. 12), 257: 'The note on Mark praises and censures the Gospel of Mark at the same time.'

280. Hengel, *Johanneische Frage* (n. 85), 86ff. = *Johannine Question*, 16ff.

281. *Die johanneische Frage* (n. 85) gives yet further reasons for this.

282. See now Hengel, 'Das Johannesevangelium als Quelle für die Geschichte des antiken Judentums', *Kleine Schriften* II (n. 120), 293–334.

283. The closest parallel to this expression is the beginning of II John:

'The elder to the elect lady and her children', see M. Hengel, 'Die auserwählte Herrin, die Braut und die Gottesstadt', in *Die Stadt Gottes/La cité de Dieu*, ed. M. H. and S. Mittmann and A. M. Schwemer, forthcoming in WUNT 2000.

284. Murdered on 18 September AD 96.

285. Eusebius, *HE* 3, 39, 16.

286. The mission discourse in Matt. 10, the community discourse in Matt. 18 and above all the apocalyptic discourse in Matt. 24 are here also in part shaped from Markan material. By contrast the Markan share in Matt. 5–7 and 23 is slight.

287. If Luke is c. 10–15 years earlier than Matthew, which seems to me to be certain, it may be that here and there in texts common to both Matthew is dependent on Luke.

288. A. von Harnack, *Sprüche und Reden Jesu, Beiträge zur Einleitung in das NT*, II, Leipzig 1907. For Harnack's theological and ethical views see above, 5f.

289. Ibid., 7.

290. The mention of the πολλοί in Luke 1.1 is to be taken quite seriously. It will hardly have been different with the later Matthew. If someone was writing a Gospel between 90 and 100 he will have assembled as many 'sources' as possible, written and oral material.

291. Matthew 9.9 replaces the name Levi for the tax-collector with Matthew and in 10.3 adds to the name of Matthew in the list of the Twelve a τελώνης, i. e. tax-collector. See W.G. Kümmel, *The New Testament, The History of the Investigation of its Problems*, 1973, 84, according to F. Schleiermacher, *Über die Zeugnisse des Papias von unseren ersten Evangelien*, 1832, *Sämtliche Werke* I, 2, 1836, 361ff.

292. Acts 4.13: 'that they were uneducated and common men', cf. John 7.15 for Jesus himself.

293. See e.g. H. J. Holtzmann, *Lehrbuch der historisch-kritischen Einleitung in das Neue Testament*, Freiburg ²1886, 387: Papias 'in his report was probably thinking of our Matthew . . .; but the Presbyter John could very well have known and meant an Aramaic collection of logia, to which the wording of the evidence points'.

294. Against J. Kürzinger, *Papias von Hierapolis und die Evangelien des Neuen Testaments*, Eichstätter Materialien 4, Regensburg 1983, 9–67. Similarly ἑρμηνευτής in the notice of the Presbyter about Mark means 'translator'. The former Galilean fisherman Peter certainly did not speak Greek fluently and faultlessly. At times a translator could have been helpful. In Rome he possibly even needed a Latin translator. We know far too little about the details to give exact answers.

295. For Davies and Allison see above, n.195. I could agree with the

argument in G. D. Kilpatrick, *The Origins of the Gospel According to St Matthew,* Oxford 1946, 138f.: 'Even after the changes of Matt IX.9, X.3, Matthew is a less important figure than Peter and if an apostolic name was to be sought for the contents of the book, it could be expected that Peter would have been chosen. The fact that this is not so makes against the possibility that the title of the book was subsequent to its production and arose out of Matt IX.9, X.3. The second possibility makes the book from the beginning deliberately pseudonymous. This view still preserves a connection between the two passages in Matthew and the title. We have seen . . . that the book was probably written about AD 90–100 and that the title cannot have even come into being later than 125. These two statements would wholly agree with the book *being imputed to the Apostle from the beginning*' (my italics). Kilpatrick conjectures that attribution of the title was not the act of an individual, but took place with the authorization of the community. One could add: the community/ies standing behind 'Matthew', the head of the school, or his circle of disciples, could have provided the copies with accompanying letters when they were disseminated in the communities. Indeed the Gospel addressed the whole church. See above, 76ff.

296. Massaux, *Influence* (n. 224); Köhler, *Matthäusevangelium* (n. 109). See already the verdict of Holtzmann, *Einleitung* (n. 293), 385, on the time of Trajan and later: 'But as far as we can go back, Matthew is the most-used book, not merely in Jewish Christianity which was turning into the church, but also with the scriptural representatives of the Gentile church. The predilection for it made the use of the two others more difficult.'

297. Matt. 13.52; cf. 23.34, see M. Hengel, 'Die Bergpredigt des Matthäus und ihr jüdischer Hintergrund', in *Judaica, Hellenistica et Christiana. Kleine Schriften* II, WUNT 109, Tübingen 1998, 219–92: 238ff.

298. For a detailed discussion of the dating see above, 170, 186ff. For the assessment of Matthew in the nineteenth century see Holtzmann, *Einleitung* (n. 293), 383f., cf. 387f. For a critical discussion of the original Hebrew document see at length A. Hilgenfeld, *Historisch-kritische Einleitung in das Neue Testament,* Leipzig 1875, 457–64: 'The canonical Gospel of Matthew refers us back even to a kind of εὐαγγέλιον καθ"Εβραίους.' In itself it indicates the difference between an old, Judaistic nucleus from the time before the destruction of Jerusalem and a later, still Jewish Christian but already universalistic revision immediately after the destruction of Jerusalem.' Thus Hilgenfeld assumes three stages: the Hebrew Gospel of Matthew, its Greek revision and the universalistic canonical Gospel of

Matthew (461ff.). H. D. Betz, *The Sermon on the Mount*,
Minneapolis 1995, 88, conjectures for the Sermon on the Mount a
Jewish-Christian author of the Gospel who wanted to address only
Jewish Christians. However, the Matthaean Sermon on the Mount
with the new 'law of the Messiah' is the theological heart of the First
Gospel and wholly stamped by the theology of the evangelist. If any-
where, his theological heart beats here. The concluding saying of the
Risen Christ in 28.20, 'teaching all that I commanded you', refers
primarily to this fulminating impact of the teaching of Jesus.
Hypotheses like that of H. D. Betz underestimate the argumentative
power of the Jewish-Christian evangelist, who was trained in a
Jewish house of teaching. In southern Syria he is familiar with mixed
communities and emphasizes that Jesus and his disciples were Jews;
he deliberately limits Jesus' activity to Israel, presupposes Mark,
Luke, special material and a 'logia source' (or sources) which can no
longer be reconstructed, and in his work addresses the whole
church. His success proved his plan right! Cf. also the criticism of U.
Luz and me by H. D. Betz, 'The Sermon on the Mount in Matthew's
Interpretation', in *The Future of Christianity. Essays in Honor of
Helmut Koester*, ed. B. A. Pearson, Minneapolis 1991, 258–75:
263f. For him the Sermon on the Mount is 'thoroughly Jewish',
whereas the author of the First Gospel was 'a Christian theologian'.
Here a completely false antithesis is constructed. Were not the first
missionaries, who also addressed non-Jews and then in time built up
predominantly Gentile-Christian communities, genuine Jews, first
and foremost the former Pharisees Paul, and can we so simply
describe Matt. 5.20 and the following antitheses as 'thoroughly
Jewish'? The one who preaches the Sermon on the Mount after all
sets his authority above that of Moses! The same goes for the universal statement in 5.13ff. and 7.21–23, where Jesus appears as the
coming judge, which can only be understood christologically. When
Matthew speaks of the law, he has in view the radical commandment to love and not the ritual law (5.43–48; 7.12; 9.13; 22.35–40).
The criticism of the demands of the Sermon on the Mount which
cannot be fulfilled is thought out from a Jewish standpoint, cf.
Justin, *Dial.* 10, 2. If Matt. 5–7 is 'thoroughly Jewish' this is also
true of Matt. 23.2ff. The separation of Christianity from its Jewish
mother cannot be described in such simple terms as Betz thinks. But
anyone who wants to see the author of the First Gospel as a Gentile
Christian does not know contemporary Judaism. See also above,
194–6, 198ff.

299. See W. G. Kümmel, *Introduction to the New Testament*, 1975,
38–79.

300. Kilpatrick, *Origins* (n. 295) 124–34, dates the Gospel with good reasons to the time between 90 and 100. I also arrive at this result, see above, 163ff.

301. In Eusebius, *HE* 4, 22, 8. His report is particularly enigmatic: 'But he also wrote much else, some of which I have already mentioned. He has quoted some things from the Gospel according to the Hebrews and the Syrian Gospel and particularly from the Hebrew language, thus showing that he came to faith from the Hebrews.' In addition, Eusebius says that he presented 'other material' from the 'Jewish unwritten tradition'. Probably Hegesippus used a Greek Jewish-Christian and an Aramaic (= Syrian) Gospel. As far as I can see, this is the earliest Christian literature we know that was written in 'Syriac'. Tatian's Syriac *Diatessaron*, the Odes of Solomon and the works of Bardesanes are later. Possibly 'Syriac' here means Palestinian Aramaic.

302. See above on Clement of Alexandria, 15ff.

303. For Papias' narrative of a women calumniated (accused?) as a sinner, which recalls John 7.53–8.11 and 'is to be found in the Gospel of the Hebrews' see Eusebius, *HE* 3, 39, 17; for Hegesippus see 4, 22, 8 (see above, nn. 179 and 301); for the Gospel of the Hebrews, the authenticity of which is disputed, see 3, 25, 5 (cf. 25, 1). See also his reference to a 'Gospel of the Hebrews' which is the only one that the Ebionites use: 3, 27, 4; cf. above, n. 301.

304. For the Jewish-Christian Gospels see the survey by Vielhauer and Strecker in *NTApoc* I, 1987, 134–78 (with bibliography), though this is unsatisfactory, and the introduction there: 'Thus the number of the Jewish-Christian Gospels – whether there be one, two or three such Gospels – is uncertain as is the identification of the individual fragments and, finally, the character and the relationship to one another of the several Gospels.' There is nothing to add to this.

305. See Josephus, *BJ* 1, 6.

306. T. Zahn, *Das Evangelium des Matthäus*, Leipzig/Erlangen 1922, 14ff. Zahn interprets Irenaeus 3, 1, 1 (see above, 10f.) to mean that Matthew (like John) left Judaea after the execution of James, the brother of the Lord, shortly before the Jewish War and the expelled Jewish Christians took their Aramaic Gospel to Asia Minor, where it was translated *ad hoc* in worship. But that rests on totally unprovable presuppositions. The introduction to the Homily on the Pasch by Melito of Sardes (ed. O. Perler, SC 123, 1966, 60), 'The scripture of the Hebrew Exodus has been read out and the words of the mystery have been expounded', refers to the reading and exposition of the narrative of the exodus of the 'Hebrews' from Egypt; after the Bar Kochba revolt the now negative designation

'Jews' was largely displaced by 'Hebrews'. This is certainly not about the reading of the original Hebrew text, which would have been incomprehensible to the hearers, but about the LXX, even if Melito took trouble to get to know the writings of the Jewish canon on his journey to Palestine: Eusebius, *HE* 4, 26, 13f. Hebrew was largely unknown in the first and second centuries in the synagogues of the Diaspora and therefore also in Asia Minor.

307. Ibid., 15. For the knowledge and use of Mark and Luke see 19. Cf. Zahn, *Einleitung in das Neue Testament* II, ³1907, 265f.

308. Eusebius, *HE* 3, 39, 11 and 14. See above, n.275. Eusebius' report with the few fragments is quite deliberately fragmentary, see the additional information from the church history of Philip Sidetes, e.g. about the killing of James and John the sons of Zebedee by the Jews, cf. Hengel, *Johanneische Frage* (n. 85), 88ff.

309. In the early Middle Ages there was then again a Hebrew translation of the Gospel of Matthew, though there is a dispute as to when it was made. See W. Horbury, 'The Hebrew Matthew and Hebrew Study', in W. Horbury (ed.), *Hebrew Study from Ezra to Ben-Yehuda*, Edinburgh 1999, 122–31; id., in W. D. Davies and D. C. Allison, *St Matthew* (n. 195), 2, 729–38; W. L. Petersen, 'The *Vorlage* of Shem-Tob's "Hebrew Matthew"', *NTS* 44, 1988, 490–512.

310. See e. g. J. D. Crossan, *Jesus* (n. 22) with its miraculous multiplication of Jesus sources, 427ff.; H. Koester, *Gospels* (n. 50), 75ff., 173ff., 187ff., 205ff., 216ff., 293ff., etc.

311. Cf. Körtner, *Papias* (n. 273), 185ff., 194ff.; Hengel, *Johanneische Frage* (n. 85), 76–8.

312. Eusebius, *HE* 3, 39, 12f.: σφόδρα γὰρ σμικρὸς ὢν τὸν νοῦν. Cf. the verdict of the Origenist Bishop Dionysius of Alexandria (c. 190/200–264/5) on the Apocalypse of John in connection with the Roman presbyter Gaius (c. 190/200) in Eusebius, *HE* 3, 28, 1–5; 7, 24f. The discovery of an early papyrus of the Apocalypse from the third/fourth century which is to appear in POx 1999 is a sensation.

313. Justin, *Dial.* 12, 2f.; 14, 3: 'this is the new lawgiver'; 18, 3; cf. 'new law', 11, 4; 122, 50; Origen, *In Matt.* 30, 26, 22 = MPG 11, 601a.

314. Clement of Alexandria, *Hypotyposes*, in Eusebius, *HE* 6, 14, 7; see above, 43 and n. 185.

315. See Kilpatrick, *Origins* (n. 295), 59ff., 72ff. 'Mark, Q and M(atthew) had been read and expounded in the same way as the Old Testament in Judaism' (59). Here, however, I would prefer to say 'in a new way'. For Mark see above, 122–5. In the case of the Our Father, the third petition which has been added in Matthew expounds the second and the seventh the fifth and sixth.

316. The three-membered baptismal formula does not appear again in the New Testament. Luke in Acts, like Paul, has only the one-membered christological formula. See in detail above, 199.

317. Matt 5.13f. For the problem see the fundamental studies collected by R. Bauckham (ed.), *The Gospels for All Christians. Rethinking the Gospel Audiences*, Grand Rapids and Cambridge 1998.

318. For the Latinisms see the long list of examples in U. Schnelle, *Einleitung in das Neue Testament*, ³1999, 217f. They could easily be increased in number. They are unique in Greek literature, cf. P. Dschulniggg, *Sprache, Redaktion und Intention des Markus-evangeliums*, SBB 11, Stuttgart ²1986, 265–8, 620; see also M. Hengel, 'Mc 7, 3 πυγμῆ. Die Geschichte einer exegetischen Aporie und der Versuch ihrer Lösung', ZNW 60, 1969, 182–98; also *Mark* (n. 10), 29f., 137f. nn. 161–4; against G. Theissen, *Lokalkolorit und Zeitgeschichte in den Evangelien*, Freiburg and Göttingen 1989, 247–51. The Palestinian 'local colouring', which Theissen rightly stresses is connected with the fact that the author comes from Jerusalem and the author standing behind him is a Galilean. Had the Gospel originated in Syria one would expect more references to this fact and a better knowledge of the situation (but cf. Matt. 4, 24: 'So his fame spread throughout all Syria.' There is nothing like this in Mark!).

319. See Hengel, *Mark* (n. 10), 1–30, 117–38 and above, 190ff.

320. Mark 8.34; Luke 9.23 reinterprets it and thus weakens it: καθ' ἡμέραν, cf. 14.27 = Matt. 16.24.

321. Tacitus, *Annals* 15, 44: *aut crucibus affixi flammandique, ubi defecisset dies, in usum nocturni luminis urerentur.* Cf. I Clem. 6 and M. Hengel, *Crucifixion*, London 1977, 26f.

322. John 21.18f.; cf. 13.36; I Clem. 5.4; Acts of Peter 37.8; Tertullian, *Scorp.* 15, 3; Eusebius, *HE* 3, 2, 1; see also R. Pesch, *Simon Petrus*, Stuttgart 1980, 113–34. P 109 = POx 65, 1998, No. 4448 on 21.8 (first half of the third century) probably has the short reading ἄλλοι [ζώσουσιν καὶ οἴσ]ουσιν σε, cf. P 59 (seventh century), i.e. the plural, which appears with considerable variants in Sin, C², D, W, 1 pr, 33, 565pc sy^hmg, pbo and refers to the action of the executioners who crucify Peter. This must be a very old textual variant.

323. The first crucifixion in Syria attested in our sources is the martyrdom of Symeon son of Clopas in the time of Trajan under the proconsul Atticus, around AD 107: Eusebius, *HE* 3, 32, 6 according to Hegesippus. Cf. Hengel, *Crucifixion* (n.323), 32 and 27: in the second century we have far more testimonies. Matt. 23.34 possibly refers to the action of Jewish opponents directed against Christian prophets which perhaps led to their execution by the Romans, an

event which could fit into the late period of Domitian, but which cannot clearly be verified.

324. See H. P. Rüger, 'Die lexikalischen Aramaismen im Markus-evangelium', in H. Cancik (ed.), *Markus-Philologie*, WUNT 33, Tübingen 1984, 73–84: 'The large number of lexical Aramaisms in the Gospel of Mark and the relative uniformity of their rendering with the help of the Greek alphabet suggests that Mark knew Aramaic.' These lexical Aramaisms, which are unique in Greek writing, definitely indicate the author is a Jew from the motherland. It is absurd in this context to suppose that in Mark 5.41 or 7.34 there is the 'barbaric speech' of a Christian magician. Mark knows the meaning of these Aramaic expressions and renders them appropriately. They are the counterpart to the numerous Latinisms which demonstrate the place of origin, see above, n.318.

325. Col. 4.10; cf. Acts 12.12, 25; 13.5, 13; 15.37, 39; Philemon 24; I Peter 5.13; II Tim. 4.11.

326. However, it does not say there that Mark was the 'secretary and interpreter' of Peter, thus H. Conzelmann and A. Lindemann, *Arbeitsbuch zum NT*, [12]1998, 320; the interpreter appears only with Papias and Irenaeus. Nowhere is there mention of 'secretary', for example in the sense of Rom. 16.22; in that case one would think of Silvanus (5.12) here. The greeting from 'Mark, my son', indicates rather a teacher-pupil relationship; that is also maintained by the whole church tradition of Papias, Irenaeus, Clement of Alexandria, Eusebius and later figures.

327. Cf. still Philemon 24; II Tim. 4.11. Not being an apostle, he dis-appears in the Apostolic Fathers, the apologetic literature and even the apocryphal Acts of the Apostles in the second century. In *NTApoc* he appears only once in the Apocalypse of Paul, ch. 51 (II, 742). Only in Irenaeus is he mentioned again as the Second Evangelist (and also the detested Gnostic and contemporary of Irenaeus with the same name). The Latin name Marcus was not all that widespread in the Greek speaking East. Hippolytus, *Refut.* 7, 30, 1, has the old and strange nickname κολοβοδάκτυλος, 'the one with mutilated fingrers'; cf. the prologue to Mark in Aland, *Synopsis*, [15]1996, 548; J. Regul, *Die antimarkionitische Evangelien-prologe*, Freiburg 1969, 29.

328. Acts 13.13; cf. 15.37ff., the abrupt form of the conflict with Barnabas; see Hengel and Schwemer, *Paulus* (n.9), 330 = *Paul*, 216.

329. See R. Morgenthaler, *Statistische Synopse*, Zürich and Stuttgart 1971, 189: 'that according to our basic statistics of the total of 885 sentences and fragments from Mark, 709 are taken over by Matthew and 565 by Luke.'

330. To some degree this absurd theory still haunts the New Testament textbooks, introductions and commentaries on Mark. One of the pseudo-arguments is that Mark 7.3f. does not report the Jewish customs relating to cleanness exactly. Certainly, Mark had not read either Strack-Billerbeck or Josephus, nor had he taken part in any undergraduate seminars on the New Testament. The criticism that he is 'not familiar with the details of the geography of Palestine' and that 'Jewish customs' are 'alien to him' fails to recognize the character of his work in a predominantly Gentile Christian milieu. He is not interested in Samaria, nor is Matthew. Mark 7.31 is geographically quite correct, as the region of Sidon borders on that of Damascus (see Hengel and Schwemer, *Paulus* (n. 9), 91 = *Paul*, 57, and Josephus, *Antt.* 18, 153), but of course Mark had never seen a map of Palestine. 14.12 presupposes the Roman calculation of the day, where the day does not begin in the evening but with sunrise. Mark wants to write in an understandable way for his predominantly 'Gentile-Christian' hearers and readers and not in the style of New Testament seminar work. For the whole question see already Hengel, *Between Jesus and Paul*, 92ff. and 127f.; *Studies in Mark* (n. 10). In my presence a well-known Tübingen theologian confused the villages of Pfrondorf and Wankheim before the gates in Tübingen and the Goldersbachtal with the Ammertal. Is Mark to be said not to have been a Jerusalemite because of the sequence Bethphage and Bethany' (11.1) – quite apart from the fact that we do not know precisely how the road from Jericho went at that time? In particular, textbooks for students were not meant to be too clever. There is a kind of criticism which is again in danger of sometimes turning into uncritical folly.

331. Dibelius, *From Tradition to Gospel*, 192, 242.

332. Mark 1.16: ' he saw Simon and Andrew, Simon's brother.'

333. Mark 16.7; cf. Matt. 28.7. Matthew has all that is needed, in the right order. The Markan 'and Peter' deliberately disrupts the narrative thread.

334. Only Paul (I Cor. 15.5) and Luke 24.34 speak of this; the latter shifts this vision to Jerusalem, against Mark and Matthew: Mark 14.28; 16.7 = Matthew 26.32; 16.7, cf. 28.10, 6; Jesus meets only the two women in Jerusalem, 28.9f. In Matthew the fourfold reference to Galilee is particularly striking. I would see this as a deliberate contradiction of Luke 24.49, 52, cf. Acts 1.12. The mount of revelation in Galilee takes the place of the Mount of Olives, see above, 182.

335. John 1.35ff.; 20.24–29; 21.22f. Cf. my *Johanneische Frage* (n. 85), 210ff. = *Johannine Question*, 74ff. As in Papias, Andrew is mentioned first here and only then Simon Peter.

336. 16.7; cf. 14.28 and 8.31; 9.31; 10.32–34; cf. 9.9.
337. On this see R. Feldmeier, 'Die Darstellung des Petrus in den synoptischen Evangelien', in P.Stuhlmacher (ed.), *Das Evangelium und die Evangelien*, WUNT 28, Tübingen 1983, 267–71.
338. Only in 9.38 does John address Jesus alone.
339. 1.16, 29; 3.18; 13.3.
340. 3.19; 14.10, 43.
341. See Feldmeier (n. 337), 267: Mark contains 11, 078 words and for Peter the ratio is 1:443 (including the inauthentic ending 16.9–20, which does not mention Peter); Matthew 18, 298 words and a ratio of 1:772; Luke, who mentions Peter thirty times, with 19, 448 has a ratio of 1:648 (figures from R. Morgenthaler, *Statistik des neutestamentlichen Wortschatzes*, Zurich and Frankfurt am Main 1958, 164). We should also not forget here that both Gospels are literally dependent on Mark.
342. Simon, Mark 1.16, 29, 30, 36; 3.16: 'whom he surnamed Peter'; in 14.37, in Gethsemane Jesus 'says to Peter, "Simon, are you asleep?"'.The evangelist knows that Jesus addressed Peter with his proper name. After the reception of the new name Πέτρος alone is mentioned 17 times. The use of Σίμων and Πέτρος is thus very well planned.
343. I Cor. 1.12; 3.22; 9.5; 15.5; Gal. 1.18; 2. 9, 11, 14; Gal. 2.7, cf. also John 1.42: 'Cephas which means Peter'. Acts uses 'Peter' 56 times, more than any of the Gospels. Only 'Paul' (128 times) is used more often there.
344. 9.38ff.; John 10.35ff., the sons of Zebedee.
345. 8.29, 32f.; 9.5; 10.28; 11.21; 14.29f.
346. 14.37; 14.66–72: but cf. John 18.15f. and on this Dibelius, *From Tradition to Gospel* (n. 331), 217f.; Hengel, *Johanneische Frage* (n. 85), 36, 215f., 309.
347. 'Die Verleugnung des Petrus', in *Rekonstruktion und Interpretation*, BEvTh 60, Munich 1969, 49–98; cf. the self-confident statement, 74: 'Bultmann's statement that this is "legendary and literary" (*History of the Synoptic Tradition*, 269) has been proved from every possible aspect and against any relevant objections.' Such pseudo-historical self-assurance discredits itself. See, rather, with the sharp eyes of the real historian, M. Dibelius, *From Tradition to Gospel* (n. 331), 214–16; 'For there is no objection to the assumption that Peter reported about himself' (his denial). One notes throughout that Dibelius' work, which is concerned with historical plausibility, comes from a pupil of the brilliant historian A. Harnack .
348. Σίμων καὶ οἱ μετ' αὐτοῦ.

349. I Cor. 9.5; cf. M. Hengel, 'Apostolische Ehen und Familien', *INTAMS Review* 3, 1997, 1, 62–77 = *Interpretation of the Bible. The Slovenian Academy of Sciences and Arts. University of Ljubljana*, Sheffield 1998, 257–76.

350. M. Hengel, 'Literary, Theological and Historical Problems in the Gospel of Mark', in *Studies in Mark* (n. 10), 31–63, 155 n.72.

351. R. Bultmann, *History of the Synoptic Tradition*, Oxford ²1968, 350. This tendency is also still widespread today. It rests on the fact that scholars can no longer can and will perceive the real event in space and time but favour ideological premises and therefore devalue it. 'Fact' has become a taunt; see Hengel and Schwemer, *Paulus* (n. 9), 38 n.139 = *Paul*, 20f.

352. Cf. 14.28ff.: walking on the sea; 16.18: saying about the rock; 15.15: Peter asks for an interpretation of the simile = Mark 7.17: the disciples; 17.24 the pericope about the temple tax. In Luke the mentions of names are concentrated above all around 5.3–10; cf. also 22.31 and 24.34. It is striking that the brothers of Jesus fade right into the background. Mark gives their names only in 6.3 = Matt. 13.55 and mentions them negatively as a group in the framework of the family of Jesus, 3.31–35 = Luke 8.19–21 = Matt. 12.46–50. The complete retreat of James shows that the greater part of the Synoptic tradition had already reached the predominantly Gentile Christian West at the latest in the 40s, when James took over the leadership in Jerusalem, and here Peter played the central role; in other words, he is the most important mediator of Jesus tradition in the West. That is already evident from his prominent role in the letters of Paul.

353. In addition to the passages mentioned above (n.352), the brothers of Jesus also appear in John 2.12 and quite negatively in 7.3, 5 as members of the earliest communities in Acts 1.14. In Acts 12.17 Luke does not even say that this James who emerges immediately after the death of James the son of Zebedee, in 12.2 is the 'brother of the Lord'. That can only rest on a certain aversion. See Hengel, 'Jakobus, der Herrenbruder – der erste Papst' (n.273), 101. But cf. the logion Gospel of Thomas 23, which is influenced by Jewish Christianity and the traditions about the kinsfolk of the Lord in Hegesippus.

354. I married forty-three years ago, and can still very well remember the time when I left Tübingen with a half-finished dissertation on the Zealots, apparently to devote myself for ever to a job in industry. But cf. above, 6, on the huge chronological distance between Muhammad and his first biographers.

355. 14. 51f.; 15.21; 15.40; 16.1.

356. Bultmann, *History of the Synoptic Tradition* (n.351), 370f. But see the objection by Lars Hartman, 'Das Markusevangelium, "für die lectio sollemnis im Gottesdienst abgefasst"', in *Geschichte – Tradition – Reflexion. Festschrift M. Hengel*, ed. H. Cancik, H. Lichtenberger and P. Schäfer, Tübingen 1996, III, 147–71; 163. W.Marxsen, *Mark the Evangelist*, 131, calls for a radical separation between kerygma and historiography: 'From the outset that means that his work is to be read as proclamation, and not as a "report of Jesus". From this aspect, it is almost accidental that something in the way of a report *also* appears. In any case, it is only raw material. Paul can largely discard this raw material.' Against this see J. Roloff, *Das Kerygma und der irdische Jesus. Historische Motive in den Jesus-Erzählungen der Evangelien*, Göttingen 1970, above all the conclusion, 270ff.: 'Some basic features of the earthly activity of Jesus have deliberately been maintained by the tradition, largely keeping their distance from the post-Easter church' (277): 'The Christ event was not taken up into the present experience of the spirit but also brought about events in history, here by analogy with the Old Testament saving events.' See also Hengel, 'Kerygma oder Geschichte?', *ThQ* 151, 1971, 323–36 (especially 329ff.), and E. E. Lemcio, *The Past of Jesus in the Gospels*, SNTS.MS 68, 1991, on all four Gospels.

357. For the messianic secret see Hengel, *Studies in Mark* (n. 10), 41–5, 146f.

358. 1.1, 11; 3.1; 5.7; 9.7, 14, 61; 15.39; see also Dibelius, *From Tradition to Gospel* (n. 331), 233, 261. 'Thus Mark took up a small part of the sayings tradition from limited perspectives; however, he made no secret of the fact that this was only a selection.' Mark certainly emphasizes Jesus' activity as a teacher endowed with divine authority, but 'what he offers here is only a selection, only an example' (236).

359. Mark 6.7f., 12f., 30, but cf. 9.14–27 and, related to Jesus, 6.5.

360. By Gentiles is primarily to be understood the 'God-fearers' and 'sympathizers' in the first thirty or forty years of the church, who had positive contact with the synagogue. Luke, for example, comes from this milieu, see above, 101, 103 and below, nn. 416, 614, and Hengel and Schwemer, *Paulus* (n. 9), 80–139 = *Paul*, 50–90; B. Wander, *Gottesfürchtige und Sympathisanten*, WUNT II/104, 1998.

361. Bultmann, *History* (n. 351), 220: 'Moreover the *Hellenistic* origin of the miracle stories is overwhelmingly probable.' 'In Mark he is a θεῖος ἄνθρωπος, indeed more: the Son of God walking on the earth' (cf. E. Käsemann, *The Testament of Jesus*, London 1968, 11, following F. C. Baur on the 'Johannine Christ, as the God striding over

the earth.' Does not the christology of both evangelists become a cliché here?); 247: 'Mark could have been the normal Gospel for the Hellenistic Christianity of the Pauline sphere.' The author aims at the 'union of the Hellenistic kerygma of Christ, the essential content of which is the Christ myth as we know it from Paul (esp. Phil 2.6ff.; Rom. 3.24), with the tradition of the history of Jesus'. By contrast I cannot establish a fundamental difference between 'Jewish-Palestinian' and 'Hellenistic' miracle stories. This division, radical and at the same time artificial, which dominated Bultmann's view of history, has meanwhile been dropped as a result of my own work. At most, the essential element is the linguistic frontier which runs through Jewish Palestine itself. In contrast to Bultmann, Dibelius, *From Tradition to Gospel* (n. 331), has kept pointing this out: 30–6, 172–4. But he too is wrong in speaking of a 'unilingual Jerusalem' (20), and wanting to presuppose a knowledge of Greek only in Northern Palestine (34). See my *Kleine Schriften* I, 1–90 und II, 115–56. For the questionable nature of the θεῖος ἄνθρωπος scheme see B. L. Blackburn, *Theios Aner and the Markan Miracle Traditions,* WUNT II/40, 1991, and now D. S. du Toit, *THEIOS ANTHROPOS,* WUNT II/91, Tübingen 1997.

362. *Einleitung in die ersten drei Evangelien,* ²1911, 155.

363. *Ursprung und Anfänge des Christentums* I, 121, 159 n.1; for the problem see Hengel, *Studies in Mark* (n.10), 1–30: 17f. Here the lives of the saints composed by contemporaries and sometimes going back to eye-witnesses, like that of Sulpicius Severus on Martin of Tours, are particularly interesting. The life of Symeon Stylites in the *Philothea Historia* of Theodoret of Cyrrhus (no. XXVI, SC 257, ed. P. Canivet and A. Leroy-Molinghen, 1979, II, 158–215) and Theodoret's remarks about eye-witness (SC 234, 1977, prol 11 I, 142f.) could also be compared. See also the introduction by the editor, I, 22–8; also R. Doran, *The Lives of Symeon Stylites,* CiSt 112, Spencer, Mass. 1992, 36ff.

364. The apostle himself speaks in the first person only in the Gospel of Peter. The completely miraculous nature of the account is miles away from the masterly, theologically thought-out narrative art of Mark.

365. Rom. 15.19.

366. II Cor. 12.12, cf. e.g. I Cor. 14.24f.; also Gal. 3.5 and I Cor. 2.4f. See now S. Alkier, *Wunder und Wirklichkeit in den Briefen des Apostels Paulus* (forthcoming 2000 in WUNT).

367. Origen, *Contra Celsum* 1, 46 (cf. 1, 2, the proof of the spirit and power, I Cor. 2.4, in the church): 'Traces of the Holy Spirit . . . are still preserved among Christians. They charm demons away and

perform many cures and perceive certain things about the future according to the will of the Logos. Even if Celsus . . . ridicule what I am about to say, nevertheless it shall be said that many have come to Christianity as it were in spite of themselves, some spirit having turned their mind suddenly from hating the Gospel to dying for it by means of vision by day or by night. We have known many instances like this. But if we were to commit them to writing, although we were eyewitnesses present at the time, we would bring upon ourselves downright mockery from the unbelievers, who would think that we were inventing the stories ourselves . . .' Translation by H. Chadwick, *Origen Contra Celsum*, Cambridge 1953, 42 cf. 7, 8 and ibid., 402 n. 1.

368. For the much-discussed question of the literary genre of the Gospels see the informative work by R. A. Burridge, *What are the Gospels? A Comparison with Graeco-Roman biography*, SNTS.MS 70, 1992. By the standards of antiquity they are βίοι, but as 'saving event' they have a unique, one might almost say incomparable, character. Ordinary biographies do not contain a message of faith which is decisive for eternal life and the last judgment. That is what is completely new about the 'genre' Gospel. But this 'theological inspiration' can also make them 'works of art'. See here the philologist Günther Zuntz, 'Ein Heide las das Markusevangelium', in *Markusphilologie*, ed. H. Cancik, WUNT 33, Tübingen 1984, 205–22: 'a masterpiece of amazing originality . . . which shook the world under his name, the name of Mark' (222).

369. In addition one could think of Gen. 1.1, ἐν ἀρχῇ, but that goes in another direction. Perhaps John as opposed to Mark was inspired to take his 'Beginning' from Gen.1.1. Thus in John the meaning of ἀρχή shifts in a significant way.

370. Hos. 1.2 (after the introductory verse 1.1, which served as a title): Ἀρχὴ λόγου κυρίου ἐν Ὡσηε, cf. Aquila: ἀρχὴ ἦν ἐλάλησεν, MT: *t*ᵉ*hillat dibber YHWH* . . .

371. For '*initium*' and '*incipit*' as the beginning of a discourse or a book see *Oxford Latin Dictionary*, 1968, 867: incipio 2b; 913: initium 3b, the opening (of a book, speech . . .). Cf. Tacitus, *Hist.* 1, 1, 1 Initium *mihi operis* . . . As in Mark, this indicates the chronological beginning of the narrative; see also *Ann.* 1, 1: *Urbem Romanam a principio reges habuere*; Pomp. Trog. (Justin, *Epitome*), 1, 1: Principio *rerum gentium* . . . *imperium penes reges erat*. Terence, *Andria* 709: *narrationis incipit mi initium*, cf. Hecyra, 361f.; Varro, *Ling. lat.* 5, 17: *initium librorum*; Sallust, *Cat.* 4, 5; *initium narrandi*; Cicero, *Brutus* 297: *longi sermonis initium*, cf. Livy 32, 39, 9; Tacitus, *Ann.* 6, 6, 1: *Caesaris litterarum initium*, cf. Cicero, *Attic.*

12, 23, 1 and *ad Quintum fratrem* 2, 14; Plin. min., *Paneg.* 1, 1: *ita dicendi initium a precationibus capere*; Statius, *Silvae* 2, 1, 1–3: *et ad huc vivente favilla ordiar* (How can I begin . . . while the ashes still glow); Sil. It., *Pun.* 1, 1: *Ordior arma . . .* (Here I begin the war . . .); Val. Flacc., *Argon* 1, 1 '*Prima deum . . . canimus.*' This somewhat random list could easily be continued. This phenomenon does not seem to me to be so striking in Greek literature. For the whole question see *Thesaurus linguae Latinae* VII, 1, Leipzig 1964, col. 1654.

372. See *Itala. Das Neue Testament in altlateinischer Übersetzung*, ed. A. Jülicher . . ., I *Matthäusevangelium*, Berlin ²1970, 1; IV *Johannesevangelium*, 1963, 1; II *Markusevangelium*, Berlin ²1970, 1.

373. See the few not always relevant examples in Arndt/Gingrich/Bauer, *Lexicon*, ad loc.: Ion of Chios, *FGrHist* 392 fr. 24 n., Harpocrates, ἀρχὴ δὲ μοι λόγου; Diog. Laert. 3, 37: the beginning of the *Politeia* has often appeared in an altered form; Diodore 17, 11: reference back to the beginning of Book 16; but only in the first instance does ἀρχή introduce a work. The examples from Greek patristic literature about the beginnings of books with ἀρχή and references to scripture are not particularly frequent either; see P. Chrysostomos Baur OSB, *Initia Patrum Graecorum* I, StT 180, Rome 1955, I, 97ff.

374. For εὐαγγέλιον in Mark see Hengel, *Studies in Mark* (n. 10), 53ff. In Mark 1.1 it should be noted that only a comma is to be put after υἱοῦ θεοῦ, against Nestle-Aland and with Irenaeus, Origen and Epiphanius, since as a rule καθὼς γέγραπται does not introduce a main clause but explains a protasis. The full stop is to be put at the end of v. 3. For Mark, the 'beginning of the message of salvation' corresponds to the appearance of John the Baptist as predicted by the prophets. For him, John the Baptist is the 'prophetic herald' of the 'Gospel of Jesus Christ'.

375. 1.14f.

376. Therefore he rejects the 'imminent expectation' which was flourishing at the time of the Jewish War (13.7).

377. See *Studies in Mark* (n. 10), 14ff., 126ff.

378. Matt. 4.23, cf. 9.35 = Mark 1.14; Matt. 24.14 = Mark 13.10.

379. Matt. 26.13; cf. 24.14. The written Gospel here appears as a special form of the generally preached oral Gospel.

380. 15.40f. = Matt. 27.55f.; cf. Luke 23.49. John deliberately introduces the beloved disciple here. He does not fail as the other disciples do. For the role of the women see M. Hengel, 'Maria Magdalena und die Frauen als Zeugen', in *Abraham unser Vater. FS O. Michel zum 60. Geburtstag*, AGSU 5, Leiden 1963, 243–56.

381. In contrast to Matt. 26.13 (see above n. 379).

382. 14.9; cf. 13.10.

383. Probably Mark is thinking here – from Rome – above all of the whole Roman empire. In my view both passages are an argument for the disputed trip of the apostle Paul to Spain, say between 62 and 64; cf. Rom. 15.24. Both Markan texts suggest that Paul, as I Clem. 5.6f. reports, really did travel to Spain: 'He was a herald both in the East and in the West; he gained the noble fame of his faith, he taught righteousness to all the world, and reached the limits of the West.' Only after that did his martyrdom take place. For Paul's trip to Spain see also *Can. Mur.* 35–6 (n. 41) und *Actus Vercellenses, Acta Apostolorum Apocrypha* I, 45, 10; 51, 26 = *NTApoc* II, 288; see Lona, *1 Clem* (n. 219), 165 n. 4f.: only against this background does the bold information in Mark really make sense; at the same time it is an indication of his Roman perspective.

384. Cf. 13.14 and Rev. 1.3, see below, n. 501 and above, 34 (n. 154).

385. Cf. already 13.10, which prepares for 14.9.

386. For the 'dramatic' form of Mark see Hengel, *Studies in Mark* (n. 10), 35–41.

387. M. Kähler, *The Der sogenannte 'historische Jesus' und der geschichtliche, biblische Christus*, ThB2, Munich 1953, 60, n. 0.

388. 21 out of 58 Nestle pages: the shorter form 14.1–16.8 has twelve pages, i.e. around one-fifth.

389. Cf. R. Feldmeier, *Die Krisis des Gottessohnes. Die Gethsemaneerzählung als Schlüssel der Markuspassion*, WUNT II/21, Tübingen 1987; id., 'Der Gekreuzigte im Gnadenstuhl. Exegetische Überlegungen zu Mark 15, 37–39 . . .', in *Le Thrône de Dieu*, WUNT 69, Tübingen 1993, 213–32. See also Hengel, *Studies in Mark* (n. 10), 36f., 44, 124 and 24.

390. 12.36; 13.26; 14.62; cf. 8.38 and 9.1.

391. Mark 4.38, 40; 6.49–51; 7.18; 8.14–21, 32f.; 9.5f.; 10.18f., 32, 34; 10.32, 35–45; 14.26ff., 37f., 50. It is significant that John keeps quiet about the flight of the disciples in Gethsemane. The key phrase 'incomprehension of the disciples' is too little to describe the behaviour of the disciples in Mark. Their incomprehension is sin. With Easter they experience the forgiveness of their guilt. Heckel, *Evangelium* (n. 12), 60 n.119, accuses me and Feldmeier (n. 389) of 'taking too little notice of the ambivalence of the disciples and thus also of Peter as fixed by the open ending'. In reality, however, the ending is not ambivalent but clear, because the twofold promise in 14.28 and 16.7 is unequivocal. The disciples will see the Risen Christ in Galilee and thus come to real faith. Without this faith of the first messengers of Jesus there would be no Gospel at all. Nor is

Mark writing (a few years after the martyrdom of Peter) from a lofty standpoint a criticism of the disciples and Peter; with the reference to the incomprehension, indeed the sinful failure of the disciples and especially of Peter, he is expressing the 'justification of the sinner' which Peter and the disciples have themselves experienced through their encounter with the Risen Christ and the understanding of his death which has been disclosed to them in this way as a saving event. The testimony to this failure comes from Peter himself, just as Paul can refer to the 'justification of the godless' which he, the former per- secutor, has experienced. It too continues to have an influence in the Pauline school, see I Tim. 1. 3; Acts 8.3; 9.1ff.; 22.3ff.; 26.9ff. It is also absurd to believe that Mark was not interested in the problem of the guarantor of tradition: the relatively numerous names in the con- text of the passion tell against this. Heckel is in danger, as are so many today, of making the evangelist a theological romance writer who is remote from reality. That may be modern, but it does not correspond to the historical reality between AD 70 and 100.

392. Cf. 8.17–21, 32f.; 9.34; 10.41ff.; 14.28–50, 54f., 66–72.

393. Mark 9.9, 32; 10.32; cf. 14.29. See also John 2.22; 12.16; 14.26; 20.9.

394. Jesus' forgiveness of sins, his fellowship with tax-collectors and sinners and the raising of the dead which is related of him are for Mark narrative anticipations of his victory over sin and death. That does not exclude the possibility that here Mark is reporting memories – selected carefully and worked over theologically.

395. I Cor. 15.8–10; cf. 9.1; Gal.1.13–17; Phil. 3.4a–11; see Hengel and Schwemer, *Paulus* (n. 9), 91ff., 98ff.

396. In the LXX usually translated καὶ ἰδου; but cf. Gen. 15.4; 38.29 and Symmachus on II Sam. (II Kingdoms) 3.22, according to the Field Hexapla. By this Mark also wants to express the radical progress of the event in the narrated story. I owe this hint to Pastor P. Katz; see *ThZ* 55, 1999, 57–75. I count 32 occurrences of καὶ εὐθύς and a further ten of εὐθύς/εὐθέως.

397. For Herder and Mark see Hengel, *Studies in Mark* (n. 10), 157 n. 78. The quotation comes from J. G. Herder, *Vom Erlöser des Menschen*, 1796, in: *Sämtliche Werke*, ed. B. Suphan, Vol.19, Berlin 1880, 216f. Cf. ibid.: 'No gospel has so little of the written about it and so much of the living voice of the narrator . . . it is the most popular tone of a Palestinian narrator.' Herder recognized the real situation far better than modern pseudo-criticism, which wanted to see the author as an unknown Gentile Christian. See now Hartman (n. 356), 146–71: 163f., who emphasizes the liturgical function of Mark and refers to Col. 3.16: 'Let the word of Christ dwell in you

richly, as you teach and admonish one another in all wisdom.'
Reading at the same time implies instruction and admonition. Cf.
also Luke 1.4, the instruction of Theophilus. For the rhythmical
language of Mark cf. J. A. Kleist, *The Gospel of Saint Mark*, NY,
etc., 1936, 125. on Mark 4.2f.: 'The very rhythm, even apart from
the meaning of the words, puts the hearer in a solemn and attentive
mood'; 126f.: 'knowing that the memoirs of St Peter would be
read aloud and in full assembly, even he must have hoped that they
would penetrate to the Christian heart without stumbling at
the portals of the ear'. See also G. Lüderitz, 'Rhetorik, Poetik,
Kompositionstechnik im Markusevangelium', in Cancik (ed.) (n.
368), 201: 'The text . . . consists of short rhythmic colons.' It is 'rich
in rhetorical figures: congeries, alliteration, geminatio, anaphora,
epiphera, chiasmus, word-play', but it does not follow the learned
rules of rhetoric. For Mark's narrative arts see also the homage of
the philologist G. Zuntz to the evangelist (n. 368).

398. Cf. Zuntz's personal impression on reading the Gospel (n. 368),
207: 'that this is not history like other histories, not biography like
other biographies; but the depiction of the actions, sayings and
sufferings of a higher being on his way through this narrow world of
human beings and demons'. That was the impression that Jesus, the
Risen One who is exalted to the right hand of God, must have made
later on his disciples and their pupils. The cliché 'cult legend' used by
Bultmann (n. 356) does not do justice to this otherness.

399. This applies to the infancy gospels and to the Gnosticizing Gospels
according to Thomas, Philip, etc. See above, 59f.

400. 14.28f.; 17.24ff.; cf. also Peter's question in 18.21f. special material.

401. Simply in terms of words alone, around 70% of Mark has been
taken over by Matthew.

402. According to Morgenthaler, *Statistik* (n. 341), 164, Luke has 19,
428, Matthew 18, 305, John 15, 416 and Mark 11, 242 words.
With almost 38, 000 words Luke-Acts surpasses even the Pauline
corpus, including the Deutero-Paulines. Here we note the most
experienced author in the New Testament.

403. For εὐαγγελίζεσθαι cf. Psalms: 39(40).10; 67(68). 12; 95(96).2;
Deutero-Isaiah: 40.9; 52.7 (cf. Nah. 1.15 [2.1]) 60.6; 61.1; Joel 2.32
(3.5); cf. also the victory message in II Kingdoms (II Sam.) 18.19f.,
27, 31, see above, 3f. In my view the use of the verb in Matt. 11.5 is
dependent on Luke 7.22 and points to Isa. 61.1ff. Cf. the
messianic texts 4 Q 521 (especially line 12, which Isa. 61.1 quotes)
und 11Q Melch 18, see J. Zimmermann, *Messianische Texte von
Qumran*, WUNT II/104, Tübingen 1998, 344ff., 391ff.

404. Ten times in the Gospel and fifteen times in Acts; twenty times in the

authentic letters of Paul.

405. See Hengel and Schwemer, *Paulus* (n. 9), 9–26 = *Paul*, 6–15.

406. Acts 15.7.

407. Cf. Acts 15.11: 'But we believe that we shall be saved through the grace of the Lord Jesus'; 11.23; 13.43; 14.3: the 'word of grace' is identical with the Gospel, see also 20.32. Luke, being a conscious theologian of mediation, is nevertheless not so totally un-Pauline as is sometimes supposed.

408. I Peter 4.17: 'those who do not obey the Gospel of God', cf. the Deutero-Pauline formulation in II Thess. 1.8.

409. Primarily in Mark 1.14f., cf. 8.35; 10.29: because of me and my message.

410. Cf. also Matt. 26.13, 'this Gospel', and 24.14.

411. 1.19; 2.10; 3.18; 4.18 = Isa. 61.1; cf. 7.22; 4.43; 8.1: καὶ κηρύσσων εὐαγγελιζόμενος τὴν βασιλείαν τοῦ θεοῦ; cf.16.16; 9.6: the twelve disciples by Jesus, 20.1.

412. Only in Papias and then again in Justin do we encounter the literary use of dedications corresponding to the time, which presuppose a higher level of education; see Hengel, *Studies in Mark* (n. 10), 174 n. 68.

413. I believe that Luke had an additional 'passion source' besides Mark, see the pupil of J. Jeremias, F. Rehkopf, *Die lukanische Sonderquelle*, WUNT 5, Tübingen 1959, and V. Taylor, 'Rehkopf's List of Words and Phrases Illustrative of Pre-Lukan Speech Usage', *JTS* 15, 1964, 59–62; cf. also J. Jeremias, *Die Sprache des Lukasevangeliums*, Göttingen 1980, 8: 'It still seems to me that Luke's passion narrative is to be counted as non-Markan material, even if no ultimate certainty is to be attained here.'

414. 1.1.

415. Aristeas 1, 1; Apoc.Bar.gr. 1, 1; Vit. Adae 1, 1; II Macc. 2.32; 6.17; seven times in Sirach; Josephus, *BJ* 7, 42.274; *Antt.* 9, 214; 11, 68; 12, 136f.; 20, 157.

416. However, Luke is a political apologist at best on the periphery, as are later Quadratus, Aristides, Justin, Melito etc. (cf. e.g. Luke 20.20–26; 23.2–5, 14–16, 47; Acts 17.7; 26.31f.; see Jervell, *Apostelgeschichte* [n. 28], 87 n. 215). His two-volume work is addressed, rather, to Christians, Gentiles (God-fearers) and Jews who are interested in the new faith and (in Acts) in the unique, indeed controversial person of Paul, i.e. initially above all Theophilus and his circle of friends. The later apologists, too, among other things also write for educated Christians and sympathizers. Despite all the great differences, what he has in common with Eusebius is that he wants to be the first to write 'Christian

history'; here the impetus came from his Jesus story. However, Eusebius had a far more comprehensive education, a unique library in Caesarea and above all great ambitions in church politics and literature. However, with him, too, the missionary endeavour is clear. See D. Mendels, *The Media Revolution of Early Christianity. An Essay on Eusebius's Ecclesiastical History*, Grand Rapids and Cambridge 1999.

417. See Hengel and Schwemer, *Paulus* (n. 9), 17–22; L. Alexander, *The Preface to Luke's Gospel*, MSSNTS 78, Cambridge 1993, is now a basic work.

418. Such a difference in time becomes necessary because of certain tensions in content, above all the fundamental difference between the account of the ascension in Luke 24.44–52 and that in Acts 1.3–14. However, it is probable that with the formula περὶ τῶν περπληροφορημένων ἐν ἡμῖν Luke was already thinking of a second book describing the activity of Peter and Paul up to the time when he was Paul's companion on the journey to Rome. Cf. Jervell, *Apostelgeschichte* (n. 28), 85: 'Acts was written later than the Gospel.' 'We are to presupposes a certain interval in time between Gospel and Acts' (86). I myself would put the Gospel between 75 and 80 (see above, 169ff.), and Acts between 80 and 85.

419. Acts 1.1. Here the Gospel appears as πρῶτος λόγος.

420. Thus in Quintilian's *Institutio oratoria* to a Tryphon, who pressed him to write it; in Statius' *Silvae* to his friend Stella; in Books 2, 8, 9 and 12 of Martial's *Epigrams* and later in Ausonius to the second book of his *Cento nuptialis* (references from H. Cancik and W. Speyer).

421. See sentences like Luke 5.8; 18.4a, which has a quite Pauline formulation or the christological statement 19.10, but also Acts 13.38–41 and the statement of faith in 13.39: ἐν τούτῳ πᾶς ὁ πιστεύων δικαιοῦται. Cf. Acts 20.21, 24, 28b, 32; see Jervell, *Apostelgeschichte* (n. 28), 71: 'Most exegetes assume that in the speeches we also have elements from the tradition.' Luke himself was present at the farewell speech in Miletus (72f.).

422. The fictitious Letter of Aristeas and the writings of Josephus dedicated to Epaphroditus (*Antiquities*, *Life* and *Contra Apionem*) are exceptions here.

423. B. H. Streeter, *The Four Gospels*, London 1924, 559: 'Indeed, it is not impossible that Theophilus was the secret name by which Flavius Clemens was known in the Roman Church.' Of course this remains an unprovable hypothesis, but it could perhaps be related to the milieu from which Theophilus comes. Flavius Clemens and his wife were not the only Roman aristocrats whom Domitian per-

secuted for 'Jewish tendencies'. For Titus Flavius Clemens and his wife Domitilla, the nephew and niece of Domitian, see Dio Cassius 67, 14, 2; Eusebius, *HE* 3, 18, 4 and on this Hengel, *Judaica, Kleine Schriften* II (n. 120), 173f.; Lampe, *Christen* (n. 158), 166ff. See already the enigmatic case of the Roman aristocratic lady Pomponia Graecina in Tacitus, *Ann.* 13, 32, the wife of A. Plautius, the former governor of Pannonia and Britannia, who – accused under Nero of *superstitio externa* and acquitted by her spouse in a family judgment – led a completely withdrawn, ascetic life.

424. Perhaps the governor of Cyprus, Sergius Paulus, Acts 13.7ff., could serve as the model of an ἀνὴρ συνετός, see Hengel and Schwemer, *Paulus* (n. 9), 11, 17f., 116. The same goes for the 'impartiality' of Gallio (Acts 18.12–17) and the assertion of Paul's innocence by Festus (Acts 26.32, cf. however 25.9, which indicates the ambivalence of Roman officials). Here Luke – as a companion of Paul – had collected concrete experiences which do not fit in later times.

425. Cf. Mark 16.9 = Luke 8.2; 16.12f. = Luke 24.13–35; 16.14 = Luke 24.36–43; 16.18 = Acts 28.3–6; 16.19 = Acts 1.11.

426. John would probably have been closer to him. But this Gospel was probably already attributed in his time to an apostle who for him was 'anti-Pauline'. See above, 31ff.

427. Probably he knew the Gospel of Mark and was not very content with it because it did not meet his higher demands. The prologue to Luke sounds as if the evangelist is fulfilling a wish of the person to whom the work is dedicated. The last sentence of the dedication, 1.4, is vital for understanding it and is more than a mere literary cliché.

428. For the originality of the title of Acts see, with good arguments, J. Jervell, *Apostelgeschichte* (n. 28), 56ff. The title is unanimously attested in the great majuscules and is only expanded somewhat in later minuscules. The form πράξεις in Codex Sinaiticus is probably an abbreviation; cf. Irenaeus, *Adv.Haer.* 3, 13, 3; Tertullian, *Bapt.* 10, 4; Clem. Alex., *Strom.* 5, 81, 4: καθὸ καὶ Λουκᾶς ἐν ταῖς πράξεσι τῶν ἀποστόλων ἀπομνημονεύει. The 'apostles' are Peter and Paul.

429. See I Clem. 5; Ignatius, Rom. 4.3; Smyrn. 3.2; Eph. 12.2; Polycarp, Phil. 3.2; 9.1; cf. also II Peter 1.1; 3.15f.

430. See M. Hengel, *Property and Riches in the Early Church*, in: *Earliest Christianity*, London 1979, 156f., 171ff., 179ff., 212.

431. M. Hengel, 'Luke the Historian and the Geography of Palestine in the Acts of the Apostles', in *Between Jesus and Paul*, London 1983, 87–126, 190–210: 101–10, 194–200.

432. Compare his account of Jewish customs and Jewish worship with the pagan witnesses from antiquity in M. Stern, *Greek and Latin*

Authors about Jews and Judaism, Vols. I–III, Jerusalem 1974–84.

433. Luke knows him, but indirectly repudiates him: Acts 16.20; cf. 17.6; 24.5: the same charge is made against the Christians as is frequently made against the Jews, namely that they cause unrest wherever they go. For the phenomenon of ancient antisemitism see P. Schäfer's fine book with a title which describes the ancient situation: *Judeophobia*, Cambridge, Mass and London 1997. Similarly, in later polemic against the Christians one can discover a 'Christianophobia' .

434. See J. Jervell, *Luke and the People of God*, Minneapolis 1972; *Apostelgeschichte* (n. 28), 92–105; M. Klinghardt, *Gesetz und Volk Gottes*, WUNT II/32, which is perhaps rather too one-sided, see Paul, Acts 13.38f. and Peter's speech, 15.7–11. The significance of the ritual law also clearly fades into the background in Luke. In the farewell discourse to the elders of Miletus there is no longer talk of the law but of repentance and faith in the Lord Jesus (20.21) and, at the end, of the divine word of grace (20.32) and the 'sayings of the Lord Jesus', which refer to the commandment to love: 'To give is more blessed than to receive.'

435. 9 times Simon, 17 times Peter and twice Simon Peter. In the first half of Acts up to ch.15 he mentions him 57 times and in the whole book Paul 128 times, Saulus 15 times and Saul 9 times. By contrast John the son of Zebedee appears in the Gospel 7 times and in Acts 9 times, almost always with Peter.

436. For Peter and Luke see Hengel and Schwemer, *Paulus* (n. 9), 9–18 = *Paul*, 6–11. The radical criticism which wants to deny any personal connection between the *auctor ad Theophilum* and the apostle to the Gentiles on the basis of divergent theological views from Paul shows a certain lack of knowledge about the historical reality of teacher-pupil relationships. Think how considerable the theological difference is between the later Melanchthon, who was concerned for harmony, and Luther, not to mention modern teacher-pupil relationships where in the twentieth-century some theologians have often swung round ninety degrees.

437. It is significant that Matthew omits these texts, see below. It may be that Luke, on the other hand, with his 'harmonizing' tendency and his interest in the Palestinian-Petrine Jesus tradition of c. 75–80, is also already opposing a 'hyper-Paulinism' und 'antinomianism' which flourished again powerfully after the destruction of Jerusalem, sharpened its criticism of Judaism and the law, and forms a prior stage to that development which ends with Cerdo, Marcion's teacher, Marcion himself or in the anti-Judaism of the letter of Barnabas (see below). The outbreak of the 'Jewish War' in 66 and the destruction of Jerusalem in 70 could be the sign of the beginning

of the fundamental 'anti-Judaism' in certain Christian circles, which it encouraged in the same way as the tendency of Jewish circles in the Diaspora to regard the new messianic sect as dangerous eschatological enthusiasts and to denounce them to the Roman authorities. Luke opposes both. Matthew does so even more strongly.

438. Later, say from around the middle of the second century, this tendency in connection with the developing orthodoxy can sometimes be reversed, as there were too many 'apocryphal' new compositions under this title (see above, 53f.). Thus between 140 and 150 we find in the *Epistula Apostolorum*, a work which presupposes all four Gospels and Acts, anti-Gnostic revelations of the risen Christ to his eleven disciples that have been preserved in Ethiopic and sometimes Coptic and Latin, according to the Latin version as a letter. The editor Carl Schmitt therefore accepts as the title ἐπιστολὴ τῶν ἀποστόλων; later copyists made it into a *Testamentum Jesu Christi*; see *Gespräche Jesu mit seinen Jüngern*, Leipzig 1919, reprinted Darmstadt 1967, 156ff., 168–77.

439. Marcion, *ad Laodicenses* cf. 1.1: ἐν Ἐφεσῷ is missing in P 46, A* B* 6, 1739 cf. *subscriptio*.

440. Or at least between 100 and 110; see Hengel, *Johanneische Frage* (n. 85), 204–9 = *Johannine Question*, 74ff.

441. The only exception is Rev. 14.6, the εὐαγγέλιον αἰώνιον of the angel; here there is still the simple meaning 'message', like the Aramaic *beśōrā* (see Stuhlmacher, *Evangelium* [n. 7], 210–18), which does not yet have the meaning 'message of salvation.'

442. Cf. the formula (ὁ πατήρ) ὁ πέμψας με, which is used about 27 times with slight variations.

443. See now M. E. Boring, 'Markan Christology: God-Language for Jesus', *NTS* 45, 1999, 451–71: 'To state the matter somewhat provocatively: John, Nicaea, and Chalcedon understood and developed Mark's Christology in a more profound sense than was done either by Matthew or Luke.' That does not exclude the possibility that Mark is substantially closer to the 'history of Jesus' than John, in whom the christology has largely 'swallowed up' the history.

444. Thus in Gnostic texts, but also in the more 'orthodox' *Epistula Apostolorum*, which presupposes all four Gospels and Acts (see above n. 438).

445. One might most likely think of the letter of the Romans to the Corinthians, in which it is Clement who wields the pen for the whole community, or the writing in Acts 15.23–29 which has been shaped by Luke. Only the later reports of the martyrdom of Polycarp or the persecution in Lyons are real 'community letters', although in the Martyrdom of Polycarp 20.1f., too, a Marcion is mentioned as

author and Euaristus as scribe (I am grateful to Dr A. M. Schwemer for this reference). However, the first person plural indicates the community as the sender. The letter to the church in Philomelium im eastern Phrygia is then to be sent on to other communities from there. This Marcion was probably an eye-witness of the martyrdom. The invitation to send on (διαπέμψασθε) the letters to communities lying even further east indicates the many contacts between communities through messengers. Presumably this happened by further copies.

446. I conjecture that there were several partially rival versions of collections of sayings of Jesus. See above, 169ff.

447. Certain experiences in Ephesus or Corinth may lie behind this (cf. e.g. I Cor. 8–10; Rom. 14), but also those in Antioch, Galatia, indeed the theological fruits of mission work over almost twenty-five years – including bitter disappointments.

448. Cf. Luke 24.47 and Acts 26.14–16. For the journey to Spain see n. 383 (and 41) above.

449. *Epitome de Tito Livio* I, 2. Florus is writing in the second century AD.

450. Gal. 3.28; Rom. 1.14f.; Col. 3.11; Rev. 5.9.

451. Cf. Rom. 16.1f.; II Cor. 8.17ff.; Phil. 2.25; III John 5–8, 12; Ignatius, Smyrn. 10.12; Polycarp 8.2; Polycarp, Phil. 14, etc.

452. For the lively exchange between the primitive Christian communities from the beginning see A. von Harnack, *Die Mission und Ausbreitung des Christentums in den ersten drei Jahrhunderten*, Leipzig ⁴1924, I, 200–20, 379–89. Closely connected with this is the admonition to show hospitality to travelling brothers; see III John and my *Johanneische Frage* (n. 85), 127, 132–34, 145; O. Hiltbrunner, 'Gastfreundschaft', *RAC* VIII, 1972, 1061–123: 1103ff.; M. B. Thompson, 'The Holy Internet: Communication Between Churches in the First Christian Generation', in R. Bauckham (ed.), *The Gospels for All Christians*, Grand Rapids 1998, 49–70.

453. Harnack, *Mission und Ausbreitung* (n. 452), 380. In the period between c. AD 130 and 250 he counts more than twenty-five names of Christians, above all of teachers, who travelled to Rome. One could expand this list further, see *RAC* I, 1950, 12–17, the great Christian traveller around AD 200, Abercius from Hierapolis in Phrygia.

454. The significance of the martyr James even after 70 tends to be under-estimated because he does not play a positive role in the Gospels. But his ongoing influence is shown not only by the reception of the Letter of James, which is perhaps authentic after all and could contain a clear criticism of Paul, but also by Acts. Texts like Gospel

of Thomas 12, the Apocryphon of James (NHL I 1, 1–16, 30, a letter to Cerinthus?), the two Nag Hammadi Apocalypses of James (NHL V 24, 10–44, 1; V 44, 11–63, 32), the texts of Hegesippus, of Clement of Alexandria and of Epiphanius, the Syrian Didascalia and above all the Pseudo-Clementine romance indicate its persistent and deep influence; see Hengel, 'Jakobus der Herrenbruder – der erste 'Papst'? (n. 273); id., 'Der Jakobusbrief als antipaulinische Polemik', in *Tradition and Interpretation in the New Testament. Essays in Honor of E. Earle Ellis*, ed. G. F. Hawthorne and O. Betz, Tübingen and Grand Rapids 1987, 248–8; W. Pratscher, *Der Herrenbruder Jakobus und die Jakobustradition*, FRLANT 139, 1987; and now the composite volume *James the Just and Christian Origins*, ed. B. Chilton and C. A. Evans, Leiden, etc. 1999.

455. Cf. e.g. Rom. 16.3–16 (the house community of Prisca and Aquila in Rome); III John; Philemon; in Corinth the 'house of Stephanas' seems to have been a special support to Paul: I Cor. 1.16; 16.15–17. Similar 'houses' or families may have favoured Peter or Apollos.

456. See Hengel, *Johanneische Frage* (n. 85), index s. v. 'Johanneische Gemeinde(n)' or 'Schule', 469.

457. See above, 40, n. 169.

458. The various house churches in Rome were probably brought more firmly together as a unity as a result of the fearful persecution of the year 64 and the reconstitution of the community which was necessary afterwards. In I Clement the Roman community speaks as a unitary authority (cf. n. 445), and we also encounter it in this form in the second century from Ignatius to Irenaeus, despite the sometimes different doctrinal views which are expressed there.

459. Eusebius, *HE* 3, 5, 3 see Hengel and Schwemer, *Paulus* (n. 9), 313 n. 1298.

460. The earliest anti-Marcionite prologue to the Gospels, see Aland, *Synopsis*, 532f., speaks of composition after the death of Peter '*in partibus Italiae*'. This information is adopted by the later composition of the so-called 'Monarchian Prologue' (Aland, 537: '*in Italia*'). Perhaps Mark had fled from Rome to another part of Italy for a while because of the persecution in Rome. Nevertheless his work was probably disseminated by the central community in Italy, i.e. from Rome.

461. If the letter of James is authentic, it would probably have been written between 60 und 62, i.e. still earlier. But this remains uncertain. See Hengel, 'Der Jakobusbrief als antipaulinische Polemik' (n. 454).

462. See Jörg Frey, *Die johanneische Eschatologie*, II *Das johanneische Zeitverständnis*, WUNT 110, Tübingen 1998, see above all Part II: 'Die Zeitbehandlung im Johannesevangelium', 153–207.

463. That does not exclude the possibility that much that is reported in the Gospels is not historical. The criteria of modern historical research were completely alien to the evangelists. They must be seen in their ancient context; they could not separate 'history' and 'interpretation', nor did they want to, see n. 356 above.

464. For this basic problem see Roloff, *Kerygma* (n. 356); B. Gerhardsson, *Memory and Manuscript*, Lund 1961, ²1964, reprint with a new preface by the author, and his essay *Tradition and Transmission in Early Christianity*, 1964, Grand Rapids, etc. 1998, and the investigation by his pupil S. Byrskog, *History as Story and Story as History*, WUNT 123, 2000, see the Summary, 300–6.

465. See Thompson, 'The Holy Internet' (n. 452).

466. Heckel, *Evangelium* (n. 12), has depicted this, largely convincingly, in extensive comparisons.

467. Already in Corinth not only Paul but also Cephas and Apollos were treasured, and the same goes for other names in Antioch, Galatia and Rome.

468. Here for the first time we meet the 'historical' reference to the trial before Pilate, I Tim. 6.13 (see H. Stettler, *Die Christologie der Pastoralbriefe*, WUNT II/105, Tübingen 1998, 117f., 120f., 327, who points out the reference to John 18.37), as also several times in the letters of Ignatius, where Pilate is mentioned three times for the sake of historical reality: Magn. 11; Trall. 9.1; Smyrn. 1, 2: ἀληθῶς ἐπὶ Ποντίου Πιλάτου . . . καθηλωμένον. The reference to Pilate, which found its way into the Roman baptismal creed, indicates a fundamental interest in the 'historical fixation' of the message of faith which distinguishes this from the timeless myth, see above, n. 356.

469. II Peter 1.16–18 = Matt. 17.5f.; cf. II Peter 1.16, the key word ἐπόπται. The letter, around 120–130, may have been written about two decades before the Gospel of Peter and the Apocalypse of Peter, which similarly make the eye-witness Peter speak in the first person. (It is in turn dependent on the letter of Jude, which may have been composed around 100 and for its part takes up the earlier and perhaps authentic letter of James: Jude 1 presupposes James 1.1, which in my view could go back to James: see above nn. 273, 454 und esp. 461.) Peter also speaks in the first person in the non-Gnostic 'Acts of Peter and the Twelve Apostles' from Nag Hammadi (NHG VI, 1, 1–12, 22), which has some features in common with the Shepherd of Hermas; see *The Nag Hammadi Library in English*, revised edition, London 1988, 287–94. This massive claim is absent from the Synoptic Gospels. There the authorship of the work itself is somewhat veiled. Here the title or, in Luke's case, the preface, is enough. For John see Hengel, *Johanneische Frage* (n. 85).

470. See M. Hengel, 'Die Ursprünge der Gnosis und das Urchristentum', in *Evangelium – Schriftauslegung – Kirche. Festschrift für Peter Stuhlmacher,* ed. J. Ådna et al., Göttingen 1997, 190–223.

471. Cf. the term παραθήκη in I Tim. 6.20 (cf. II Tim. 1.14) against 'the godless chatter and contradictions of what is falsely called gnosis' and the objectified term πίστις in the Pastorals, which is strongly bound up with tradition.

472. 67, 3–7; for the liturgy of the word see 3; the widespread form can be inferred from the introduction: an assembly takes place of all those who live in the cities or in the open countryside (κατὰ πόλεις ἢ ἄγρους) this cannot mean Rome alone. See also above, 19f. The description probably did not apply only to the Western churches dependent on Rome but at least also to Asia Minor, where Justin was converted around AD 130 and was first active.

473. For the liturgy of the word in the synagogue see Hengel, *Kleine Schriften* I, 171–95; J. C. Salzmann, *Lehren und Ermahnen*, WUNT II/59, Tübingen 1994, 450–9; P. Schäfer, 'Der synagogale Gottes-dienst', in *Literatur und Religion des Frühjudentums. Eine Ein-führung*, ed. J. Maier and J. Schreiner, Würzburg 1973, 391–413; Jutta Leonhard, *Worship in Philo*, forthcoming TSAJ, Tübingen 2000.

474. See the criticism of the apostle in I Cor. 14.13–40, 'let all things be done for edification' (26) and the admonition to 'order' (40). This was evidently there in Rome.

475. In the time of I Clement the great closing prayer 59.1–61.3 with few alterations and expansions derives from the synagogue and similarly shows how in Rome c. AD 100 worship was dependent on the pro-ceedings in the synagogue. The use of scripture in I Clement also attests an intensive paraenetic use of the Old Testament in the com-munity assembly.

476. For the ancient book cupboard see T. Birt, *Die Buchrolle in der Kunst*, Leipzig 1907 (reprinted 1976), 248–68 on scroll chests, bun-dles of scrolls – with or without chest – and the book cupboard. Large works consisting of numerous scrolls caused particular prob-lems (264ff.). Livy's *History* had 142, and the *World History* of Nicolaus of Damascus, written in Jerusalem, 144. For the Torah shrine see E. R. Goodenough, *Jewish Symbols in the Greco-Roman Period* I–III, 1953, under the indices I (Palestine), 296; II (Diaspora), 211; III (Illustrations), 7 also nos. 58–61 and above all the Roman gilt glasses, 964–68, 973f. etc. In contrast to the Christian book cup-board the Torah shrine after 70 attracted attributes of the Holy of Holies in the destroyed temple; the shrine became a copy of the ark of the covenant of the *'aron hab-b^erīt*, which contains the Torah as

the form of the 'divine presence' that is now normative for Israel. In Christianity, instead the altar, the table where the eucharist was celebrated, took central place. The Christian book cupboard, for which we have relatively little evidence, had a purely functional role; see e.g. the *capsa* (the book chest or basket) in the possession of the martyrs of Scili (nn. 223, 496) and the wall cupboard with the four Gospels on the mosaic of Galla Placidia in Ravenna, see C. Wendel, 'Bibliothek', *RAC* 2, 1954, 266–72 (pl. 4) and H. Leclercq, 'Bibliothèques', *DACL* 2, 1, 1925, cols 842–904 (pls 1553f., 1556: the writing Ezra in Codex Amiatinus; 1557: Galla Placidia mosaic).

477. A Greek Jewish Esther scroll has now been published by K. Luchner in POx 65, 1998, no. 4443 from the first or second century. It is the earliest text of Esther that we have.

478. I Clem. 55.4–6; further in Hengel, 'Septuaginta' (n. 1), 273f.

479. It is strange that the Samaritikon, the Samaritan Greek translation of the Torah, seems to have taken over the *nomina sacra*. See the Giessen papyrus fragment and the Samaritan synagogue inscription of Thessalonica with the priestly blessing in E. Tov, *The Greek and Hebrew Bible. Collected Essays on the Septuagint*, VT.S 72, 1999, 459–75: 461–4 and 513–17.

480. See the numerous early Old Testament Christian codices, as a rule with *nomina sacra* (*n.s.*), in K. Aland, *Repertorium* (n. 205): No. 03 Ex, *n.s.* (second century); No. 05 Num., Deut. c. 50 foll., *n.s.* (second century, time of Hadrian, 117–138); No. 06 Proverbs/Wisdom/Sirach, *n.s.* (third century); No. 07 Hosea/Amos, Greek/Coptic, school copy? (second/third century); No. 08 Minor Prophets 34 foll., *n.s.* (third century); No. 010 Ezekiel/Daniel/Esther, 109 foll., *n.s.* (second/third century); OT 6 (early second century) Gen.14.5–8 = p.Yale 1, probably Christian because of the way the number 318 is written in Gen.14.14 and because of its codex form; OT 8 Gen.(second/third century); OT 10, Gen.(beginning third century); OT 14, Gen (third century); OT 19, Ex, *n.s.* (second/third century); OT 20, Ex, *n.s.* (third century); OT 38, II Chron., *n.s.* (third century); OT 39, II Chron., *n.s.* (second/third century); OT 43, Ps 2, *n.s.* (third century); OT 53, Ps, *n.s.* (third century, according to Roberts second century); OT 68, Ps, *n.s.* (second century); OT 72, Ps, *n.s.* (third century); OT 78, Pss. 81f., *n.s.* (second century); OT 86, Ps, 118 (second/third century); OT 100, Job, *n.s.* (c. 220); OT 129, Isa., *n.s.* (beginning third century); OT 138, Jer, *n.s.* (third century); OT 139, Jer, *n.s.* (second/third century). The number of the early LXX-papyri is greater than that of the Gospels. See also further LXX papyri published since the Aland collection: POx 65 (1998), No. 4442 (pp.1–4), an Exodus codex of the early third century with

nomina sacra.

481. I Cor. 16.2; Acts 20.7ff.; Rev. 1.10; cf. Hengel and Schwemer, *Paulus* (n. 9), 311.

482. Ibid., 311; see also above, 116ff.

483. C . H. Roberts, 'The Codex', *PBA* 4, 1954, 169–204, substantially expanded in C. H. Roberts and T. C. Skeat (n. 204); cf. also already T. C. Skeat, 'Early Christian Book-Production: Papyri and Manuscripts', in G. W. H. Lampe (ed.), *The Cambridge History of the Bible*, Vol. 2, *The West from the Fathers to the Reformation*, Cambridge 1969, 54–79: 65–79. See also Roberts, *Manuscript* (n. 186), Index, 86 s.v. 'Codex'; for the *nomina sacra* 27ff., 75ff., 83ff. The development of the codex on the basis of papyrological evidence is described by E. G. Turner, *The Typology of the Early Codex*, University of Pennsylvania Press, 1977; for a survey of papyrus and parchment codices of the second and third centuries see 89ff. Michael McCormick, 'The Birth of the Codex and the Apostolic Life-Style', *Scriptorium* 39, 1985, 150–8, rightly emphasizes the practical side of the introduction of the codex among Christians. On the other hand, J. van Haelst, 'Les origines du codex', in A. Blanchard, *Les débuts du codex*, Turnhout 1989, 13–35, has disputed Roberts und Skeat and made the Christian codex dependent on the literary use of the parchment codex in Rome attested by Martial. The significance of Rome after 70 as the 'geographical centre' of the Christian churches in the Roman empire must not be underestimated, but 'new literary discoveries in the book trade' for which Martial writes propaganda will hardly have influenced the community there; people did not want to know about this kind of literature. The stimulating article by G. H. R. Horsley, 'Classical Manuscripts in Australia and New Zealand and the Early History of the Codex', *Antichthon* 27, 1993 [1995], 60–83, which indicates the relative cultural isolation of the Christians from outsiders tends to be overlooked, but shows the right direction.

484. In themselves the Pastoral Epistles were composed relatively late, probably hardly before AD 110. However, we cannot exclude the possibility that in II Timothy the author used earlier fragments of Paul's letters, thus perhaps in II Tim. 4.9–16, or follows models which are unknown to us. Presumably Paul wrote substantially more letters than have come down to us. Timothy is to bring with him 'the scrolls, and especially the parchments', together with the travelling cloak which Paul had left with Carpus in Troas. The parchment (book)s are particularly important for the author and are therefore stressed. For the whole matter see Roberts and Skeat, *Birth* (n . 204), 22, 60; McCormick, *Codex* (n. 483), 155: 'the parchment

notebook in codex form' or 'parchment literary codices' decisively indicates 'that the author of II Timothy expected his audience to identify writings in the novel format with St Paul'. On the basis of various parallels, T. C. Skeat, *JTS* NS 30, 1979, 173–7, proposes the translation 'the books – I mean the parchment notebooks' (174).This would make the meaning clearer; Paul is not asking for various written works, but only the 'parchment notebooks'. E. R. Richards, 'The Codex and the Early Collection of Paul's Letters', *Bulletin for Biblical Research* 8, 1998, 151–66, refers to the connection between the collection of Paul's letters and the codex. Cicero already wrote copies of letters in his 'notebook while at the dinner table' (*Fam.* 9, 26, 1). Paul could likewise have collected his copies on the μεμβράναι. That does not of course exclude the possibility that such copies were later, around AD 100, combined with Deutero-Pauline letters like Colossians, II Thessalonians and Ephesians and the enigmatic letter to the Hebrews in a collection and published in a codex. This collection, too, may have been disseminated from Rome soon after I Clement (this could explain the inclusion of Hebrews).

485. I, 2; see Roberts and Skeat, *Birth* (n. 204), 24ff.
486. Martial 14, 184, 186, 188, 190, 192. Even in the case of Livy with the 142 books of his *Annals* Roberts und Skeat presuppose that the whole work took up comparatively little space: 'Narrowed into scanty skins is bulky Livy, the whole of whom my library does not contain' (190; translation by W. C. A. Ker, LCL, 1920, 2, 50f.), see Roberts and Skeat, *Birth* (n. 204), 27 and H. Blanck, *Das Buch in der Antike*, Munich 1992, 93f.
487. Blanck, *Buch* (n. 486), 100.
488. See the collection and critical assessment in Roberts and Skeat, *Birth* (n. 204), 45–53.
489. I Cor. 7.31; I John 2.17; Rom. 13.12f.
490. Paul speaks both of the eucharist and of worship only once, because there were difficulties in Corinth. Without I Cor. 10f. 'critical' scholars would assert that Paul did not know the eucharist, as they do not want to believe Luke (Acts 20.7ff.).
491. Cf. at length Turner, *Typology* (n. 483), 55–71; cf. Blanck, *Buch* (n. 486), 86f. If people wanted something bigger it was possible to put several layers of individual signatures together and sew them into a book block.
492. P 75 around 200 with Luke and John consisted of one signature; 51 leaves have been preserved; possibly this signature was bound together with another one containing Matthew and Mark to make a four-Gospel codex.

493. See above, 53ff. and 116ff. The conditions in Egypt – rather later – here will not have been fundamentally different from those in other provinces of the empire. We know nothing at all about Christianity in Egypt before the devastating Jewish revolt in 115–117 and little in the decades after. See Hengel and Schwemer, *Paulus* (n. 9), 392–4.

494. Cf. Col. 4.16; Rev. 1.3; see also below, n. 501.

495. It follows from the reference to the authors of the reminiscences (see n. 12 above) and also from the reference to the account of the eucharist in 66, 3, where Gospels and 'reminiscences of the apostles' are identified, that this is about the four Gospels. That like II Clement a little earlier he often does not quote verbatim and is fond of harmonizing is connected with the catechetical purpose of his Gospel quotations. In the early period of the church, when oral teaching still wholly predominated over literary work, verbatim, exact quotation was more the exception.

496. See already the Scillitan martyrs; around 180 they were asked by the proconsul about the contents of their book basket (*capsa*). They answered: 'Books and letters of a just man named Paul'; see H. Musurillo, *The Acts of the Christian Martyrs*, Oxford 1972, 88f. (§12): *libri et epistulae Pauli viri iusti. libri* could have denoted the Gospels. In the Diocletian persecution the Roman authorities attached prime importance to the handing over and destruction of the Christian books, see W. H. Frend, *Martyrdom and Persecution in the Early Church,* 1967, 364, 371–7. The confessors in Carthage regarded officers who handed over the scriptures as *traditores*, i.e. as apostates (374f.).

497. Significantly the designation ἐκκλησία is lacking in the prescript in 1.7; there is mention only of 'all the beloved of God' and 'called to be saints' 'who are in Rome'. We find the word ἐκκλησία referring to Rome only in 16.5 as the house community of 'Priscilla and Aquila'. See Lampe, *Christen* (n. 158), index 431 s. v. 'Hausgemeinde', and 301ff. on the 'formation of parties' within Christianity in the city of Rome. Unfortunately the author does not go into the question of Mark. I Peter 5.13 is not mentioned. He mentions Philemon 24; Col. 4.10 only peripherally; for the problem see also Hengel and Schwemer, *Paulus* (n. 9), 389ff. = *Paul*, 257ff.

498. For example Pauline, Petrine or emphatically Jewish Christian types of teaching. See the enigmatic formulation in Rom. 6.17b. A certain diversity of teaching governed by the size of the city, the various house churches and the influence of numerous visitors to Rome becomes evident throughout the second century.

499. 13, 9–20(13); Tacitus, *Ann.* 15, 44, 4; here charges originally made against the Jews are transferred to the Christians, see *Hist.* 5, 5, 1

about the Jews: *adversus omnes alios hostile odium*. The effect of the Neronian persecution also become evident in the picture of Rome in Rev. 13–18. Perhaps an earlier version was written at that time.

500. Cf. Mark 9.1; John 21.20–23, see Hengel, *Johanneische Frage* (n. 85), 212ff. = *Johannine Question*, 76ff.

501. ἀναγινώσκειν means both reading privately and reading aloud in worship, but the difference is relative, since as a rule people read aloud personally, so that others could overhear: Acts 8.28, 30, 32. For the exception of silent reading see A.Gawrilow, 'Stilles lesen in Altertum', *Hyperboreus, Studia Classica* (Petropolis), Vol.1, 1994/5, Fasc. 2, 17–33 (German summary 32f.). We must also remember that the majority of members of the community were illiterate and therefore dependent on reading aloud. With the Gospel the author wants to address all. Cf. also Rev. 1.3; Luke 4.16; Acts 15.21; II Cor. 3.2, cf. 3.15–18, but this probably also presupposes a reading and interpretation of Christian scripture; Col. 4.15f.; I Thess. 5.27; I Tim. 4.13. For the problem see also above, 116ff.

502. According to Morgenthaler, *Statistik* (n. 341), in the New Testament Moses is mentioned 79 times, Isaiah 22 times (cf. Luke 4, 17: βίβλιον τοῦ προφήτου Ἡσαίου; 3.4 βίβλος λόγων Ἡσαίου); Jeremiah three times; Daniel once; Hosea once; Amos 3 times; Joel once; Psalms (of David) or David as Psalmist around ten times (cf. Luke 20.42: Δαυὶδ λέγει ἐν βίβλῳ ψαλμῶν). The scriptural experts Matthew and Paul have the most frequent names of Old Testament 'authors'; as well as of David, Luke also speaks of the book of Psalms: Acts 1.20; 13.33, cf. the Old Testament canon; Luke 24.44: the law of Moses, the Prophets and Psalms and also the prologue to Sirach: 'The Law and the Prophets and the other writings.'

503. 1. 22, 27; 2.10; 11.28; cf. generally chs 11–13.

504. *Arbeitsbuch zum Neuen Testament*, Tübingen ¹¹1995, 318, cf. 328: 'Like Mark, Matthew is an anonymous writing; the author does not make himself known.'

505. See above, 61f. When Lona, *1 Clem* (n. 219), 93 assumes on the basis of Clement of Alexandria, *Strom.* 5, 80, 1 πρὸς Κορίνθιους Ῥωμαίων ἐπιστολή that this is the original address without the name of the author Clement, he overlooks the fact that the Alexandrian scholar names Clement of Rome four times. His name had been associated with the letter from the beginning. It would not have been preserved without the name and the authority. Clement of Alexandria uses the letter so often, not because the Roman community wrote it to the Corinthians, but because behind it stood the well-known authority of Clement of Rome, which in *Strom.*4, 105, 9 he designates as ὁ ἀπόστολος Κλήμης. For him it had 'apostolic'

authority because he was regarded as a direct disciple of the apostles, i.e. Peter and Paul, and because the content of his letter was very useful in paraenesis. Therefore no other writer of the early church uses the letter as profusely as Clement of Alexandria. Around 200 he still had no completely clearly fixed notion of 'the New Testament canon'. Polycarp, two generations earlier, had often referred to I Clement (see above, 61f. and nn. 219, 255, 256).

506. In Matthew at any rate indirectly indicated in 9.9. and 10.3; in John according to 21.14, cf. 19.35 and I John 1.1ff., it is the anonymous beloved disciple's game of riddling, see Hengel, *Johanneische Frage* (n. 85).

507. Rom. 2.16; secondarily, 16.25; cf. also Gal. 1.6; 1 Thess. 1.5.

508. Presumably in two successive stages, so that initially it was not regarded as a uniform two-volume work. See above, 101 n. 418.

509. Hermas 8, 2 = *Vis.* 2, 4, 2. See Hengel, 'Evangelienüberschriften' (n. 10), 6f.; id., *Mark* (n. 10), 81, 182 n. 110; N. Brox, *Der Hirt des Hermas*, KAV 7, 1991, 106–9.

510. Lona, *1 Clem* (n. 219), 9: 'only knowledge of I Corinthians and Romans can be demonstrated . . . with certainty'; cf. I Clem. 35.5f. = Rom. 1.29–32: probably known from readings in worship and cited with small alterations from memory in a paraenetical context. The same is the case with references to the divisions in Corinth, I Cor. 1.10–13 = 47.1–3; here Clement knows that this letter is also in the Corinthian community archive. Cf. also 34.8 = I Cor. 2.9; 37.5 = 12.21f.; 49.5 = 13.4–7; 37.3 = 15.23. II Cor. 9.8 = 2.7; 33.1; 34.4 and Phil. 4.15 = 47.2 must be quotations. Because of the free use without an introductory formula it is difficult to distinguish between quotation and allusion.

511. 1.3–5.13 = 36.2–5; 11.37 = 17.1, and countless allusions; cf. already Eusebius *HE* 3, 38, 1. I cannot understand how Lona, *1 Clem* (n. 219), 22–55, can deny that Clement is acquainted with Hebrews and can only conjecture an 'influence of Alexandrian Jewish Christianity' on the two epistles 'without contact between them' . We know absolutely nothing about 'Alexandrian Jewish Christianity' in the first century and its influence in Rome. We are to presuppose a good 'Hellenistic education' in the upper classes of the large Jewish community in Rome (cf. Josephus, *BJ* I, 80–3 = *Antt.* 17, 299–302, and the new Schürer, III, 1, 75ff.). References to Philo are quite sparse and limited to commonplaces of Jewish synagogue preaching. Unfortunately the author has not investigated the closer relationship to the language of Josephus (in Rome) (58–61). The restraint towards Hebrews in the West is simply connected with the fact that the letter was included in the Pauline collection *anony-*

mously. Perhaps Clement still knew the author. Many works which were highly respected in the second century were later rejected. In the case of Hebrews, despite its acceptance into the collection of Paul's letters some people knew from the start that the letter was not directly Pauline. That caused difficulties later, particularly in the West, during the formation of the canon, see also above, 52.

512. 13.1f. see above, 61f.

513. In I Clem. 23.3f. under the key word γραφή an apocryphal saying is quoted which is introduced in a partially altered form in II Clem. 11.2 as προφητικὸς λόγος. Since – as I have already emphasized above – Judith and Esther (55.4f.; 59.3f.; 55.6) and probably also Tobit, Wisdom and Sirach were in the Roman book cupboard and later Eldad and Modad are quoted in Hermas (*Vis.* 7, 4 = II 3, 4; cf. Num.11.26f.), we can assume that it contained yet further 'apocrypha'. Unlike with Josephus in Rome (*c.Ap.* I, 37–41), in the Christian communities the 'Old Testament canon' was still far from being clearly established; cf. also I Clem. 46.2, where perhaps a saying from the psalms reshaped by Christians is introduced with γέγραπται γάρ; also Ps. 17.26f. and II Sam. 22.26f.LXX. Clement probably believed that these were two different Psalm texts. Perhaps a collection of texts designed for catechesis and paraenesis lay behind them. For the LXX canon see Hengel, 'Septuaginta' (n. 1), 182–284.

514. 47.1: Ἀναλάβετε τὴν ἐπιστολὴν τοῦ μακαρίου Παύλου τοῦ ἀποστόλου; cf. I Ezra 9.45: ἀναλαβὼν Εσδρας τὸ βιβλίον τοῦ νόμου ἐνώπιον τοῦ πλήθους on the public reading II Ezra 11.8.

515. The 'many' in the Prologue of Luke remain unknown and in Acts 1.1 Luke refers only to his 'first writing'. By contrast, Paul's references to earlier letters in I and II Cor. are signs of a constant exchange with the problematical community, of which the first letter has been lost, perhaps because of its sharp rebuke (I Cor. 5.9f.).

516. Accordingly, later church tradition makes him the disciple of Peter or Paul, Lona, *1 Clem* (n. 219), 66–9. Above all the Pseudo-Clementine romance spreads his praise.

517. 13.1f.: 'Especially remembering the words of the Lord Jesus which he spoke when he was teaching gentleness and longsuffering. For he spoke thus: "Be merciful, that you may obtain mercy. Forgive, that you may be forgiven. As you do, so shall it be done to you. As you give, so shall it be given to you. As you judge, so shall you be judged. As you are kind, so shall kindness be shown you. With what measure you mete, it shall be measured to you.' With this cf. Matt. 5.7; 6.14f.; 7.1f., 12; Luke 6.31, 36–38. See the extended discussion by D. A. Hagner, *The Use of the Old and New Testaments in Clement*

of Rome, NT.S 34, 1973, 138–51, who conjectures an 'oral extra-canonical tradition' as a source. But perhaps here 'written' and 'oral' rests on a false opposition.

518. 46.7f.

519. I Clem. 46.8; Mark 14.21; Matt. 26.24; Luke 22.22.

520. Cf. Lona, *1 Clem* (n. 219), 497: I Clem. 46.8; Mark 9.42; Matt. 18.6f.; Luke 17.1f.

521. See Mark 4.3ff.; cf. 4.26 and 4.8; Luke 8.5, 8; Matt. 13.3: ἐξῆλθεν ὁ σπείρων . . . see also Justin, *Dial.* 1, 25, 1 = Luke 8.5. However, Clement, like Theophilus of Antioch, *ad Autolyc.* 1, 13, later, who here is probably dependent on Clement of Rome, refers the text to the resurrection and connects it with formulations from I Cor. 15.37f.; see Hagner, *Use* (n. 517), 64f.; Lona (n. 219), 302: 'The text forms a new unit which is to be interpreted in its context.' As the relationship to I Cor. 15.37 hardly rests on oral tradition, the Synoptic references too seem to presuppose a knowledge of the Gospel texts, above all Mark: 'The author knows this tradition (which need not only be oral), but he shapes it a new narrative, drawing on memory.'

522. Lona, *1 Clem* (n. 219), 290; cf. Hagner, *Use* (n. 517), 165; see II Clem. 11.3. Behind this perhaps stands an apocryphal text which is introduced with γραφὴ αὕτη (I Clem. 23.3) (see above, n. 517).

523. And with a slight change, Matt. 15.8; see Hagner, *Use* (n. 517), 172ff.

524. Ibid., 175.

525. See the thorough investigation by H. Löhr, forthcoming in WUNT 2001.

526. This would above all be a matter of course if Theophilus, as I conjecture, was a prominent Roman, see n. 423 above.

527. See above, 53ff. and 116ff.

528. Cf. Matt. 22.14; cf. also Matt. 10.30 and 20.16. The dispute over whether the author of Barnabas here is deliberately introducing a passage from Matthew as a scriptural saying or whether he wrongly believes that he is quoting an Old Testament saying is pointless. The author is quoting this eschatological threat from memory. See now F. R. Prostmeier, *Der Barnabasbrief*, KAV 8, 1999, 226f., n. 154. It is not a clear 'proof' that here Barnabas is quoting Matthew as 'holy scripture', but still less can the opposite be 'proved'. Individual manuscripts add the saying in Matt. 20.16 still early in the second century, and others later in Luke 14.24. Until the opposite is proved, we must assume that it comes from Matthew. In no way should it be doubted that Barnabas, which was written around a generation after I Clement, knows Matthew or Mark; cf. Barn. 5.9 = Mark 2.17 and Matt. 9.13; 7.3, 5 = Matt. 27.34, 48, cf. Mark 15.36; John

19.29; 12.10–12 presupposes Mark 12.37 par. Nor may it be overlooked that the Synoptic Gospel tradition does not always clearly correspond to the concerns of the anti-Judaistic letter of Barnabas.

529. 5.9: 'But when he chose out his own apostles who were to preach his Gospel', cf. Barnabas 8.3, where he speaks of 'the twelve', 'to whom he gave authority to (proclaim) the Gospel': οἷς ἔδωκεν τοῦ εὐαγγελίου τὴν ἐξουσίαν, οὖσιν δεκαδύω (thus Vaticanus, Hierso: δώδεκα, Sin: ιβ) . . . εἰς τὸ κηρύσσειν; cf. Luke 6.13 ἐκλεξάμενος . . . δώδεκα, οὓς καὶ ἀποστόλους ὠνόμασεν (cf. Acts 1.2 = John 6.70) and Luke 9.1f. ἔδωκεν αὐτοῖς . . . ἐξουσίαν . . . καὶ ἀπέστειλεν αὐτοὺς κηρύσσειν, cf. also the expansion of the Western text: D W (lat) bo pt, which goes back into the second century: Mark 3 ἵνα ἀποστείλῃ αὐτοὺς κηρύσσειν τὸ εὐαγγέλιον καὶ ἔδωκεν αὐτοῖς (ἐξουσίαν). It has close connections with Barnabas and derives from an ongoing interpretation of Synoptic tradition in the second century. See Prostmeier (n. 528), 328. 'For the author, the Lukan construct of the "twelve apostles" already seems to be regarded as a fixed entity of the beginning, for which the number twelve can be used as *pars pro toto* and as a synonym of apostle.' One can readily agree with this; however, contrary to the questionable theses of G. Klein the twelve apostles are not merely a 'Lukan construct', cf. Matt. 10.2, 5 and 28.19, the mission command for the eleven and Rev. 21.14. Matthew knew Luke, but on this point he does not simply copy him.

530. 5.9 ἐξελέξατο ὄντας ὑπὲρ πᾶσαν ἁμαρτίαν ἀνομωτέρους, ἵνα δείξῃ ὅτι οὐκ ἦλθεν καλέσαι δικαίους, ἀλλὰ ἁμαρτωλούς; cf. Mark 2.17: οὐκ (Matt. 9.13: οὐ γὰρ) ἦλθον καλέσαι δικαίους ἀλλὰ ἁμαρτωλούς. The dependence on Mark/Matthew is clear here. However, H. Koester, *Synoptische Überlieferung bei den apostolischen Vätern*, TU 65, Berlin 1967, 145, comes to the apodeictic judgment: 'none of the . . . motifs in Barnabas 5.8f. can derive from a Gospel'; rather, he argues, they have come to the author 'from free community tradition'; Prostmaier (n. 528), 247 n. 75, agrees. Certainly, not just one *but all the Gospels*, including the Johannine tradition, stand behind the author; cf. the threefold coming of the Son of God ἐν σαρκί, 5.6, 10f. and his mediation at creation 5.10.

531. *Actus Petri cum Simone* 20 (Lipsius/Bonnet 2, 66). The earliest Greek version of the Acts of Peter is to be dated as roughly contemporaneous with Irenaeus, *NTApoc* 2, 235, 275, 283. The Gospel which Peter himself wrote could refer either to the Gospel of Mark or the Gospel of Peter. Cf. also II Peter 1.17f. For the 'apostolic we' see nn. 538–41.

532. Cf. Barn. 8.3; 11.1; 16.8 and on this Luke 1.77; 24.47; Acts 2.38; 26.18; cf. the reference to baptism in Barn. 8.3 and the baptismal

command, Matt. 28.19 and the Matthaean version of the saying over the cup, 26.28.

533. The book of Enoch could also not quote the Torah of Moses and the prophetic writings, nor the Christian Ascension of Isaiah New Testament writings. If the contemporary Papias and, fifty years later, Irenaeus, had historical knowledge about the relatively late origin of the Gospels, why not also the author who wants to write in the name of Barnabas?

534. The remarks by Prostmeier (n. 528) on the place of origin and the title (119–34) are unsatisfactory, but one may accept his reflections on the time of origin: spring 130–February/March 132 (118). In giving the place of origin as Alexandria he is taking too little account of the murderous rebellion of the Jews in Egypt in 115–117 with its fearful consequences. Not a word in the letter indicates this catastrophe. Therefore Syria or Asia Minor is a more likely origin. If 'the introduction of the *inscriptio* or one of the various *subscriptiones* took place at the latest on the inclusion . . . in a collection', in order to 'demarcate the work from others' (132), the title was given to the work at a very early stage, since this was written 'for inclusion' in Christian community and private libraries and was certainly first disseminated as a single codex. We know nothing of an early acceptance into larger collections of writings. The earliest witness is Codex Sinaiticus. Here the 'high regard' for this work as late as the fourth century is clear (Prostmeier, 14). Since the designation as 'Letter of Barnabas' in the manuscripts is unanimous and it is already taken for granted by Clement of Alexandria that Barnabas is known to be the author, and also later this is attested time and again (see Prostmeier, 34–63), we must assume that it was not the later Christian tradition 'which inscribed this anonymous writing with ΒΑΡΝΑΒΑ ΕΠΙϹΤΟΛΗ' (ibid., 132), but at the latest those who disseminated this letter by copies: in my view it was the author himself. Only in this way could he give this work the necessary authority in the second century. Here too the uniformity of the attribution should be noted. On the other hand, at this time it would already be too late for a 'canonization' of the work.

535. II Clem. 2.4f.: 'And another scripture also says, "I came to call not righteous, but sinners"', cf. 2.7 and on this Luke 19.10.

536. See K. Wengst, *Didache (Apostellehre), Barnabasbrief . . ., Schriften des Urchristentums* II, Darmstadt 1984, 221ff.; above all on II Clem. 5.2–4, where texts from Matthew and Luke are combined (223); G. N. Stanton, 'Matthew: ΒΙΒΛΟϹ, ΕΥΑΓΓΕΛΙΟΝ or ΒΙΟϹ', in *The Four Gospels. Festschrift Frans Neirynck*, ed. F. van Siegbroeck et al., II, 1992, 1197–201: 1191f.

537. Eusebius, *HE* 4, 3, 2f.; cf. Mark 5.35–43 par.; Luke 7.11–15; Luke 7.22 par.; John 11. The report can similarly be found in Papias in respect of the Risen Christ according to a fragment from the church history of Philippus Sidetes and, if this information is also thought to come from Papias, be an indication for the dating of his work (see above, n. 273); see Kürzinger, *Papias* (n. 294), 116f. fr. 16. Hadrian reigned from 117 to 138. 'Barnabas', Polycarp, Papias, Quadratus, Basilides and probably also Aristides (see above, nn. 241, 247) were writing in his time.

538. II Peter 1.14. This is a reference to the expected martyrdom.

539. II Peter 1.16: 'We made known to you the power and coming of our Lord Jesus Christ.'

540. II Peter 1.17f.; see also above nn. 50, 210, 218 and 469 on the Peter apocrypha which accumulated in his time.

541. II Peter 3.15. The 'other scriptures' may be a hint at the Gospels, cf. n. 531.

542. διεγείρεν ὑμᾶς ἐν ὑπομνήσει.

543. II Peter 1.13, 18.

544. H. von Schubert, *NTApoc*, 589, quoted in K. Wengst, *Schriften des Urchristentums* II, Darmstadt 1984, 215 n. 40, cf. also J. C. Salzmann, *Lehren und Ermahnen. Zur Geschichte des christlichen Wortgottesdienstes in den ersten drei Jahrhunderten*, WUNT II/59, Tübingen 1994, 219–32.

545. R. Knopf, *ZNW* 3, 1902, 266–79; id., *Das Nachapostolische Zeitalter*, Tübingen 1905, 235, 239: 'The relationship between the teaching and the sections of scripture read out must be imagined as more of a free one. That already follows from the fact that the sections of scriptures, as was indicated above, were extended. So there can be no question of a treatment in accordance with the text, of the kind that took place in the synagogue, and which is already demonstrated, for example, in the homilies of Origen. Therefore we cannot determine with any certainty the kind of reading which preceded II Clement' (239). Knopf conjectures that the reading took more time than a sermon with a paraenetic orientation. Cf. Salzmann, *Lehren und Ermahnen* (n. 544), 221f.

546. 'Attend to the public reading of scripture, to preaching, to teaching.' The Pastoral Epistles were written around 110/115.

547. Irenaeus, *Adv.Haer.* 3, 3, 3 and 4 = Eusebius, *HE* 4, 10–11, 2. He is said to have been influenced by the Simonians. Like Valentinus, he is further said to have come from Syria to Rome under bishop Hyginus, i.e. in the last years of Hadrian.

548. Cf. in addition to I Clement, Ignatius, Rom. Prologue; 3.1: ἄλλους ἐδιδάξατε, 4.3 P.1; 10.2; Hermas, *Visions* 2, 4, 3 (8, 3); Eusebius, *HE*

4, 11, 1.7; 14, 5; 23, 10f.; see also above, 34ff., on Irenaeus. The importance of the Roman community at the end of the first and in the second century can hardly be overestimated. What has been said also applies, with a pinch of salt, to the establishment of the Christian Septuagint, at least in the West, see Hengel, 'Septuaginta' (n. 1); 280ff.

549. However, 'book of the genesis of Jesus Christ, son of David, son of God' is certainly not the title of the whole work, but only of the genealogy and the birth story. For Matthew the whole work is already εὐαγγέλιον; cf. the twofold τοῦτο τὸ εὐαγγέλιον in Matt. 24.14 and 26.13: τὸ εὐαγγέλιον τοῦτο, thus with Stanton, 'Matthew' (n. 536), 1187–201 (only this title is not new, but has been taken over by Mark), against D. Dormeyer, 'Matt. 1, 1 als Überschrift zur Gattung und Christologie des Matthäusevange-liums', ibid. (n. 536), 1361–93. The term' ideal biography' also seems to me to be inadequate. It is an unconditional 'message of salvation', in which case it is neither a 'model' nor an 'ideal' but has immeasurable soteriological significance. I do not believe that the author had read a 'foundation biography' of Greek philosophers (1379).

550. A last, relatively artificial and marginal offshoot of these logia texts is the Gospel of Thomas, which receives all too much praise today. Alongside its own largely gnosticizing but also in part Jewish-Christian tradition, at the same time it represents a further develop-ment of the Synoptic Jesus tradition, which presupposes the earlier Gospels. See also above, 59ff. Its designation as 'Gospel of Thomas' and its introduction already indicates its secondary character.

551. Ignatius, too, does not quote the Gospel of John, though he very probably knew it, see Hengel, *Johanneische Frage* (n. 85), 68–71, and an expert on the theology of Asia Minor like F. Loofs, *Leitfaden zum Studium der Dogmengeschichte*, Halle/Saale ⁵1950, 1, 76, could already remark: 'The affinity to the circle of Johannine ideas is so close that what in my view is the unmistakable knowledge of Ignatius does not explain it. Before his episcopate, Ignatius must have had connections with the Johannine circle in Asia Minor.' Perhaps there were also relations between the Christian teaching authority in southern Syria which is expressed in Matthew, and Rome.

552. See above, n. 157. For Valentinus see Markschies, *Valentinus* (n. 239), 293–336: Valentinus' prosopography, 303f.; Tertullian, *Adv. Val.* 4, 1 *'sperauerat episcopatum Valentinus . . .'.*

553. Hengel, *Johanneische Frage* (n. 85), 26ff., 37ff., 41ff. See also above, 21.

554. Eusebius, *HE* 5, 15; 20, 1–7; see also above, n. 157; cf. further *HE*
5, 13, the controversy between Tatian's pupil Rhodon and Apelles
and other adherents of Marcion, and 5, 28, 6ff., on the cobbler
Theodotus and his school in Rome, who were excommunicated in
the time of Bishop Victor or his successor Zephyrinus for their
'Monarchian' heresy; cf. A. Harnack, *PRE* 13, 1903, 311ff.

555. Absolute use: Rom. 1.16; 10.16; I Cor. 4.15; 9.14, 18 (twice), 23;
15.1; II Cor. 8.18; Gal. 1.11; 2.2, 5, 7, 14; Phil. 1.5, 7, 16, 27
(twice); I Thess. 2.4; Philemon 13; 'my (our) Gospel': Rom. 2.16;
16.25; II Cor. 4.3; I Thess. 1.5, cf. II Tim. 2.8 and according to
Eusebius, *HE* 3, 7, the Gospel of Luke with Marcion, above n. 42
and 151. 'Gospel of God': Rom. 1.1; 15.19; I Cor. 9.12; 4.4; 9.13;
10.14; Gal.1.7; Phil. 1.27. 'Gospel of Christ': Rom. 15.19 (cf. 1.9);
I Cor. 9.12; II Cor. 2.12; 9.13; 10.14; Phil. 1.27; I Thess. 3.2.

556. With the exception of Mark, the written sources of Luke cannot be
reconstructed. For the difficult, as yet insoluble, problem of the
Logia source see above, 169ff.

557. Luke 1.2: καθὼς παρέδοσαν ἡμῖν οἱ ἀπ' ἀρχῆς αὐτόπται καὶ ὑπηρέται
γενόμενοι τοῦ λόγου. Luke still knew such αὐτόπται. Later II Peter
1.16 makes Peter speak as an eye-witness (ἐπόπτης), see above, 114
and n. 469. Αὐτόπτης plays an even greater role in medical literature
than among the historians, see Hengel and Schwemer, *Paulus* (n. 9),
21 n. 61, and L. Alexander, *The Preface of Luke's Gospel*, MSSNTS
28, Cambridge 1993, 34–41, 120–5. There is a typical example of a
very short medical prologue based on personal autopsy, which
describes a written summary of his researches with ἀνατάσσεσθα, a
dedication and at the end an indication of use in the *Corpus
Hippiatricorum Graecorum*, ed. Oder and Hoppe, Vol. 1, 1, Leipzig
1921 as an introduction to the *Hippiatrica Berolinensia* (text below,
n. 678). Justin, *Dial.*115, 3 sets αὐτοψία in direct opposition to
seeing ἐν ἐκστάσει on the basis of a revelation.

558. Cf. Acts 1.21f.; 10.37; cf. Luke 24.47ff.; Acts 1.8; 13.31.

559. See Hengel and Schwemer, *Paulus* (n. 9), 37f.

560. Both references in Jeremias, *Sprache* (n. 413), 9.

561. For the problem of eye-witness see now the fundamental work by S.
Byrskog, *Story as History – History as Story. The Gospel Tradition
in the Context of Ancient Oral History*, WUNT 123, 2000.
Probably the most impressive example of this is the introduction to
Plato's *Phaedo* 57a with Echecrates' question: 'Were you yourself,
O Phaedo, present with Socrates on that day when he drank the
poison in prison, or did you hear it from someone else?' *Phaedo:* 'I
was there myself . . .' *Echecrates:* 'And what did the man say before
his death? And how did he die?' In the *Phaedo* we have a 'passion

narrative' preceded by a long farewell discourse, though of course of quite a different kind from that in John or Luke. See also n. 567.

562. Heb. 2.3f.

563. See above, 65ff.

564. The problem has been much discussed. At all events we should not overlook the fact that in Luke's special material, texts about the justification of the sinner like Luke 15; 18.9–14 or 19.1–10, and also Acts 13.38f.; 16.14, 31; 20.24 and Peter according to 15.11 show that he was not totally ignorant of Paul's theology and preaching. I think that the theological difference between Paul and Luke was certainly no greater than that between colleagues in any theological faculty today. How many formerly 'narrow Barthians' or 'orthodox Lutherans' have changed their views, sometimes fundamentally, between 1950 and 1980? The same goes for the theological 'old 1968ers' in the present. Are we not to allow Luke to change his mind – just a little? He deliberately wanted to be a 'mediating theologian' and this was also probably to some degree necessary in the church situation after 70. The church should not fall apart. Among other things, his work is also an indirect appeal to the unity of the church. See Hengel and Schwemer, *Paulus* (n. 9), 15f., 23ff.

565. There were also sociological reasons for this, see above, 101–4.

566. Acts 21.7–30 and 27.1ff. The interval is around two years. Luke may have spent part of this time in Jerusalem or Caesarea. Cf. Hengel, *Between Jesus and Paul* (n. 431), 97–128: 126ff.

567. Mark 15.21, 40, 43; cf. 10.46; 14.3; Luke 8.3; 10.38ff. The list of the Twelve in Mark 3.16–19; Luke 6.13–16; Acts 1.13; Matt. 10.2–4 is also to be seen from this perspective. Cf. *Phaedo* 58c: 'Which of his friends was with the man? Or did the authorities not allow it? Did he die without the presence of friends?' It is no chance that the eye-witnesses appear particularly in the 'passion narrative', cf. also 59b-c. Phaedo wants to narrate everything ἐξ ἀρχῆς, cf. the ἀπ' ἀρχῆς and the ἄνωθεν in Luke 1.2f.

568. A fine example is the impressive work by G. Theissen and A. Merz, *The Historical Jesus*, London and Minneapolis 1997. The fundamental importance of memory for the tradition of the sayings of the Lord is emphasized by J. Schröter, *Erinnerung an Jesu Worte. Studien zur Rezeption der Logienüberlieferung in Markus, Q und Thomas*, WMANT 76, Neukirchen 1997. Here 'memory' always at the same time means 'assimilation' – 'change'. However, it must not be replaced by the postulate of the free 'new creation'.

569. This applies above all to the works of Bultmann and some of his pupils. Here Dibelius showed a better understanding, see *From Tradition to Gospel* (n. 331), 242, on the importance of the 'authori-

tative sayings of the Lord' and the 'evaluation of tradition, authenticity and authority'. This also applies to the authority of the tradents, in the first place Peter. See at length, above, 78ff.

570. *DLZ* 1922, nos.7/8, 128–34:132: Among other things he accuses Bultmann of 'overstepping the limits of pure form-critical method' associated with 'a particularly large degree of scepticism' and 'unbounded subjectivism', *DLZ* 1932, no.24, 1105–11: 1109f.: 'It must be said quite emphatically that Bultmann's scepticism on all matters historical is not necessarily connected with form-critical criteria but with his view of the nature of the primitive Christian community and emphasis on the difference between Palestinian and Hellenistic Christianity.' In reality 'the Gospels show most clearly . . . how slight the influence of new theological notions on the Gospel material basically was; otherwise belief in the Kyrios and sacramental theology would have made themselves felt much more strongly.' By now the historical foundations of Bultmann's picture of primitive Christianity which led to his radical verdicts and which Dibelius criticized have collapsed. The sharp opposition between 'Palestinian' and 'Hellenistic' community cannot be maintained any more than the complete splintering of the tradition, as if there had been neither eye-witnesses nor real memory, and the fundamental anonymity of the tradition and writing of the Gospels. Jerusalem and the cities of Galilee also had their own 'Jewish-Hellenistic culture' with a distinctive stamp, quite different from Alexandria, see Hengel, *Kleine Schriften* I, 1–90.

571. See Hengel, *Johanneische Frage* (n. 85), 264ff., 318ff.; id., *Kleine Schriften* II (n. 120), 293–334.

572. Within the Bultmann school it is to the credit of E. Käsemann that he demonstrated this in his much-noted article 'The Problem of the Historical Jesus', in *Essays on New Testament Themes*, London 1964, 15–47.

573. See Hengel and Schwemer, *Paulus* (n. 9), 72ff., 174–94 = *Paul*, 43ff., 106–47. Cf. also Isa. 42.11 (LXX): εὐφρανθήσονται οἱ κατοικοῦντες Πέτραν . . . δώσουσιν τῷ θεῷ δόξαν. I am grateful to my colleague Seyoon Kim for this reference.

574. Gal.1.12–17. See Hengel and Schwemer, *Paulus* (n. 9), 60–101 = *Paul*, 24–49.

575. I Cor. 15.1–11: v.1: 'I would make known to you . . . the Gospel that I gospelled to you, which you also received'; v.11:'Whether it was I or they, so we preach and so you believed.'

576. I Cor. 15.3–5.

577. I Cor. 1.23; cf. 1.13; 2.2; Gal. 2.2.

578. Mark 16.6 = Matt. 28.5. Only Heb. 6.6; 12.2 and Rev. 11.8 are

exceptions. In Acts cf. 2.36; 4.10: σταυροῦν; 5.30; 10.39: κρεμάσαντες ἐπὶ ξύλου; cf. Gal. 3.13.

579. Thus Conzelmann, *Theology of the New Testament*, London 1969, 196, 'From the beginning faith expresses itself in stereotyped formulae. These undergo a historical change. The Apostles' Creed already . . . represents a final stage.' Against this it needs to be said that at the very beginning we do not have the formulae but the saving event itself, which has to be narrated and explained. The formulae are only the necessary theological summary and interpretation of the underlying record of the event, not the matter itself. That matter is Jesus' death on the cross as a historical event on Golgotha and the appearance of the Risen Christ to the disciples. The formulae 'undergo a historical development'; only the 'fact' of the saving event in the past is and remains 'unique', ἐφάπαξ (Rom. 6.10). Therefore the statement about the saving event in the formulae in Paul is usually in the aorist, which emphasizes this ἐφάπαξ. In I Cor. 15.3f. the formula about dying is in the aorist (ἀπέθανεν), while resurrection by God is in the perfect (ἐγήγερται), because the Risen One lives in eternity. However, all these formulae about the saving event of the death and resurrection of Christ are necessarily in the preterite.

580. R. Bultmann, *Faith and Understanding* (1933), New York and London 1969, in his discussion of Karl Barth, *The Resurrection of the Dead*, Munich 1926, 66–94: 83f., initially directed against Barth and then also against Paul: 'All of that interpretation seems to me (for better or worse) unacceptable. I can understand the text only as an attempt to make the resurrection of Christ credible as an objective historical fact. And I see only that Paul is betrayed by his apologetic into contradicting himself. For what Paul says in vv.20–22 of the death and resurrection of Christ cannot be said of an objective historical fact.' Here Bultmann shows his complete failure to understand the historical situation of the apostle. Here Paul is basically being accused of not thinking, like Bultmann and his teacher Wilhelm Herrmann, from the lofty standpoint of neo-Kantian scheme, of having a 'mythical', necessarily 'objectifying', view of the world. Both the fall of Adam and its consequences (15.21) and the death and resurrection of Christ are for Paul indirectly or directly 'objective factors of human history brought about by God'. However, he does not understand this history as a web of purely immanent causal connections. Therefore these 'facts' break through the perception of space and time which is available to human beings and fundamentally govern the relationship between God and human beings. For Paul, with a pinch of salt, they are 'the

most objective thing' that has happened in this world, because all human beings are affected by it: I Cor. 15.22; II Cor. 5.14; Rom. 5.12–19. Precisely for that reason this 'fact' *must* be attested by the narration of eye-witnesses. How else could it be preached?

581. See above, n. 367, Origen on the ambivalence of the miracles brought about by the Spirit of God which evoke only mockery among unbelievers. That is the very reason why Paul can say that the preaching of the crucified (and risen) Christ is 'folly' for the Gentiles. According to them God does not act in this way. There is no better example of this in the ancient world than the mockery of the Christian message by Celsus (e.g. *c.Celsum* 2, 55) or Julian.

582. Cf. Matt. 28.17; Luke 24.37, 41; John 20.15, 25. Cf. John 21.4; Luke 24.16; see A. M. Schwemer, in *Die Auferstehung*, ed. F. Avemarie and H. Lichtenberger, forthcoming in WUNT, 2001. See also Mark 16.8.

583. See already Luke 24.37–39; cf. Mark 6.49 = Matt. 14.26; see M. Hengel, *La crucifixion dans l'antiquité et la folie du message de la croix*, Lectio divina 105, Paris 1981, 70f.: *Martyrium Pionium* (ed. H. Musurillo, *The Acts of the Christian Martyrs*, Oxford 1972) 13, 8; 14, 1; cf. Origen, *c.Celsum* 3.22; 7, 35f.; Mart., *Konon* 4, 6; Mart., *Arethas*, ed. I. F. Boissonade, *Anecdota Graeca* 5, p. 24; Sozomen *HE* 2, 1, 6).

584. Origen, *c.Celsum*, 2, 55.

585. Here J. Jeremias in his learned study *The Eucharistic Words of Jesus*, London 1967, goes a step too far; by contrast the history-of-religions school completely alienated it. For the history of research see now the survey by Theissen and Merz (n. 568), 406–37, which points out the cultic character of the meal. However, that is only an incidental aspect by comparison with the eschatological saving significance of his death, connected with Isa. 53. In the last resort the words of institution go back to an act of Jesus at the last supper.

586. I Cor. 7.10; 9.14; 1 Thess. 4.15, cf. I Cor. 14.37.

587. Rom. 12.14, 17, 19f.; 13.8; Gal.5.14; I Cor. 13.2, etc.

588. The preaching of Peter (Acts 2.22–36) and Paul before Jews (13.23–40) with the combination of argumentation on the basis of Old Testament texts and Jesus tradition are typical, whereas Peter's preaching in 10.34–43, which is addressed to Gentiles, mixes up Old Testament allusions and Jesus tradition. Indeed Jesus' own ethical preaching had a wealth of Old Testament references. Here Luke indicates schemata which have been familiar to him for a long time and attempts in this way to characterize the 'historical situation' of the speech.

589. That also applies to I Cor. 15. In Corinth it was not the – bodily –

resurrection of Jesus that was disputed, but that of believers at the parousia.

590. *Theology* (n. 579), 166.

591. Acts 9.20, 22; 17.2, 19; 18.4; 19.8f.; 24.12. Luke is thus describing historical circumstances. At the time of the composition of his two-volume work these discussions in the synagogue had probably already ceased. The 'messianic trouble-makers' had been expelled and had founded their own communities.

592. See M. Hengel, '"Christos" in Paul', in *Between Jesus and Paul*, London 1983, 65–77, 179–88.

593. See Gal. 4.4. Just as the community knows about the brothers of Jesus, James and his other brothers (Gal. 1.19; I Cor. 9.5, cf. Acts 1.14; Mark 6.3 par.; John 7.3ff.), so too it will also have known the name of his mother. Paul was not the first docetist, who attributed to Jesus only an apparent humanity, even though some modern interpreters seem to suggest this, cf. below, n. 604.

594. Rom. 1.3; 15.12.

595. I Cor. 9.5; 15.7; Gal. 1.19; 2.9, 10. Cf. also John 7.2ff. and Acts 1.14; 12.19; 15.13; 21.18.

596. Rom. 15.8.

597. Gal. 2.7–9; cf. I Cor. 3.10f.: in my view Christ as θεμέλιος is also an indirect allusion to the rock man. Not Peter but Jesus is the 'foundation stone' on which the church is built; cf. Matt. 16.18.

598. Hengel, *The Pre-Christian Paul*, 1991, and Hengel and Schwemer, *Paulus* (n. 9).

599. Gal. 4.4: 'born of a woman, born under the law'; cf. Rom. 8.3; I Cor. 8.6; 10.1ff.; Phil. 2.6ff.

600. Acts 17.2, 17; 18.4, 19; 19.9; 20.7, 9; 24.12: διαλέγεσθαι.

601. Psalm 110.1 is alluded to only once, in Rom 8.34; Paul does not quote elsewhere what is probably the most important text interpreted christologically alongside Isa. 53 in the New Testament. See M. Hengel, *Studies in Early Christology*, Edinburgh 1995, 137–143. Cf. also II Cor. 12.1ff. and on this U. Heckel, *Kraft in Schwachheit. Untersuchungen zu II Cor. 11–13*, WUNT II/56, Tübingen 1993, 52ff.

602. Phil. 2.9: the Philippians hymn may very well come from Paul himself, since in exalted language the choice of words is different from those used in prose: moreover the 'death on a cross' is not a secondary addition. It is the phrase which gives the whole first strophe its point, performing the same function as 'to the glory of God the Father' at the end of the second. See O. Hofius, *Der Christushymnus, Philipper 2, 6–11*, WUNT 17, Tübingen ²1991.

603. II Cor. 8.9. Cf. Rom. 15.3; 8.3 and on them M. Hengel, 'Präexistenz

bei Paulus?', in *Jesus Christus als die Mitte der Schrift*, ed. C. Landmesser et al., BZNW 86, 1997, 479–518.

604. Nor is II Cor. 5.16 evidence of a lack of interest in the history of Jesus on the part of Paul. This text has only been misused in this sense. Bultmann wrongly believed that such an inference could be made from the verse, cf. his exegesis in id., *Der zweite Brief an die Korinther*, ed. E. Dinkler, Göttingen ²1988, 158. In this verse 'according to the flesh' is not an attribute relating to 'Christ' but is an adverbial determination of 'know'. Paul is not saying here that he no longer wants to know anything about the history of (the human) Jesus Christ, but that he now no longer knows Christ (the undertone of a title can still be detected here) in a fleshly way as at the time when he was a persecutor (of which he has been accused) (cf. F. Lang, *Die Briefe an die Korinther*, Göttingen 1986, 293f.).

605. See A. Schlatter, *Atheistische Methoden in der Theologie*, BFCTh 105, 5, 229–50 = id., *Zur Theologie des Neuen Testaments und zur Dogmatik*, ed. U. Luck, ThB 41, Munich 1961, 134–50.

606. Cf. also Rom. 11.28f. in respect of the 'conversion of Israel at the parousia'.

607. Acts 12: presumably at Passover AD 43.

608. Cf. Acts 12.17: 'Then he departed and went to another place' means outside the kingdom of Agrippa I, i.e. outside Palestine, possibly Rome, see Hengel and Schwemer, *Paulus* (n. 9), 388f.

609. H. Lietzmann, *Petrus und Paulus in Rom*, AKG 1, ²1927, 245: 'In all probability, Peter and Paul died a martyr death under Nero in Rome'; cf. R. Pesch, *Simon-Petrus*, Stuttgart 1980, 109–34. See also above, 35f., 39f., nn. 165, 322.

610. We already see this in a very concrete way from the prehistory of the interlude in Antioch, where according to Gal. 2.11ff. Cephas-Peter visited the already strongly Gentile-Christian community and first of all made no objections to sharing a (eucharistic) table with uncircumcised 'Gentile Christians', until Jewish-Christian visitors coming to him from James in Jerusalem unsettled him. The result was that he acted against his innermost convictions and broke off table fellowship. However, the term 'Gentile-Christian' sounds too one-sided. These were above all godfearers, see below, n. 615.

611. Gal. 2.7f., see above, 87f.

612. Cf. I Cor. 15.11. This is a normative text to indicate the uniform basis of the primitive Christian message, for all its diversity brought about by the Spirit. It is all too readily overlooked, although it is one of the most important theological statements in the whole of the New Testament, see Hengel and Schwemer, *Paulus* (n. 9), 73, 156, 164, 438, 313: 'On the basis of I Cor. 15.11 we must speak of one

fundamental Gospel (1.Cor. 15.1ff.) despite Gal. 1.6, 11.' It is significant that this text is not cited in the index of biblical references in the more recent New Testament Theologies by Bultmann, Conzelmann/Lindemann and Strecker, nor does Berger's *Theologie-geschichte des Urchristentums* take note of it.

613. Gal. 2.15ff.: the first person plural points to the shared basis of faith in Paul and Peter and its consequences for the whole community in Antioch, Jewish and Gentile Christians, cf. Acts 15.9–11 (n. 622).

614. R. H. Bell, *Provoked to Jealousy*, WUNT II/63, Tübingen 1994.

615. Hengel and Schwemer, *Paulus* (n. 9), 80–6, 101–32 und index, 532 under 'Godfearer' = *Paul*, 50–5, 61–71; B. Wander, *Gottesfürchtige und Sympathisanten*, WUNT 104, Tübingen 1998.

616. Luke 7.22 = Matt. 11.5 = Isa. 61.1.

617. Stuhlmacher, *Evangelium* (n. 7), 153; it is still the most important work on the subject.

618. Like Paul, Peter too will have had quite a few missionary collaborators. Paul's difficulties in Corinth, above all according to II Corinthians, might be connected with them: cf. II Cor. 11.5, 22; 12.11. Possibly here the conflict in Antioch at the end of the 'second missionary journey' (Gal. 2.11ff.) and before the 'third missionary journey' had a direct effect. Cf. also II Cor. 10.7 and the enigmatic ἄλλον Ἰησοῦν (11.4): is this about Jesus as a miracle worker? Paulus is writing in extreme, quite subjective, agitation as one who has been deeply wounded and in part with a refined use of rhetorical stylistic means. See now L. Thuren, *Derhetorizing Paul*, WUNT 124, 2000. II Corinthians is the 'most human' and most rhetorical of all the letters of Paul. Despite the fundamental unity in respect of the christological foundations of the one Gospel, the severe conflict in Antioch must later have led to considerable tensions. It is significant that in II Corinthians (as opposed to I Corinthians) no names of 'rivals' are mentioned. Does Paul deliberately avoid mentioning the name of Peter in II Corinthians, Romans und Philippians, i.e. his late letters? Among the charges levelled against Paul was that his preaching critical of the Law could lead to libertinism (Rom. 3.8). That becomes visible in Corinth, cf. also the tensions in Phil 1.15ff. (either in Rome or Caesarea) and the concluding fundamental v.18, which indicates that the opponents, too, 'preach Christ', i.e. after all, '*no* other Gospel'. It may be that imprisonment and his stay in Rome again made Paul more conciliatory. But we do not know how his relationship to Peter developed in the unknown period after AD 60. Both suffered martyrdom, presumably both during the Neronian persecution. Then they are again really reunited a generation later with Clement of Rome and Ignatius, and in the Roman

tradition. Did perhaps Mark and the author of I Peter, some twenty-five to thirty years later, and also in his own way Luke, who knew more about the tension between the two than he wrote, contribute to this posthumous reconciliation?

619. I Cor. 1.12ff.; Gal. 2.11ff. I assume that Peter himself visited Corinth and that he had been in Rome, presumably before Paul. There he probably suffered martyrdom with Paul, see above, n. 609.

620. Acts 20.24 and 15.7.

621. Acts 15.9: 'cleansing their hearts by faith'. This fundamental statement is closely connected with the description of the vision and the word of God in 10.11–16 and 11.5–10. After the preaching of Peter in 10.34–43 which narrates the story of Jesus has brought about faith (the decisive statement is the last one, 10.43), the Spirit falls on the Gentile hearers as a 'divine judgment' (10.44; 11.15). God brings this about as one who 'knows the heart' (15.8, cf. 1.28). The 'cleansing of the heart' by faith corresponds to the 'circumcision of the heart', Rom. 2.29, cf. Acts 7.51.

622. Acts 15.11: 'we believe that we shall be saved through the grace of the Lord Jesus, just as they will.'

623. Gal. 2.5, 14.

624. See Hengel and Schwemer, *Paulus* (n. 9), 214–36 = *Paul*, 133–50: Paul's visit to Jerusalem and Peter.

625. Deut. 34.10ff.: 'And there has not arisen a prophet since in Israel like Moses, whom the LORD knew face to face, none like him for all the signs and wonders the LORD sent him to do in the land of Egypt . . . and for all the mighty power and all the great . . . deeds, which Moses wrought in the sight of all Israel', cf. John 21.25.

626. See Hengel, *Kleine Schriften* II (n. 120), 18f., cf. Deut. 26.28.

627. Mark 9.11ff. = Matt. 17.10ff.; Matt. 11.14; cf. Justin, *Dial.* 49, 3–5; Luke 1.47. Only John 1.25 is an exception here. The passage shows that the – late – Fourth Gospel is attacking a widespread earlier primitive Christian version. For it John the Baptist (like the whole of the Old Testament) is alone the witness to Jesus (1.32–34).

628. Mark 1.13, cf. Matt. 4.1–11; Luke 4.1–13; on this cf. also I Kingdoms 19.5–9. For the forty days see Ex. 24.18; 34.28, etc. (Moses); I Kingdoms 19.5–8 (Elijah).

629. *hay-yad hag-gᵉdōlāh*; LXX: τὴν χεῖρα τὴν μεγάλην. Cf. Mark 6.2 and Luke 11.20, and on this M.Hengel, 'Der Finger und die Herrschaft Gottes in Luke 11, 20', in *La Main de Dieu/Die Hand Gottes*, ed. R. Kieffer and J. Bergmann, WUNT 94, 1997, 87–106: here too there is a clear reference to the Exodus.

630. MT *wayaʾᵃmīnū bᵉYHWH ubᵉmōšeh ʿabdō*; LXX: καὶ ἐπίστευσαν τῷ θεῷ καὶ Μωϋσῇ τῷ θεράποντι αὐτοῦ.

631. See B. Ego, 'Gottes Weltherrschaft und die Einzigkeit seines Namens. Eine Untersuchung zur Rezeption der Königsmetapher in der Mekhilta des R. Yishmael', in *Königsherrschaft Gottes und himmlischer Kult*, ed. M. Hengel and A. M. Schwemer, WUNT 55, 1991, 257–83; H. Merkel, 'Die Gottesherrschaft in der Verkündigung Jesu', in ibid., 135–8.

632. μετανοεῖτε καὶ πιστεύετε ἐν τῷ εὐαγγελίῳ.

633. Mark 8.4 Ἡλίας καὶ Μωϋσεῖ, Luke 9.30 and following him Matt. 17.3 turn it round. In a christological respect Elijah was even more important than Moses as a 'forerunner' for Mark. In Mark and Matthew he appears nine times, in Luke seven times, in John twice. By contrast Moses appears in Mark only eight times, but in Luke ten times and in Matthew seven times.

634. Mark 14.27; cf. 6.34, also Ex. 24.8–11; Num. 17.27 and Zech. 13.7.

635. Cf. Gal. 3.13; Deut. 21.23; 27.26. It is striking that for Luke and John, Mark's description was so offensive that they interpreted this last cry of Jesus theologically and thus weakened it: Luke 23.46 = Ps.31.6, the dying prayer of the pious Jew and fundamentally John 19.30, see A. M. Schwemer, 'Jesu letzte Worte am Kreuz', *ThBtr* 29, 1998, 5–29: 18–28. Only Matthew, bound by theological conviction and the authority of Mark and his tradent Peter, takes over from the offensive account in Mark with slight alterations (Mark 15.33–39 = Matt. 27.45–54). He deserves great credit for this.

636. See K. Haacker and P. Schäfer, 'Nachbiblische Traditionen zum Tod des Mose', in *Josephus-Studien. Otto Michel zum 70. Geburtstag gewidmet*, Göttingen 1974, 147–74.

637. Ex. 32.30–34; cf. Mark 8.37b.

638. Mark 10.45; 14.24.

639. Mark 12.29–34; Deut. 6.4f.; Lev. 19.18.

640. Matt. 23.2, cf. above, 161, 163.

641. Ex. 3.1, 6, 15: 'This is my name for ever, and thus I am to be remembered throughout all generations.'

642. Luke 20.34 appropriately makes the interpretative addition to Mark, 'for in him they all live' cf. Rom. 14.7–9.

643. Cf. e.g. Mark 2.28: 'the Son of man is Lord even of the sabbath.'

644. However, Luke, the former 'godfearer', is more restrained in his criticism of the law: he omits Mark 7.14ff. See Jervell, *Apostelgeschichte* (n. 28), 100ff.

645. See R. Watts, *Isaiah's New Exodus and Mark*, WUNT II/88, Tübingen 1997, especially 381ff.

646. Ibid. 96–102, 167f.

647. Matt. 28.19f.; cf. 18.20. Cf. I Cor. 10.1–4, 9.

648. Luke 16.16. Cf. also his verdict on John the Baptist, 7.28: '. . . yet he

who is least in the kingdom of God is greater than he'.

649. *Apol* I 67, 3–5: 'And on the day called Sunday there is a meeting in one place of those who live in the cities or in the country, and the reminiscences of the apostles or the writings of the prophets are read as long as time permits. When the reader has finished, the president in a discourse urges and invites us to the imitation of these noble things. Then we all stand up together and offer prayer. And, as said before, when we have finished the prayer, bread is brought, and wine and water, and the president similarly sends up prayers and thanksgivings to the best of his ability, and the congregation assents, saying the Amen; the distribution and reception of the consecrated elements by each one takes place and they are sent to the absent by the deacons', cf. 66, 3, above 116f. See J. C. Salzmann, *Lehren und Ermahnen. Zur Geschichte des christlichen Wortgottesdienstes in den ersten drei Jahrhunderten*, WUNT II/59, Tübingen 1994, 235–57 and on the prophets Hengel, *Kleine Schriften* (n. 120) II, 335–80: 337–47 on Justin's understanding of scripture: the 'Prophets' mean all Old Testament writings including the Torah and the 'hagiographa'; they were all translated by the seventy for King Ptolemy.

650. The term 'books of the old covenant' appears a little later in Melito of Sardes, see Eusebius, *HE* 4, 26, 14.

651. See M. Hengel, 'Schriftauslegung des 4. Evangeliums auf dem Hintergrund der urchristlichen Exegese', *JBTh* 4, 1989, 249–58, in Hengel and Schwemer, *Die Septuaginta* (n. 1), 182–284: 183ff., 188ff., 198ff., 212ff

652. See above, 63, n. 263. It needed a long development.

653. II Cor. 3.6ff., 14; Gal.4.24; cf. I Cor. 11.25. That the 'old covenant' continues to maintain its dignity in the history of the canon 'in Christ' is shown by Rom. 9.4; 11.27. For II Cor. 3 see O. Hofius, *Paulusstudien*, WUNT 51, Tübingen 1989, 75–120; for Rom. 9–11 see ibid., 175–202.

654. Cf. e. g. John 1.17, 45; 5.39f., 45ff.; 10.34–38; basically see Hengel, *Kleine Schriften* II (n. 120), 211–16; for the relationship to Jesus see id., *The Charismatic Leader and his Followers*, Edinburgh 1981, and specially on John, *JBTh* 4, 1989, 258–88.

655. Hengel, 'Jesus the Messiah of Israel', in id., *Studies in Early Christology*, Edinburgh 1995, 1–72, and 'Jesus as Messianic Teacher of Wisdom and the Beginnings of Christology', ibid. 73–117.

656. 2.10, 17, 19, 21f., 27 or sayings and actions critical of the law and the temple like 7.15 or 11.15ff.

657. Mark 12.34–38; reinforced in Matt. 22.34–40 in 'rabbinic' language: 'On this commandment hang the law and the prophets',

cf. 6.12, where Luke 6.31 is deliberately expanded, see 9.13; 12.17.

658. Hengel, *Kleine Schriften* II (n. 120), 219–92: 249–54, 287–90: 'Matthew has to be brought into conversation with Paul, even if he himself would rather have evaded it' (289). The perspective from which he is considered is decisive here; whether he is regarded in the light of statements like Matt. 1.21 and 26.28, where he inserts the formula εἰς ἄφεσιν ἁμαρτίων from Mark 1.4 (cf. also 9.13 and 20.28, which are taken over from Mark), or whether one sees him in the light of the Sermon on the Mount and 28.20b, or how one interprets the term δικαιοσύνη in him. But even in the Sermon on the Mount, the centre which supports it is the Our Father with the decisive verses 6.12f. In the book of Revelation, which is similarly not without problems, reference is made to 1.5; 5.9; 7.14; 12.11; 13.8; 14.1 and consequently 21.3ff.

659. I Cor. 3.11; Eph. 2.20, cf. Mark 12.10f. = Matt. 21.42 = Luke 20.17; Acts 4.11; I Peter 2.4, 6–8.

660. See P. Stuhlmacher, *Theologie des Neuen Testaments* II, Göttingen 1999, § 41 on the 'Centre of Scripture' (304–21).

661. K. Beyschlag, *Grundriss der Dogmengeschichte*, I, *Gott und Welt*, Darmstadt ²1987, 155f.

662. That also applies to the thesis of Ernst Käsemann, which was provocative in its time: 'The New Testament canon does not, as such, constitute the foundation of the unity of the church. On the contrary, as such (that is, in its accessibility to the historian) it provides the basis for the multiplicity of the confessions', *Essays on New Testament Themes* (n. 572), 103. In reality it does both. See also id., *New Testament Questions of Today*, London and Philadelphia 1969, 37, directed against H. Braun: 'the constant' in the primitive Christian anthropology of believers is 'the element of belonging to Jesus'. In my view that applies to the whole course of the church as long as one can still call it church. See his confession on p.45 of Christ as the 'Lord of faith'. But all four Gospels – just like Paul – seek to lead us to this 'Lord of faith' (John 6.68).

663. C. G. Wilke, *Der Urevangelist oder kritische Untersuchung über das Verwandtschaftsverhältnis der drei ersten Evangelien*, Dresden and Leipzig 1838, 685–93: 'The insertions in Matthew which are the same or related come from none other than Luke, as borrowings.' The author demonstrates: (a) that in his links Matthew goes by Luke; (b) that he even uses words characteristic of Luke; (c) that he has taken up passages in the same spirit as blows in other accounts, characteristic of Luke; (d) that he has given the passages a context and here and there an expression which they could not have had originally or before his revision of them, whereas the originals are in

Luke.' The detailed reasons which Wilke gives, for example in comparing the Lukan and Matthaean versions of the Sermon on the Mount, are almost always worth considering. He sees above all that the Lukan parallel text gives the impression of being more original than that of Matthew, which has been worked over more strongly in redaction. Cf. also 693 on the ordering of the material: in contrast to his attitude towards Mark as his 'original Gospel', Matthew did not want 'to copy out Luke in its entirety. The order was in the possession of the Gospel of Mark before he had news of Luke's writing, or he knew it as the older work and was aware that Luke had simply made additions to this work. Therefore he inserted what he had to insert into his original document [= Mark, M.H.] and began from there to supplement the discourses of Jesus which appear in it with similar discourses,' so he 'did not need the whole apparatus which Luke . . . offered him.' See also id., *Die neutestamentliche Rhetorik, ein Seitenstück zur Grammatik des neutestamentlichen Sprachidioms*, Dresden and Leipzig 1843, 445f. For Wilke's theory of the Gospels see W. Schmithals, *Einleitung in die ersten drei Evangelien*, Berlin and New York 1985, 166–73.

664. *Das Evangelium nach Matthäus*, [4]1922, 19: 'It would not be surprising if for the Greek translators . . . the Gospels of Mark and Luke had not been normative here or there.' See also above, 74, n. 307. O. Pfleiderer, *Das Urchristentum*, [2]1902, I, 612, concedes Matthew: 'Rather than thinking of the use of Matthew by Luke one might think of the use of the Gospel of Luke by Matthew; however, I cannot leave this still open question on one side, since there is no way in which the Gospel of Matthew would be explicable *merely* from Luke and Mark as sources.' He therefore tends towards a common 'original source' translated into Greek and sees in Matthew 'not the unitary work of an individual author; rather, different hands, indeed different generations of primitive Christianity worked on it' (614). Here the influence of his teacher F. C. Baur, who was far removed from history, is perceptible.

665. H. P. West, 'A Primitive Version of Luke in the Composition of Matthew', *NTS* 14, 1967/68, 75–95, cf. John Knox, *Marcion and the New Testament*, Chicago 1942, 85–88. While Morgenthaler mentions the order Mark, Luke, Matthew in his *Statistische Synopse* he does not go into it and remarks that 'the only serious competition to the Q hypothesis is the scheme Mark – Matthew – Luke'. However, on closer inspection this is quite improbable.

666. R. V. Huggins, 'Matthean Posteriority: A Preliminary Proposal', *NT* 34, 1992, 1–22. I came across this article only after finishing my own studies.

667. Ibid., 5f.: 'But when it is assumed to the contrary that Matthew stands last in line instead of Luke, the argument from the phenomenon of order loses its force, because the actual number of instances where Matthew might have departed from the Marcan outline in favour of Luke is reduced to only five for the double-tradition, each of which when taken over is easily accounted for from the point of view of Matthean redaction.' Cf. also the comparison of the insertions of the common material into the Markan thread. In the case of Matthew there are 15, in the case of Luke only 5.

668. Ibid., 4, 14f.

669. Ibid., 17–22.

670. See the result of this process of subtraction down to individual characters in the private printing by the Institute for Antiquity and Christianity, Claremont, Calif. 91711, 1985, under the significant title 'Pap. Q', with the introduction: 'This print-out, like a unique papyrus, contains the only extant vestiges of the otherwise lost collection of Jesus' sayings familiarly known as Q.' Why should there not at least in part some literary dependencies (as I think of Matthew on Luke)? Must one common source always lie in the background, especially as the agreements in extent and wording are so very different? This question has never been satisfactorily explained on the basis of the 'Q' hypothesis (see below, n. 671, the work of Bergemann).

671. See the Introductions to the New Testament. The literature on 'Q' is legion. Here I shall mention only some more recent monographs. A basic work for the earlier literature is F. Neirynck and F. van Siegbrock, 'Q-Bibliography', in J. Belobel (ed.), *Les paroles de Jésus – The Sayings of Jesus*, BETL 59, 1982, 561–86. There is a survey of the further bibliographies in A. Denaux, 'Criteria for Identifying Q-Passages', *NT* 37, 1995, 105 n. 1. Given this wealth of monographs one might almost speak of a distinctive 'literary genre'. Individual titles are: J. S. Kloppenborg, *The Formation of Q. Trajectories in Ancient Wisdom Collections*, Philadelphia 1987, who wants to filter out different strata of tradition; M. Sato, *Q und Prophetie. Studien zur Gattungs- und Traditionsgeschichte der Quelle Q*, WUNT II/29, Tübingen 1988, a shrewd work which, however, concludes with what to my mind is the completely misguided 'question of the historical continuity of prophecy since the Old Testament – the tradents of the Q source' = Ch. 5, 314–405. Is not the question here rather that of a 'messianic prophet' Jesus? A. D. Jacobson, *The First Gospel, An Introduction to Q*, Sonoma CA, 1992; D. Catchpole, *The Quest for Q*, Edinburgh 1993, who in a first section (which is unfortunately too short) goes into those who dispute the existence of Q (1–7). T. Bergemann, *Q auf dem Prüfstand*, FRLANT 158,

Göttingen 1993, a work which really takes research forward, rightly criticizes the all too simple process of subtraction and emphasizes that this is a hypothesis. Bergemann offers a thorough survey of research and then concentrates on a 'basic discourse' as a common source for Luke's Sermon on the Plain and the Sermon on the Mount. Here – and this is a substantial step forward – he states 'that the Sermon on the Mount and the Sermon on the Plain in the material that they have in common are not based on pieces of tradition from Q', as 'the core material of the basic speech' only demonstrates 'an agreement in wording of . . . 30%, whereas well over 75% of all differences are . . . massive discrepancies', and the 'agreements mostly have the character of proof texts' (230f., cf. 235). These critical findings of Bergemann's deserved to be noted more widely. C. M. Tuckett, *Q and the History of Early Christianity*, Edinburgh 1996, similarly contains an extended introduction. Jens Schröter, *Erinnerung* (n. 568), is a thorough work of around 600 pages; it ends by comparing a reconstruction of 'Q' with parallels from Mark and the Gospel of Thomas and with the Logia tradition. But could not this 'reconstruction' of 'Q' at least be in part originally Lukan, if, as I believe, Matthew has, among other sources, also used Luke? U.Schnelle, *Einleitung in das Neue Testament*, Göttingen [3]1999, 194–212, gives the most recent, brief conventional survey, with predominantly German literature (these passages are not in the English translation, U. Schnelle, *The History and Theology of the New Testament Writings*, Minneapolis and London 1998, which is of an earlier edition). The wealth of hypotheses and possibilities is reflected even more clearly by the new series Documenta Q, of which four volumes have appeared since 1996 and which has the character of a catena of research. There have been more conjectures over 'Q' than over any other real New Testament document. So even I will allow myself to offer some hypotheses in criticism of Q – albeit not unfounded.

672. Schnelle, *Einleitung* (n. 671), 184, 196, following R. Morgenthaler, *Statistische Synopse*, Zurich/Stuttgart 1971, 81. Still according to Morgenthaler, Matt. 'Q' has 3,869 words and Matt. 'Q' doublets, and 5,596 special material; Luke-'Q' 3,663 words and 108 Luke-expansions and 8,887 special material. Schnelle, 196 n. 85, arrives at substantially higher figures. J. S. Kloppenborg, *Q Parallels*, 209, who counts 'for the common material in Matthew 4,464 and in Luke 4,652 words'. This already shows the relative uncertainty in the demarcation of Q. Of course an explicit 'Q'-specialist is interested in the widest possible extent of the subject of his research.

673. *Sprüche und Reden Jesu*, Leipzig 1907. See also above, 5 and n. 17.

His work, which is still a basic one, is far removed from the most recent investigations, in which the daydreams about a new picture of Jesus are all too evident, cf. e.g. the still numerous publications of J. D. Crossan or B. L. Mack; above n. 22.

674. Thus e.g., in the older work of S. Schulz, *Q. Die Spruchquelle der Evangelisten*, Zurich 1972, who wanted to distinguish between the 'kerygma of the earliest Q-communities on the frontier of Palestine-Syria' and a 'kerygma of the later Q-community in Syria'. Would it not be simpler to derive the 'independent sphere of tradition' and the 'relatively self-contained conception of the kerygma' which he postulates (486) from Jesus' preaching and the Jesus tradition of the primitive community generally? There is absolutely no trace in the material attributed to the Logia source that the Jewish Christianity standing behind the Q material was 'soon to lead a sectarian existence'. The whole of primitive Christianity began as an offensive messianic and a little later also a 'universal' Jewish 'sect'.

675. In my view F. Neirynck, *The Minor Agreements of Matthew and Luke against Mark*, BETL 37, 1974 (with a detailed history of research) is right in criticizing one-sided conclusions from the 'minor agreements'; cf. also id., 'Evangelica', in *Collected Essays*, BETL 60, 1982, 769–810 (above all his critical discussion of the theses of A. Fuchs, 769–80). There are even fewer convincing indications of the existence of a 'Deutero-Mark', available to Luke und Matthew. Granted, A. Ennulat, *Die 'Minor Agreements'. Untersuchungen zu einer offenen Frage des synoptischen Problems*, WUNT II/62, Tübingen 1994, again assumes a 'revision of Mark before Matthew and Luke'. However, despite his tremendously diligent work, his arguments do not convince me.

676. Cf. e.g. Koester, *Gospels* (n. 50), 13: 'It is quite possible that a later scribe added this phrase in order to indicate the point in his manuscript at which the text of another writing began.' There is no basis in the text for such a conjecture and it goes against all the rules of sound literary and textual criticism.

677. Cf. e.g. Luke 3.21f. and Matt. 3.16 the ἀνεῳχθῆναι/ἠνεῳχθήσαν and ἐπ' αὐτόν against Mark 3.10; Luke 9.29f. and Matt. 17.2f. against Mark 9.3f.; Luke 22.64 = Matt. 26.28: τίς ἐστιν ὁ παίσας; Luke 22.62 = Matt. 26.75: καὶ ἐξελθὼν ἔξω ἔκλαυσεν πικρῶς. For Luke 10.25 and Matt. 22.36 against Mark 12.28 see above, 196 and n. 767.

678. Arndt/Gingrich/Bauer, *Lexicon*, on ἀνατάσσεσθαι: 'compose a narrative (from material handed down); it can therefore also be synonymous with συντάσσεσθαι, cmpose, be taken.' See also Loveday Alexander, *The Preface of Luke's Gospel*, SNTS.MS 78,

1993, 110f., who points out that here Luke (the physician) is speaking less the language of historical literature than that of scientific-technical literature. See the similarity of the prologue of Luke to the prologue in *Corpus Hippiatricorum Graecorum* (n. 557), 1, 1: Στρατευσάμενος ἐν τοῖς τάγμασι τοῖς ἐπὶ τοῦ Ἴστρου ποταμοῦ ἔγνων τὰ συμβαίνοντα τοῖς ἵπποις, ἐν οἷς καὶ διαφωνοῦσιν. ἀναταξάμενος οὖν ταῦτα καὶ τὰ πρὸς αὐτὰ βοηθήματα προσφωνῶ σοι, φίλτατε Ἀσκληπιάδη, τοῦτο τὸ βιβλίον, ὄντι μοι πολίτῃ καὶ ἰατρῷ μεγίστῳ. ἐν ᾧ μὴ ἐπιζητήσῃς λογιότητα, ἀλλὰ τὴν ἐκ τῆς πείρας φυσικὴν ἐμπειρίαν ἐπίγνωθι.

679. See n. 672 above: 8, 887 words as against Matthew's 5, 596.

680. H.Schürmann, *Traditionsgeschichtliche Untersuchungen zu den synoptischen Evangelien*, Düsseldorf 1968, 111–56, sought in the 'special material' of Matthew and Luke 'reminiscences' of the discourse source, and in so doing made valuable observations. However, it remains questionable whether there was only one such 'discourse source'. 'Q material' could derive from different and partly overlapping 'sources' of this kind.

681. See Huggins, 'Posteriority' (n. 666), 5–14 and above, 68ff.

682. Jeremias, *Sprache* (n. 413), 9: '. . . that the degree of Luke's revision of the material he had before him is to be reckoned considerably less than is generally assumed. It is largely limited to stylistic improvements of the material in the tradition; here Luke is not afraid to polish the style even of LXX quotations. Luke has revised stylistically everything . . . that belongs in the framework. Compared with that, I find Luke's restraint in redactional interventions into the sayings of Jesus all the more impressive.'

683. Cf. M. Reiser, *Syntax und Stil des Markusevangeliums*, WUNT II/11, Tübingen 1984, though he takes too little note of the possibility of semitisms in Mark. I have demonstrated in many investigations that many people had a command of Greek in Jerusalem, and also in the towns of Galilee, see e.g. *Kleine Schriften* I, 1–90.

684. See Morgenthaler, *Statistik* (n. 341), 128–62. Here it is significant that in Matthew – which in my view is later – the doublets predominate by comparison with Luke (157f.): 'In Matthew we read almost twice as many logia doublets as in Luke', cf. 162, the same observation in the case of the 'non-logia like' doublets. In the case of Luke the – rare – doublets come from Mark and from sources unknown to us.

685. Huggins, 'Posteriority' (n. 666), 3f.: 'Luke is *usually* more primitive than Matthew'.

686. So now again in the perceptive but not always convincing work by M. D. Goulder, *Luke. A New Paradigm*, JSNT.S 20, 1989, I, 27–71,

in criticism of the 'Q' hypothesis. See also the literature given in Huggins, 'Posteriority' (n. 666).

687. See R. Laufen, *Die Doppelüberlieferung der Logienquelle und des Markusevangeliums*, BBB 54, 1980 and H. T. Fleddermann, *Mark and Q. A Study of the Overlap Texts*, BETL 122, 1995. We might even ask whether Mark did not compose his narrative account, which contains relatively little logia tradition, in connection with earlier Peter tradition which he held to be authoritative and with the focus on the passion narrative as the necessary 'complement' to the earlier collection(s) of Logia attributed to Matthew. At all events, he treats the sayings tradition eclectically. Luke, and in his footsteps even more impressively Matthew, would then have made the combination which the subject-matter needed.

688. Cf. Mark 2.14 = Luke 5.27 (Luke omits the name of his father, Alphaeus) with Matt. 9.9: the addition λεγόμενον in Matthew indicates a clear 'critical' correction: the toll collector was really called Matthew and not Levi, i.e. here Mark (and Luke) are wrong. Such corrections of names can also be found, for example, in the rabbinic haggada and with tradents of the halakhah. Cf. also the change of names in the case of the women in Luke 24.10 (cf. 8.2) over against Mark 15.40 und 16.1. Here too there could be a hidden reference to a guarantor of the tradition.

689. In the Jewish-Christian Gospel of the Ebionites, according to Epiphanius, *Panarion* 30, 13, 3, Jesus names the disciples he has chosen and then at last addresses them directly: 'and I called you, Matthew, when you sat at the receipt of custom, and you followed me.' According to Epiphanius this was 'an abbreviated and falsified Gospel of Matthew', see *NTApoc* I, 166, 170, cf. 140.

690. Indeed we have no Gospels under the names of Clement, Ignatius, Polycarp or Hermas; their authority was simply no longer enough to 'canonize' even their letters or writings. In the case of a Gospel that would have been even more impossible.

691. See above, 132ff.

692. Sato (see above, n. 671), 17–65, conjectures a gradually growing collection in the form of a 'parchment volume' (64). But in that case there must have been not only two ($Q^{Matt.}$ and Q^{Luke}), but a larger number of volumes passing from hand to hand and being copied. This would fit Luke 1.1ff. well.

693. See Schröter, *Erinnerung* (n. 568), who, because of his orientation on early research, in his 'reconstruction process' goes far beyond what can really be demonstrated and all too readily assumes 'Q' as one source with a firm outline.

694. See above, 60 and nn. 249, 550.

695. That happens emphatically with the use of statistical methods in Bergemann, *Q* (n. 671).

696. P.Vassiliadis, 'The Nature and Extent of the Q-Document', *NT* 20, 1978, 49–73, gives as the first 'principle' for what in my view is the impossible 'Reconstruction of the Q-Document' (66): 'All extensive or consecutive sayings in Matthew and Luke which show an almost verbatim agreement in wording *quite certainly* belong to Q.' Precisely here we must ask whether Matthew did not take over such passages from Luke. This is the only criterion of seven that Bergemann (n. 671) agrees with in his investigation *Q auf dem Prüfstand*. On the basis of earlier investigations by W. Bussmann und O. Linton he keeps emphasizing rightly the problem that tends to be overlooked, that Matthew and Luke treated the source in such an inexplicably variable way, which ranges from extreme freedom to complete dependence (i.e. from around 8% to 100%). The complete dependence is best explained by a partial adoption of Lukan texts by Matthew, and the differences by markedly divergent Logia versions which could perhaps go back to a common source 'which each translated as he was able'.

697. In what follow I am referring to the admirable collection by F. Neirynck, *Q-Synopsis. The Double Tradition Passages in Greek*, SNTA XIII, Leuven 1988.

698. See Bergemann, *Q* (n. 671), 61–306, who wants to construct a 'basic discourse' from 6.20–49 and Matt. 5.3–7.27 (with great gaps, 283ff.). However, this is a very uncertain operation.

699. For the much-discussed question of doublets which could derive from 'Q' and Mark and have been recorded above all in Matthew and less in Luke, see n. 684 above.

700. Cf. Mark 9.50; Luke 14.34f.; Matt. 5.13 | Mark 4.21; Luke 8.16; Matt. 5.15 | Luke 16.16f.; Matt. 5.17ff.; Mark 11.25; Matt. 5.23 | Luke 12.57–59; Matt. 5.25f. | Mark 9.43–48; Matt. 5.27–32 | Luke 16.18; Matt. 5.32 | Luke 11.2–4; Matt. 9.13 (here Matthew is probably independent of Luke and is handing on the liturgical prayer of his communities) | Luke 12.33f.; Matt. 6.20f. | Luke 11.34f.; Matt. 6.22f. | Luke 12.22–32; Matt. 6.25–34 | Luke 11.9–13; Matt. 7.7–11 | Luke 13.23f.; Matt. 7.13f. | Luke 13.25–27; Matt. 7.22f. The differences between these texts are sometimes quite considerable and sometimes relatively small: the dependence of Matthew on one or more logia sources, Mark or Luke can be determined only in each individual instance and only with very different degrees of probability.

701. For the Sermon on the Mount see Hengel, *Kleine Schriften* II (n. 120), 219–99. H. D. Betz, in my view wrongly, conjectures a Jewish-

Christian source with a still quite Jewish character, independent of the evangelist, as the basis used by the evangelist, see above, n. 298.

702. We New Testament scholars constantly attempt this.

703. Even in the account of the baptism the ἠνεῴχθησαν and the ἐπ' αὐτόν in Matt. 3.16 derive from Luke 3.21f. ἀνεῳχθῆναι and ἐπ' αὐτόν (instead of Mark 1.10 σχιζομένους and εἰς αὐτόν).

704. The toll collector Matthew leaves his toll gate and follows Jesus, Matt. 9.9. On this see the negative evaluation in Matt. 5.46; 18.17. The text Matt. 21.31f., which is probably redactional, could presuppose knowledge of Luke 3.12f. (cf. also Luke 7.39). Here Matthew took it for granted that 'toll collectors and prostitutes' gave up their previous occupation as 'fruits of penitence'. Therefore he also had to reject texts like Luke 18.10ff.; 19.1ff. The combination of the threat of judgment to the Pharisees and Sadducees in 3.7–10 (Luke 3.7, 10 speaks only of ὄχλοι) with the announcement of the 'Stronger One' as judge gives his preaching at baptism greater sharpness and unity. Here the moral admonitions to the crowd in Luke 3.10–14 would only have been disruptive.

705. The εἰς τὴν ἁγίαν πόλιν in 4.5a reappears word for word in the miracle of the resurrection after the death of Jesus in Matt. 27.53 (cf. also 5.35). That too is certainly a redactional change, brought about by theological reflection. Jesus enters the Holy City, there to suffer and through his resurrection symbolically to introduce the general resurrection, not to perform a public miracle. His messianic activity is focussed on this goal and initially is wholly limited to Israel.

706. The rejection of the temptation to perform a messianic miracle to legitimate himself also is particularly important in Matthew: 12.38f.; 16.1–4; cf. 24.24 and on πειράζειν 4.1, 3; 19.3; 22.18, 35.

707. Cf. 4.8–10; 28.18f.; see also already 11.29a. (Luke's more 'naïve' account contains less theological reflection.) The very high mountain (Matt. 4.8) contrasts with the mountain of the Sermon on the Mount (5.1), and of the transfiguration (17.1) and above all of the concluding sending of the disciples from the Mount of revelation in Galilee (28.16), where the rule of the Son of God over the world is revealed. The ὕπαγε Σατανᾶ is dependent on Matt. 16.23 = Mark 8.33; 4.4c is an expansion of the scriptural quotation from Deut.8.3b. At no point is it suggested that Matthew is more original than Luke.

708. 13.42, 50; 22.13; 24.51; 25.30. Of course it could also have occurred in one of the 'sayings sources' which he used.

709. 9.34; cf. the doublet 12.24. Mark has – with more historical accuracy – 'the scribes coming down from Jerusalem' (3.22), Luke –

presumably in accordance with the most original narrative version –
τίνες. See Hengel, 'Finger' (n. 629), 87–106. Here I would still quite
naturally have assumed an original Q version. Luke clearly has the
earlier text.

710. 12.22–30, cf. 43–45 and Luke 11.14–26. In 12.31–37 Matthew
inserts the sin against the Holy Spirit, which in content belongs there
for him (cf. Mark 3.28f.) and the good and bad fruits of the tree (cf.
Luke 6.43–45). In Matt. 12.24–29/Luke 11.14f., 17–23 we addi-
tionally have the influence of Mark 3.22–27. The question is
whether here Matthew could not have shaped his text on the basis
of Mark and Luke and whether we must still unconditionally presuppose Q as the common source in Matthew und Luke.

711. In Hengel and Schwemer, *Paulus* (n. 9), 14, we already assumed that
the later Matthew knew Luke, and pointed out that he could be
dependent on Luke in the minor agreements, but we still believed
that Matthew ignored the work of the Pauline Luke, which was
suspect to him; we still simply presupposed the logia source (15, 53,
59, 146), but emphasized its open, uncertain character.

712. See Byrskog, *Story* (nn. 464, 561).

713. In Acts 8 Philip acts directly towards him, cf. 8.5, 26, 40. For the
Samaritans in Luke see now the comprehensive study by Martina
Böhm, *Samarien und Samaritai bei Lukas*, WUNT II/111, 2000. For
Matt. 10.5 see 95–100 and the index.

714. More precisely 8, 555 of 11, 078 words in Mark, of these 128 from
Matthew-Mark doublets and 68 Matthaean expansions of Mark in
the in all 18, 298 words of the first Gospel. That is around 50% of
his vocabulary. In the longer Luke (19, 448 words, i.e. 6% more) the
Markan share is only around 29%.

715. See above, 29 and esp. n. 125.

716. See the survey of the relevant texts in Streeter, *The Four Gospels.
A Study of Origins* (n. 423), 295–331, who points out that the
'minor agreements' are not least a problem of the harmonizing
textual tradition. Nevertheless his invitation, 'Renounce once for all
the chase of the phantom Ur-Marcus' (331), should still be taken to
heart.

717. See the survey in Davies and Allison, *Matthew* (n. 195), I, 127.

718. That is striking, even if we assume that basic Jewish phenomena and
Matthaean texts with parallels in the Synoptic Gospels have all
already been discussed in Volume 1.

719. U. Luz, *Das Evangelium nach Matthäus*, EKK I, 1, [3]1992, 76.

720. Ibid., 127–38: 138. I believe that with a good conscience we should
bring this date down to around 90–95 and perhaps even extend it to
c. 100. The question is whether I Clement, at the latest around 100,

knows Matthew (see above, 128ff.); the problem of the relation of Matthew to John is similar.

721. Schnelle, *Einleitung* (n. 671), 238.

722. See the survey in Holtzmann, *Einleitung* (n. 293), 418.

723. H. Marshall, *The Gospel of Luke*, NIGTC, Exeter 1978, 35.

724. *The Gospel According to Luke* (I–IX), AncB 28, 57; cf. Barrett, *Acts* (n. 28), XLIII, who conjectures for Acts a date 'hardly . . . before 80; quite possibly some years later', Koester (n. 50), 334, still 'as late as the first decades of the second century'. His conjecture that 'apart from Marcion, a harmony of Matthew and Luke was apparently the earliest form through which the text of the Gospel of Luke came to be used', is adventurous. He finds this harmony in Justin und II Clement and in the Gospel of the Ebionites. The name Luke, he argues, appears for the first time in Irenaeus. He passes over the *Epistula Apostolorum*, which knows the Gospel and Acts and says nothing of the fact that Justin already speaks of disciples of the apostles as the authors of Gospels (see above, 19f.) and that Basilides probably knows the Gospel and Marcion accepts it because it comes from a disciple of Paul. On this see Schmithals, *Einleitung* (n. 663), 363, who refers to the admiration 'that Marcion in particular used the Gospel of Luke as the basis of his canon of New Testament writings, although other Gospels, above all John, would have caused his theology far fewer difficulties'. Schmithals himself (367) has it written 'in the sphere of influence of pre-Marcionitism and under the influence of vigorous persecutions of Christians in northern or western Asia Minor towards the end of the emperor Domitian'. All these assumptions are historically extremely questionable.

725. Schnelle, *Einleitung* (n. 671), 259.

726. Hengel and Schwemer, *Paulus* (n. 9), 9–26 = *Paul*, 6–21.

727. For the 'we-reports' and Luke as a contemporary witness see Thornton, *Zeuge* (n. 144).

728. Luke 19.41–44. The details of this text may be influenced by LXX quotations of which Luke has an excellent knowledge and which he imitates (Isa. 29.3; II Sam. 17.13; cf. also Hos. 10.14; 14.1; Nahum 3.10). However, he clearly alludes to the Roman *circumvallatio* in the siege of the city and depicts its complete destruction and the sorry fate of its population (see e.g. Josephus, *BJ* 5, 248ff.; 6, 502ff.).

729. Luke 21.6: 'The days will come when there shall not be left here one stone upon another *that will not be thrown down.*' Matthew initially goes with Mark 13.2, but then improves it at the end with Luke, by following Mark to 'on another' and then like Luke puts 'which shall not be thrown down'. We get the impression that here

too he also read Luke and in ch.24 inserted various bits of Lukan material. However, the destruction of Jerusalem was no longer so important for him, see below, nn. 753–4.

730. Mark 13.14: τὸ βδέλυγμα τῆς ἐρημώσεως ἑστηκότα ὅπου οὐ δεῖ. Here the grammatically offensive masculine ἑστηκότα instead of the neuter refers to the Antichrist in the form of Nero *redivivus*, who is still expected; cf. II Thess. 4; see Hengel, *Mark* (n. 10), 18–20, 258. Matthew has the correct neuter participle ἑστός. For the abomination of desolation cf. Dan 11.31 und 12.11 LXX and Th.

731. 'But when you see Jerusalem surrounded by armies, then know that its desolation (ἐρήμωσις) has come near.' For the key word ἐρήμωσις see Dan. 9.2 Th; Jer. 22.5, see I Ezra 1.55 (58); II Chron. 26.27.

732. 'Then let those who are in Judaea flee to the mountains, and those who are inside the city depart, and let not those who are out in the country enter it.'

733. Josephus, *BJ* 6, 384: the Romans grant a pardon only to the citizens of Jerusalem who came over to them, not the country population in the city, which was sold into slavery; 421–430: at Passover 70 a large number of Jews flocked into the city: 'A large number (of the visitors) assembled from abroad. At that time the whole nation had been shut up by fate as in a prison, and the city when war encompassed on it was packed with inhabitants. The victims thus outnumbered those of any previous visitation, human or divine' (427–29).

734. The Aramaic version was written around AD 75; the Greek was completed around AD 79/81; see I. Wandrey, *Der Neue Pauly* 5, 1998, 1089f.

735. There may be an allusion here to the Roman Civil War in 68/69.

736. Josephus gives the number of Jewish prisoners of war as 97, 000 and the victims of the siege as 1.1 million, an exaggeration. This denotes all the Jewish losses. The numbers must be based on Roman military sources, *BJ* 6, 420f. For the prisoners of war see 414ff.; 7, 24.37.118.137f.; cf. also the triumphal procession in Rome, 7, 123ff.

737. Luke 21.22–24.

738. Cf. Luke 21.23 and Mark 13.19 = Matt. 24.21. Here too (see above, 176) the somewhat abbreviated form of Matthew, although in content it follows Mark, could have made a stylistic borrowing from Luke: the ἔσται γὰρ τότε θλῖψις μεγάλη οἵα corresponds to the ἔσται γὰρ ἀνάγκη μεγάλη in Luke 21.23; cf. at greater length Mark 13.19: ἔσονται γὰρ αἱ ἡμέραι ἐκεῖναι θλῖψις οἵα, cf. Dan. 12.1 LXX: ἐκείνη ἡ ἡμέρα θλίψεως, οἵα . . ., Th.: καὶ ἔσται καιρὸς θλίψεως, θλῖψις οἵα, cf. Ex 9.18 and Joel 2.2.

739. The formula καιροὶ ἐθνῶν is also orientated on the apocalyptic language of Daniel and could be translated '*years of the Gentiles*': Dan. 4.13 (16), 20(23), 22(25), 29(32), cf. 11.13 (Th); the LXX translates in 4.16, 32 ἔτη instead of καιροί; 9.27 (LXX); 7.25; 12.7 (Th/LXX). It is the time when the Gentiles in the form of the legionaries of the Tenth Legion, whose sign was the pig, 'trampled' the destroyed city with their military boots and thus desecrated it, but were also to listen to the message of the Gospel all over the world. For the καταπατεῖν of Jerusalem see Dan.8.13 (LXX); I Macc. 3.45, 51; III Macc. 2.18; cf. II Macc. 8.2 and Ezek. 26.7–14(11).

740. See Hengel, *Studies in Early Christology* (n. 601), 84–6.

741. For the difficult ὑμῖν see F. Bovon, *Das Evangelium nach Lukas*, EKK III, 2, 1996, 456f.; he refers to Arndt/Gingrich/Bauer, *Lexicon*, ad loc., cf. Diodore 17, 41, 7.

742. Cf. Jer. 7.4 (and against this 12.7; 22.5); see the prophecy of salvation immediately before the storming of the temple in Josephus, *BJ* 6, 285f., and his argument with John of Gischala 6, 96–110. Against the argument of the Zealot leader that 'he fears no conquest, for the city (and the temple) belong to God', Josephus refers to Jeremiah, among others.

743. Cf. Luke 21.22f.: ἡμέραι ἐκδικήσεως and ὀργή. This is ultimately about God's punishment and God's anger.

744. Cf. 24.30.

745. The destruction of the temple has already anticipated the judgment on the 'scribes and Pharisees' who have now attained spiritual rule. The ruins of the temple are an abiding sign against them.

746. 23.27–31 (28); but cf. the quite different tone of the curse that the Jews bring down upon themselves in Matt. 27.25: could Matthew have been prompted to this addition by the parallel in Luke?

747. Cf. 19.11; 17.20f.; Acts 1.6ff., on this, however, cf. 2.17.

748. Hengel, *Studies in Mark* (n. 10), 14–28.

749. 21.22: ἡμέραι ἐκδικήσεως, only πάντα τὰ γεγραμμένα is fulfilled. Josephus could also have put it like that.

750. 1.4ff.; 24.52; cf. 24.47, 49; Acts 1.8, 12.

751. It is the particular merit of Jervell, *Apostelgeschichte* (n. 28), to have opposed this tendency.

752. For the last Roman series minted in AD 79 cf. H. Mattingley, *Coins of the Roman Empire in the British Museum, II, Vespasian to Domitian*, Oxford ²1976, 256 nos. 164–170. Later, on individual mintings, 266 no. 211; 279 no. 259; 294 no. 308 in AD 79. See also the index s. v. Jewess und IUDAEA CAPTA. For the building of the Colosseum from the plunder from Jerusalem see the building

inscription *ex manubiis* reconstructed by G. Alföldy, *ZPE* 109, 1995, 195–226, and the Antiochene inscription on the temple of Apollo in Daphne *ex praeda Iudaea,* see Hengel, *Kleine Schriften* II (n. 120), 123f.

753. Cf. Matt. 24.2, which abbreviates Mark 13.2. In 24.15 = Mark 13.14 he corrects the masculine ἑστηκότα in Mark 13.14, which refers to the Antichrist, into the grammatically correct neuter, and changes the enigmatic ὅπου οὐ δεῖ into ἐν ἁγίῳ τόπῳ, by which he means the temple square (cf. II Thess. 2.4) or *pars pro toto* the Holy City. In the first and second years of the first revolt coins bore the legend 'Jerusalem is holy' (*yrslm qdwsh*), see Y. Meschorer, *Jewish Coins of the Second Temple Period,* Tel Aviv 1967, 154, nos 148–152, cf. the story of the temptation in Matt. 4.5 und 27.53 with the designation of Jerusalem as ἁγία πόλις. Elsewhere the term appears only in Rev. 11.2 with a reference to the destruction and in 21.2, 10 for the heavenly Jerusalem. Presumably Matthew is also referring this prophecy of Daniel – he particularly emphasizes the name of the prophet – no longer so much to the destruction of the city, which now lies further in the past, as on the approaching eschaton. In other words he, too, understands by the 'abomination of desolation' the rule of terror by the Antichrist before the parousia. Matthew's gaze, like that of Mark, is directed more towards the future than towards the past. For Matt. 23.38 = Luke 13.35 see above. In Matt. 21.41 the answer of the hearers (according to 21.23 the high priests and the elders) to Jesus' question about the reaction of the owners of the vineyard, Κακοὺς κακῶς ἀπολέσει αὐτούς, could amount to a curse on themselves (cf. 27.25), which could then possibly refer to the judgment of the year 70.

754. See e.g. R. Kampling, *Das Blut Christi und die Juden,* NTA NF 16, 1984, who discusses the exegesis of the passage in the Latin fathers up to Leo the Great and in Origen.

755. See Hengel and Schwemer, *Paulus* (n. 9), 82–4.

756. In John there is a clear allusion to the destruction of Jerusalem in 11.48, cf. also the bitter irony in the answer of the chief priests (ἀρχιερεῖς) to Pilate, 19.15. Cf. also the prediction in 4.21.

757. See Hengel, *Johanneische Frage* (n. 85), 288–98 = *Johannine Question,* 114ff.

758. In Matt. 13.52 he is referring not least to himself; he is also probably including himself in 23.34 in that chain of 'prophets, wise men and scribes' who are persecuted and driven out by their opponents. He has deliberately inserted a 'wise men and scribes' by comparison with the 'prophets and apostles' that he found in Luke. Both terms

are opposed by Matthew to the proud self-designation of his scribal Pharisaic opponents as '*hakhamim* und *sopherim*'. At the same time, 13.52 speaks for the hardly lesser self-confidence of the Christian 'scribe' and author of the Gospel. The author of John and I–III John had no less a claim to authority. Here Mark and Luke are still more restrained.

759. 23.2, 13, 15, 23, 25, 27, 29. Verse 14 is secondary, formed by analogy on the basis of Mark 12.40, which was inserted at a relatively early stage.

760. We still find the double formula in the redactional admonition 5.20, and again in 12.38, where the 'Pharisees' of Mark 8.11 is supplemented.

761. Cf. also Mark 3.22: 'And the scribes who had come down from Jerusalem . . .' Pharisees appear in Mark only together with the Herodians (cf. 3.6) in 12.13. In the Matthaean parallel the initiative is shifted entirely to the Pharisees (22.15); for him the Herodians are still merely the 'fellow-travellers' (22.16); they appear in Matthew only here, but cf. still Mark 3.6 with Matt. 12.14, where Matthew deletes the Herodians and has only the Pharisees seeking Jesus' life. In general their attacks (21.45 together with the high priests, cf. 27.62; 22.15, 34, 41) prepare for the attack of Jesus in ch.23. By contrast Luke has delegates of the 'scribes and chief priests' (10.19) laying a trap for Jesus. Luke's account gives the impression that he is attempting to paint a historically realistic picture of conditions in Jerusalem, cf. 23.2.

762. Cf. also Mark 2.16, 'the scribes of the Pharisees', i.e. the scribes as a mere leading group of the Pharisees, a formula which presupposes also scribes of other Jewish groups, and the whole scene Luke 11.37–54 with the polemic sparked off by an invitation from a Pharisee (see already 7.36ff.) against the Pharisees (11.37–39, 42–44), followed by the intervention of a νομικός, who differentiates between the Pharisee and his own state: 'Master, in saying this *you shame us also*'. Thereupon Jesus attacks the 'teachers of the law', 11.45f., 52. Only at the end are they brought together again, cf. also 7.30. It follows quite pertinently from Acts 23.9 that Luke knows that the groups are not simply identical: 'some of the scribes of the Pharisees' party'. The μέρος here corresponds to the term αἵρεσις which is used elsewhere: 25.5; 26.5 the religious party of the Pharisees; 5.12 the Sadducees. The Christians too are still a *Jewish* αἵρεσις: 24.5; 28.22. In Matthew these fine distinctions are levelled out. He still only envisages a close group of opponents. That also applies to the formal use of 'Pharisees and Sadducees' (always in this order) in Matt. 3.7; 16.1, 6, 11f. In Matthew the Sadducees have

yielded the leading political role which they had before 70 to the Pharisees.

763. 8.31; 10.33; 11.18, 27; 14.1, 43, 53; 15.1–31, i.e. 9 of the 21 examples. For Jerusalem as the world-wide centre for the study of the Torah see M. Hengel and R. Deines, 'Der vorchristliche Paulus', in *Paulus und das antike Judentum*, WUNT 58, Tübingen 1991, 177–293: 212ff., 222ff., 239–56 = *The Pre-Christian Paul*. The same is true for important parts of Diaspora Judaism.

764. 19.47; 20.1, 19; 22.2 etc.

765. Cf. Matt. 21.45; 27.62.

766. The relatively rare term appears in IV Macc. 5.4; in the original passage γραμματεύς is used for Eleazar, see II Macc. 6.18.

767. Luke 10.25: καὶ ἰδοὺ νομικός τις ἀνέστη ἐκπειράζων αὐτὸν λέγων. διδάσκαλε . . . This is one of the most striking minor agreements. See also above, n. 677.

768. See Billerbeck I, 901–8; Hengel, *Kleine Schriften* II (n. 120), 282–7.

769. As well as the parallels from Luke 11.39–51 in a very changed order he has also worked in Mark 12.39. The Markan parallel prompts him to put the discourse before the great eschatological discourses.

770. H.-J. Becker, *Auf der Kathedra des Mose. Rabbinisch-theologisches Denken und antirabbinische Polemik in Matt. 23, 1–12*, ANTZ 4, Berlin 1990, 45–51. Becker, a theologian and Judaist in Göttingen and a pupil of P. Schäfer, is one of the leading Talmudic experts in Germany.

771. Ibid., 49–50.

772. In Mark 12.37 a large crowd of people (ὄχλος) hears Jesus; in Luke 20.45 the whole people (λαός) listens while Jesus speaks to his disciples (τοῖς μαθηταῖς αὐτοῦ). In Matthew Jesus speaks to the ὄχλοις καὶ τοῖς μαθηταῖς αὐτοῦ. Here Matthew seems to combine Mark and Luke. The Lukan προσέχετε ἀπὸ τῶν γραμματέων in the twofold meaning 'listen to the scribes' and 'beware of the scribes' perhaps stimulated Matthew to his formulation in v. 3.

773. Becker, *Auf der Kathedra des Mose* (n. 770), 50 n. 155, criticizes the datings of R. Hummel, *Die Auseinandersetzung zwischen Kirche und Judentum im Matthäusevangelium*, BEvTh 33, Munich ²1966, 32, 'not much later than . . . AD 85', and Luz, *Matthäus* (n. 719) I, 76, 'not long after . . . 80' as too early and follows G. Strecker, *Der Weg der Gerechtigkeit*, FRLANT 82, Göttingen ³1971, 36, around 90–95. There is a survey of attempted datings from 40–50 to after 100 in Davies and Allison, *Matthew* (n. 195), 127f. They note the references to years and conjecture a date 'in all probability between 80 and 95'. Here the first date is certainly too early.

774. I Peter was composed in Asia Minor or Rome around the same time

as or a little later than Matthew, perhaps among other things as an answer to the collection of the letters of Paul: the pseudepigraphical letter to the communities in Asia Minor seeks among other things to provide a counterbalance to the excessively powerful Pauline communities. Perhaps the collection of Paul's letters were also edited at that particular time. It was the time of a last very great *theological* effort before the dark first decades of the second century. R. Metzner, *Die Rezeption des Matthäusevangeliums im 1. Petrusbrief*, WUNT II/74, Tübingen 1995, points to theological connections between Matthew and I Peter. But he puts Matthew too early (4 n. 14) and conjectures a literary dependence. Here he does not consider sufficiently the possible relationship between Mark and I Peter and also the common logia tradition that becomes visible in I Clement. The investigation of the influence of Matthew in Rome and Asia Minor, 266–71, certainly does not confirm an early dating of the Gospel of Matthew.

775. Mark 10.51; John 20.16: a Palestinian intensifying form which appears in Judaism as a courteous form of address in the phrase *ribbōn šāēl 'ōlām*, see Hengel, *Leader* (n. 654), 42f. n. 19. 'Rabbi' appears in Mark a further three times and in John a further eight (!).

776. Matt. 26.25, 49: accumulated four times in the two verses!

777. The closest parallel to Matt. 23.8–10 is John 13.13–15, cf. also Matt. 10.24 and by contrast the 'trinitarian' basis of the episcopate in Ignatius ten to twenty years later: Eph. 6.1; Magn. 2.1; 3.1; 6.1; 7.1; 13.2; Trall. 2.1; 3.1 etc. In Rom. 2.2 Ignatius even calls himself ἐπίσκοπος Συρίας, Eph. 11.1 = Matt. 3.7. This shows that he knew Matthew in around AD 110–114. Nevertheless Matthew does not fit Antioch! For James the brother of the Lord as the first 'bishop of Jerusalem' see Hengel, 'Jakobus' (n. 454), 81–5, in connection with Clement of Alexandria according to Eusebius, *HE* 2, 1, 3, cf. Ps.Clem., *Recog.* 1, 43, 3 and Jerome, *Vir ill.* 2, see Eusebius, *HE* 7, 19, 1.

778. Didache 7.1, 3 (but cf. 9.5). After that we only find the baptismal formula again in Justin, *Apol.* I, 61, 3, cf. 61, 10–13. However, Matt. 28.16–20 is already presupposed earlier in the conclusion to Mark 16.15f., but without the formula. For the problem see L. Abramowski, 'Die Entstehung der dreigliedrigen Tauformel – ein Versuch', *ZThK* 81, 1984, 417–46: 422–40, who derives it from the three-membered Aaronite blessing.

779. In different forms: Acts 2.38; 8.16; 10.48; 19.5; cf. Rom. 6.3; Gal. 3.27. Even the Didache (9.5) also knows the simple form alongside the trinitarian form. The same is probably also true of James 2.7 and Hermas: see Abramowski, 'Entstehung' (n. 778), 434f.

780. I Clem. 46.6; 58.2; Ignatius, Eph. 9.1; Magn. 13.2; Phil., prologue, etc.; cf. also the presbyters in Asia Minor and Irenaeus, *Adv.Haer.* 5, 36, 2. F. Loofs, *Leitfaden der Dogmengeschichte*, ed. K. Aland, [5]1980, I, 75, sees in it a 'multiple allusion to the trinitarian baptismal formula'. However, we have isolated albeit less developed formulae without reference to baptism already in Paul, cf. II Cor. 13.13; I Cor. 12.4–6, see J. N. D. Kelly, *Early Christian Creeds*, London 1982, 23ff. G. Kretschmar, *Studien zur frühchristlichen Trinitätstheologie*, BHTh 21, 1956, 121f., points out that – apart from Matt. 28.19 – in the New Testament 'the Holy Spirit is clearly depicted in personal terms and distinguished from the exalted Christ only in the Paraclete sayings' in the roughly contemporaneous John. He connects trinitarian notions with Isa.6, i.e. God and the two seraphs, and refers to the Christian apocalypse Ascension of Isaiah 9.27–40 – which in my view belongs in the first decades of the second century with the vision of God and Christ on the right hand and the angels of the Holy Spirit on the left. See also Odes of Solomon 23.22. Perhaps the formula emanated from Syria, where there was a quite deliberate concern to include God the Father alongside Christ, then a threefold formula was created through the Spirit. Paradoxically, the incorporation of (God) the Father and the Spirit made the baptismal formula more 'monotheistic'. Echoes of the trinitarian baptismal formula then occur relatively frequently in the Apologists: Justin, *Apol.* I, 6; 13, 1–3; 65, 3; 67, 2; Athenagoras, *Suppl.* 10, 2; 12, 2; 24, 1; Theophilus, *Ad. Autol.* 2, 15; F. Loofs, *Leitfaden der Dogmengeschichte.*, 95. The Matthaean baptismal formula largely established itself by the end of the second century. Fundamentally it is already completely related to the development of the second century.

781. Against E. Klostermann, *Das Matthäusevangelium*, HNT 4, [3]1938, 232. Cf. also Davies and Allison, *Matthew* (n. 195), III, 684f. Perhaps more attention should be paid to the fact that the triad of God, Christ and Holy Spirit is decisive for the Matthaean birth narrative. God brings about through the Spirit the miraculous birth of Christ and thus salvation for Israel and now, in 28.19, through Christ and the Spirit, in baptism for all believers. However, it is not just the unusual baptismal formula but the baptismal command in the mouth of the Risen Christ that contradicts the earlier tradition which we meet in Luke-Acts or leads beyond it. Luke is still aware that the invitation to baptism 'in the name of Jesus Christ' first belongs in the preaching of the primitive community in Jerusalem, and accordingly makes it appear in the Peter's Pentecost speech (Acts 2.38). Here too one could speak of a deliberate theological

correction of Luke by Matthew, just as John corrects Luke in connection with the bestowal of the Spirit on the disciples by the Risen Christ (John 20.22f., but cf. Luke 24.49; Acts 1.4f.). By contrast with Luke and John, Matthew attaches greater value to the handing on of the 'commandments' of Jesus (28.20). The coming baptism in the Spirit is mentioned only in Matt. 3.11 which is dependent on Luke 3.16b. Matthew is extremely sceptical about unattached 'bearers of the Spirit' or 'miracle-workers': 7.21ff. That makes the presence of the Kyrios in the community through his commandment and word all the more important (28.20, cf. 18.20).

782. For Celsus' Jews see Origen, *c. Cels.* 1, 28–2, 29; Tertullian, *de spect.* 30, 6; see S. Krauss, *Das Leben Jesu nach jüdischen Quellen*, Berlin 1902, reprinted Hildesheim 1977, 3.

783. Tal Ilan, 'Man Born of Woman (John 4.1): The Phenomena of Men Bearing Metronymes at the Time of Jesus', *NT* 34, 1992, 23–45, points out that in Jewish sources in some circumstances only the name of the mother can be mentioned if she was highly regarded. That was certainly the case with Mary in the community (Acts 1.14; John 19.25–27, cf. also Gal.4.4). Presumably Jesus' father Joseph had long been dead at the time of Jesus' public appearance. The mention of his numerous brothers and sisters (Mark 6.3) tells against the view popular among exegetes who think themselves 'progressive', that Jesus was a son born out of wedlock.

784. Such a detail did not fit into a work dedicated to the 'most excellent' Theophilus.

785. Origen, *c. Cels.* 1, 28, 32.39: 'The craftsman hated her and cast her out.' For the name Panthera see Chadwick, *Contra Celsum* (n. 367), 31 n. 3. In my view this name can be explained as a distortion of παρθένος. According to Epiphanius, *Pan.* 78, 7, 5, Jesus' grandfather, Jacob, had been given the nickname Panther, a report which perhaps goes back to Hegesippus. Tertullian, *De spect.* 30, 6 speaks of 'the son of a craftsman and a prostitute.'

786. Luke mentions Mary twelve times in chs.1 and 2; there he speaks a further five times of the mother of Jesus; cf. also Acts 1.4. By contrast Joseph is mentioned only three times; in addition there are two mentions of him as father. The ratio is 17:5.

787. Joseph appears in Matthew in his infancy narratives seven times by name and Mary only four times, with one exception together with Joseph. In addition 'the child and his mother' is mentioned four times in the invitation to Joseph.

788. Matt. 27.63 ὁ πλάνος; 64 καὶ ἔσται ἡ ἐσχάτη πλάνη χείρων τῆς πρώτης. Cf. also the accusation against Jesus in bSanh 43a: Jesus is executed 'because he did magic, led people astray (*whysyt*) and

321

invited Israel to apostasy'.

789. 27.62–66; 28.1–4, 11–15.

790. In Matthew this still happens in a restrained way in 28.1–4; in the Gospel of Peter it is fantastically elaborated. I find it quite impossible to understand how Koester and Crossan can give this late and crudely anti-Jewish hotch-potch such a dominant role in the Gospel tradition.

791. John 7.12: πλανᾷ τὸν ὄχλον, cf. 47; for Jesus as one who leads people astray and is a deceiver see *c. Cels.* 1, 68, 71: γόης; 2, 1: ἐξαπατήθητε; 12: ἀπατήσας τοὺς μαθητάς; Justin, *Dial.* 108, 2: Γαλιλαῖος πλάνος; and 69, 7.

792. John 20.15. This motif recurs in Tertullian, *Spect.* 19, 6 and then frequently in the versions of the Jewish *Toledot Jeshu*: Krauss, *Leben Jesu* (n. 782), 45f., translation 58f., 80ff., (102ff.), 129; G. Schlichting, *Ein jüdisches Leben Jesu*, WUNT 24, Tübingen 1982, 152ff.: in this late version the disciples appear as deceived deceivers.

793. 9.32–34 = 12.22–24; see above, 183). This is matched in Celsus' Jews by the defamation of Jesus as a magician who learned his magic art in Egypt: *c.Cels.* 1, 68 cf. 66; cf. Justin, *Dial.* 69, 7.

794. Matt. 1.2–17.

795. Luke 3.23–38; see M. D. Johnson, *The Purpose of the Biblical Genealogies*, SNTS.MS 8, 1969, 229–52; Fitzmyer, *Gospel* (n. 126), I, 488–505 (with bibliography); D. L. Bock, *Luke*, Baker Exeg. Comm., Grand Rapids 1994, I, 348–62. The problem is the names between Eli, the father of Joseph (in Matt. 1.2 this is Jacob), and Nathan, the third son of David (II Sam. 5.14; I Chron. 3.5; 14.4; Zech. 12.12; in Matt. 1.6f.: Solomon); here the 'royal' names Zerubbabel and Shealtiel (Luke 3.27), which agree with Matt. 1.12f., complicate the riddle to a point where it becomes completely insoluble. Perhaps Luke avoids the royal line between Solomon and Jechoniah because of the oracle of disaster in Jer.22.28–30 and 36.30f., but that does not make the riddle of his genealogy any the less. The Davidic descent itself could go back to Jesus' family tradition, cf. Rom. 1.3; 15.12 and Eusebius, *HE* 3, 20, 1f.; cf. 32, 5f.; however, along with Matthew, the Lukan genealogy gives the impression of being a construct: Matthew 'constructs' his genealogy more scripturally and more artistically and in so doing shows himself to be a scriptural scholar of Jewish-Christian origin writing later.

796. His geographical knowledge of Judaea and the coastal plain are amazingly good for a foreigner, see Hengel in *Between Jesus and Paul* (n. 431), 97–128, 190–210, and now Böhm, *Samarien* (n. 713), passim.

797. Acts 4.1ff.; 5.17ff., cf. 23.7f. and Josephus, *BJ* 20, 200ff. Cf. also the trial of Paul carried out by the high priest Ananias in Acts 24.1ff.

798. Luke 6.15; Acts 1.13; see M. Hengel, *The Zealots*, Edinburgh 1989, 59–73, 388–96 for the absolute use, which appears elsewhere only in Josephus and represents a Jewish parallel tradition.

799. Acts 21.38; cf. Hengel, *Zealots* (n. 753), 46–53, 397–401; cf. also the conspiracy in Acts 23.12ff.

800. Acts 5.36f. It is a forgivable mistake that Luke confuses the order and puts Theudas anachronistically far too early. He had not yet read Josephus. For Judas see Hengel, *Zealots* (n. 753), 76–145, 330–7 and index 479; for Theudas, 229–33, 293.

801. Acts 21.38; Hengel, *Zealots* (n. 753), 231f.

802. In 24.24 presumably he also knew that she was the sister of Agrippa II. 24.25 refers discreetly to the life-style of the two. For the venality see 24.26. The picture painted here in a few strokes corresponds completely with Josephus, whom Luke does not know – otherwise he would have made use of him quite differently. Moreover Acts 21–26 are painted in a far more lively way as 'historical-dramatic scenes' than the reports of the Jewish historian. They are a living 'commentary' of a contemporary on the last book of the *Antiquities*.

803. Suetonius, *Titus* 7, 1f. of Titus: *Berenicam statim ab urbe dimisit invitus invitam*: 'Berenice he sent from Rome at once, against her will and against his own.' It was said that he had promised to marry her.

804. Acts 21–26; see Hengel, *Between Jesus and Paul* (n. 796), 97–128, and Thornton, *Zeuge* (n. 144), passim.

805. Luke 3.1f.; cf. Acts 18.2, 12ff.

806. Cf. Luke 3.2 und Acts 4.6: together with Caiphas, according to John 18.13 the father-in-law of Caiphas and the really dominant figure in the clan of Annas. All his five sons received the high priesthood, see Hengel, *Kleine Schriften* II (n. 120), 1999, 322–34.

807. Matthew has the key word διώκειν five times, especially emphasized in the Sermon on the Mount, 5.10–12, 44; Luke only twice in the meaning 'persecute', 11.49 and 21.12, referring to a persecution by Jews. Cf. also the reference to crucifixions in Matt. 23.24, the accentuation of Mark 13.2 in Matt. 10.21 (cf. the more restrained Luke 21.16), and the doublet on Mark 13.13 in Matt. 10.22 und 24.9f., which radicalizes the situation of persecution: a stronger wind from the state side was blowing against the church in the time of Matthew than in the time of Luke. Evidently Christians were again being put on trial by the state.

Index of References to the Bible and Early Christian Writings

330

Index of Modern Authors

General Index

351